To my dear colleague Ann,

with my best wishes,

Jack   March 20, 2015

TRADE SHOWS IN THE GLOBALIZING KNOWLEDGE ECONOMY

Trade Shows in the Globalizing Knowledge Economy

by

HARALD BATHELT, FRANCESCA GOLFETTO,
AND DIEGO RINALLO

OXFORD
UNIVERSITY PRESS

Great Clarendon Street, Oxford, OX2 6DP,
United Kingdom

Oxford University Press is a department of the University of Oxford.
It furthers the University's objective of excellence in research, scholarship,
and education by publishing worldwide. Oxford is a registered trade mark of
Oxford University Press in the UK and in certain other countries

© Harald Bathelt, Francesca Golfetto, and Diego Rinallo 2014

The moral rights of the authors have been asserted

First Edition published in 2014

Impression: 1

Published in the United States of America by Oxford University Press
198 Madison Avenue, New York, NY 10016, United States of America

British Library Cataloguing in Publication Data
Data available

Library of Congress Control Number: 2014931563

ISBN 978-0-19-964308-0

Printed and bound by
CPI Group (UK) Ltd, Croydon, CR0 4YY

For Waltraud, Tommaso, and Cassiano

Preface

This book focuses on providing an understanding, conceptualization, and investigation of the role of trade shows in the globalizing knowledge economy. Trade shows have long been seen as marketing or sales events, where firms from a particular industry or technology group showcase their products to current and potential customers. Alternatively, they have been viewed as events that bring business tourists and related activities to certain trade show cities/regions, providing jobs and income to a segment of the local/regional economy that specializes in servicing them. Relatively little research has treated these events as places where international business networks are created and maintained, where both technical and creative inputs for innovations are collected and generated, or where decisive knowledge is created, circulated, exchanged, and negotiated.

Indeed, studies in business management, economic geography, and other disciplines have only recently begun to conceptualize and explore the role of trade shows as key nodes in the global knowledge economy that enable the generation and dissemination of decisive knowledge flows connecting agents/firms, clusters, and regions in different parts of the world. Building on and extending these contributions, this book draws on a knowledge-based perspective to develop a coherent conceptual understanding of the nature, extent, and structure of interaction and learning at trade shows. Based on empirical evidence regarding different trade shows in a variety of underlying industries in different geographical contexts, we highlight the following aspects of knowledge generation: (i) the knowledge acquisition and dissemination processes carried out by participating firms (i.e. exhibitors and visitors); (ii) the types of knowledge that are exchanged and co-produced by the actors involved in different industry groups; and (iii) the knowledge strategies through which trade show organizers affect learning processes at their events.

Our main goal is to investigate how trade shows contribute to the establishment of new geographies of circulation (Thrift 2000; Amin and Cohendet 2004), which enable knowledge creation and exchange between different locations around the globe, across different industries, and without permanent or even frequent face-to-face contact. To understand this dynamic, we develop a clear account of how these events operate in the knowledge economy, and how they have become major building blocks in innovation and globalization processes, despite important differences from country to country. This is done from both a conceptual and empirical standpoint.

The book aims to demonstrate that trade shows are a key factor in understanding globalization, innovation, and local/national economic development processes. These processes engage a wide range of research questions from different disciplinary traditions. The book is thus directed to researchers and students across the social sciences; yet we anticipate that it will also be relevant to policy-makers, regional planners, public managers, local economic governments, as well as organizers in the trade fair industry:

(1) Policy-makers. The book provides important insights into how local and national governments can use trade shows to avoid the institutional lock-in and self-referential behaviour of firms overly embedded in local industrial clusters. It also speaks to the ways in which governments might support the development of marketing competencies and market-based innovation, and foster the competitive advantage of regional/national economies.

(2) Trade show industry. The book highlights the ways in which trade shows may become knowledge-rich spaces that foster the competitiveness of their exhibitors and visitors. It should, thus, be of primary interest to trade show organizers who employ knowledge-based strategies to increase the competitiveness of their events.

(3) Firms and business associations. The book complements the mainstream perspective in the business literature, which typically views trade shows as individual promotional events. On the one hand, this literature highlights the critical role of trade shows in product innovation and in matching technological competences to evolving market needs. On the other hand, it emphasizes their role in collective marketing initiatives, which enable cooperation among competitors (i.e. coopetition—Brandenburger and Nalebuff 1996) to achieve common promotional goals.

(4) Economic organizations and policy-makers from new manufacturing countries and emerging market economies. Most of the existing scholarship on trade shows focuses on Western European and North American contexts. This book departs from this long-standing preoccupation to present a systematic overview of trade shows' activities, structures, and developments across many industries and countries. In doing so, it offers a comprehensive perspective of these events and their role in the world economy.

Needless to say that this book would not have been possible without valuable feedback and help from ongoing collaborations and regular exchanges with many friends and colleagues. Its limitations and imperfections, however, are solely the responsibility of the authors. We have greatly benefited from inspiring and insightful suggestions from Enrica Baccini, Stefania Borghini, Cristian Chizzoli, Emanuele Guido, Sebastian Henn, Sufyan Katariwala, Nina Knippen (formerly Schuldt), Peng-Fei Li, Ben Spigel, Guido Zakrzewski, Gang Zeng, and Fabrizio Zerbini. Rachael Gibson, in particular, provided invaluable input at all stages of this project, for which we are most grateful. Furthermore, we would like to thank Alexandra Eremia and Yuefang Si for superb research support. We are also indebted to the various trade show organizers that assisted us in collecting data and shared their insights about these events, their strategic challenges, and their role in the world economy. We are especially indebted to Fondazione Fiera Milano, which, by continuously soliciting new research, allowed us to better understand trade show activities and functions. Finally, we thank Oxford University Press, particularly David Musson and Emma Booth, and the anonymous advisers for helpful comments on earlier drafts of the book and for managing this project so effectively. Last but not least, we wish to thank our loved ones—Cassiano, Clare, Fiona, Mauro, and Tommaso—for joining in our enthusiasm for this book and for providing continuous support throughout the entire project.

As a last remark, we wish to emphasize that this project is an example of how relationships can be created over distance based on shared interest in a novel research perspective, how this process would not have been possible without occasional face-to-face communication and temporary get-togethers, and how ongoing interaction in professional relations can produce personal trust over time.

Toronto, Milan, and Marseille, December 2013

Harald Bathelt,
Francesca Golfetto,
and Diego Rinallo

Contents

List of Figures

List of Tables

Permissions

Like many academic publications, parts of this book draw from earlier work and publications. The arguments developed in several of its chapters are based on or develop from ideas established in former research. We wish to acknowledge the following original sources, in particular, and thank the publishers and editors of the respective works for allowing us to use this material in building our argument.

Permission to draw on ideas from prior publications are gratefully acknowledged from the following sources: *Journal of Business Research*, 59 (2006), 1151–9 (Elsevier B.V. <http://www.elsevier.com>) with respect to Chapter 2; *European Planning Studies*, 14 (2006), 997–1013 and 18 (2010), 1957–74 (Taylor & Francis Ltd. <http://www.tandfonline.com>) in the context of Chapter 3; *Economic Geography* 87 (2011), 453–76 (Clark University and John Wiley & Sons, Inc. <http://onlinelibrary.wiley.com>) in the context of Chapters 3, 4, and 11; *Canadian Geographer*, 56 (2012), 18–38 (Canadian Association of Geographers and John Wiley & Sons, Inc. <http://onlinelibrary.wiley.com>) with respect to Chapter 7; *Regional Studies*, 42 (2008), 853–68 (Taylor & Francis Ltd. <http://www.tandfonline.com>) in the context of Chapter 9; and *Industrial Marketing Management*, 35 (2006), 856–69 (Elsevier B.V. <http://www.elsevier.com>) with respect to Chapters 11 and 12. Permission to reproduce tables and figures are kindly granted by SAGE Publications Ltd. <http://www.sagepub.co.uk> for Figure 3.1 (*Progress in Human Geography*, 28: 46), Taylor & Francis Ltd. <http://www.tandfonline.com> for Figure 3.2 (*Regional Studies*, 42: 856), and Clark University and John Wiley & Sons, Inc. <http://onlinelibrary.wiley.com> for Table 11.3 (*Economic Geography*, 87: 460).

Permissions

Like many academic publications, parts of this book grew from lectures and presentations. The arguments developed in several of the chapters draw on or develop ideas published in earlier articles. We wish to acknowledge the influence of that process, in particular, and thank the publishers that authorized the respective works for allowing us to use this material in building this book.

Permission to draw on ideas first published as is gratefully acknowledged from the following sources. Journal of B. Cruz, chapters. 33 items.

1

Introduction

1.1. BACKGROUND OF THE BOOK

Trade shows are temporary marketplaces where suppliers from a given industry convene to showcase their products and services (Black 1986; Rinallo and Golfetto 2011). Research on these events has been largely dominated by studies in management and marketing. This body of work, which dates back to the late 1960s, generally views trade shows as promotional or sales instruments. Over time, these studies have produced a wealth of knowledge on how firms, typically preoccupied with the 'exorbitant cost of exhibiting', can effectively select and manage trade shows and maximize their return on investment (e.g. Carman 1968; Cavanaugh 1976; Bonoma 1983; Shoham 1992; Gopalakrishna and Lilien 1995; Clausen and Schreiber 2000; Smith et al. 2004). Another group of studies, of mostly applied nature, sees trade shows as a boost to business tourism, and has developed a body of knowledge on how to employ these events as local economic development and city marketing tools. These studies focus on measuring the economic impact of trade shows on host areas, linked to exhibitor and visitor expenses (e.g. Golfetto 1991; Braun 1992; Schätzl et al. 1993; Hodur and Leistritz 2006; Lee 2006).

In recent years, trade shows have been the focus of renewed interest in a variety of disciplines, and from a different perspective than in the past. In sociology, for instance, scholars have drawn on the work of theorists such as Bourdieu and Goffman to analyse how these events render visible the boundaries and relational positions of agents in their respective fields (Entwistle and Rocamora 2006; Skov 2006). In organization studies, moreover, trade shows have been characterized as a type of 'field-configuring event', emphasizing their ability to lead the development of technologies, industries, and markets (Lampel and Meyer 2008). And, in political science, a field that is largely quiet about such events, recent studies have linked trade shows to the persistence and ongoing specialization of capitalist varieties (Gibson and Bathelt 2010; Gibson 2015).

Deviating from conventional approaches, recent studies in marketing and economic geography have highlighted the nature and scope of information search and knowledge exchange processes at these events, drawing on the knowledge-based view of the firm and industrial clusters (Borghini et al. 2004,

2006; Maskell et al. 2004, 2006; Bathelt and Schuldt 2008; Rinallo and Golfetto 2011; Bathelt and Gibson 2014). Despite differences in the types of questions raised, the scope of analysis, and the methodology used, these studies espouse a similar view of trade shows, that is, as places that are conducive to an 'industrial atmosphere', à la Marshall (1927), which facilitates learning and innovation. In the realm of marketing, this 'knowledge turn' is evident in a new generation of studies that investigate how exhibitors and visitors learn from each other at these events (Tanner et al. 2001; Borghini et al. 2006; Li 2006; Rinallo et al. 2010). Research in this field reveals that industrial buyers (visitors) use trade shows to obtain critical knowledge about technologies and supplier competencies, as well as select partners for new product development activities (Borghini et al. 2006). Moreover, studies of exhibitors demonstrate that these firms disclose valuable knowledge for promotional reasons at trade shows and gather feedback on how to adapt their innovations to ever-changing market needs (e.g. Golfetto and Mazursky 2004; Zerbini et al. 2010).

In economic geography, trade shows have become valuable research sites for scholars interested in the relative importance of internal and external sources of knowledge for firms embedded in industrial clusters (Bathelt et al. 2004). In this context, it has been suggested that local buzz, obtained by 'being there' (i.e. located in a cluster context), and trans-local pipelines, which require specific investments in other localities, are important mechanisms in explaining a local cluster's vitality and success in globalizing and hyper-competitive marketplaces. From this perspective, trade shows are conceived as relational spaces that foster forms of organized, temporary proximity between actors that are otherwise geographically and, possibly, technologically distant (Maskell et al. 2006; Bathelt and Glückler 2011). These spaces are viewed as temporary clusters, characterized by knowledge creation and exchange mechanisms similar to those found in permanent clusters—albeit in a short-lived and intensified form (Bathelt and Schuldt 2010). Trade shows provide rich opportunities for learning through face-to-face interaction and the physical inspection of products, technologies, and other artefacts. Such learning opportunities are, perhaps, the main reason why trade shows and similar temporary community gatherings continue to thrive in the age of the World Wide Web and social media, despite experimentation and commercial attempts to substitute these events with virtual trade fairs and other forms of online professional interaction (Damer et al. 2000; Geigenmüller 2010).

1.2. GOALS OF THE BOOK

The central goal of this book is to develop a knowledge-based understanding of trade shows and their roles in globalization, innovation, and local economic development processes. More specifically, the book builds on previous studies in the fields of management/marketing and economic geography to show that these events are crucial for their contribution to inter-firm learning, knowledge exchange, and innovation processes, rather than for trade-related motivations alone.

The point of departure for the book is our own previous conceptual and empirical work on international trade shows, globalization processes, global–local tensions, and knowledge-based perspectives of economic development. Yet the book extends beyond classical disciplinary boundaries to provide a broad problem- and practice-related, inter-disciplinary understanding of trade shows and their role in the globalizing knowledge economy.

We do this by developing a conceptual understanding of trade shows as temporary clusters and temporary markets in the knowledge economy, and propose a typology of trade shows according to the nature of knowledge flows that occur during these events. The typology describes how different information and communication patterns develop during specific types of trade shows and illuminates the consequences of these patterns from a spatial perspective. This conceptualization is used to analyse the nature and dynamic changes of trade shows in different industry groups and in different parts of the world, drawing from examples in Europe, North America, and the Asia-Pacific region.

The book relates to a number of ongoing academic debates, addressing the current resurgence in interest on trade shows and similar events in management, marketing, sociology, organization studies, and economic geography. Our work attempts to systematize the debate in these fields by offering a comprehensive conceptual framework explaining the role played by different kinds of trade shows in the global knowledge economy, the knowledge dynamics at play during these events, and their relationships with local clusters (which can be either healthy or dysfunctional). The rich empirical material gathered for the book provides a substantive contribution to the discussion of trade shows in the different academic debates.

The book draws on relational and practice perspectives of economic action, which pay particular attention to the context of socio-institutional relations and the practices of economic interaction to understand how economic structures develop in a spatial perspective (Bathelt and Glückler 2011, 2012). In this context, trade shows are viewed as 'relational spaces' where firms of an industry or technology field interact intensively over a short period of time (Bathelt and Spigel 2012). Focusing on knowledge flows, and processes of learning by observation and interaction regarding products, markets, and technologies, the book builds upon a resource-based—or, more precisely, a knowledge-based—view of the firm. This view suggests that competitiveness crucially depends on the knowledge resources of firms (Penrose 1959; Wernerfelt 1984; Grant 1996; Nonaka et al. 2000). Our discussion of trade shows as events that establish critical links between actors around the globe relates to discussions about the learning or knowledge economy in a global context (Lundvall and Johnson 1994). In addition, the analysis of these events in terms of opportunities to build and maintain pipelines between different regions and clusters addresses existing gaps in the literature on industrial clusters and global value or production chains (Bathelt et al. 2004). As such, this book explores critical mechanisms in establishing global relationships and networks and making connections across regional industry settings.

1.3. DISTINGUISHING TRADE SHOWS FROM OTHER EVENTS

Modern trade shows of the kind investigated in this book are events that bring together different groups of suppliers (referred to as exhibitors) from a particular industry or technology field with the primary goal to showcase, promote, and/or market their products and services to buyers and other relevant target groups (i.e. visitors) (see Chapter 2). These events last from one to a few days, and take place periodically—typically annually, but more or less frequently—depending on the innovation cycle of the respective industries (e.g. bi-annually in the case of fashion and textile trade shows; once every two, three, or four years in the case of mechanical engineering/machine tool trade shows, and so on; see Golfetto 2004). Such temporal frequencies, coupled with repeated participation of a large number of exhibitors and visitors, make trade shows 'interorganizational rituals' that foster a sense of community among actors, who often view attendance as a social necessity that goes beyond utilitarian motivations (Borghini et al. 2006). Depending on the geographical origin of visitors and exhibitors (see Chapter 4), the community that gathers at a specific event may be local, regional, national, international, or even global in nature. This makes trade shows highly reactive to changes in import/export flows across countries and to the geographical distribution of their underlying industries.

Knowledge exchanges are crucial reasons for attending trade shows, ranging from the operational information required to conduct business to broader sense-making about key trends affecting markets and industries. Due to their focus on specific industry or technology fields, trade shows represent important meeting places for occupational/professional communities (Rinallo et al. 2007) that share similar or complementary knowledge bases and working practices. Learning at trade shows mostly occurs through face-to-face communication and interaction with/observation of artefacts (e.g. product samples, innovative solutions, or stand architecture), which provides an effective means for participants to transfer tacit knowledge (Kreiner 2002; Borghini et al. 2006; Rafaeli and Pratt 2006). Trade shows thus become relational spaces for focused interactions (see Chapter 3) that form an ideal basis to prepare economic transactions and enable knowledge creation and circulation over distance. In other words, these events play a critical role within the context of the emerging and deepening 'geographies of knowledge transfers over distance' (Bathelt and Henn 2014).

Trade shows have characteristics that set them apart from other types of events: (a) they are commercial events (i.e. arts, entertainment, education, or politics are not core elements, even though they are present in many shows); (b) trade shows of the type discussed in this book target professional audiences (i.e. not primarily the general public or consumers); (c) they constitute a form of collective, rather than individual, promotion (as they bring together many firms from the same industry or technology field); and (d) the experience they provide is based on showcasing physical exhibits and interacting with and around them.[1] These characteristics set them apart from other types of events.

(i) Events (in a broad sense): Events take place for a variety of different reasons and occur in many forms (Getz 1997), such as cultural celebrations, sport competitions, or educational, scientific, recreational, and political meetings. Trade shows often borrow elements from other types of events. They may be inaugurated by celebrities or politicians, for example, or they might involve arts exhibitions to celebrate an industry's history and tradition. In addition, trade shows sometimes include a programme of educational workshops, or conclude with a final party or concert. Nevertheless, these aspects are of marginal importance with respect to the main activities at the trade show, which are business driven. This is not to downplay the economic aspects of other events, which can be significant, as in the case of sports competitions (Masterman 2012) or cultural events, such as festivals (Moeren and Pedersen 2011) or award ceremonies (Anand and Watson 2004). It should also be noted that some cultural events adopt a trade show format, as in the case of arts or book fairs (Moeren and Pederson 2011; Yogev and Grund 2012). Consumers are often the primary targets of such events and commercial exploitation is mediated by the logic of arts (Caves 2000).

(ii) Business-to-business shows: With respect to audiences, trade shows differ dramatically depending on whether they target professional audiences or consumers (Golfetto 2004). Business-to-business events (trade shows in a strict sense—also known as B2B, business, or professional shows) link economic actors from different stages of a value chain to each other (i.e. producers of manufacturing technology, raw materials, and semi-finished products to producers of end products, and to distributors and retailers). Aside from marketing and product promotion information, these events generate critical knowledge flows related to production, technology development, the institutional environment, and market needs. This book centres on business-to-business trade shows because it is at these events that linkages and networks in production over space are prepared, maintained, or where they crystallize.

(iii) Business-to-consumer shows: These shows (also B2C or consumer shows), where exhibitor-producers showcase end products to consumers, are the heirs of

the old sample and agricultural fairs (see Chapter 2). After decades of decline linked to the modernization of distribution systems and the diffusion of mass communication, some of these events are now experiencing an era of renewed success thanks to the adoption of experiential formulas (Pine and Gilmore 1999; Schmitt 1999) based on product 'spectacularization' and consumer entertainment that aims to strengthen brands (Rinallo 2011a; Zarantonello and Schmitt 2013). While business-to-business shows are focused on learning opportunities, business-to-consumer shows are more hedonistic in character (i.e. visitors often attend to have pleasant experiences that are ends in themselves). The value-chain character of these events sometimes disappears and, as a result, these shows become less important for the development of the respective industry or technology fields.[2]

(iv) Corporate events: The collective nature of trade shows sets them apart from individual corporate events targeting professional audiences, such as incentive/reward events offered to top clients, corporate seminars and meetings, branding events, and product launches (Rinallo 2011a). While these individual business-to-business events may offer rich opportunities for interaction and learning, from a knowledge-based perspective, their scope is more limited. And from the visitors' standpoint, they do not enable the same type of learning by interaction and learning by observation as trade shows.

(v) Conferences: In the context of collective events, trade shows are often discussed together with conferences as business tourism events. Often occurring in the same dedicated spaces as trade shows, conferences are also sometimes termed congresses, conventions,[3] or, more generically, meetings (Rogers 2007). Some of these events (i.e. individual corporate events) are organized by larger firms for promotional or internal reasons, whereas others represent the periodic meeting places of professional associations and scientific societies. Learning and knowledge exchanges are often a central focus of conferences, and take place through formal presentations and papers that are relevant to business or scientific topics (Bathelt and Henn 2014).

(vi) Field-configuring events (FCEs): Like trade shows, certain types of conferences are viewed in organization studies as field-configuring events, especially those that affect the evolution of industries, markets, and technologies in discontinuous and more radical form (Garud 2008; Lampel and Meyer 2008; Hardy and Maguire 2010).

In sum, other event types do not focus on the kinds of physical artefacts that are at the core of trade show interactions. Nevertheless, many conferences and other events have developed trade show elements over time and display related products and technologies in a specific part of the event space. Producers of surgical precision instruments, for instance, exhibit their products at an international convention of surgeons. We thus find hybrids and mergers across different event formats, as trade shows also dedicate part of their space to conference presentations and convention meetings.

1.4. TRADE SHOWS, GLOBALIZATION, AND THE KNOWLEDGE ECONOMY

Trade shows may be viewed as instruments or mechanisms of globalization. Serving as important export promotion tools and necessary first steps in the internationalization strategies of firms (Bello and Barksdale 1986; Evers and Knight 2008; Golfetto 2004), trade shows have long provided the material conduit for firms in contacting and establishing a commercial presence in foreign markets. The development of international trade shows—and, consequently, their geographical distribution—is therefore closely related to the ups and downs of production cores and the growth or decline of long-distance exchanges between regions, countries, subcontinents, or continents.

By the late nineteenth century, economic processes, corporate production networks, and trade were already fairly international in nature. The popularity of world exhibitions during this period was thus no accident (see Chapter 2). Such exhibitions attracted thousands of visitors from around the world to see and inspect the technological progress of highly developed economies. This was a direct outcome of industrialization and driven by the goal to access new resources and markets. World exhibitions were an expression of associated growth patterns and reflected the progress that had been made (Findling and Pelle 2008). Industrial organization also became quite internationalized, with extensive international production networks developing in major manufacturing sectors. At the beginning of the twentieth century, however, the degree of economic internationalization decreased due to protectionist policies and the two World Wars, which destroyed many of the formerly established global connections (e.g. Held et al. 1999).

The levels of internationalization enjoyed in the late nineteenth century did not return until the 1970s and 1980s. Yet, this new wave of globalization differed from its predecessor due to reduced protectionism, new trade regimes, and the development of modern transportation, storage, and information and telecommunication technologies. As a consequence, international production, market, and technology structures became closely integrated, with production structures becoming increasingly decentralized and truly intertwined—to an extent never witnessed before (for an overview, Bathelt and Glückler 2012). It is during this current stage of globalization that knowledge flows and knowledge linkages have become pre-conditions to fostering innovation processes and producing product varieties targeted for the specific needs of different markets.

Parallel to this development, knowledge circulation and knowledge flows have become core components of trade show activity. These events are increasingly important in a globalized world because they assume the role of central nodes in the global economy (Bathelt and Zakrzewski 2007). They enable worldwide actors and firms to get together, physically inspect new products as benchmarks for their own activities, create and sustain new linkages, and reduce the uncertainty surrounding the extremely diverse cultural, institutional, economic, technological, social, and political structures in different countries and production settings (e.g. Maskell 2014). In a sense, globalization has fostered a further widening of the horizon of exchanges and a stronger fragmentation of supply chains across a multitude of geographically dispersed economic actors. While trade shows have been instrumental in accelerating globalization tendencies, they provide a means to temporarily recompose key nodes in supply chains and align the behaviours of distant actors (Rinallo and Golfetto 2006). As a consequence, learning and knowledge exchange processes at trade shows have reached an unprecedented level.

As documented in Chapters 6 to 8, globalization is accompanied by an international redistribution of trade show activities. After decades of growth, trade shows in Western European economies, in particular, are severely affected by the global restructuring of supply chains in manufacturing industries, the development of trade shows in Eastern Europe, South America, and Asia (limiting visitors from these countries at Western European events), and the need of exhibitors to attend non-European trade shows (Golfetto 2013). North America, as a whole, has suffered less from globalization, given the more self-contained nature of local/national markets. In contrast, trade shows localized in Eastern Europe, South America, and Asia, are growing at a very fast rate. There are, however, remarkable differences in the ecologies of trade shows and the interaction and learning opportunities they enable across geographical regions and industries. This is most obvious in the knowledge environments generated by different Asia-Pacific trade shows (Bathelt and Zeng 2014c).

With the foreseeable emergence of a new 'global shortage economy' (e.g. Giddens 1990) associated with the effects of global climate change, peak oil, and the resulting increase in transportation and mobility costs, trade shows could become even more significant in the future as crucial relational spaces through which international production networks can be sustained when other routinized regular direct exchanges become rare.

1.5. STRUCTURE OF THE BOOK

This book systematizes novel theoretical and empirical insights surrounding the role of trade shows in the globalizing knowledge economy by providing the foundations of a knowledge-based theory of trade shows. It consists of four parts and fifteen chapters.

Part I presents a knowledge-based understanding of industrial trade shows. It begins with a discussion of the functions played by trade shows in the past and their current role in the knowledge economy. Following a historical introduction to the evolution of such events, the core elements of a knowledge-based perspective of trade shows are outlined. Part I illustrates the fundamental two-way impact of trade show specialization on territorial economic specialization and vice versa. It also provides a knowledge-based categorization of trade shows based on exhibitor and visitor origin as local/national, export, import, and truly international hub events.

Chapter 2 focuses on the functions of trade shows in historical perspective. It provides a historical sketch of the development of trade shows since the Middle Ages and demonstrates how the nature of these events has changed over time. This includes shifts in the sets of participants, both in terms of exhibitors/sellers and visitors/buyers, as well as shifts in the nature of exchanges and interactions, with a general increase in the significance of knowledge flows. The chapter demonstrates that trade shows have developed from periodic markets where products are traded to events where knowledge exchange and dissemination, impulses for innovation and creativity, and the construction of networks have become increasingly important. This is evidenced by the changing roles of visitors (including 'atypical visitors'), exhibitors, and trade show organizers over time, which leads us to develop a specific knowledge-based view of trade shows.

Chapter 3 begins by conceptualizing trade shows as temporary markets in which vertical interactions along the value chain dominate and horizontal interactions between competitors occur as a side effect. The nature of these market relations is structured by trade show organizers in ways that facilitate exhibitors' promotional endeavours. While the role of sales and contract negotiations during these events has declined, knowledge flows have become more important over time, suggesting a knowledge-based conceptualization of trade shows as temporary clusters that are characterized by specific vertical, horizontal, and institutional dimensions. This multi-dimensional structure gives rise to a complex information and communication ecology that we refer to as 'global buzz'. The interdisciplinary conceptualization developed in this chapter integrates perspectives from economic geography and management studies.

Chapter 4 presents a knowledge-based typology of trade shows. It introduces a model of trade show types that builds upon an analysis of the degree of internationalization of visitors and exhibitors. This allows us to distinguish four types of trade shows: import shows, export shows, national/regional shows, and international hub shows. The chapter conceptualizes these different events by developing ideal types that are characterized by different patterns of knowledge flows.

Chapter 5 discusses how economic and cultural influences impact trade shows in particular places and how the resulting characteristics of these temporary events feed into permanent industry structures. After examining paradigmatic views of the relationship between trade shows and their underlying economic geographies, grounded in the structure–agency debate in the social sciences, we propose a two-way model of reciprocal influences between trade show specialization and territorial specialization. On the one hand, trade shows and their specialization patterns depend on the characteristics of firms located in the local/regional catchment basin, the image and cultural heritage of the hosting regions, and the national institutional set-up. On the other hand, trade shows impact hosting areas by generating local economic multiplier effects and regional development, facilitating the establishment of vertical pipelines with non-local business partners, and contributing to the reproduction of national specialization patterns. We also discuss how the link between trade shows and territories is stronger in some phases of the trade show life-cycle and for certain types of trade shows, as opposed to others. In aggregate terms—as industrial specialization depends on wider institutional settings and structures that are often defined at the national level—such reciprocal effects encourage ongoing specialization patterns within political economies instead of enforcing the dissemination of standardized best-practice solutions across them.

Part II provides a geographical analysis of trade show dynamics in Europe, North America, and Asia. This is based on secondary sources that provide statistical indicators regarding the size of trade show activity (e.g. surfaces sold or attendance levels), analysed from a globalization and knowledge perspective.

Chapter 6 analyses trade show dynamics in the mature European markets. The chapter describes the nature, structure, and evolution of the trade show business in Europe. The presence of export-oriented small- and medium-sized enterprises, in particular, has given rise to many export and hub trade shows, characterized by global knowledge flows. In this context, the chapter discusses geographical shifts within Europe, trends in trade show activity by country and industry group, typical trade show stakeholders and governance models, and the rise of competitive environments.

Chapter 7 investigates trade show dynamics in another set of mature markets in North America. The chapter compares the rise and structure of trade shows in North America to those in Europe. Different ideal types of trade show development are identified, and changing patterns in trade show attendance and size are discussed according to industry group, hosting city, and country. The analysis finds that the nature of these events and their stakeholders differ from those in Europe and that these variations relate to underlying differences in the manufacturing system. The large internal market and large size of manufacturing firms have led to the development of demand trade shows, with a mainly regional or continental focus.

Chapter 8 turns to the emerging or developing trade show markets in the Asia-Pacific region. By investigating variations in the status of trade show activity and the different specializations of events in different countries, we demonstrate that the trade show business in the Asia-Pacific region is highly heterogeneous. The chapter also looks at how trade shows play a different role in various political economies and how policies to support the trade show business follow different national strategies. This, in turn, contributes to their development and to specialization patterns. Specific attention is paid to the recent development of trade show activity in China, where events have grown exponentially as a consequence of the increasing local/national demand and the relocation of traditional manufacturing activities from Western Europe and North America. Overall, the restructuring of the trade show industry worldwide, and its implications for the global circulation of knowledge, brings forth a new era of polycentric knowledge circulation processes. This is characterized by a situation in which the key trade shows in each continent attract worldwide manufacturers to present innovations that match specific local/national/continental market needs.

Part III of the book focuses on the knowledge acquisition and creation practices enabled by trade shows in different industries, including lighting, meat processing, fashion, fabrics, furniture, machinery, tiles, and marbles. This part is based on primary studies conducted by the authors. More specifically, the chapters document interaction practices and patterns of knowledge flows across events in the same industry groups. We also highlight the importance of trade shows in the affirmation of technological standards and style innovation, and their role in supporting the origin and growth of industries. The analysis documents the knowledge generation, dissemination, and acquisition practices carried out by organizers, exhibitors, and visitors in contexts driven by different knowledge bases, from high technology to style and design.

Chapter 9 discusses different knowledge practices in hub shows, comparing the cases of lighting versus meat processing technology. It investigates design-intensive versus technology-oriented hub shows to explore the nature of interaction practices and knowledge flows, noting how these vary across different industry and design contexts, creating different types of temporary clusters. The discussion is based on a comparison of two hub shows: Light and Building (L + B) and IFFA in Germany.

Chapter 10 explores cyclical meetings and varying knowledge practices at trade shows in different countries by analysing three international lighting shows: L + B (Germany), LightFair International (US), and IIDEX/Neocon Canada (Canada). The chapter compares the nature of knowledge practices and interaction patterns and the linkages between the shows. Although the events are bound together in the context of cyclical meetings involving ongoing developments and technology discussions within industry/technology fields, they attract different sets of exhibitors and visitors that attend these events for different purposes. The participants take part in the events as members of loosely connected knowing communities, contributing to the reproduction, rather than configuration, of their industry and technology fields.

Chapter 11 describes the evolution and knowledge practices of export and import shows in the case of fabrics. Using the example of fabric shows in Italy, it explores the connection between temporary and permanent clusters, and finds that industrial districts have given rise to specific close-by import or export trade shows that are directly related to the regional industry specialization at hand. The chapter discusses patterns of knowledge flows during such import or export shows and identifies problems for future development that may require shifts, relocations, or mergers of some of these shows.

Chapter 12 demonstrates the impact of the knowledge practices applied by trade show organizers by analysing the 'concertation processes' in fashion that shape design innovation in the industry. It finds that knowledge practices are structured and actively shaped by the role of trade show organizers in pre-arranging parts of the field. Using the example of fashion fabrics, what appears to be an emerging fashion trend during a trade show has actually been planned and orchestrated long before the event. The case of Premiere Vision is used to demonstrate that trade show organizers can have a distinct impact on the nature of knowledge flows and the resulting practices that take place during a show.

Chapter 13 presents the cases of ceramics and marble technologies as examples of knowledge flows and competition between export shows in an international context. The chapter focuses on the rivalry between events and venues and how this shapes the dynamic geographies of trade show development. It is demonstrated how increasing global competition in ceramics and marble technologies puts pressure on trade shows and their associated knowledge practices in Germany and Italy.

In Chapter 14, the dynamics of knowledge flows in export shows are illustrated, focusing on the affirmation processes in the furniture industry. Using the case of Italian furniture shows, it is demonstrated how knowledge practices are in a constant state of emergence and reconstruction due to geographical competition between different exhibition centres.

Part IV discusses the policy implications of a knowledge-based view of trade shows for key actors involved in or affected by those events. Chapter 15 demonstrates the implications of a knowledge-based understanding of trade shows by highlighting the main findings of the book and drawing policy conclusions regarding the role of trade shows in the context of globalization. Policy conclusions are directed towards industrial firms and their knowledge acquisition practices, organizers of trade shows, national industry associations, as well as regional and national economic policy-makers and their programmes.

NOTES

1. Depending on their market position, trade shows dedicated to consumer goods may target professional audiences, consumers, or both. In the latter case, mixed trade shows result. In contrast, trade shows dedicated to industrial products and technology are only directed to professional audiences, as these product categories

do not trigger consumer interest. From an exhibitor's perspective, mixed shows can be problematic, as exhibition philosophies behind communication with consumers versus professional audiences are very different. Audience heterogeneity may also be problematic for professional audiences that get annoyed by overcrowded exhibition spaces. Some large trade shows that are primarily business events deal with this by opening up for consumers on the last day only.

2. Trade shows are sometimes also referred to as exhibitions or expositions. In the context of this book, we do not employ this terminology, but reserve it for other, often singular events such as arts or photographic exhibitions or world fairs (also known as expos). While the history of world fairs is intertwined with that of trade shows (see Chapter 2), the former are less commercial in nature and present countries as 'exhibitors' (Findling and Pelle 2008).

3. While conventions are sometimes simply viewed as large conferences, they are better defined as total membership-meetings. They focus on the reproduction of associations, clubs, or other specific communities, but, like conferences, also involve presentations and keynote speakers (Kerr and King 1984; Bathelt and Henn 2014).

Part I

Towards a Knowledge-Based Understanding of Trade Shows

2

Functions of Trade Shows:
A Historical Perspective

2.1. INTRODUCTION

This chapter discusses the historical evolution of the functions of trade fairs. Since ancient times, fairs have provided a significant opportunity for the exchange and dissemination of production knowledge between populations living in different geographic areas. However, for a long time, these functions were inherent and not immediately recognized by the firms or in the scientific literature. In fact, they took a back seat to critical functions, such as the exchange, presentation, and marketing of products, which were the primary reasons for the existence of fairs.

Especially since the nineteenth and twentieth centuries, the organizational models for fairs have changed substantially. Initially the organizational model of fairs was limited by the need to organize the physical distribution of the goods. With the rise of sample fairs in the nineteenth century, products were displayed as examples of merchandise that could be manufactured and delivered at a later date. With this development, the core function of fairs shifted towards showcasing innovations made within a specific period by individual companies and entire industries. Another milestone in this evolution concerns the range of technologies and products represented. While fairs were originally general in nature—their main purpose sometimes being to highlight the progress of a given economic area—they narrowed their focus in the twentieth century to highlight innovations in specific sectors. Consequently, fairs targeting professionals (now often called trade shows, rather than fairs or trade fairs, to differentiate them from consumer shows for end users) have become prime places for exhibiting 'available capabilities'. For exhibiting firms, this objective takes precedence over the sale of products. From the perspective of visitors, such events are now seen as an opportunity to obtain a close-up view of industry trends—a function that is more important than making purchase decisions. As a result, trade shows have become a highly specialized, professionalism-building experience for all participants, and are attended by industrial buyers or distributors, often separated from the end consumer. But more than anything else, trade shows have become dedicated events for specific sectors, where learning opportunities are offered through physical contact with products and manufacturers. Here, trade show participants have a chance to become fully immersed in an environment that mimics the target market, with all its associated issues and opportunities.

While it is true that knowledge exchanges also occurred in the past, in the less evolved types of trade shows (commodity fairs), contemporary exchanges tend to be more substantial and efficient and take place during highly specialized shows. At the heart of these knowledge exchanges, there has always been—and continues to be—the presence of artefacts, along with the technical production staff, as well as buying firms and their respective technical staff. This has given rise to important material practices. For instance, trade show participants are able to touch the products that are being presented, notice who is buying, engage in discussions with technicians, and so on. These material practices reinforce cognitive processes and encourage dialogue between firms. Finally, since these exchanges take place in a material context, where it is possible to perceive hundreds and sometimes thousands of other exchanges, an opportunity for collective sense-making is created. This not only enables participants to sharpen their view of the state of the industry and its recent developments, it also encourages convergent interpretations regarding the future direction of the industry.

The next section of this chapter analyses the evolution of fairs, from the ancient market fairs to the specialized trade shows that we see today. The following section then looks at the functions of events for both exhibitors and visitors. It also examines the ways in which these functions have evolved due to changes in the parallel development of information and communication technologies and the evolution of industries. The last part of the chapter discusses the functions of trade shows for local industries or business networks and for hosting areas.

2.2. ORIGIN AND EVOLUTION OF TRADE SHOWS

2.2.1. Commodity Fairs

The origin of fairs dates back to ancient civilizations and to trade across various continents. In Europe, for instance, many significant fairs of the past originated even before the founding of Rome, in the era of the great Celtic pilgrimages. At that time, many fairs were also organized in Egypt and Greece, in cities whose location put them in a prime position for international trade. In India, fairs have been reported as far back as 4000 BC, while in China the first such events date back to 3000 BC (Allix 1922).

From the very beginning, fairs stood out from other kinds of markets because of their singularity and the unique products traded. Whereas markets were frequently held and the products traded were of local origin, fairs were usually held annually, bringing together goods and merchants from distant lands. This stimulated the 'break-up of the traditional circle of trade' (Braudel 1979: 56). These fairs also accepted the exchange of different national currencies, leading to the name 'exchange fairs' as well as 'commodity fairs'. At the time, everyday exchanges were limited due to political isolation and high customs or, simply, by challenges associated with the means of communication. In places where there were fewer such barriers, there was no need for large fairs (Turgot 1757; Lanaro 2003). Thus, these events were organized around special incentives, such as exemptions from customs duty (primarily with Roman and Chinese fairs), and held at the same time as religious festivals or athletic games, during which hostilities between territories were suspended. During the Middle Ages in Europe, the 'peace of the fair' was protected by kings and feudal lords who wanted to ensure that merchants travelled safely and met their contracted obligations. This form of peace influenced the earliest systems of commercial law and international agreements, as well as certain forms of advertising about the legal affairs of individual merchants, which served to instil confidence in buyers (Milgrom et al. 1990). Fairs also enjoyed the support of the large monarchies, which realized great gains from the commercial traffic and cultural exchanges on their lands (Allix 1922).

Among the fairs whose histories have been well-documented are those in Europe, held between the twelfth and thirteenth centuries CE, including the French fairs in Flanders, Champagne, and Lyon, the German ones in Hamburg, Leipzig, and Frankfurt, and those of the English Midlands (Verlinden 1963; Bautier 1970; Moore 1985; Munro 2001). Many handcrafted items and livestock products made their way to these fairs, which had a great impact on European commerce (Allix 1922; Braudel 1979). Towards the end of the fifteenth century, European fairs went into a steep decline that initially affected the fairs in France and then those in Germany. This decline was precipitated by a number of factors, including the termination of exemption from customs duties, plagues, and the many local wars which kept foreign merchants away and curtailed local trade. The surviving French fairs acquired a primarily agricultural focus, while the hub of commodity fairs moved to southern Russia. This fair complex, which promoted exchanges between Europe and Asia, survived until the Russian Revolution in 1917. But it was the evolution of fixed locations for wholesalers and retailers, along with improvements in communications and shipping, that most affected the decline of commodity fairs. Orders could now be placed from a distance, based on samples, without rigid geographical limitations or the need for merchandise to be physically present (Allix 1922; De Roover 1942; Weber 1961; Epstein 1994).

2.2.2. Expositions, Sample Fairs, and Industrial Trade Shows

The industrial revolution brought about a new chapter in the evolution of fairs. This evolution took the form of a cycle of large expositions (Ley and Olds 1988; Roche 1999)—or expos, for short—during which physical products were not sold. These one-off (non-periodic) expos were designed primarily to focus the public's attention on industrial and scientific progress in specific countries. While they initially were domestic events, expos soon broadened to become international in scope. Among the first events of this kind were the Parisian expositions of French industrial accomplishments (1798–1849), the expositions in London (1756 and 1761), and the Geneva expo (1789). Perhaps the top international exposition of this period was the one held in London in 1851, which boasted at least 50 per cent foreign visitors. This was soon followed by many international expos in Paris and other major cities in Europe (Dublin, Munich, etc.) and beyond (Chicago, Melbourne, and New York). In essence, however, these expos retained mainly political and social content, and had the primary goal of demonstrating the production and the progress of the country, in which they were organized.

A major development occurred when some of the traditional commodity fairs changed their format to differentiate themselves from the retail markets by allowing only the display of samples. Thus, the new 'sample fairs', which recurred periodically, took on the role of events for placing orders, rather than a market configuration where goods were delivered directly to customers. The new formula was introduced at the Leipzig Fair in 1894, but was quickly followed by fairs in Lyon, London, Paris, and gradually all the others. Many of these shows were also created to promote international trade in the aftermath of the First World War (Allix 1922; Carreras and Torra 2005).

After this transformation, fairs regained their vitality, taking the lead in the area of trade relations in and between industrialized nations. For some time, however, fairs were still highly general in nature. Exhibitors from many sectors worked side by side, and the visitor pool included both professional buyers and end users. From the perspective of exhibitors, the fair was a vehicle for presenting the firm's products and acquiring purchase orders; for visitors, fairs were the easiest way to stay informed about the technical advances and industrial output of each sector. These particular functions, based on non-specialized promotion–information exchange at generic sample fairs, lasted until the late 1950s (Golfetto 1988).

In the years that followed, fairs underwent two other important transformations. First, professionals became the primary (or even only) attendees at these events, as mass consumers increasingly turned to mass communication to replace fairs as a source of updated information. Secondly, in keeping up with the growing complexity and diversity of manufacturing sectors, fairs became increasingly specialized in nature. Trade show specialization also led to differentiation between visitor types (consumer fairs and business fairs), which was further divided by manufacturing sectors, production stages, and distribution channels. These new shows are now known as industrial shows or trade shows.

2.2.3. Specialized Trade Shows, Buying Time, and Global Circuits

Between the 1970s and 1980s, there was dramatic growth in trade shows, particularly in Europe. This expansion later extended to North America and other industrialized countries, albeit to a lesser degree. More recently, the rapid growth of trade shows has also extended to newly developed areas, most notably China, India, and South America (see Part II).

The trend towards increased specialization was accompanied by the periodic recurrence and regular scheduling of fairs. These patterns focused on the timing of purchasing and replacement processes for industrial buyers and distribution channels, each one quite different and specific to its sector and sub-sector. Eyewear fairs, for example, are held at the beginning of the year or at the end of the summer, depending on whether they are more focused on corrective eyewear or on sunglasses. The timing of yarn fairs is related to their subsequent applications in knitwear, fabrics, and clothing or furniture, and so on, and their dates consequently depend on the buyers they are devoted to. The periodic cycle also takes into account the typical pace of innovations. Consequently, in industries tied to fashion and clothing, trade shows are predominantly semi-annual to reflect the fast rate of innovation in those industries, while for most products, trade shows are held annually. In the areas of machinery and production technologies for traditional manufacturing, trade shows are typically held every two or three years. Generally, trade fairs in new technologies occur more frequently than in mature technologies (Golfetto 2004).

Importantly, the scheduling of individual exhibitions also takes into account the dates of other trade shows in the same industry held around the world, in a very sophisticated system of balance and competition between global, national, and local reference fairs. In the scheduling, trade show organizers aim to allow international buyers to visit the leading trade shows for the various production sectors, in the ongoing search by industrial buyers (Borghini et al. 2006; Power and Jansson 2008; Bathelt and Gibson 2014). This enables them to visit numerous events serving their own sector in any given year.

Even consumer shows, following the difficulties associated with the decline of general fairs, have experienced an impressive revival and are still thriving both in Europe and North America and in less industrialized countries worldwide. Certain consumer segments (such as sports, food, or automotive) are good examples of this, as are some other product segments that are linked to local traditions, religious festivities, and agriculture. The former, in particular, benefit from the recent spread of experiential marketing (Pine and Gilmore 1998; Schmitt 1999; Rinallo 2011a; Golfetto and Rinallo 2013). This type of marketing has transformed many trade shows into places where firms have an opportunity to get close to their consumers, allowing for sensory and relational experiences that emphasize the specificity of the brand. Events that celebrate local traditions are more similar to retail markets. In any case, consumer shows represent worlds that are quite different from those where the coordination of industrial processes and knowledge transfer, discussed earlier with regard to business fairs, takes place. In some ways, however, they can be a source of inspiration for industrial innovations, thanks to the observation of the behaviours of end consumers (Golfetto 2004). Consumer shows are not included in the schedules and cycles of the purchasing process. In many countries they often take place during time periods of good weather or are associated with agricultural and religious traditions.

It is important to note that the sharp distinction between business and consumer fairs is primarily found in Western countries with highly specialized production. With respect to business fairs, this distinction extends further to fairs representing different industry sectors and stages in the supply chain (CERMES 2012a). In newly developed countries, business fairs are often open to consumers and cover many different sectors and supply chains at the same time. It is likely that these countries will also experience processes of increased specialization similar to what occurred in Europe at the end of the last century.

2.3. FUNCTIONS OF TRADE SHOWS FOR VISITING AND EXHIBITING FIRMS

The evolution of trade fairs occurred at the same time as important changes were taking place in the functions of these events for participating businesses. Visitors repeatedly changed their motivations for attending these recurring events, causing a shift in the way exhibitors chose to participate in fairs as well.

2.3.1. Functions for Visitors: Learning Processes of Buyers and Non-Buyers

The first stage in the transformation of fairs, namely, the transition from periodic markets (which included the physical exchange of goods) to sample fairs (where exhibitors from various industries took orders but deferred delivery to a later date) provided more space for exhibitors. It also made the fairs run more smoothly for visitors. This change led to the discovery of a greater number of products, manufacturers, and technologies from different geographic areas, making it easy to compare products and place orders with existing and new suppliers. The next stage, namely, the specialization of fairs by industry and stage of production, completed this process. End consumers were no longer part of the mix of visitors at a normal business fair and the increased focus on the business community opened up more possibilities for vertical relationships, where visitors met with exhibitor-manufacturers, as well as horizontal relationships between suppliers and other exhibitor-suppliers or between visitors and other visitor-buyers. At specialized trade shows today, visitors often recognize each other and have conversations about their own actions and impressions. These types of interactions are an important part of the information-gathering and knowledge-exchange processes underlying their participation at trade shows.

Following the evolution of fairs into trade shows, some important changes in visitor profiles have occurred. At present, visitors are much more diversified than in the past and have objectives that extend well beyond buying or gathering information about buying. First of all, we now see large numbers of trade show attendees who are non-buyers or not linked to industry buying centres (atypical visitors); instead, these atypical visitors attend trade shows to glean important information and expertise about the industry. Second, the prevailing interest of visitor-buyers is no longer driven by the goal of short-term buying, but rather by a desire to conduct 'learning expeditions' to better understand developments in the competitive and demand environments (Borghini et al. 2006). Next, we examine how trade shows work for typical and atypical visitors and describe the associated learning environments.

(i) Typical visitors

For a long time, the trade show literature focused on a single type of visitor, the so-called 'typical' visitor (Borghini et al. 2006). This type presents the key target audience for exhibitors because they make or influence buying decisions for customer firms. Marketing studies have shown that, unlike consumer behaviour, corporate purchasing decisions are subject to long, complicated procedures that involve people from different departments (e.g. purchasing, product development, and marketing) with different levels of influence in the decision-making process (Robinson et al. 1967; Gingold and Wilson 1998). Influenced by studies of cognitive and social psychology, the literature on this subject has made several attempts to model the purchase process of industrial buyers and the most useful sources of information (including trade shows) for each of the phases in that process (see Figure 2.1).

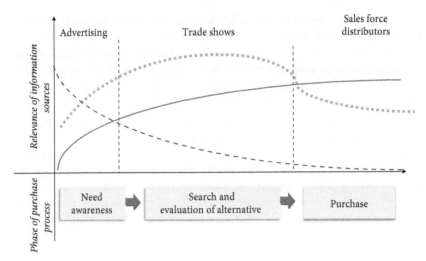

Figure 2.1. The role of trade shows in the industrial buyer information mix (Golfetto 2004)

Based on one of the most well-known models (Gopalakrishna and Lilien 1995; Golfetto 2004), the buying process can be segmented into three phases: awareness of need, search for information, and purchase. The empirical literature points out that advertising is particularly effective in stimulating new needs that buyers may not be aware of (such as more powerful technology). Because it is not impartial and is mediated by media and therefore impersonal and less direct, advertising becomes less useful in the later stages of the purchasing process, giving way to other tools such as trade shows. Because of the associated agglomeration of competing sellers in one place (Florio 1994), trade shows are most effective when industrial buyers are looking for information about available alternatives. Information gathering through trade shows is more efficient than many other common sources because it is not mediated by the media; indeed, the information acquired during these events is experiential in nature. Direct contact with the sales network and distributors of preferred suppliers is very useful in finalizing purchases.

While it does not adopt a knowledge-based vision, the model qualifies trade shows as places of learning for short-term purchase decisions. Recent marketing studies have demonstrated how typical visitors often fall short of exhibitors' expectations because many are not necessarily interested in making immediate purchases. According to Borghini et al.'s (2006) analysis of a large visitor sample, only 22–34 per cent of buyers, industrial users, and retailers attended trade shows with the intention of making purchases within the next few months (see Table 2.1). Typical visitors are, instead, more interested in building a stock of

Table 2.1. Main attendance motives for visitors from buying firms, 2004

Trade shows	Main attendance motives		
	Making purchases (share of firms)	Getting informed; knowing the market; seeing novelties (share of firms)	Total sample (number of firms)
Trade shows dedicated to trade (retailers, wholesalers, importers, etc.)			
Micam	29%	71%	78
Mipel	21%	63%	80
Momi	34%	63%	71
Moda Prima	52%	43%	21
Mifur	32%	68%	40
Salone del Mobile	35%	63%	112
Macef	44%	54%	118
Average	34%	62%	520
Trade shows dedicated to industrial users			
Xylexpo	20%	78%	187
Fluidtrans Compomac	9%	86%	95
Sasmil	16%	75%	152
Moda In[1]	67%	31%	61
Average	22%	73%	495

Source: Borghini et al. 2006.

Note: [1]Investigated in 2003.

knowledge about products, suppliers, and solutions for future reference; meeting with and paying courtesy visits to known and regular suppliers; updating professional skills and thus improving their credibility within their organization; drawing 'inspirations' for product innovation; taking part in an important industry event; being part of the professional community that convenes at the show; and being reassured, in times of crisis, by the presence of suppliers and customers (Borghini et al. 2006). In other words, information search is not necessarily motivated by short-term purchase motivations and is interpreted by many visitors as an opportunity to remain current or buy time to reflect on broader issues. Visits to trade shows thus result in new ideas and unexpected knowledge for future use (Rinallo et al. 2010; Bathelt and Gibson 2014). While previous studies in marketing identify such motivations (e.g. Rothschild 1987; Morris 1988; Dudley 1990; Sharland and Balogh 1996; Godar and O'Connor 2001), recent research points to a more complex and nuanced view of visitor motivations, paving the way for the conceptualization of trade shows as focal points in the global knowledge economy covered in this book (Bathelt and Zakrzewski 2007).

Finally, a meaningful aspect of the knowledge-based view of trade shows can also be found in the business functions of visitors and their behaviour following the visit. In recent years, the share of visitors from purchasing departments seems to have dropped, while the proportion of research and development engineers, production engineers, designers, and marketing and sales managers who make regular visits to trade shows has increased—each with their own goals and perspectives (opportunities for new products, new markets, sales channels, etc.). At the end of their visits, they often write reports and bring back samples to share with their firm, along with whatever they saw or found at the show that was innovative and thought-provoking (Rinallo 2011a). The members of the various departments are, in fact, the main channels of 'absorptive capacity' in the firms' learning processes (Cohen and Levinthal 1990; Zahra and George 2002).

(ii) Atypical visitors

The presence of many 'atypical visitors' emerged in various research studies at American and European shows (e.g. Bello and Lohtia 1993; Rosson and Seringhaus 1995; Godar and O'Connor 2001). Recent findings indicate that, at many European shows, the atypical visitor share is higher than in the past, sometimes exceeding 50 per cent of the total number of visitors (Borghini et al. 2006; see Table 2.2).

Atypical visitors are mostly exhibitors' suppliers, exhibitors' competitors, and firms in related industries. There are different reasons why trade shows attract this type of visitor (Borghini et al. 2004). Exhibitors' suppliers, for example, collect market intelligence on downstream sectors and try to establish

Table 2.2. Composition of trade show audiences, 2004

Trade shows	Share of buyers or influencers	Share of atypical visitors	Total sample (number of visitors)
Trade shows dedicated to trade (retailers, wholesalers, exporters, etc.)			
Micam	77%	23%	101
Mipel	78%	22%	103
Momi	71%	29%	100
Moda Prima	42%	58%	50
Mifur	80%	20%	50
Salone del Mobile	41%	59%	274
Macef	77%	23%	153
Average	63%	37%	831
Trade shows dedicated to industrial users			
Xylexpo	81%	19%	231
Fluidtrans Compomac	95%	5%	100
Sasmil	77%	23%	198
Moda In[1]	81%	19%	75
Average	82%	18%	604

Source: Borghini et al. 2006.

Note: [1]Investigated in 2003.

contacts for future sales. They also visit their customer-exhibitors in a sort of relational rite common to all industries. By visiting downstream market trade shows, these suppliers can glean an insight into the customer's end market, which inspires ideas for their own innovations. Exhibitors' competitors, on the other hand, typically undertake competitive intelligence activities and look out for innovation ideas. They range from firms belonging to the same regions or industrial districts (which send their designers, technicians, and representatives to gather information about new products), to producers from other countries and low-cost imitators. Operators from related industries try to verify whether their own strategic choices are aligned with those of exhibitors (e.g. fashion accessory producers may assess to what extent the colours and patterns of their new collections are in line with those of apparel producers) and, like the others, they are on the lookout for inspiration and cross-fertilization (Borghini et al. 2004).

Classic marketing studies viewed atypical visitors as marginal targets that were of little importance and were not conducive to the goal of making contacts for future sales. At best, these 'curious' visitors were considered a waste of time, which at this time could have been better invested in interactions with potential customers; at worst, they were viewed as competitors in disguise, digging for confidential information about new products. From a knowledge-based viewpoint, however, atypical visitors contribute to further qualifying the role played by trade shows as nerve-centres of knowledge-based economies bringing together an increasingly fragmented and geographically scattered value chain. This concept will be more thoroughly discussed in Chapters 3 and 4.

A key point is that a significant proportion of trade show visitors do not repay exhibitors in terms of their marketing investments. Thus exhibitors can be considered as providers of free externalities to all visitors that are not (at least potentially) customers. Because of this, overall visitor attendance statistics published by trade show organizers do not necessarily mirror the size of the target groups whose presence motivates exhibitors' participation (Borghini et al. 2004). Some exhibitors react to this situation by adopting countermeasures, such as creating a booth design that prevents visitors from seeing the products from the outside if this is a sensitive topic—but this is not possible in many industries. Such measures, which make sense from the individual exhibitor's perspective, reduce the trade show's learning potential, which is at least partially based on visual stimuli.

(iii) Learning at trade shows

In essence, visitors (both typical and atypical) at trade shows are engaged in real 'learning expeditions'. These processes are based on live experiences of immersion in stimulating environments (sometimes excessively so), which are much more intense than those experienced through other means of information, such as advertisements or websites. Trade shows plunge industrial buyers into a physical and cognitive experience that requires their active participation. The quest for information, which is viewed as a purely cognitive activity in the first generation of marketing studies, is instead an embodied experience that takes place under conditions of reduced attention. Indeed, it amounts to sensory and information overload and physical fatigue (Rinallo et al. 2010), connected to the overwhelming amount of information and stimuli to be processed in limited time, while moving around inside the trade show centre. Thus visitors have developed their own learning and relational practices involving the various learning elements of trade shows.

Here are the results of ethnographic research on the behaviour and evaluations of visitors at a sample of international trade shows, with reference to the elements that they consider most important for learning (Borghini et al. 2004, 2006; Rinallo et al. 2010).

- Leaders and regular suppliers: Despite some variance, there are remarkable similarities in the route followed by visitors and the time dedicated to different types of exhibitors. A typical visit: (i) starts with a visit to the stand of market leaders, (ii) continues on to regular suppliers, and (iii) devotes residual time to other exhibitors. The impressions picked up in-between are much less systematic or predictable, however (Bathelt and Gibson 2014). The stands of market leaders are often considered worth a visit, even when these firms are not regular suppliers. Visitors say that leaders are often among the main innovation carriers in the industry. Only after these stands have been checked out do visitors meet their regular suppliers. This is a crucial moment, as they can evaluate and compare the innovation activity of their partners with the innovation provided by the leaders. Finally, industrial buyers search for new suppliers only if time allows. This behaviour confirms the idea that buyers visit trade shows with the main objective of being reassured about the quality and the innovative capacity of their current supplier and not so much to identify possible new partners (Godar and O'Connor 2001; Blythe 2002).
- Trend areas: Some trade shows have 'trend areas' where innovative products or technologies (selected by the organizer) are arranged in creative and visually appealing ways. These areas are frequently visited by industrial buyers to gain an immediate impression of new trends and to quickly identify the suppliers of the most interesting products. Technical seminars or conferences during trade shows are also considered good sources of learning. However, these initiatives offered by organizers do not replace a visit to leaders.
- Vertical and horizontal relational experiences: Besides cognitive elements, relational opportunities are an important aspect of a valuable trade show

experience. They allow visitors to establish or maintain social bonds with key actors in their business networks and to explore technical information in greater depth. Visitors appreciate the opportunity to meet members of the suppliers' staff with whom they do not usually interact. They might, for example, ask for technical help from the engineer who designed the machine they have bought, or have informal conversations on future fashion trends with creative designers. With respect to horizontal relations, interaction among visitors involves engaging with people in similar positions in other firms (e.g. other technicians, buyers, or designers). By providing occupational communities with a neutral setting for these interactions, trade shows represent important sources of knowledge via informal conversations that contribute to the dissemination of knowledge about products and suppliers, but also through rumours and gossip (e.g. Bathelt and Schuldt 2008). However, unlike exhibitors, other visitors are difficult to locate at trade shows. Therefore, any opportunity to interact informally with colleagues in the sector is much appreciated (e.g. cocktail hours at the exhibitor stands and technical seminars or social events provided by trade show organizers).

• Stand contents—experience with products: When visiting stands, visitors particularly welcome the presence of products and competent personnel. The option to see and touch products is important as products are often considered tangible evidence of firms' competencies, and as firms from different parts of the value chain employ different strategies to demonstrate such competences. In the fashion value chain, for example, producers of fabrics and machinery often display clothing items made with their products (Golfetto and Mazursky 2004). In this way, visitors can evaluate the supplier knowledge of trends in consumer fashion (the end market) and derive inspiration for their own new collections. Visitors like to take away samples or prototypes, in order to bring a part of their experience back to their firms. Samples, prototypes, and the accompanying documentations serve as artefacts that recall the competencies of the producers inspected. They can also be shared more easily with colleagues who did not attend the event (Bechky 2003a; Lorenzoni and Narduzzo 2005; Stigliani and Ravasi 2012).

• Stand contents—experience with people: Interaction with competent personnel is the second element which makes a visit to a stand a valuable experience. The opportunity to speak to the exhibitor's technical personnel is in itself an important return on the investment to visit the firm. In one remarkable instance, for example, a large Japanese machine producer drew substantial attention by bringing research and development staff from the parent firm to meet local visitors during the main European trade show. Finally, the 'leisure' interaction opportunities offered by exhibitors during, for instance, cocktail hours, invitations to dinners, social events, and so on, provide relief from the tiring visit and serve to create and reinforce social bonds with the producers' staff. Moreover, interactions with other buyers are also fostered.

- Off-site events: In the pursuit of stimulating experience, visitors bask in the atmosphere that surrounds the events, fuelling phenomena like off-site events. Businesses and cities are well aware of these phenomena and often respond by organizing spaces and opportunities for interaction. These are not only commercially oriented activities but also recreational and cultural events that palpably enhance the climate and trade show experience tied to the participants' fields of interest. An example is the case of Berlin, many years ago, when visitors from the fashion world went in search (outside the 'official' show facilities) of the perspectives of taste and traditions of the expanding Europe. It also happens today at the Salone del Mobile in Milan, where the 'fuori salone' (off-site events) have become a fixture. These largely attract professionals and young people who cultivate a passion for design and are looking for inspiration and ideas for new products by participating in the rites and rituals of their community, as well as by observing the behaviour of the most sophisticated consumers, namely the Italians (see Chapter 14).

2.3.2. Functions for Exhibitors: Impartive and Absorptive Activities

In recent years, there have also been important developments in the functions of trade shows for exhibitors. The traditional functions are to write orders, promote sales, and strengthen the firms' images. These are flanked by some functions that the literature has only recently begun to highlight. On the whole, these functions pertain to the role that trade shows play in focusing on knowledge-based activities. Exhibitors learn at the show, by observing competitors and by asking their technicians to interact with potential customers (absorptive activities). At the same time they also disseminate knowledge about themselves and their products with a promotional purpose. Such kinds of knowledge dissemination are referred to as 'impartive activities' (Golfetto et al. 2004; Zerbini et al. 2006), as the knowledge voluntarily flows from the exhibitors to potential customers.

(i) *The sales promotion function: from product communication to competence release*

Exhibitors bear the costs of trade shows with the main objective of promoting the sale of their products. By exhibiting at trade shows, manufacturers are considered by buyer-visitors as potential suppliers in exploring their selection alternatives, or in deciding whether to make a repurchase if considered competitive enough.

The sales function is especially crucial for small- and medium-sized businesses that do not have their own sales organization or specific distributors in the area. In this case (and despite the importance of non-buyers), trade shows serve the primary purpose of taking direct orders, which happens on a regular basis, either during the show or in the months immediately afterwards. Many firms exhibit at multiple trade shows (even twenty to thirty per year) with the aim of getting orders from different geographical areas or in market segments where they do not yet have distributors.

When a firm is well-established and its main customers are already well-known, as is the case with many European firms in continental European markets, sales-related activities fade into the background. The primary objectives then revolve around strengthening the firm's corporate image and its customer relations. In this context, even the stands assume a different look. When sales are the primary goal, stands focus on presenting the latest products; the sales staff is on hand; and there are office spaces dedicated to negotiations. The transition to the relational phase requires greater attention to image, focusing only on new products, and the presence of areas for socialization and entertainment (see Table 2.3). This change has taken place in many trade shows in leading manufacturing countries, but a third change is also taking place—namely, towards the promotion of the manufacturers' competencies (Barney 1991; Hamel and Prahalad 1994) rather than their products only (Golfetto and Mazursky 2004; Golfetto and Gibbert 2006; Zerbini et al. 2007).

In this instance, change is again motivated by new needs of the visitor-buyers. On the one hand, thanks to the internet, information about firms and their products is much more accessible and routine purchases no longer require physical contact with producers. On the other hand, potential buyers express the need for more complex information, or to understand where the industry as a whole is headed, how demand is performing, and what innovations

Table 2.3. Stand space distribution at textile/apparel trade shows by exhibited products, 2004–2007

	Consumer products	Intermediate products	Capital goods	Average stand space distribution
Product exhibition	73%	44%	61%	60%
Professional interaction	20%	53%	30%	34%
Relaxation and socialization	7%	3%	9%	6%
Total	100%	100%	100%	100%

Source: Rinallo et al. 2010.

will be offered in the next years. They also need to add to this perspective the selection of new suppliers and their relationship with the current ones, their skills in partnering and innovation, and knowledge of end markets. Due to their physical nature and the simultaneous presence of different actors, trade shows seem to have all the necessary elements to meet these new requirements. In such interaction, participation in trade shows may have a greater impact on corporate image than on immediate or short-term sales.

Many exhibitors have begun to show off their competence as specialized innovators by filling their stands not with products, but with prototypes, product concepts, and ideas for their customers. Moreover, they frequently offer free samples and solutions for customers, disclosing their ability and innovation capacity in a way that also exposes them to imitation. Essentially, their goal is to encourage interaction based on their skills as a means of promotion (so-called impartive activities). For example, instead of the sales force and the current product portfolio (the core offering), exhibitors at capital goods trade shows tend to have the technical staff from their research and development department to discuss prototypes built to customer specifications. Similarly, events for yarn producers present fashion shows and ideas for clothing collections for the coming seasons (future products of their customers), rather than the balls of cotton or wool to be sold. While there is less demonstration of competence at shows exhibiting consumer products, the exhibitors' stands frequently offer aids for retail sales, window displays, and communications designed to cater to new consumer behaviours. To summarize, instead of focusing on products, exhibitors increasingly display the competencies underlying these products (Barney 1991; Hamel and Prahalad 1994), competencies that might be instrumental in the future to add value to the customers' processes. Such competencies may also dovetail neatly with the customer's specific competence gaps. Moreover, during the events, part of the know-how related to these competencies is freely passed on in order to support a credibility that is difficult to demonstrate otherwise (Zerbini et al. 2006; Zerbini and Borghini 2012).

These new presentation models are, however, more costly and risky than previous models, and they are not used by all exhibitors at all events. Instead, they are reserved for presentations at major industry events, so-called 'reference events' (see Chapter 5), because they represent the frontiers of innovation in a specific sector. More than anything else, they repay the exhibitors by powering up their image since these events generate great visibility, media attention, and a large international audience.

(ii) The knowledge absorption function

Although exhibitors are mostly geared towards promoting sales, for many firms learning from the market and from the competition is also critical

(Borghini et al. 2004; Bathelt and Schuldt 2008). Trade shows offer critical and easy-to-access feedback on the development of new products. Firms some-times claim that, for months after participating in trade shows, their research and development departments are buzzing with ideas and new initiatives. The technical staff is, in fact, one of the primary vehicles of absorptive capacity with respect to customers (Cohen and Levinthal 1990), yet opportunities to directly interact with buyers in distant markets on a daily basis are rather limited for small businesses. Consequently, trade shows provide exhibitors with the opportunity to gather crucial downstream knowledge by matching their core competences with different market needs. Small firms are typically oriented towards product or process quality and generally find it difficult to acquire knowledge about market needs and marketing opportunities from non-local, distant markets (Day 1993, 1994). By exhibiting at trade shows, with their tech-nicians on-site, firms can tap into specific pockets of market knowledge that point at innovations suited to a variety of foreign needs and preferences.

Exhibitors further refine their marketing skills by observing the promotional efforts of competitors serving similar markets. However, an important element of the learning processes is related to interaction with the markets. Many firms exhibiting at trade shows have interesting stories about how, through more or less random meetings with potential customers, they are able to understand the specific nature of and the distribution channels in foreign markets. They also describe how they are able to recognize new segments of demand after receiv-ing requests for product changes from visitors from other industries. The 'jour-ney' of small businesses through various trade shows thus supports the development of competencies, especially in approaching international mar-kets. It is consistently observed that firms start participating in trade shows by mostly exhibiting at local events and then move on to international events in their own country, where they begin to interact with foreign customers. During these contacts, they notice initial reactions to their products and decide in which foreign markets to specialize and what changes to make to their prod-ucts. In the next stage, they participate in import-focused trade shows held in foreign countries, where they further their relations with local distributors and customers (Golfetto 2004).

Consequently, the development of the portfolio of trade shows in which to participate allows smaller firms to align with various markets (Kohli and Jawor-ski 1990; Narver and Slater 1990) and acquire knowledge about the needs of clients from different sectors and geographical areas. In this manner, trade shows support firms in the development of so-called 'complementary assets' (Teece 1986), referring to the resources and competencies needed to support the successful commercialization and marketing of innovations. Such market-ing capabilities are fundamental for effective innovation and competitive advantage, since innovative firms lacking complementary assets can easily be outperformed by market-savvy imitators (Day 1993, 1994).

2.4. FUNCTIONS OF TRADE SHOWS FOR NETWORKS OF FIRMS AND COMMUNITIES

It is impossible to fully understand the evolution of trade shows, and the role they play in the current knowledge economy, without considering the functions of groups of actors. These are networks of firms (often organized through trade associations), which use trade shows as marketing tools, and regional authorities, which use the same events as part of territorial marketing strategies. For both, trade shows are a useful tool for locally based businesses to expand their horizons beyond the local economy (Cox and Mair 1988) by attracting firms from other geographical areas. It is possible, however, that the marketing efforts of local governments and manufacturers' trade associations are in conflict with each other, potentially leading to the formation of different types of events (see Chapter 4 and the empirical chapters in Part III).

2.4.1. Collective Marketing by Networks of Firms

In some European countries, trade shows represent one of the main activities of trade associations—an often profitable activity, which makes it possible to finance other initiatives for the benefit of member firms (e.g. lobbying, market research, and communication campaigns). Often, this is the only form of cooperative activity between firms that are otherwise competitors. Such relationships can be described as cooperative competition (or 'coopetition', according to Brandenburger and Nalebuff 1996), which works well but is not entirely without tension.

(i) Sales promotion

The main functions of collective marketing efforts at trade shows are analogous to those of individual exhibitors; yet, they also point to the competitiveness of the entire industry, locally or nationally. The primary goal is to promote sales by member firms, specifically export sales. This function is particularly strong during trade shows (especially those that are labelled as 'supply or export shows' in Chapter 4) that bring together exhibitors representing local or national production. The presence of a large group of such exhibitors with a good reputation can attract many international visitors and buyers. To attract such an audience, associations take charge of the communication campaigns in major markets, seek government attention and grants, and endeavour to leverage production knowledge and relationships with large and small businesses, for the benefit of all. Manufacturers sometimes make strong efforts, and often gain surprising results, in terms of achieving international visibility for a local industry. The control of such shows by local or national trade associations can, however, lead to the adoption of protectionist practices. As such, to avoid direct confrontation with less desirable competitors, event organizers sometimes restrict access for certain types of firms, such as national firms or those that meet certain quality standards, and exclude others. The widespread application of antitrust measures has reduced the prevalence of these practices, but it has not prevented inclusion of certain exhibitor selection parameters that, for instance, allow for the exclusion of low-price producers, or mechanisms that guarantee members better access conditions to the events (e.g. price discounts or prime locations).

(ii) Image strengthening

A second function of trade shows for business networks involves image strengthening. Since these events support strong communication streams related to both the exhibits and the host territory (typically the region or city), they characterize the entire host region as one that is specialized in a certain activity or industry. The reverse process also occurs, when exhibitors at a specialized trade show benefit from the territory's image and reputation. The international marketing literature has long recognized that the geographical origin of a product has a substantial impact on perceptions of the product's quality, as well as on the willingness of the customers to pay a premium price. Examples of this are German technology or Italian design. This 'country-of-origin effect' (Peterson and Jolibert 1995; Khalid and Baker 1998; Verlegh and Steenkamp 1999; Pharr 2005) is, at least partly, based on the existing expertise of local businesses or, at a more collective level, on the specialization of the region/city (see Chapter 5). Trade shows can help strengthen the country-of-origin effect (Golfetto 2004) directly upon the participants (live audience), as well as indirectly on a broad audience that is reached by media reports (indirect audience). The image of trade shows becomes stable over time from one edition to the next, thanks to the repetition of these events.

(iii) Pushing product styles/technology standards

A third collective function (only possible with relatively strong trade associations that are able to effectively steer the innovative activities of member firms) is the ability to establish product styles and technological standards over those of competing trade associations. The mechanisms that make this possible relate to the processes of selecting standards and emerging styles during trade shows, and to speedily propagate these among upstream and downstream businesses to ensure they are adopted and successfully established ahead of other standards and styles. The literature regarding innovation cycles views this as a strategy of standard affirmation, especially for large firms (Abernathy and Utterback 1978; Anderson and Tushman 1990; Tushman and Rosenkopf 1992), but trade shows offer this strategic opportunity also to fragmented industries (Cappetta et al. 2006; Rinallo and Golfetto 2006; Rinallo et al. 2006; Golfetto and Rinallo 2008). The organizational literature also emphasizes that shows and other types of events, so-called 'field-configuring events', can influence the evolution of professions, technologies, markets, and industries (Anand and Watson 2004; Lampel and Meyer 2008). For example, Garud (2008) shows how conferences are events where the struggle between different technological standards takes place and how they can help speed up the transition from competing standards to the affirmation of a dominant design (Bathelt and Henn 2014). Similarly, shows controlled by trade associations can steer the path of innovation to the benefit of their members (see Chapters 11 and 12).

The struggles or 'wars' for supremacy between exhibitions that recur in the history of many industrial sectors are often motivated by the rivalry between different regional industries looking to make their specific local event the prevailing one at a national or international level (see Chapters 12 and 14), in order to control the evolution of their sector and gain a region-based competitive advantage.

Overall, the differences in size between the member firms of associations—and thus the differences in their ability to access international markets—cause some problems in the use of trade shows as a tool for collective marketing. After initial periods, during which regional firms bond because they share difficulties of approaching foreign markets, the larger firms (which enjoy greater international recognition, are often the most innovative, and bring greater drawing-power to the events) start contacting foreign customers individually at exhibitions in their target markets. Smaller firms, although greater in number, continue to rely on domestic trade shows and the collective marketing approach due to their limited capacity. This can undermine relationships and lead to conflict within regional trade associations, to the point of rendering them ineffective. It can also change the rationale behind events, which then end up serving imports rather than exports.

2.4.2. Trade Shows as Marketing Tools for the Hosting Areas

While the trade shows described are communication tools that exploit the host region as a key resource, they bring, at the same time, wide-ranging benefits to the region in which they are held. As a result, trade shows are often seen as valuable marketing tools, encouraging economic growth in the regions where they take place. This impact includes the stimulation of business travel and hospitality services, and the strengthening of the region's image.

The effects of direct sales on hospitality systems and local support services are beneficial to both the vendors of visitor services (e.g. transportation, hospitality and restaurants, entertainment, and shopping) and exhibition services (exhibit spaces, outfitting, stand management, communication services, and so on). Some research reports the weight of spin-off services at an approximate value of fifteen to twenty times the turnover generated for the trade show organizers of major international business events. In the case of consumer events, which are typically more focused on regional-local audiences, the spin-off effect is still estimated at three to five times the turnover (Golfetto 1991).

Most trade show economic impact studies cover a single event or an entire trade show facility (e.g. Golfetto 1991; Sternberg and Kramer 1991; Schätzl et al. 1993; Chambre de Commerce et d'Industrie de Paris 2001; AUMA 2006; Penzkofer 2008). As trade show centres sometimes operate at a loss and are financially supported by local governments, such impact studies are often used to demonstrate the value of the trade show industry to the public, to governmental shareholders, and other local stakeholders. In terms of methodology, these studies are frequently based on input-output models that generate multipliers, which are then applied to exhibitor and visitor expenditures to determine the overall impact of trade shows on the economy and employment rates (see also Chapter 5). Benchmarks for event impact assessments are borrowed from tourism and travel research, where procedures are debated as improved methods are proposed (e.g. Dwyer et al. 2005), and critics point to the tendency to produce exaggerated impacts to legitimize both the events and governmental sponsors. Besides the local economic impact, trade show contributions to regional and urban development attract public funding from higher levels of government for the development of support infrastructure and the promotion of a city's/region's image (Rubalcaba and Cuadrado 1995; Golfetto 2004).

Territorial competition through trade shows involves the construction of larger and improved trade show centres (UFI 2012a) and the launch of new shows that replicate successful events located elsewhere—within or outside the boundaries of the same state. Rubalcaba and Cuadrado (1995: 396) emphasize that territorial competition has resulted 'in the appearance of clone fairs, mere replicas of fairs held in competitor cities that are usually of greater fair-hosting weight and tradition'. In essence, local governments and regional authorities use trade shows as tools of territorial competition, in order to break free of economic dependence on local/regional trade and establish 'trade pipelines' to other geographic areas. Regional marketing initiatives and group marketing by businesses may, however, have conflicting aims. While collective marketing views trade shows as a means to generate benefits for local businesses (as exhibitors), territorial marketing has no interest in protecting specific business groups. The goal is to attract a maximum number of exhibitors and visitors, even if this involves massive admission of firms that are competitors to the local businesses. Industry associations may be interested in more selectively organized events in terms of granting controlled access to foreign exhibitors, as a form of protectionism. The tensions between collective and territorial marketing can be resolved in favour of one or the other function depending on the importance of community or association stakeholders within the frameworks of trade shows. Such phenomena are examined further in Chapters 4 and 12.

2.5. CONCLUSIONS

This chapter investigates the evolution of fairs over time: from market fairs, where merchandise was delivered to consumers on site, to sample fairs and modern trade shows, where presentations of symbolism, exhibitors' displays of competencies, and knowledge exchanges become increasingly important. This evolution, however, goes beyond the development of the functions of trade shows for exhibitors and visitors. It directly addresses the core model of trade show exchange: a shift from a model of promotion–information to one of promotion–experience and, finally, promotion–knowledge.

At trade shows, traditional exchanges took place as promotion–information exchange: visitors received (accepted) the exhibitors' promotion in return for the information they received (requested) by comparing the varieties and features of the supply in a certain market. This model characterized trade shows since the earliest general sample fairs, which end users and industrial buyers alike attended in order to gather information about the latest developments in products and technologies. The promotion–information exchange model for visitors-consumers started to falter when information about products became more easily accessible through mass communication and large-scale retailing. General sample fairs, which focused especially on consumers, quickly declined, leaving the stage to trade shows that were specialized by sector and dedicated to industry professionals. The contemporary quest for information by business buyers focuses on highly specific aspects of production that are difficult to communicate and aimed at a limited number of buyers. For this reason, mass communication has not reduced the need to be there in person to examine the samples before making purchase decisions. As a result, industrial trade shows have not become obsolete settings for economic exchange and trade— in fact, they continue to thrive.

Nonetheless, in recent years, developments in information communication technologies and internet-based communication have greatly facilitated contacts and the availability of information about products and technologies, again changing the framework of potential buyers. Surveys conducted at leading international trade shows (Borghini et al. 2006; Rinallo et al. 2010) have demonstrated that, increasingly, visitors are only marginally motivated to acquire information related to purchase decisions or to make such decisions at trade shows. They reveal that, instead, the experiential exchange of expertise between firms that have not yet established a direct relationship has become extremely important. The presence of finished products, prototypes, and other artefacts, along with skilled technicians, are crucial tools of manufacturers to display their skills, and effectively disseminate expertise and innovative ideas to the participants. This aspect is fundamental because, first, it offers visitors a prime selection basis to find new suppliers and validate existing ones; it also makes the experience of trade show participation indispensable in terms of the selection and design of products. Second, visitors, mainly at European trade shows are especially driven by the need to understand where their industries are heading, to search for new ideas, and to ensure they are making informed choices for the future. But visitors do not simply develop new ideas through imitation of the things they have seen. The ideas are generated through intellectual stimulation, sensations, perceptions of the market climate, contact with trends taken to extremes, and from interaction with and perceptions of the behaviour of others. In short, ideas flow from this vast sensory immersion and open a window to understanding the future. In essence, what visitors expect at exhibitions today is the exchange of promotion for professional knowledge.

Exhibitors have adapted to new demands of visitors by organizing stands that are geared towards the presentation of their skills and their ability to partner, rather than only towards the promotion of products. Such new modes of presentation are used primarily for presentations at the leading industry exhibitions, which are often referred to as 'reference events' or 'flagship events' because they offer sense-making on the frontiers of industry innovation. At other events, particularly those oriented towards the penetration of local markets (trade marketing), exhibitors make simple presentations that are primarily aimed at bringing in orders or supporting customer relations.

Reference, flagship, or for-the-innovation trade shows are sometimes used as a means of collective marketing where exhibitors participate individually with their own marketing objectives but also pursue a common goal. These objectives include enhancing the visibility of a country/region's industry and validating specific product styles or technology standards over those of competing industries in other territories. This chapter explained the functions of these events for cities/regions in terms of local marketing. The direct sale of services in the host area (economic spin-offs) and the image of competence and visibility gained by local firms (image spin-offs) are both important for local development and create competition among local governments/regional authorities to attract trade shows.

3

Temporary Markets and Temporary Clusters

3.1. INTRODUCTION

Based on the traditional role of industrial districts as industry agglomerations and export hubs, this chapter begins developing a knowledge-based conceptualization of trade shows by discussing their nature as temporary markets, where supply meets demand and rich learning and interaction opportunities are provided. The theoretical foundation presented is derived from the disciplines of marketing and economic geography, which, albeit starting from different premises, have looked at the same objects: the trade show and the interaction patterns between participants at these events. In this chapter, we integrate the different trade show perspectives by offering a view of these events as learning platforms for intervening economic actors. Marketing scholars, while traditionally emphasizing the value of trade shows in sales promotion and export support, have recently highlighted the role of these events in enabling producers to learn from their markets. Conversely, economic geographers have started mapping the different forms of interaction and communication patterns at trade shows, depending on the specific type of market configuration found (e.g. Li 2014a).

The first part of this chapter reconstructs the evolution of industrial districts in Europe and the role of trade shows in their internationalization. These events, we argue, were instrumental in allowing manufacturing firms, embedded in local production systems, to extend their sales to customers that were localized in other regions and countries. This paves the way for our discussion of trade shows as temporary markets, where the most important knowledge flows take place between suppliers and customers (Borghini et al. 2006), while other communication streams are less relevant or even an annoyance for exhibiting firms.

The second part of this chapter is dedicated to analysing trade shows from an economic geography perspective, which increasingly views these events as important places where knowledge circulation and creation take place in a condensed form and over a limited time period. This has been expressed in characterizations of such events as temporary assemblages of human beings (Zelinsky 1994), periodic events of the social economy (Norcliffe and Rendace 2003), organized anarchies (Bathelt and Gibson 2014), or temporary clusters (Maskell et al. 2004) where forms of organized proximity (Rallet and Torre 2009) reproduce some of the knowledge dynamics found in permanent industrial clusters. After engaging with the knowledge-based view of permanent clusters, this chapter examines the multifaceted information flows and communication activities at trade shows beyond those between suppliers–exhibitors and buyers–visitors, which represent the core of the marketing research. From this, we conceptualize the specific communication and knowledge ecology, or 'global buzz', which develops during some of these events, through a set of interrelated characteristics or components.

We suggest that the notions of temporary markets and temporary clusters are highly complementary as they provide a more nuanced view of the central role of these events in the globalizing knowledge economy (Amin and Cohendet 2004). This conceptualization provides the basic framework from which we develop a knowledge-based typology of trade shows in Chapter 4 and discuss different trade show patterns in Part III of the book.

3.2. TRADITIONAL INDUSTRIAL DISTRICTS AND THE EXPORT-PROMOTION FUNCTION OF TRADE SHOWS

The need to expand sales beyond local or regional markets that are typically not large enough to ensure economic survival has accompanied economic actors ever since industrial agglomeration and specialization tendencies emerged in medieval times. In Italy, for instance, so-called Marshallian 'industrial districts' (Marshall 1920)—the ancestors of the modern industrial districts—developed in cities such as Prato near Florence with a focus on textiles (Piore and Sabel 1984), Santa Croce with a focus on leather tanning (Amin and Thrift 1992), or Montebelluna in the production of mountain shoes (Belussi 2003). Primarily involving small firms, production in these industrial districts was organized in the form of the so-called 'putting-out system' (Lazerson 1993), through a distributed network of subcontractors who completed work in their own homes or at workshops. During this proto-industrialization stage, industrial districts developed a distinct division of labour, with some actors responsible for securing access to wider markets. In Prato, this task was accomplished by specific traders, the 'impannatori'. Like travelling salesmen later on, they packed locally produced goods to tour through European cities and travel from one trade fair to the next. Not only did they sell the Italian products at these events, these traders also acquired important information and knowledge about European fashion markets and changing consumer preferences. They would bring this information back to their home base, share it with local producers, and then order particular designs within the local production systems for the next trip (Scott 1988; Sabel 1994; Maskell et al. 2004).

The modern industrial districts that developed after the Second World War in Italy, while building on a rich industrial cultural heritage, were somewhat different. Although sharing some parallels with the former production systems, they were based on new technologies and increasing market segmentation, and developed in reaction to the Fordist crisis of the large firms (Bathelt 1998). This opened up possibilities for small and mid-sized firms to specialize in selected production stages of an industry, while collectively developing a broader competence across the value chain through an extended locally based division of labour (Brusco 1982; Becattini 1990). Through spatial proximity, firms were able to reduce their transaction costs in this complex social division of labour (Scott 1988). The development of trust relationships and a joint understanding of the technologies and industries at hand supported a stable social order within the districts, enabling firms to collectively react to market challenges and learn continuously (Harrison 1992; Belussi and Pilotti 2002). As Becattini and Coltori (2006) demonstrate, this model of the modern industrial district became quite pervasive in Italy and led to strong export growth in personal/household goods and light mechanically engineered products. This competitive strength went along with the establishment and success of 'Made in Italy' as a brand. The number of industrial districts with this type of production system continuously increased in the post-Second World War period and, at the turn of the millennium, went far beyond the former 'Third Italy'.

To be able to sustain such specialized production systems, firms needed to be able to access markets beyond their regional reach. Trade shows provided structured solutions to this problem. Local firms and industry associations in the Italian districts organizing collective events for local firms to showcase their products and invited their customers from regions throughout Europe to attend. The success of some of these districts thus went along with the establishment of trade shows that were designed to support regional exports (see Chapter 4). In Italy, many trade shows that originated from industrial districts in the 1950s and 1960s still exist, despite remarkable changes in formats and in some cases even relocation (see Chapters 11 to 14 for historical aspects of these events and their evolving relationship with local districts). For example, the textile districts of Prato, Como, and Biella established trade shows that were initially reserved for members of the eponymous industrial districts (i.e. Prato Expo, Ideacomo, or Ideabiella). These separate events have recently been united in Milan to better face competing European events. Similarly, most of the Italian furniture districts centralized their trade shows and relocated to Milan, despite the fact that some smaller district-level events still exist, for instance in Pesaro (i.e. Domo—a furniture fair specializing in kitchen furniture and furnishings) and Udine (i.e. Promosedia, the International Chair Exhibition).

The relationship between industrial districts and local trade shows has thus changed over time. These events were originally very important in the internationalization processes of industrial districts, as they provided much-needed export opportunities to firms that otherwise would not have been able to contact foreign customers. As firms grew, however, they tended to migrate from small local events to larger international ones, where they were able to interact with a more diverse international clientele and learn how to customize their offers to local tastes and needs. The final step in this process was to invest in attending trade shows held in the largest or most promising geographical markets they wanted to export to (Golfetto 2004). At first, this happened through participation in collective stands; in later phases, individual firms participated through the representation of local resellers or through their own stands.

This sequential use of trade shows resulted in a dynamic portfolio of participation often comprising dozens of events per year, each of which attributed to different marketing goals. In this process, new trade shows were constantly added to the portfolio based on evolving market opportunities, whereas others were abandoned. More recently, industrial district-level trade shows have ceased to provide commercial benefits to the most successful exhibiting firms, which need to rationalize their overall trade show participation and allocate promotional investments to growth markets. Faced with deficiencies in their exhibitor base, such industrial district-level trade shows have entered a state of crisis, which has forced them to join forces with other events in better locations in order to ensure their survival.

Overall, trade shows provide a solution to the problem of reaching international markets, even in the absence of international commercialization competence and sales force. Like industrial districts, participation in trade shows presents small firms, in particular, with opportunities to survive and cope with large multinational firms.

3.3. TRADE SHOWS AS TEMPORARY MARKETS

As the reconstruction of the historical evolution of trade shows demonstrates (see also Chapter 2), these events have long been recognized for their ability to expand the commercial horizon of market transactions and exchanges, putting suppliers and buyers from different geographical origins in contact with each other. As a consequence, previous conceptualizations have long described these events as temporary marketplaces. In economics, trade shows are viewed as institutions that reduce the transaction costs associated with searching for information under imperfect market conditions; that is, when prices do not convey enough information to the potential buyers about differences in product quality (Florio 1994). The marketing literature more directly addresses the commercial aspects of these events, that is, the vertical relationships between suppliers and buyers. Its emphasis is on providing exhibiting firms with guidance on maximizing sales and returns on investments from trade show participation (Golfetto 2004; Rinallo 2011a). Chapter 2 shows that exhibitors try to focus their limited time and attention on current and potential buyers during trade shows, as well as visitors that can potentially influence purchasing decisions. In comparison, 'atypical visitors' (Borghini et al. 2006) are considered to be a distraction from more productive uses of their time, or even an annoyance. In this section, we conceptualize these observations with reference to Storper's (1997) distinction between traded and untraded interdependencies in the innovation process. We employ these terms to better understand the nature of trade shows as temporary markets, and the characterization of knowledge exchanges during these events.

Traded interactions are interactions during which knowledge exchanges are embedded into commercial exchanges. In vertical traded interactions, knowledge reified in products, services, solutions, or other commercial offerings is sold by one party and purchased by the other. We also find horizontal traded relationships (e.g. innovation partnerships between competitors or suppliers of complementary products) that involve different forms of compensation (monetary or otherwise) for the exchange or development of knowledge. In contrast, untraded interactions are informal in character, do not need to evolve into formal relationships, and are not the object of monetary transactions. Participation in trade shows is conceived by some as a realization of untraded interdependencies (e.g. Trippl et al. 2009). This includes interactions among actors during these events and the corresponding learning outcomes, which are characterized as knowledge spillovers.

While this is true to a certain extent, such views downplay the fact that the raison d'être of trade shows is the facilitation of vertical traded relations between exhibitors and typical visitors. However, firms in today's knowledge economy realize that transactions are increasingly complex and require manifold considerations. As such, decisions about purchases require time and planning, and increasingly cannot be made on the spot. At their stands, exhibitors mostly engage with current or potential customers. For the former, relationships with suppliers include a series of traded interactions, carried out before, during, and after the shows. For the latter, interactions at the show correspond more closely to the untraded and informal variant. That being said, most exhibitors hope that such interactions will be the first step towards converting prospects into customers (Gopalakrishna and Lilien 1995; Golfetto 2004; Smith et al. 2004; Stevens 2005; Lee and Kim 2008; Rinallo 2011a). Despite their importance from a knowledge-based perspective, other untraded interactions at the shows (whether they be vertical, between exhibitors and atypical visitors, or horizontal, in the form of exhibitor-to-exhibitor and visitor-to-visitor interactions) are not the main reason for the organization of trade shows. Exhibitors would not allocate their promotional investments to trade shows if they did not provide commercial returns or opportunities for future returns. Accordingly, organizers would not break even—and most trade shows, unless heavily funded by local governments or other stakeholders, would not be sustainable.

The temporary market nature of trade shows also makes it possible to specify the nature of the knowledge obtained during these events. Trade shows provide exhibitors with a unique opportunity to gather crucial downstream knowledge by matching their core competencies, which are often embedded in artefacts (product samples, prototypes, and so on), with market needs (Pavitt 2005). Firms that are embedded in local clusters in peripheral regions, or in areas with small local markets, find it difficult to acquire knowledge about the needs of non-local, distant markets. This requires what Cornish (1997) refers to as marketing intelligence. By exhibiting at trade shows, firms may tap into specific bases of market knowledge and develop innovations that are suited to a variety of foreign needs and preferences. Moreover, exhibitors refine their marketing skills by observing the promotional efforts of competitors serving similar markets. Here, the concepts of temporary markets and temporary clusters begin to merge. Consequently, trade shows support firms in the development of so-called complementary assets (Teece 1986); that is, the resources and competences needed to support the successful commercialization and marketing of innovations, and assist firms in the transition from product to market orientation (Kohli and Jaworski 1990; Narver and Slater 1990). Research has found that marketing capabilities are fundamental for effective innovation and the development of competitive advantage and that, conversely, innovative firms lacking complementary assets tend to be outperformed by market-savvy imitators (Rothaermel 2001a, 2001b). Such complementary assets are difficult to obtain in local industrial districts or permanent clusters because knowledge is often dominated by existing technological/productive assets and marketing know-how regarding nearby customers has grown to become quite homogeneous so that little deviant knowledge can be acquired locally.

To fully develop our knowledge-based view of trade shows, the next section turns to examine industrial districts or clusters from a knowledge-based perspective. This will help us illustrate how trade shows can be conceived as temporary clusters that provide economic actors with learning opportunities that are structured in a way that is similar to those in permanent clusters. It is perhaps ironic that exhibitors' commercial investments and production decisions result in knowledge externalities that are beneficial for many other local firms. While this leads us to conceptualize trade shows as temporary clusters, this role is a direct consequence of their nature as temporary markets.

3.4. PERMANENT CLUSTERS AND GLOBAL MARKET ACCESS: A KNOWLEDGE-BASED PERSPECTIVE

While specialized industrial agglomerations or clusters are pervasive in the world economy (Porter 1990, 2003), the reasons that explain why they prosper and remain competitive have shifted. Also, their requirements regarding global market access and access to knowledge from other regions and nations have changed—and generally increased. In fact, it appears that regional input-output relationships and inter-firm networks based on traded interdependencies are not as important as observers once thought (see Bathelt 2007). Recent conceptualizations of industrial clusters take this into consideration and suggest that the existence and growth of clusters should be viewed in relation to processes of knowledge creation and circulation. Such processes appear to be central to the success of industrial agglomerations in advanced economies (Maskell 2001; Malmberg and Maskell 2002; Pinch et al. 2003; Bathelt 2005). These approaches view 'clusters' as local or regional concentrations of industrial firms, as well as their support infrastructure and institutions, which are closely interrelated through both traded and, especially, untraded interdependencies.

Recent conceptualizations have recognized that the prior focus on regional collaboration and networking in a localized industry setting is not sufficient to understand cluster dynamics. Regional learning processes—as argued in conventional approaches—serve to generate product and process innovations and increase the collective competitiveness of the regional firms. Meanwhile, many studies and reviews have shown that conventional conceptions underestimate the importance of supra-regional connections for cluster success (e.g. Oinas 1999; Bathelt and Taylor, 2002; Britton 2004; Clark and Tracey 2004).

The need to draw on a knowledge perspective, while also conceptualizing cluster-external relationships, has led to the development of the local-buzz-and-global-pipelines approach. This approach emphasizes the knowledge flows that occur between cluster firms and also those with agents outside the cluster (Bathelt et al. 2004; Bathelt 2007). It argues that clusters must systematically combine internal and external knowledge flows in order to be successful (see Figure 3.1). On the one hand, cluster firms greatly benefit from constant knowledge flows and updates of news, gossip, and information about the industry or value chain at hand. Such knowledge flows exist almost automatically within a cluster (Crevoisier and Maillat 1991). Firms do not have to invest huge amounts of money to gain access to much of this 'local buzz' (Storper and Venables 2004). They benefit from just 'being there' (Gertler 2004). On the other hand, it has become clear that the economic success of a cluster and the richness of its buzz depend on the establishment of external linkages with outside technology leaders, foreign customers, and suppliers, as well as access to international markets. Firms thus establish trans-local

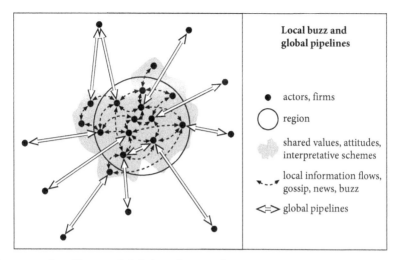

Figure 3.1. Local buzz and global pipelines in clusters (Bathelt et al. 2004: 46)

linkages, or 'global pipelines', which provide access to crucial information, new markets, and technologies (Owen-Smith and Powell 2004). The knowledge that flows through these pipelines is, however, different from that found in local buzz. As the establishment and maintenance of pipelines is timely, associated with uncertainties, and requires substantial investment, these external linkages tend to be pre-structured, goal-oriented, and more focused than local-buzz linkages.

An important question that arises from this research is, of course, how firms select 'pipeline partners' and get access to information and technology on a global scale. Aside from linkages that are established through third-party referrals and reputation networks (Glückler 2007), pre-existing international networks (Dicken et al. 2001), or virtual social networks and internet search engines (von Hippel 2001; Jeppesen and Molin 2003; Grabher et al. 2008), relatively little is known about the processes by which such pipelines are generated. We do not know, for example, how contact with potential future transaction partners is made, how suppliers are found and selected, or how complex transaction relations with international partners are established (see Maskell 2014). In this book, we suggest that trade shows, especially international 'flagship fairs' or hub shows (see Chapter 4), play a decisive role in this respect (Borghini et al. 2004; Maskell et al. 2004). These events can be viewed as temporary clusters that support processes of interactive learning and knowledge creation for those firms which participate in them. Such events, which bundle together agents and firms from all over the world, define temporary spaces of presentation and communication between the suppliers, producers, and customers of a particular industry or technology field.

3.5. TRADE SHOWS AS TEMPORARY CLUSTERS

Although the most prominent relationships during trade shows are vertical in character, linking producers with their respective users (Rinallo and Golfetto 2011), trade shows generate both vertical and horizontal knowledge flows and encompass a strong institutional dimension. Like permanent industrial clusters (Maskell and Malmberg 1999b; Bathelt and Taylor 2002), trade shows are characterized by distinct communication patterns across various dimensions. Internal and external relationships and communication patterns can no longer be easily distinguished during these flagship events, as internal and external knowledge circles overlap, are constantly being reconfigured, and are in a state of flux.

Vertical interaction with suppliers and customers consists of information exchange about recent trends, experiences, and requirements for future products and services. Firms set up meetings with established suppliers, located in different regions and countries, to discuss technological changes in product specifications, developments in markets, and future conditions. At the same time, they also look for suppliers that might offer opportunities for new applications. Systematic customer contact is a key component of vertical interaction during trade shows (Rinallo and Golfetto 2011). Firms intensify social relations with their customers and address new customers to market their products, display new developments, and discuss potential contracts (Backhaus 1992; Meffert 1993). Scheduled meetings between producers and their customers are a vital source of information for further product improvements.

Trade shows also bring together firms that compete against one another and normally do not interact. At this horizontal level, trade shows provide multiple opportunities for firms to observe and compare their products and strategies with those of their competitors (Borghini et al. 2004). Firms systematically look through the exhibits of their competitors, and make note of product designs, innovations, and new fields of application. Parts of the screening and observation processes are less systematic, however, as firms try to get an overview of what is going on in their business and what trends exist (Bathelt and Schuldt 2008). This information is of great importance because it enables firms to evaluate their products and technological sophistication in relation to what goes on in other parts of the world. Along with the information gathered from customers and suppliers, firms obtain a broad overview of state-of-the-art technologies and market trends, which they use to review their own practices and strategies (Rosson and Seringhaus 1995). It is sometimes even possible to discuss general technological problems or industry trends with representatives of competing firms during these events. At such times, the show grounds may be viewed as a 'neutral space' for open exchanges about the competitive context.

Trade shows provide firms with multiple opportunities for interactive learn-ing and problem solving, especially when the same specialists from different firms meet regularly during these cyclical events (Power and Jansson 2008). They are places where members of communities of practice and epistemic communities with partly overlapping and complementary knowledge bases get together (Brown and Duguid 1991; Wenger 1998; Knorr Cetina 1999). This temporary intermingling provides a basis for common interpretations and mutual understandings through intense communication (Bathelt and Schuldt 2008). As common interpretative schemes and visions about technological tra-jectories are reproduced through knowing communities, the institutional dimension of trade show interaction unfolds.

Overall, the vertical, horizontal, and institutional cluster dimensions facilitate an intensified circulation of information and knowledge between participants. New ideas and projects in an industry or technology field can be identified through scouting and monitoring. Knowledge exchange occurs in scheduled meetings with business partners, as well as accidental meetings with former colleagues. Just as certain off-work social spaces seem crucial for knowledge exchange in permanent clusters, we find that the corridors, cafés, and bars at trade shows are sometimes places where important knowl-edge circulates. During a trade show, people are surrounded by a thick web of specialized knowledge from which they can hardly escape. The respective information and communication ecology can be characterized as temporary 'global buzz' (Maskell et al. 2006; Bathelt and Schuldt 2010). Through this, knowledge flows at trade shows are simultaneously planned and spontane-ous in nature. Since knowledge is constantly being transmitted from one agent to another, it is repeatedly interpreted, evaluated, and enriched with additional relevant knowledge (Storper and Venables 2004). This reduces uncertainties and helps firms distinguish important from less important news and trends.

Global buzz helps to identify interesting firms, acquire information about them, and make initial contacts with new partners (see Figure 3.2). Over time, through consecutive trade shows (Power and Jansson 2008), potential partners become familiar with one another and trust may develop. This pro-cess is supported by the multiplex nature of social relations (Uzzi 1997) between the people who attend trade shows. Such individuals interact with one another as competitors, experts of the same community, long-term part-ners, or 'old trade show buddies'. In the end, international trade shows not only help maintain and intensify networks with international customers and suppliers (Prüser 1997), but they also allow firms to identify and select other firms from different national or regional contexts that may become partners later on. This can, in turn, lead to the establishment of new 'trans-local pipe-lines' between firms from different territories (though not necessarily between firms from different clusters).

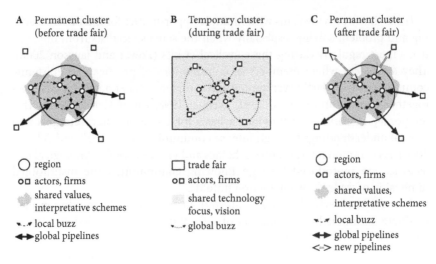

Figure 3.2. Pipeline creation and the complementary relation between temporary and permanent clusters (Bathelt and Schuldt 2008: 856)

3.6. GLOBAL BUZZ AT INTERNATIONAL TRADE SHOWS

The discussion of temporary markets and temporary clusters highlights the significance of the specific communication and knowledge ecology at international trade shows. Indeed, this is central to understand the importance of trade shows in generating critical knowledge flows about industries, technologies, and world-wide markets, as well as their decisive role in establishing and maintaining international networks with other firms and corporate units. 'Global buzz' is a complex concept that is difficult to measure and does not merely refer to a certain way of communication, such as an informal, group-based conversation, as suggested by Asheim et al. (2007). Rather, it represents an all-embracing constellation of different components inherent to such events that generate a professional knowledge and communication ecology. In the following, we describe five different, yet overlapping, components of global buzz. The discussion emphasizes how different components of communication and interaction processes support one another in mutually reflexive ways. They are particularly relevant to international trade shows.

3.6.1. Dedicated Co-Presence of Global Supply and Demand

The show grounds establish a spatial constellation through which a specific ensemble of agents meet and interact both sequentially and simultaneously. International trade shows are events that bring together leading and less well-known agents from an entire industry branch, value chain, or technology field. Suppliers, producers, users, interested experts, media representatives, and other multipliers get together to exchange news about the present and future development of their industry, centred around the displays of existing products, prototypes, and innovations. The co-presence of many specialized firms of a particular value chain and constant face-to-face communication between specialists from these firms generate a unique milieu for the exchange of experience and knowledge. Specific information about technologies, markets, strategies, and solutions is discussed in a variety of ways in the context of both planned and unplanned meetings (Bathelt and Schuldt 2008). From the view of an exhibitor, this exchange includes discussions about business transactions with customers and suppliers, general conversations with interested agents about the character of products and the development of the industry, specific possibilities for problem solving or improvements, and negotiations with long-term customers from different parts of the world (Borghini et al. 2004).

Despite their diverse roles and expectations, the individuals that attend international trade shows have a shared dedication to, and focus on, the activities that take place on the show grounds (Blythe 2002; Bathelt and Zakrzewski 2007). To be away from the normal workplace for several days in a row creates time slots that are not blocked with particular tasks. Agents can concentrate on all aspects of the trade show without the typical interruptions found in day-to-day work situations.

Because of the specific atmosphere of these 'get-togethers' and the exclusive focus on exploring an industry's state of the art, participants at trade shows tend to be more relaxed than in their ordinary work situations. Free of routine administrative issues, they are likely open to new ideas and are willing to critically compare their own economic practices with those of others. This environment is highly conducive to the adaptation of different experiences and for processes of learning and knowledge dissemination (Borghini et al. 2006; Schuldt and Bathelt 2011). Media representatives and other multipliers, such as specialized user groups who are usually not in direct contact with the producers, also play an important role in these events (e.g. Entwistle and Rocamora 2006; Rinallo and Golfetto 2006). These agents have a substantial impact on the success of trade shows and the wider image of the exhibitors because they transmit their impressions to a larger audience after the events.

3.6.2. Intensive Temporary Face-to-Face Interaction

As opposed to other modes of communication, attendance at international trade shows automatically involves face-to-face contact with a multitude of participants who assume different roles, through which a diverse mix of information and knowledge can be sorted, classified, and interpreted. Storper and

Venables (2004) have pointed out the importance of face-to-face interaction in transferring complex messages, getting immediate feedback, and responding further. Face-to-face communication helps reduce information asymmetries, as there are many ways of inquiring about the reliability of new information and the trustworthiness of other agents. Non-verbal cues in communication also help to evaluate potential future partners and reduce risks in interaction (Short et al. 1976). Firm representatives grasp important additional information when talking to their peers and observing their facial expressions and gestures; this greatly assists firms in making judgements and sorting information (e.g. Watzlawick et al. 2000). Overall, it is possible to interpret the mind-sets and opinions of other agents and check their compatibility for future business relations at a low cost.

The fact that firms do not necessarily require direct contact with a specific source of information to access to that information makes participation in a trade show particularly valuable. Participants may hear from other agents about new developments and then decide for themselves whether or not it would be useful to personally inspect these innovations. Firms greatly benefit from the decentralized character of knowledge exchanges and the multiplicity of channels through which such knowledge flows during these shows.

In design-intensive industries, the symbolic and emotional value of exhibits is particularly important and depends heavily on face-to-face contacts in acquiring knowledge, which is largely tacit and contextual in nature. Discussions with peers provide a stimulating arena for the development of new visions, uncoupled from corporate routines and pressures for homogeneity. In technical trade shows, in contrast, the interest in the actual exhibits is often (yet, not always) more limited as it is difficult to evaluate technical properties through visual inspection alone. Studies have shown, however, that personal meetings are important in maintaining positive business contacts with customers and suppliers from other parts of the world (Backhaus 1992; Sharland and Balogh 1996; Prüser 2003).

3.6.3. Temporary Possibilities for Dense Observation

Important insights during international trade shows also result from observing exhibitors and visitors. Through practices—such as close inspection of other exhibits, peer observation, 'being part of the crowd', and watching the reaction of other visitors—agents collect ideas and impressions that are used to revise or confirm existing strategies regarding the production programme. Trade shows are events that attract leading, 'unusual', and 'exotic' agents from an industry or technology branch, providing plenty of opportunities for learning-by-observation (Blythe 2002; Borghini et al. 2006). In the area of consumer products, the possibility of directly experiencing, feeling, or smelling the products exhibited is of great importance for participants. In creative industries, on the one hand, particular colour and design variations stimulate associations and help observers imagine reconfigurations involving their own products and designs. Firms in technology-oriented shows, on the other hand, are more interested in exchanges that involve strategic information on system architecture, which could affect medium- and long-term policies.

While looking through the exhibits of competing or complementary firms, agents can also evaluate the goals of other firms' trade show participation and their corporate identities. Such goals and identities might be in line with the firms' existing views of their competition, or they might deviate from these, indicating, for instance, that a competitor might have begun to operate in a different market context. Similar to gestures and facial expressions in face-to-face communication, the observation and experience of a competitor's trade show exhibit can be understood as a visualization of the firm's broader philosophy within the industry. Overall, the unique combination of developing and exchanging arguments about new developments, while at the same time being able to observe the effects on other agents, can be applied to one's own production context. This provides instant insights that are extremely difficult to acquire through other means.

3.6.4. Intersecting Interpretative Communities, Shared Understandings, and Overlapping Visions

In general, international trade shows attract different, yet closely interrelated communities that have in-depth knowledge about many aspects of the products, technologies, and value chains portrayed (Entwistle and Rocamora 2006; Skov 2006). Both communities of practice and epistemic communities meet during international shows (Wenger 1998; Knorr Cetina 1999), turning them into large conglomerates of shared understandings, repertoires, and visions about an industry, value chain, or technology field.

As these communities draw on similar specialization and work experience, and meet regularly or periodically (Power and Jansson 2008), they share a similar institutional basis. This allows them to efficiently exchange and interpret knowledge, generate new ideas, and further develop competencies. They may also share 'swift trust' related to the norms and goals acquired through their training (e.g. Knorr Cetina 1999). Focused communities provide a valuable source of knowledge that cuts across the strict boundaries of corporate structures (Lawrence et al. 2006).

By no means, however, do the participants of trade shows share the same identical background. In fact, their backgrounds are often fairly heterogeneous, reflecting differences in technology, specialization, and business focus. Some participants who are experienced in production might, for instance, be interested in discussing problems of product quality or production failure, while others, such as sales specialists, interact mostly with customers and are likely eager to get to know more about demand changes and new trends. The decisive point is that the visitors and exhibitors at international trade shows are characterized by some degree of common knowledge basis, or 'cognitive proximity' (Nooteboom 2000), which enables efficient transfers of information and knowledge. Due to this unique mix of similar, overlapping, and complementary knowledge, important learning processes are stimulated. Overall, active participation and membership in focused knowing communities enables firms to distinguish more from less valuable knowledge, and to sort through innovations of others that could be worth exploring further.

3.6.5. Multiplex Meetings and Relationships

Within these networks of contacts, agents are linked in different ways with each other as business partners, colleagues, peers, or community members. As a result, resources can be transferred from one type of relationship to another. Multiplex ties and diverse possibilities for meetings at international trade shows help firms gain access to new information and relevant knowledge pools, while also speeding up the transfer of such knowledge (Uzzi 1997). During a trade show, information is constantly being transmitted from one agent to another. While acquiring new knowledge, participants act simultaneously as recipients and broadcasters of global buzz. Participants derive tremendous benefits from the large number of different types of meetings with diverse agents.

Firms that aim to enter new markets and search for partners to support this move particularly benefit from such meetings, which are often spontaneous and not planned long in advance. These encounters also assist in testing the 'chemistry' between two parties and establishing some initial basis of communication, or perhaps ruling out further communication. These events involve feelings and emotions (Massey 2004); and participants generally expect to 'have a good time'. Although the development of conventional trust between business partners may take a long time, the existence of so-called 'swift trust' and repeated meetings during international trade shows serve to form a favourable basis for the stimulation of business relations. In conclusion, trade shows enable participants to constantly switch from negotiations to observations, from business talks to private exchanges and back. And all of this takes place within a short period of two or three days. In this sense, flagship shows provide unique opportunities for truly multiplex encounters on a global scale. Despite these processes, we still have to keep in mind that all of this transpires within the context of temporary market interactions that provide the key triggers for this knowledge ecology.

3.7. CONCLUSIONS

Despite—or, perhaps, thanks to—their nature as temporary markets, trade shows have emerged as important nodes in the global knowledge economy. In this chapter, we have identified the important role played by trade shows in the internationalization of traditional industrial districts, and the typical process through which small industrial district-level trade shows have been abandoned by local firms in favour of more international trade shows that provide direct contact with foreign markets. Based on scholarship in economics and marketing, trade shows have been characterized as temporary markets, or events focused on the facilitation of traded vertical knowledge linkages between suppliers/producers (exhibitors) and buyers (typical visitors). Other informal knowledge spillovers—horizontal (exhibitor-exhibitor and visitor-visitor) and vertical (exhibitor-atypical visitor) alike—exist as well and play an important role; yet they result as side effects of the exhibitors' promotional investments. Instead of simply treating these effects as by-products, however, we argue that trade shows have become important ways for firms to find and access remote knowledge directly relevant for investment and production decisions. Building on the knowledge-based view of industrial clusters, and the local-buzz-and-global-pipelines approach, we therefore conceptualize trade shows as temporary clusters *and* temporary markets, describing the different, yet mutually supporting, constituent elements of global buzz, which characterize most major international trade shows.

Temporary markets and temporary clusters, in this view, are two sides of the same coin, and not alternative paradigmatic views on trade shows and their functions. The market functions of trade shows help to better characterize the knowledge exchanges typical of trade shows, which set them apart from other types of temporary clusters (e.g. fashion weeks, medical conferences, film festivals, or art biennales) not covered in this book. The knowledge flows regarding value chains, competitors, and technology trends also help overcome a functionalist perspective of transactional relations that underestimates the broader knowledge effects of trade shows for the development of entire industries and the globalization processes of these industries.

This previous discussion also indicates that there may be differences among trade shows in terms of their learning potential and the nature of knowledge flows to be expected. We make, for example, references to international flagship or hub trade shows and to local events established to foster the export activities of industrial districts, as well as to the differences between design-oriented and technology-oriented shows. This is developed much further in Chapter 4, where we turn to a more systematic analysis of the main types of trade shows from a knowledge-based perspective and discuss the active role played by the organizers of these events in structuring interaction and learning.

4

A Knowledge-Based Typology of Trade Shows and Knowledge Strategies of Trade Show Organizers

4.1. INTRODUCTION

Chapters 2 and 3 have outlined the fundamental conceptualizations associated with a knowledge-based view of trade shows. Applying this further, this chapter turns to explore the ways in which trade shows differ in terms of their learning potential for participating firms. Our focus is here on vertical learning processes during events in developed economies. Of course, not all trade shows in developed economies represent central hubs in the globalizing knowledge economy. Some shows of a smaller scale and smaller geographical reach offer learning opportunities that are almost redundant as they can be easily achieved by local firms through other means. This is largely due to limitations to developing knowledge pipelines with external partners at these smaller events. In contrast, other shows with an international or global reach can offer too many exchange and networking opportunities, possibly generating an overflow of information for exhibitors and visitors alike. Yet it is not just the size of the trade show and the geographic origin of the exhibitors and visitors that determines the knowledge exchange capacity of trade shows. Other elements can lead to substantial differences among trade shows. These include the proximity to places of production or markets, the exhibition layout, the presence and involvement of leading companies, an imbalance in the ratio of producers to distributors participating in the show, the timing of the trade show with respect to innovation cycles or the development stage of a host country's economy.

The main goal of this chapter is to provide a trade show typology related to the geographic origin of its exhibitors and visitors, and to illustrate the knowledge environment of these events. Based on readily available data that are collected routinely during many trade shows worldwide, this typology allows implications to be drawn about the horizontal and vertical knowledge exchange among exhibitors and visitors across a local–global continuum. It also highlights the characteristics of trade shows resulting from different combinations of global–local shares of exhibitors versus visitors. From a methodological standpoint, this typology is useful in the design of empirical studies and in generalizing research findings about trade shows. Part III of this book has been structured according to this typology.

The discussions in this chapter also highlight the sometimes critical role of trade show organizers in understanding the knowledge dynamics of these events. While much of the literature on temporary clusters focuses on micro-level, production-related knowledge exchanges between firms during such events, there is another dimension that has been downplayed thus far. This relates to the role of trade show organizers which can be of crucial importance in structuring knowledge flows during the shows by the way exhibits are ordered, which exhibitors and visitors are supported (or not), or which innovation themes are highlighted in specific exhibits/conference presentations. Organizers have the capacity to encourage certain types of interactions while hampering others, as well as to allocate investments to create new knowledge that exhibitors and visitors have difficulty achieving on their own (Golfetto and Mazursky 2004; Rinallo and Golfetto 2011). It should be emphasized though that the influence of trade show organizers greatly varies at the micro-level. It can be extremely strong during leading design-oriented trade shows in Italy or France, to the point where the future of an industry's development is actively shaped (Entwistle and Rocamora 2006; Rinallo and Golfetto 2006); but it can also be more generic and largely indirect, as in large technology-oriented manufacturing shows in the US and Germany (Bathelt and Schuldt 2008; Bathelt and Gibson 2014). This chapter identifies the main strategies applied by trade show organizers to guide the learning processes of exhibitors and visitors. These practices, which exhibitors and visitors are not always aware of, represent an important basis for individual and collective learning.

It is important to note that the knowledge strategies used by trade show organizers are aimed at promoting the national/international competitiveness of these events. They are also used by regional/national networks of firms or industry associations that use trade shows to compete with other regional/national networks, as well as by local governments to compete with other territories (Golfetto and Rinallo 2012). Depending on the extent to which one of these interests prevails over another, the knowledge strategies used by organizers assume specific features.

The following section describes the main configurations and commercial functions of trade shows based on the geographical origin of their exhibitors and visitors. It also examines the different knowledge environments that result from these configurations. We then turn to analyse trade show organizers' preferences for certain types of events over others. These preferences are largely based on their specific trade show goals. Finally, we discuss the main strategies used by trade show organizers to foster knowledge release by exhibitors and other key players, as well as knowledge acquisition by visitors.

4.2. KNOWLEDGE-BASED TYPOLOGY
OF INTERNATIONAL TRADE SHOWS

If we consider trade shows from a market perspective as temporary markets, the most important knowledge flows involved are those generated by vertical inter-actions between exhibitors and typical visitors (i.e. existing and/or prospective buyers). Trade show organizers also base their business model on facilitating interactions between suppliers-exhibitors and buyers-visitors. By focusing on these vertical relationships, we can identify different archetypes of events based on exhibitor and visitor origins (Golfetto 2004; Rinallo and Golfetto 2011). Figure 4.1 shows four import-export function scenarios of trade shows, based on the relative share of overseas exhibitors and visitors at the trade show.[1]

4.2.1. Local Exchange Trade Shows

They are primarily attended by exhibitors and visitors from the same region or nation. This scenario is not very common among manufacturing trade shows

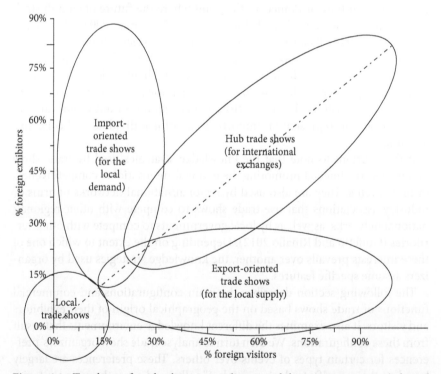

Figure 4.1. Typology of trade shows according to exhibitor/visitor origin (adapted from Golfetto 2004)

since local trade is carried out through commercial networks or routine interactions associated with permanent clusters or other forms of industrial networks. The large number of local trade shows that existed in Europe in the early stages of industrialization and even until the mid-late-twentieth century made sense when domestic markets were geographically fragmented. Today, however, globalization and the pressures of competition have led exhibitors to shun those local trade shows that do not have an international reach, at least in terms of buyer-visitors. This has resulted in the disappearance of many local events, although new local events have been established in developing economies.

4.2.2. Export-Oriented Trade Shows

This scenario is characterized by the presence of supplier-exhibitors from the host region/nation, and the predominance of non-local buyers as visitors. These events support the local manufacturers' export activities and typically emerge as collective marketing projects for these producers. Such events could be termed 'for-the-local-supply' trade shows. Such export-oriented trade shows operate at various geographical scales for exhibitors. At the regional level, most exhibitors originate from the immediate vicinity of the host region (e.g. a nearby industrial cluster), with only a minority originating from other regions of the country or from abroad. At the national level, export-oriented trade shows draw most of their exhibitors from within the same country. This is usually the result of initiatives by manufacturer associations that aggregate companies from different industrial clusters in a single exhibition.

4.2.3. Import-Oriented Trade Shows

This type helps promote imports by attracting a large proportion of non-local producers as exhibitors, while the visitors are mostly buyers from the surrounding region or nation. These events can also be referred to as 'for-the-local-demand' trade shows. Import-oriented trade shows are frequently organized by organizations that also run exhibition centres. They are also supported by local governments which regard these facilities as territorial marketing instruments that generate economic benefits from the expenditures of exhibitors and visitors in the local area (see Chapters 2 and 5). With the increased adoption of neoliberal policies and the opening of the trade show business to international competition, many for-profit firms also organize events of this type. Consequently, unlike export-oriented trade shows, import-oriented events welcome exhibitors regardless of their geographic origin: the larger the trade show, the greater its local economic impact. Similar to export-oriented trade shows, these events operate at various geographic levels with regard to visitors: from regional (with most of the visitors originating from the region hosting the event) to national (with visitors from different regions within the same country).

4.2.4. Hub Trade Shows

These are trade shows where most of the participants, both exhibitors and visitors, come from overseas. These trade shows are dedicated to international trade and serve a similar function to airport hubs because most of the trade is not conducted by participants from the host region/country. Events of this kind represent an advanced stage in the trade show life-cycle, and as such can only take place in cities with well-developed international or intercontinental accessibility. At these events, export and import functions are exercised simultaneously. Hub trade shows may be considered export-oriented at the supranational level if they mainly attract exhibitors from one geopolitical area (e.g. North America, European Union) while simultaneously attracting visitors (buyers) from other continents. Trade shows such as Première Vision (Paris, clothing textiles) and Salone del Mobile (Milan, furniture and interior design) can be considered export trade shows at the European level (see Chapters 11 and 14) because they primarily host exhibitors from Europe and mainly attract visitors from outside Europe. In terms of knowledge flows generated, these are nonetheless truly global events. In analysing the history of these trade shows, one can see how events that originally display national offerings over time open up to exhibitors from neighbouring geographical areas (if they have similar quality standards). Through this, trade shows become even more attractive for international visitors, triggering a virtuous circle of growth. As a result, such trade can develop into the mainstay events for an entire continent, or beyond.

Hub trade shows that are import-oriented at the supranational level focus on allowing suppliers from other continents to gain a commercial foothold in another continental market context. Chapter 11 discusses the case of two textiles trade shows, Interstoff (Frankfurt) and Texworld (Paris), which, at different times, have acted as a gateway to the Western European market for manufacturers from across the world, first and foremost from Asia.

At present, the market space for true supranational hub trade shows is becoming smaller across many sectors and technology fields. In Europe, where international business-to-business trade shows have existed for a long period of time, national hub trade shows have fought to become the mainstay events in the European Union. A very small number of trade shows have become supranational events, forcing the others to abandon any hopes of expanding further. With the emergence of newly industrialized countries and their trade shows, the trade show business worldwide is now being divided into large continental areas: the mature markets of Europe and North America, and the rapidly developing markets of Asia and South America (see Part II). Since the global trade show business develops a polycentric structure, trade shows have less appeal for buyers from other continental areas. Each continental area tends to develop import-based supranational trade shows based on the features of its own markets.

4.3. KNOWLEDGE EXCHANGES AT EXPORT, IMPORT, AND HUB TRADE SHOWS

In examining the various trade show types and the role of these events as temporary markets and temporary clusters, it becomes apparent that each produces specific ideal-type knowledge geographies related to where its exhibitors and visitors originate from and depending on the reach of the associated knowledge pipelines (i.e. local, national, or international). Horizontal exhibitor-exhibitor and visitor-visitor interactions also come into play here. This is because knowledge exchanges are not restricted to vertical exchanges and are not solely for market purposes. While our discussions focus on the knowledge flows from a temporary market perspective, we should keep in mind that, at a macro-level, the different types of trade shows that take place in a less developed or developing economy can also play different roles in the evolution of this economy by supporting crucial production-related knowledge flows and related learning processes, although this has thus far not been studied in depth (Bathelt and Zeng 2014a; Li 2014b).[2]

At a vertical level, export-oriented trade shows allow manufacturers to build pipelines with buyers from other territories, both nationally and internationally. At a horizontal level, the reach of these trade shows varies significantly. At one extreme, we find regional trade shows, which are often the commercial offshoots of permanent industrial clusters. These trade shows are small and can be very popular among local exhibitors that value the intimate club-like atmosphere. Local exhibitors tend to feel at ease during these events because they are sheltered from competitive pressures and comparisons with overseas competitors. These trade shows can represent pivotal moments in the development of permanent clusters as the direct comparison with 'neighbours' at these events results in local producers engaging in greater efforts to 'show off' their competencies and innovations to both rivals and non-local buyers. Horizontal interactions and comparisons with local rivals occur in a more intensified form than in everyday exchanges, during which new products cannot be examined. Yet, fear of bringing the 'enemy' (non-local suppliers) into the trade show may inhibit learning processes and limit innovation incentives, which normally arise from observing and comparing oneself to non-local competitors with different technological, organizational, and market cultures. In other words, just like the permanent clusters they derive from, these trade shows may reproduce an institutional lock-in problem (Grabher 1993; Boschma 2005) that is often found among economic actors, which are too strongly embedded in a specific geographical area, risking becoming overly self-referential and less responsive to market and technological developments (Bathelt and Taylor 2002).

When interacting with non-local visitors at events that showcase local offerings, exhibitors benefit from more in-depth, longer contacts than at trade shows with a wider and more diversified exhibitor base. The manufacturer's premises may be located near the trade show, thus generating opportunities for exchanges to continue at these sites. While this results in learning benefits for exhibitors and visitors alike, it also restricts opportunities for visitors to witness the many product varieties available in other markets. To receive a complete clear overview of international offerings, visitors thus need to attend numerous other trade shows with regional offerings. While the absence of non-local competitors protects exhibitors from undesired comparisons, it also reduces the overall information value for visitors.

National-level supply trade shows provide visitors and exhibitors with learning opportunities of limited depth, but of a greater variety than the more homogeneous local supply events. More specifically, this type of trade show reduces visitor knowledge acquisition costs and enables exhibitors to observe and compare their products with those of competitors that originate from industrial clusters located in different parts of the country. The establishment of horizontal and vertical knowledge pipelines at a global level, however, only occurs at trade shows that aggregate exhibitors from many different countries exhibiting a wide product range. Such hub events create a knowledge environment that is much richer than other export-oriented shows in an industry.[3] Exhibitors can observe and compare themselves with other participating firms that adopt similar strategies based on the quality, creativity, and innovation of their respective production contexts (such as industrial clusters or other networks), thereby ensuring robust processes of horizontal learning. Furthermore, by aggregating a large number of manufacturers, these shows attract visitors from across the world—beyond what could be achieved by a national or district-level supply trade show.

Import-oriented trade shows allow exhibiting firms to build knowledge pipelines with customers from a specific geographical market (local or national). At a horizontal level, these events allow exhibitors to observe and compare themselves with competitors from various countries that are interested in serving the same regional/national market. The reach of this trade show type can also vary. Over the years, there has been a notable increase in the number of trade shows with a regional/national focus. Exhibitors use these events when their international development has reached an advanced stage and attend trade shows held in larger or developing geographical markets. Due to the large number of different national markets, firms tend to rationalize their participation by investing less money in individual shows (e.g. small booths, fewer products, and fewer technical personnel) or by attending such events only indirectly through agents or distributors (i.e. wholesalers or importers). Consequently, the promotional knowledge exhibitors release at these events mainly involves commercial information (e.g. product range, prices, and delivery dates). As a result, knowledge flows are more limited than at large hub trade shows where manufacturers participate directly, present their latest innovations, send research and development experts, and discuss future programmes. From the visitors' perspective, import events enable local buyers to learn about product and alternative solutions from a selection of suppliers interested in interacting with them.[4] While the resulting knowledge exchanges are more limited than at international events, the reduced costs of participating in regional/national events partially compensate for this.

Import-oriented supranational trade shows enable exhibitors to observe and measure themselves against a broad set of foreign competitors. The main difference between these exhibitions and export-oriented hub events lies in the fact that the exhibiting companies are more heterogeneous. The exhibitor selection process by the organizers is less stringent because they prefer large events that can optimize their revenues and the economic impacts for the community hosting them. Horizontally, exhibitors find themselves dealing with competitors that have both similar and dissimilar strategies in terms of their market focus, manufacturing processes, technological/raw material basis, product quality, innovation, and/or price level. Vertically, visitors can access information about a broad range of products, solutions, and suppliers, as well as select the best purchase options. For both exhibitors and visitors, there is generally a great potential for knowledge cross-fertilization at these trade shows.

In contrast, the large attendance and more limited amount of time spent visiting these shows sometimes generates a sense of discomfort among participants. This pertains to the superficial nature of some of the contacts made at these events, as well as a general sense of lost opportunities. The physical fatigue and sensory and information overload seen at smaller trade shows (Borghini et al. 2006; Rinallo et al. 2011) occur here at a higher and more intensified level. This is especially true when comparing these events to niche trade shows, which focus on specific technology fields or market segments.

4.4. TRADE SHOW ORGANIZERS AND THEIR KNOWLEDGE STRATEGIES

In temporary clusters and temporary markets, the proximity among actors is organized. While many studies focus on the micro-level knowledge exchange and learning processes at large international events, they tend to neglect the role of trade show organizers in structuring these events and even actively shaping the nature of interactions that take place. This impact is similar to the role of professional organizations (e.g. Benner 2003; Faulconbridge 2007a, 2007b) and public authorities (e.g. Filippi and Torre 2003) in activating the advantages of geographical co-localization in permanent clusters by, for instance, mobilizing member firms for collective or communal projects. As will be discussed, trade show organizers can sometimes have a crucial impact on the type of knowledge flows generated during these events (see also Part III).

Trade shows have specific decision-making centres that are responsible for adapting to environmental changes and coordinating the physical proximity between actors. The role of these organizers as enablers and constrainers in exhibitor–visitor interaction has only recently been highlighted (Rinallo and Golfetto 2011). A shift towards the meso-level of analysis allows us to highlight the activities of these key actors whose practices ultimately structure the set-ups and communication contexts of trade shows. This is something that exhibitors and visitors are not always aware of.

4.4.1. Typologies, Competencies, and Main Objectives

The production of trade show services, which users see as being a single offering, is actually made up of various activities and functions provided by different firms with specific core competencies. In addition to trade show organizing activities, the main compartments include organizing activities, the management of exhibition complexes and general services, and the supply of trade show-related goods and services (see Figure 4.2; Golfetto 2004).

Trade show organization includes selling exhibitor space, physically organizing the event, attracting visitors, supplying services, and looking for sponsors. Trade show organizers are entities owned by or otherwise linked to trade associations, organizations running exhibition complexes, and/or private firms. They are generally relatively small because the organizing activity requires them to be highly specialized in given sectors. However, some larger organizers exist (such as Comexposium SAS, GL Events Exhibition, ITE Group plc, Montgomery, and Reed Exhibitions) that stage between 400 to 500 trade

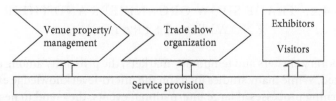

Figure 4.2. Activities of the trade show chain (adapted from Golfetto 2004)

shows in various countries and sectors throughout the world each year. Firms managing exhibition complexes (such as Fiera Milano SpA, Messe Düsseldorf GmbH, and Messe Frankfurt GmbH) can also be large-scale and, in some countries, organize trade shows while also carrying out their traditional exhibition space management activity. Some organize hundreds of trade shows, while others have a multinational structure. The various organizer types have specific competencies and competitive behaviours.

Organizers owned by or linked to producer associations primarily benefit from having a privileged relationship with potential exhibitors and a significant amount of industry-specific know-how. These are necessarily small organizations that organize a small number of trade shows. They are also extremely specialized and tend to focus more on the problems of the main exhibitors (which are members of the associations) than on those of the visitors (the potential customers of exhibitors). The aim of these organizers is often to promote and develop the local/regional industry they represent. Trade shows can be important collective projects of an association, which keeps their member firms together. In the past, these organizers often limited and controlled participation of foreign exhibitors at regional/national shows because association members were fearful of international comparison. With the onset of globalization, this has become less of a problem, as a broad and varied exhibitor base, even from overseas, has become fundamental to the competitiveness and survival of trade shows.

Aside from associations, organizations running exhibition complexes that simultaneously organize trade shows are also a common feature, especially in Europe. They typically develop their trade show expertise by organizing general industry trade shows, around which exhibition complexes are built. With the development of specialist trade shows and the growing need for industry-specific competencies, many exhibition complexes have limited their activities to the management of the exhibition space and the supply of basic technical services, instead of organizing events. Others have fine-tuned their organizing skills in order to specialize in industry/technology fields, working in cooperation with trade associations. Finally, some organizations running exhibition complexes have developed events solely for local/national markets or consumers. The main resource for these organizers is the often monopolistic control of exhibition space in a given territory and their primary goal is to develop local services and business tourism. In so doing, organizing trade shows helps to 'balance the books', as running an exhibition complex is typically a money-losing business.

Private organizers, or organizers independent of exhibition complexes and associations, were not very common in the trade show industry in the past. This is largely due to the conditions under which trade shows historically developed—i.e. the collective marketing objectives of associations on the one hand, and the goal of a local/regional economic impact of governments on the other. Since the 1990s, however, there has been a rapid increase in the number of such organizers, both locally/nationally and at a multinational level. Independent organizers are mainly from the publishing industry (such as dmg events, Informa Exhibitions, and UBM plc), where they have developed skills and relationships with producers for the sale of advertising space. Like any other firm, the goal of these organizers is profit maximization, without any special concern for the economic development of host areas or the collective marketing of local industries. Consequently, the competitive behaviour of private organizers is characterized by fewer constraints, resulting in the selection of the best venues for a given trade show concept or aggressive marketing strategies to attract foreign exhibitors.

4.4.2. Knowledge-Based Strategies

In this section, we identify the main strategies through which organizers enable and structure exhibitor and visitor knowledge-acquisition practices (see Table 4.1). Here, the term 'strategy' encompasses the knowledge-circulation solutions and activities that organizers intentionally employ for competitive purposes. The aim of organizers is to differentiate the trade shows they organize from competing events, by making them better learning places for exhibitors and visitors. As in other sectors, competition in the trade show business centres on first-mover advantages or successful imitation. In this respect, several recent developments can be observed, for instance related to new professional technologies and social media that are being used by leading trade shows to create internet portals. Related tools and practices go beyond the few days spent at live meetings, offering longer-term opportunities to interact, observe, and compare. Such strategies are not shown in Table 4.1, as it is still too early to examine their impact on trade show competition (Golfetto and Rinallo 2013).

(i) Marking the boundaries of the temporary cluster

Trade show organizers define the boundaries of their events by including some firms and excluding others on the basis of the firm's origins and types of products they represent. Attendance at trade shows sometimes closely corresponds to the shows' catchment basins, the extension of which is also based on the locations' relative accessibility (Golfetto 2004). Organizers have some freedom in determining which exhibitors and visitors will participate in their shows, as they set formal or informal guidelines to target the appropriate market segments, while excluding others. As discussed previously, this can be based on countries from where exhibitors and visitors originate, thus giving rise to export- or import-oriented trade shows with a local to global reach.

Table 4.1. Knowledge-based strategies of trade show organizers

Strategy	Associated activities

Marking the boundaries of the temporary cluster	• Selection of the actors allowed to participate in the temporary cluster by
	  o Geographic origin (import/export trade shows with a local to global reach)
	  o Product assortment and visitor segments (general/niche trade shows)

Improving knowledge release and acquisition	• Active search for, and visibility of, market leaders and innovative leader producers • Organizing market-sensitive exhibition layout solutions • Highlighting key innovations through innovation areas • Organizing technical seminars • Organizing social events
Hindering undesired knowledge spillovers	• Offering incentives to buyers and restrictions for non-buyers • Photo ban • Intellectual property protection measures
Investing in new market or technological knowledge development	• Investing in research and development activities • Mobilizing actors to generate new relevant knowledge and to support specific achievements • Supporting the affirmation of specific styles and technologies
Building culture of the industry	• Presenting the historical roots of the sector • Educating the market about differences in the functional and symbolic quality of products

Another criterion that trade show organizers use to mark the boundaries of these events is the range of products on display (for exhibitors) and the variety of market sectors addressed (for visitors). Many of the large-scale specialist trade shows that emerged in the mid-twentieth century were general trade shows in terms of the products displayed and the markets addressed. By displaying the entire range of offerings from a relatively broad sector, they attracted heterogeneous market segments. Some of these large-scale trade shows are still in operation. An example is EMO (Hanover and Milan), the world machine tool exposition, which is the oldest and largest European trade show for the metalworking industry with a broad range of products and solutions exhibited. As a consequence, visitors at EMO are firms from many different manufacturing sectors.

At large-scale trade shows, buyer-visitors are not interested in making contact with all these different product segments. Similarly, exhibitors are usually only interested in interacting with some of the segments that are presented. Despite this, visitors often comment on the importance of such large-scale events in terms of enabling cross-fertilization of knowledge between diverse sectors (Ramírez-Pasillas 2008; also CERMES 2003a, 2003b). The large number of participants and the heterogeneous nature of the actors involved can, however, accentuate problems that are associated with larger events (i.e. superficial contacts, sensory overload, and cognitive fatigue). These problems make room for niche trade shows, which specialize in single exhibition sectors or smaller market segments.

When dealing with clothing textiles, for example, specialist trade shows for specific products attract a smaller number and more homogeneous group of exhibitors and visitors, making targeted contacts easier for all participants. This also reduces the number of atypical visitors and leads to a larger extent of actual trade dealings, with fewer distractions. For buyer-visitors, this implies having a more focused overview of suppliers that address their needs than in large-scale trade shows. As a result, these events allow for the establishment of specialized knowledge pipelines.

Niche trade shows that focus on the requirements of specific segments of demand display products that are based on the assortment needs of target buyers. Unlike supply niche events, which have homogeneous products, these shows have a more heterogeneous group of exhibitors. For example, the mix of offerings at specialized health and wellbeing trade shows varies substantially, depending on whether the main market segments addressed are hospitals, pharmacies, or health product stores. These shows are also timed to cater to the purchasing needs of export markets and channels for new supplies, instead of manufacturer innovations.

(ii) Improving the release and acquisition of knowledge

Trade show organizers can facilitate knowledge circulation at their events by using strategies to improve exhibitor knowledge release and simplify visitor knowledge acquisition. In order to stimulate knowledge circulation, a critical first step is to ensure the presence of market leaders and other firms that are at the forefront of innovation. These firms are key accounts for trade show organizers, not simply because of their normally large exhibits, but also because they serve as a crucial reference point and often first step in visitor learning processes (see Chapter 2). In addition to adopting typical exhibition strategies at their booths (e.g. showcasing innovations and prototypes, engaging technical experts, and so on), these market leaders often participate in setting up the 'trend areas' in collaboration with the organizers. As a result, trade shows benefit from a large amount of knowledge that can be acquired due to the presence of leaders. Some supply trade shows have overcome their traditional aversion to foreign competition and have invited leaders from other countries in an effort to enrich knowledge flows during these events. They attract and build the loyalty of such firms by offering incentives to them (e.g. discounts or more attractive places in the exhibition layout) and by inviting them to be part of event steering committees. This is not always successful, however, as some trade shows, such as CeBIT in Hanover (Bathelt and Zakrzewski 2007), have been abandoned by leading companies, with the danger of other exhibitors following later.

In addition to encouraging the presence of leading firms, trade show organizers also conduct talent scouting, such as encouraging the participation of highly innovative emerging firms. Some fashion and furniture trade shows, for instance, allow the best graduates from design schools to exhibit free of charge. Through this, these individuals can find firms willing to pick up their designs/prototypes and produce them later (see, for example, Chapter 14).

Organizers also try to support and simplify visitor knowledge acquisition through improved exhibitor layout solutions. One of the key challenges that trade show visitors face involves the quick identification of relevant information. Unlike online supplier directories, which can be searched in real time, trade shows physically arrange exhibitors in the exhibition space by applying a few layout criteria (e.g. country of origin, market destination, and/or price/quality level). The architectures of interaction that derive from preferring one of these criteria over another and the sequence of knowledge exchanges may greatly differ.

In the past, most specialized trade shows arranged exhibitors according to nationality. Exhibitors from one country would thus find themselves together with rivals from the same country. According to this design, the economic geography of the sector was essentially reproduced at the trade show. This complicated matters for visitors, however, as buyers that were interested in a specific product needed to search different halls at the fairground in order to locate relevant suppliers, which wasted valuable time and opportunities. The first trade shows that considered changing their layout on the basis of functional criteria (e.g. technology/raw material used or market destination) faced considerable resistance from exhibitors, who feared direct comparisons with foreign competitors. Such scepticism disappeared, however, when visitors expressed their satisfaction with the new layouts. Nowadays, organizers often replan their exhibition layouts to adapt to new technological and market trends, to further simplify the visitor's search for information and knowledge, or to highlight certain innovations and emerging subsectors.

By selecting exhibitors and reorganizing their layout according to an evolving segmentation of market needs, organizers influence the micro geography of trade shows and structure sequences of interactions and knowledge exchanges. With each subsequent change, organizers can alter the nature and sequence of interactions that take place. Exhibitors can observe as well as compare themselves with different sets of competitors, and buyers that are interested in their products can more easily find what they are looking for. The exhibition layout thus has important implications that affect both the horizontal and vertical levels.

Organizers can also promote knowledge acquisition at trade shows by setting up innovation areas, market trend areas, and seminars on topics of interest for visitors. These initiatives use different ways of sharing knowledge. Innovation and market trend areas use the ability of artefacts to share tacit knowledge, given that they form the basis for individual and collective cognitive processes (Bechky 2003b; Lorenzoni and Narduzzo 2005; Stigliani and Ravasi 2012). Displaying the 'best in innovation' is one way in which organizers guide or reflect the development of the sector, particularly in cases when new products are selected with the aid of experts, by issuing formal recognition or organizing award-winning ceremonies (Rao 1994; Anand and Watson 2004). Technical seminars are mainly based on sharing coded knowledge, which is easily transferrable through language and illustrations. Many trade shows offer a broad, detailed programme of specialized seminars, the duration of which can vary. The challenge for organizers is to select the contents and strike a balance between the needs of exhibitors (speakers or sponsors), who release knowledge for promotional purposes, and visitors who, by attending, have to use some of the precious time available to visit the trade show.

(iii) Hindering undesirable knowledge spillovers

Trade shows sometimes allow the acquisition of knowledge despite the intentions of the exhibitors to prevent visitors who are not customers from gaining access to critical knowledge. To prevent undesirable knowledge spillovers, exhibitors adopt different practices, which include building closed booths and having specific staff exclusively for buyers and a few other qualified visitors. Despite such measures, it is difficult to protect intellectual property rights at trade shows, as one of the main functions of these events is to showcase new products for promotional purposes and to test the reaction of future customers (Cohendet et al. 2013). While this problem dates back to the first universal expositions (Townsend 1914; Moser 2005; Palumbo 2008), it has escalated dramatically during the period of globalization, when low-cost manufacturing countries started attending exhibitions. It is most serious in industries where innovation is more about style than technology (Cappetta et al. 2006), as legal property rights tend to be weaker and more difficult to enforce in these industries.

Trade show organizers employ various measures to limit undesired knowledge spillovers. Most importantly, they focus their attention on the most dreaded atypical visitor, that is, competitors that go to trade shows with competitive intelligence or even industrial espionage in mind (Palumbo 2008). The main measures used in this context include allowing entry to buyers only who are pre-selected through specific invitations and incentives. For example, some organizers offer VIP treatment (i.e. free entrance, no queues, exclusive previews, free bar and lunch, or special events) to those who register in advance and provide proof of having purchased a certain number of products from exhibitors at the trade show. Organizers often restrict or do not allow photographs to be taken on the fairgrounds. Enforcing this rule has become a challenge, however, in the era of the smartphone, since crowded halls make controls and timely action impossible.

Finally, organizers can fight against undesired knowledge spillovers by circulating information on legal actions that could be taken to protect intellectual property rights. The Global Association of the Exhibition Industry (UFI) recommends that organizers hand out intellectual property rights information to all exhibitors, and provide a list of local intellectual property attorneys who can represent exhibitors wishing to take legal action (UFI 2008). Organizers sometimes provide an on-site service to deal with any intellectual property rights complaints, have interpreters to help communicate any disputes, and/or offer neutral arbitration to help determine if there is a violation of intellectual property rights or to resolve disputes during the events. Such measures do not prevent imitation and espionage, but help to limit the potential consequences by allowing action to be taken against violators in blatant cases (e.g. counterfeit products or brands on display).

(iv) Investing in new technological or market knowledge development

Besides providing a relational space for the exchange of knowledge between the participating actors, trade show organizers sometimes actively develop new knowledge through specific investments. In the past, when trade show organizers understood their responsibilities as primarily renting space to exhibitors, such investments did not occur or were employed for media relations purposes only. At that time, organizers left it to the exhibitors to bring and showcase the contents. This began to change when third-party actors, such as universities or experts, became involved in preparing seminar programmes to complement the exhibition activity. There is now a growing awareness that trade show organizers compete with each other in knowledge markets. Strategic decisions to dedicate resources, even essential ones, to content development are thus increasingly justified. In trade shows where this occurs, organizers have an especially strong impact on the nature of knowledge flows.

By exploiting their capacity as relational platforms, some exhibitions are able to build new contents (e.g. new product styles for the season) via broad mobilization processes that involve a variety of actors from different locales with heterogeneous competencies and knowledge bases. Chapter 11 discusses the concerted process of fashion trends set by the main European trade shows for the clothing textiles industry. This experience, which could be defined as a form of crowd-innovation 'ante litteram', long before the advent of present-day networks and social media, means the trade show organizer must be a recognized leader and be able to put a very large number of players into action. These practices are perhaps the most complex forms of knowledge-based strategies implemented by organizers and do not occur very often. They also leverage the multiplying process of the actors involved. The ability to bring innovations to the market is, in fact, also linked to the ability to affirm them. In the case of the concerted process, which sets new fashion trends, this initiative is: (i) originally confined to a select number of leading exhibitors, who identify the information to disseminate, and the styles and products to support; (ii) shared with all exhibitors at the trade show and within the respective supply chain; (iii) transferred to all visitors in elaborate ways during the trade show; and (iv) reverberated by the press among all other actors in the sector and consumers (see Chapter 11).

By no means, however, are trade show organizers in all industries and technology fields always able to organize such processes based on comprehensive knowledge of the industry and its future development. We found many cases of events in which the understanding of the organizers about technological frontiers or the specific forms of knowledge exchanges taking place was surprisingly limited.

(v) Building culture of the industry

Finally, trade show organizers can put knowledge strategies into place by using initiatives designed to establish, explicate, or build a specific identifiable 'culture' of the respective industry or technology field. This can be done by highlighting the history and educating the market (i.e. buyers, purchase influencers, and end consumers) on differences in the quality—functional and/or symbolic—of their exhibitors' core products. Such initiatives can more easily be implemented at supply events with a relatively homogeneous group of exhibitors with deep roots in the same region or territory. The specialized production programmes of these exhibitors have resulted from historical processes which, when identified (and sometimes romanticized), can help to build a collective image for local/national groups of firms (so-called 'country-of-origin' effect; see Chapter 12). Through this, trade shows can function as platforms for a collective reconstruction of the past (Peñaloza 2000, 2001), using what the recent marketing literature calls 'commercial mythmaking strategies' (Thompson and Tian 2008). These mythmaking strategies are based on the ideological shaping of popular memories and counter-memories about a territory's past development. Italian furniture trade shows, for instance, organize retrospectives on the history of Italian design and on its relationship with artisan Renaissance furniture (see Chapter 14).

Educating the market about differences in quality has become a need for many national industries in Europe and North America to justify price differences between their products and seemingly similar products sold at much lower prices by producers from newly industrialized countries. When the differences between producers are functional ones, knowledge can be built via technical seminars, information material, and other tools aimed at demonstrating the differences in quality. When the differences are aesthetic and symbolic in character, it is necessary to educate the market in a way that allows it to perceive these differences in terms of preferences and 'develop a taste' for them.

This often takes place through processes of cross-fertilization with arts. Italian marble processing trade shows, for example, give architecture awards to link the image of marble as a material to the work of the great masters of contemporary architecture (see Chapter 13). Yarn trade shows entrust the creation of the 'trends areas' to well-known artists who present the colours and themes of new exhibitor collections creatively and emphasize their aesthetic quality (Golfetto and Mazursky 2004).

References to history and the arts can place significant cultural meaning (McCracken 1986) on the products displayed at trade shows, thereby differentiating such products in the eyes of industrial customers, distributors, and (if initiatives manage to reach the public at large) end consumers. As with knowledge-generating strategies, those aimed at educating the market are usually based on mobilizing a broad group of players, something which individual firms are unable to do. As for other types of events (Anand and Watson 2004), trade shows are also able to encourage diverse actors and institutions to become involved in the fates of their industries.

4.5. CONCLUSIONS

This chapter has focused on the main differences among trade shows in terms of their knowledge circulation potential. One of the main differentiating factors is based on the geographic origin of exhibitors and visitors. This criterion highlights the different orientation (import or export) and reach (from local to international) of trade shows. Another criterion is the extent and variety of the industries/technology fields addressed or the segments of demand involved. The various types of trade shows generate very different interaction and learning opportunities. Some trade shows are broad and diversified, while others are deep and specialized; some events offer more knowledge acquisition opportunities than others; some establish specific settings to interact with a small number of actors in great depth, while the number of potential partners at other events is so large that communication becomes superficial and short-lived; and so on. Finally, the learning opportunities are also different depending on whether production capabilities or marketing capabilities are at stake—and they further depend on the stage of economic development and technological sophistication of the respective participants—as well as host economies.

This chapter has also highlighted the role of the trade show organizers, described the main types of organizers (i.e. trade associations, organizations running exhibition complexes, and private organizers), and identified their main objectives. In addition to determining the scale, reach, and variety of products and markets at trade shows, organizers use a large number of strategies to control or increase knowledge release and acquisition among trade show participants. These strategies include, for example, involving leaders, organizing special exhibits that focus on innovation themes, holding technical or socializing events, building knowledge of the sector, and mobilizing broader processes for the affirmation of product styles and technologies. All of these activities increase knowledge circulation, in terms of both individual and collective interactions. This makes trade shows more appealing for participants. They become stronger in the competition among similar industry events organized by different organizers with different territorial interest.

NOTES

1. In Figure 4.1, a national geographic scale is used, albeit that we refer to various other geographic scales in this chapter, from regional to supranational. The so-called methodological nationalism (Beck 2005), using the 'nation–country' as the unit of analysis, can make it difficult to understand some phenomena of economic exchange, especially when dealing with globalization. One example is the smaller international reach of US trade shows compared to those in Europe, which is due to the smaller domestic markets of European countries where firms need to export in order to grow. If the statistics of European trade shows were calculated at the level of the European Union, their international reach would be similar to that of US trade shows.

2. The following discussion concentrates on vertical knowledge exchanges between exhibitors and typical visitors (buyers), using observations and interactions, as well as horizontal exchanges among exhibitors, mainly using observations and comparisons (Maskell 2001). Knowledge exchanges among exhibitors and atypical visitors are not the main focus. Horizontal exchanges among visitors, while important, are hindered by the fact that the trade show environment is not usually structured to facilitate interaction among the latter. Such exchanges are more spontaneous in nature but play an important role in the collective sensemaking processes at trade shows (see Chapter 9).

3. However, in a less developed country, local/national participants might not be able to benefit as much from such knowledge flows, as these producers may not be sophisticated/experienced enough to do so (Li 2014b).

4. Again, while this may open important learning opportunities for foreign exhibitors, those for technologically less-sophisticated regional/national firms may be limited (Li 2014b).

5

Trade Show Specialization and Territorial Specialization

5.1. INTRODUCTION

This chapter addresses two related issues that have thus far remained in the background. These aspects need to be addressed before concluding the conceptual part of this book (Part I) because they fundamentally concern the relationship between trade shows as events and the places, cities, and regions that host them and provide the venues where they take place (exhibition, convention, or conference centres). Two questions are central in this respect. First, what is the relationship between trade shows, their underlying industries, and their surrounding economic geographies? And second, in times of globalization, do trade shows in a particular industrial or technological field become increasingly similar over time in terms of the products offered and markets served, or do they retain a specific local/national character?

Depending on the theoretical perspective adopted, the answers to these questions vary. On the one hand, trade shows are seen as exerting a dominant influence on their underlying industries and markets, while, on the other hand, they are viewed merely as reflections of the underlying and surrounding industries and markets. Under conditions of globalization and ubiquitous markets, we might expect trade shows to become increasingly similar to each other, losing connections with the economic geographies of the cities and regions that host them. This could be called the 'convergence hypothesis'. At the same time, however, a different outcome might also be expected insofar as trade show organizers and firms assign specific functions to trade shows through which they maintain territorial specificities—referred to as the 'divergence and specialization hypothesis'.

These views differ markedly in terms of the degree of agency granted to the economic actors involved, such as firms, networks of firms, or organizers. While the individual chapters in this book stress the role of these agents, this chapter suggests a two-way influence between trade shows and their trajectories, on the one hand, and the structure of underlying industries and economic geographies on the other. This creates a fundamental interdependence between trade show specialization and territorial specialization.

Leaving aside for the moment our discussions from previous chapters, one might not expect a close relationship between trade shows, their surrounding economic landscapes, and territorial developments. Modernity and globalization seem to be characterized by uncoupling processes (Giddens 1990) that loosen any potential connections between territorialized economic specialization and trade show specialization. The idea that there are important interrelationships between territorial economic development and trade show development might, thus, seem counterintuitive. Anyone who has attended different trade shows in the same industry that are located in different regions and countries will easily notice, however, that despite the veneer of similarity (sometimes accentuated by look-alike brand names), trade shows are characterized by fundamental heterogeneity. This is true not only in terms of the origin of their visitors and exhibitors (see Chapter 4), but also with respect to the specific products showcased, the agendas pushed forward by the participants, and the relative representation of different industry branches in the exhibition halls. These differences, we argue, originate, to some degree, from localized (i.e. local, regional, and/or national) economic specialization. At the same time, economic specialization is also affected by the knowledge and commercial exchanges activated by local, regional, or national trade shows, as they internationalize further and attract non-local exhibitors and visitors.

These considerations call into question the permanent effects of temporary events. In terms of their overall impact, we must acknowledge that trade shows are temporary. They are fluid in nature, only taking place for a few days; their networks appear to dissolve when participants return to their daily routines in different parts of the world after the event; and, after a few weeks, hardly any traces of the artefacts and dynamics of the shows are left at the facilities where they took place. In the absence of consecutive events, there is no indication of the rich knowledge ecologies that unfolded only a short time earlier. And there is little incentive for firms to make these major trade show locations their permanent hubs for production activities (Maskell et al. 2004; Bathelt 2012), as localized capabilities and sunk costs at the original production sites encourage spatial persistence and hinder relocation.

Despite the temporality of trade shows, this chapter argues that there is a systematic interrelationship between trade show specialization and territorial specialization with respect to the local, regional, or national economy. On the one hand, trade show specialization is driven by the characteristics of the firms located in the respective catchment basins of the events, which represent captive markets for organizers. Differentiation strategies based on extant territorial specialization are obvious choices for most trade show organizers (Golfetto 2004; Rinallo and Golfetto 2011). These, in turn, affect exhibition layout decisions, which are organized accordingly. Differentiation strategies also influence promotional activities, which give prominence to the shows' unique characteristics compared to competing non-local events. Additionally, local cultural specificities in production processes, which affect the image of the host region/nation and of the firms therein (e.g. French fashion, Italian cuisine, or German precision technology), along with variations in national institutional set-ups further add to trade show specialization in idiosyncratic manners. Altogether, these factors contribute to the diversity of trade shows that take place in different cities, regions, or countries.

On the other hand, trade shows have distinct implications for economic development at different geographical scales. First, they generate economic growth and the development of a specialized service economy for such events in the local economy; second, they support regional industrial specialization patterns if they are related to or focus on the respective regional agglomerations (thus providing an outlet for regional industries); third, in less developed economies, they play a fundamental role in enabling industrialization processes and provide a forum for industries to grow and develop new specializations; fourth, at the level of national territories, the learning processes and technological choices of firms at hub shows are driven by existing industrial specialization and, at the same time, support ongoing national specialization patterns.

In aggregate terms, these processes hinder standardization processes among trade shows and their underlying national industries. Rather than becoming increasingly similar under the conditions of globalization, and developing into cosmopolitan places (e.g. Skov 2006), international trade shows maintain a distinctive character, the origins of which lie in national territorial specialization. The consequences of massive knowledge exchanges during these events, supported by actual transactions and material flows (often at a later stage), in turn, support and promote territorial economic specialization. In sum, trade show specialization and territorial specialization have a reciprocal, interdependent relationship with one another.

Our argument regarding the interrelationship between trade show and territorial specialization proceeds as follows: After a brief discussion of paradigmatic views on the relationship between trade shows and their underlying industries, we discuss, in two steps, the effect of cultural-economic territorial influences on trade shows and, conversely, the consequences of trade show activity on economic development and specialization at different territorial scales. From this, we develop a two-way influence model that describes the interrelationship between trade show specialization and territorial economic specialization. We suggest that the link between these specialization patterns is stronger in certain phases of the trade show life-cycle than in others, and stronger for certain types of trade shows as opposed to others. In conclusion, we summarize our findings and discuss avenues for future research.

5.2. PARADIGMATIC VIEWS ON THE RELATIONSHIP BETWEEN TRADE SHOWS AND THEIR UNDERLYING INDUSTRIES

The literature on trade shows, implicitly or explicitly, espouses different paradigmatic views regarding the influence of these events on their underlying industries—and vice versa (see Figure 5.1). In a broader sense, such views reflect the ongoing debate in the social sciences over the primacy of structure versus agency in shaping human behaviour. Some theories emphasize the agents' autonomy and freedom from external limitations in determining their destinies, whereas others highlight the set of economic, social, and cultural constraints that shape human behaviour, in ways that are often not realized by subjects who may instead believe they act like free agents (e.g. Giddens 1984; Taylor 1989; Hay 1995; Callinicos 2004).

The structure/agency debate has influenced many disciplines throughout the social sciences, including those that form the theoretical foundations of this book. Business studies, for instance, have typically viewed managers as strategic actors who, thanks to a variety of skills and rational decision-making processes, affect the success of their organizations (Child 1997). In economic geography, the relational approach (Dicken and Malmberg 2001; Bathelt and Glückler 2003; Boggs and Rantisi 2003) has attempted to correct the under-socialized nature of previous approaches by using the interactions of key agents as a starting point in the analysis of economic behaviour, while also recognizing the role of structure and the interrelationship between both (Bathelt 2006; Bathelt and Glückler 2011).

Do trade shows influence underlying industries? / **Do underlying industries influence trade shows?**	*Yes*	*No*
Yes	Interdependence (2-way influence)	Trade shows influence economic structure
No	Trade shows are dominated by economic structure	Autonomy (no causal connection)

Figure 5.1. Paradigmatic views of trade shows and their relationship with underlying industries (*Note:* Illustration is inspired by McQuail's 1984 categorization of theoretical positions regarding the relationship between media and society)

Depending on the academic background, the research questions at hand, and the methodologies used, studies of trade shows may adopt one of the paradigmatic views represented in Figure 5.1. A position of strong trade show influence over underlying industries (upper right quadrant in Figure 5.1) is prevalent in numerous studies in management and economic geography. This is perhaps best expressed in the literature on field-configuring events, which originates from the observations that specific events shape the evolution of professions, technologies, markets, and industries in discontinuous ways (Garud 2008; Lampel and Meyer 2008). Marketing and management studies focusing on trade show organizers similarly suggest that trade shows can affect trajectories of innovation in the underlying industries (Rinallo and Golfetto 2006; Rinallo et al. 2006; Golfetto and Rinallo 2008; 2012). In economic geography, it has also been proposed that these events affect the geographies of knowledge circulation in their underlying industries, expressed in the literature on trade shows as temporary clusters (Maskell et al. 2004, 2006; Bathelt and Schuldt 2005, 2010; Rinallo and Golfetto 2011; Schuldt and Bathelt 2011; see also Power and Jansson 2008; Ramírez-Pasillas 2008, 2010). Empirical work pertaining to this research stream adopts a variety of approaches, including case study research, participant observation, historical analyses based on archival sources, and survey-based research designs aimed at quantifying the volume of interaction and knowledge acquisition at trade shows. Although econometric studies are less prevalent, it would be possible to model the impact of trade show-related independent variables with respect to various outcomes of interest (dependent variables such as territorial specialization, degree of innovativeness, or export levels).

Other studies implicitly view trade shows as being dominated by economic structure (lower left cell of Figure 5.1). Historical economic analyses of the rise and fall of medieval trade fairs, for instance, tend to fall into this category (e.g. Weber 1961). More recently, Rubalcaba-Bermejo and Cuadrado-Roura's (1995) econometric study of the distribution of trade show activities identifies several socio-economic variables that condition the hierarchy of trade show cities in Europe at an aggregate level (see also Cuadrado-Roura and Rubalcaba-Bermejo 1998; Jin et al. 2010). Similarly, Zhu and Zeng (2014) identify economic and infrastructural factors that influence the spatial distribution of China's exhibition industry. Managerial models evaluating the market potential of trade shows and exhibition centres in a given area are also based on the evaluation of structural variables, such as the number of buyers and suppliers in the catchment basin and the international accessibility of the host city (Golfetto 2004).

In contrast to this work, this chapter proposes a two-way influence model between trade shows and their underlying industries (upper left cell of Figure 5.1). In doing so, we appreciate the influence of structural conditions and changes in underlying industries on trade shows. Since the 1990s, for example, the organizers of once-leading trade shows in Europe have been facing difficulties as global supply chains were restructuring and manufacturing industries moved from Western Europe to Asia, South America, or Eastern Europe. Such macro-economic trends have created increasingly difficult conditions for European shows, which, at an aggregate level, have to face maturity and even decline (see Chapter 6), while Asian shows are growing extremely fast (see Chapter 8; Golfetto and Rinallo 2014; Rinallo and Golfetto 2014; Bathelt and Zeng 2014b). As a result, the global geographies of knowledge circulation are changing in ways that reflect the dynamics of their underlying industries. At the same time, however, European trade shows have adopted different knowledge generation strategies to strengthen the market success of local/regional industrial clusters and slow down de-localization patterns (see Chapter 6 and the empirical studies in Part III).

Finally, it would be difficult to maintain the position that no connection exists between trade shows and their underlying local, regional, or national industries (lower right quadrant of Figure 5.1). At the most, we could expect traces of such positions, with specific reference to the issues of territorial specialization, in studies focusing on the geographical origin of exhibitors and visitors in hub trade shows (see Chapter 4) that are increasingly detached from their regional/national production bases (e.g. Skov 2006). However, historical analyses of the evolution of these events demonstrate that international attractiveness may just be a phase of the so-called trade show life-cycle. Accordingly, in early phases of the life-cycle, trade shows are more dependent on the local context than in later phases. Similarly, trade shows that successfully attract foreign exhibitors and visitors during their growth are sometimes confronted with phases of decline when multiple domestic influences become stronger.

Having categorized the paradigmatic views on trade shows and their impact on underlying industries, the remainder of this chapter focuses on the specific case where interdependent relationships exist between trade show specialization and economic specialization in the respective local, regional, or national contexts. We conceptualize this as a two-way influence, while recognizing that the nature of this relationship is not deterministic, as it varies over time and depends on the trade show context (Bathelt and Glückler 2011).

5.3. TERRITORIAL SPECIALIZATION AND ITS IMPACT ON TRADE SHOWS

Economic specialization can occur in different forms and exists at different spatial levels. We may observe, for instance, a closely intertwined local/regional industrial agglomeration of a specific industry and its related supplier and service sectors, developing into industrial clusters that dominate local/regional economies. Alternatively, we may face an agglomeration of competing firms in a specific sector, which do not collaborate with each other, but benefit from a shared labour market and high attraction to a joint customer basis. Or we may observe national specialization patterns of industries in the sense that certain national industries become globally competitive with strong export activities, resulting in the relative strength of these industries in a given country (e.g. the automobile industry in Germany). We describe these structures as expressions of 'territorial specialization' at different scales.

This section discusses how such territorial specialization affects the nature, focus, and type of trade show activity in a given territory. We refer to this as 'trade show specialization'. At the macro-level, trade show specialization relates to the relative importance of a specific merchandise sector in the trade show portfolio of a region, country, or supranational territory. At the national level, for example, Germany is specialized in industries such as machinery/machine tools, automotive, and chemicals. The leading European trade shows pertaining to these industries are localized in Germany. Similarly, many Italian trade shows reflect the industries in which the country is economically dominant, such as textile-clothing and food (see Chapter 6). At the micro-level, trade show specialization (i.e. individual events pertaining to specific merchandise segments) is reflected in the specific product/service mix showcased by exhibitors. Here, trade show specialization depends on two factors: first, the specific exhibitor mix attracted by a show and, second, the specific products/services that are showcased. This type of two-fold specialization is particularly significant when we recognize that the product assortment of most manufacturing firms is quite wide (various product lines) and deep (broad product variation) (e.g. Bordley 2003). The selection of the appropriate product mix to be showcased at a trade show in order to maximize customer response is one of the key exhibitor managerial challenges addressed in the marketing literature (e.g. Golfetto 2004; Stevens 2005; Rinallo 2011a). We propose two complementary mechanisms to explain the influence of territorial specialization on trade show specialization. The first mechanism is based on proximity to the local/regional exhibitor and/or visitor base, termed the 'local catchment basin model'. The second is based on national variations in institutional set-ups and manufacturing specialization.

5.3.1. Local/Regional Proximity Effects

Trade shows are spatially conditioned because their survival and eventual success is based on a variety of localized factors, which simultaneously enable and constrain their specialization and development trajectories. Territorial specialization affects trade show specialization since a given trade show's exhibitor base, at least in the initial phase of the trade show life-cycle, corresponds to the size of the underlying industries in the event's catchment basin (e.g. the number of firms or economic importance of the industry). The extent to which this catchment basin can be extended also depends on the location's relative accessibility (Golfetto 2004; Rinallo and Golfetto 2011). Organizers often attempt to attract exhibitors from distant locations, but firms localized in the local catchment basin represent the easiest and most defendable target market. This is especially true when we consider that geographical proximity tends to generate cultural proximity, more consolidated relationships, as well as reduced exhibiting costs (e.g. Rallet and Torre 1999; Boschma 2005).

While, historically, many trade shows developed from their local industry bases (see Chapter 3), these effects are not as strong in the modern knowledge economy—although the locations of events in traditional trade show countries still bear some affinity to these origins. The chemical machinery show, ACHEMA, is, for instance, located in the heart of the chemical industry agglomeration Rhein-Main-Neckar in Germany. Similar observations apply to Frankfurt's International Book Fair, Nurnberg's International Toy Show, and so on.[1] Even in North America, where trade shows developed in a different way from agricultural markets and other periodic markets (AUMA 2009a; Bathelt 2012), regional specializations in the economy affect trade show specialization at least to some degree (see Chapter 7). The cities of Washington and Ottawa, for instance, host a relatively large number of trade shows related to government activity that also serve to strengthen the local service economy in this field. Conversely, Chicago specializes in hosting manufacturing shows, San Francisco in electronics shows, and Fort McMurray in northern Alberta, Canada, hosts the world's largest trade show for the oil sand extraction business (Bathelt and Spigel 2012).

Additionally, with the increase of international competition, market-oriented organizers attempt to strategically differentiate their shows based on the products shown (exhibitor specialization) and market segments served (target visitors). Differentiation strategies based on extant territorial specializations are an obvious choice for many trade show organizers (Golfetto 2004). This, of course, affects exhibition layout decisions and promotional activities, which give prominence to a show's unique characteristics compared to competing events elsewhere. Trade show promotional messages often employ widely held and, therefore, highly resonant cultural stereotypes about the distinctive characteristics of a country's products, sometimes referred to as 'national imaginaries' (Reimer and Leslie 2008). It is, for example, not difficult to persuade international audiences that products showcased at Italian trade shows have high aesthetic value or that high precision technology can be more easily found at German events than elsewhere.

Whether emergent or based on the organizers' deliberate strategies, a given trade show's specialization affects not only the specific exhibitors that are attracted, but also the product mix they decide to showcase. For example, exhibitors at packaging trade shows in Italy may highlight materials and technology used in the packaging of pasta and other grain-based foods, which will be grouped together by the organizers in a specific area of the exhibition grounds and advertised in promotional material. In a similar French show, in contrast, products pertaining to the packaging of pasta would be offered by fewer exhibitors, which would likely be more scattered in different exhibition halls and be harder to find by interested visitors. The same show, on the other hand, might give greater visibility to producers of packaging solutions for perfumes. Conversely, producers at a Chinese technology show may place less emphasis on the aesthetic design of the exhibit and focus on a limited variety of practicable solutions (Young 2004; Bathelt and Zeng 2014c). During trade shows, buyer information searches may be deeply influenced by organizers in some industries and countries (Rinallo and Golfetto 2011). Because of promotional efforts and layout decisions, for instance, the demand for pasta packaging will be greater at Italian trade shows than elsewhere. As a result, foreign exhibitors at Italian trade shows will have market incentives to showcase products and innovations pertaining to such market segments.

5.3.2. National Institutional Effects

The latter aspects and some earlier examples on differences between trade shows in different countries already move beyond the local catchment basin model to include existing or perceived national differences in consumer tastes, competitive advantages, or technological skills. The influence of territorial specialization on trade show specialization is clearly related to national variations in institutional set-ups and manufacturing specialization. Since national institutional set-ups vary and lead to different national varieties of production and innovation (Lundvall and Maskell 2000; Hall and Soskice 2001), countries specialize in different industries, resulting in national differences in trade show mixes. For instance, the US is well-known for its leading electronics shows, Germany has a strong basis in machinery/mechanical engineering hub shows, and Italy is famous for its food and textile/clothing industry events. Li (2014a) explores a similar pattern in less developed and developing countries, as the trade show portfolio of emerging economies in South and South-East Asia reflects their particular mix of important/dominant industries.

But the impact of national variety on trade show portfolios goes beyond differences in the sectoral mix of trade shows. It also includes aspects related to the nature and focus of the products and technologies showcased and the way how this is done. While research on this topic is scarce, the literature on varieties of capitalism and national innovation systems suggests that countries continue to specialize in certain industries and follow particular pathways to solve the types of manufacturing/technological problems that typically occur in their respective contexts (Gibson and Bathelt 2010). This leads not only to different manufacturing foci, but also to different ways of doing things. Clearly, this is reflected in the innovation processes of national states and resonates with how major trade shows are set up. For instance, US industries that develop in a context where market changes lead to fast adjustments in employment, and where institutional conditions support quick 'hiring and firing', are encouraged to remove resources from mature manufacturing paths and engage in radical innovation processes. In contrast, German industries are situated in an institutional context that supports long-term employment relations, cumulative learning, and inclusive decision-making, which provide the basis for ongoing incremental innovation (Katzenstein 1987; Hall and Soskice 2001). By extension, the competitive advantage of Chinese industries may particularly enable the development of low-cost solutions and process innovations in low-/medium-technology industries (see Nelson 1993 for a characterization of different national innovation systems).

This dynamic contributes to differences in the product characteristics and manufacturing capabilities exhibited at trade shows in different national contexts. While certainly not detectable at each event, we find that German trade shows, for instance, tend to place a particular emphasis on consumer-specific solutions, presenting product solutions that apply to diverse contexts, and highlighting product characteristics that are feasible, improve consumer experience, and overcome design and handling problems. In contrast, US shows put more emphasis on revolutionary new technologies and new potential fields of application, while Chinese events showcase price-efficient solutions in the medium-technology range, generating platforms for firms to demonstrate their capabilities to mix quality production with cost efficiency (see the discussion of different continental trade show characteristics in Part II). While empirical support for such effects is often anecdotal, there seems to be some indication that industrial speacilization associated with national institutional variety systematically influences the set-up and internal differentiation of large, international, or hub trade shows (Gibson and Bathelt 2010).

5.4. TRADE SHOW SPECIALIZATION AND ITS IMPACT ON TERRITORIAL SPECIALIZATION

Having outlined some of the mechanisms by which territorial specialization affects trade shows, we now turn to examine the multifaceted ways in which trade shows shape economic development and specialization processes at different spatial scales—the local/urban, regional, and national levels. It is important to note that these processes are not homogeneous across different industries and events, but differ from context to context. Despite this variation, the discussion offers evidence to support our argument regarding the influence of trade shows on territorial specialization.

5.4.1. Local/Urban Effects

At the local and urban levels, trade shows are distinctly visible in the city-regions where they exist and form a significant part of the urban economy (see Chapter 2). Leading trade show cities have established large modern venues that are designed to house trade shows, conventions, conferences, and other events with similar spatial requirements. They are often designed according to ambitious architectural aesthetics to symbolize state-of-the-art technologies, openness, and progress in the context of broader urban design and place-branding initiatives (Hubbard 1995; Gospodini 2002). International trade shows take place in large spacious convention, conference, and/or exhibition centres. These centres may be located in or close to the downtown cores of metropolitan areas, in revitalized old industrial areas, or on the outskirts of the city, close to transportation hubs such as international airports. While cities such as Frankfurt/Main and Montreal are characterized by large downtown facilities, other cities, like Toronto and Shanghai, have several, partially competing exhibition centres.

These venues become landmarks of urban development and reference points for related industries. The establishment of such centres also boosts infrastructure development and modernization processes aimed at creating efficient connections with crucial transportation nodes, such as major train stations or international airports. These facilities and the international trade shows that take place within them become an important part of the local/urban communities' efforts to attract international business; indeed, they become part of world city networks, generating economic connections to other urban cores worldwide (Sassen 1994; Taylor 2004; Bathelt 2012). Examples include the co-development of a subway system and new trade show facilities in Chengdu, China, or the establishment of new, major facilities in the immediate vicinity of airports as in Shanghai or Toronto (Bathelt and Zeng 2014c). While often not easily attributable to the trade show business alone, the point is that the effects of such investments extend to many parts of the urban economy and help stimulate urban growth.

At the urban level, trade shows also generate a specialized service economy targeted towards such events. These services range from planning, design, exhibit building, catering, mechanical and electrical, and computing services to security and accommodation services (see also Chapter 2). Their size correlates with the number and size of trade shows that take place in a given location. While these are localized services with little outside effects or exports, they generate important jobs and benefit the entire urban economy, including its permanent clusters. In the large trade show cities worldwide, major events become an important source of income and stimulate the growth of the hospitality and entertainment sector. The hotel and accommodation business, in particular, benefits from such events. In cities such as Frankfurt/Main and Milan, not only are hotel capacities substantially enlarged as a consequence of their proximity to major trade shows, room rates at these establishments also tend to double in price when a major trade show occurs.

As demonstrated in the case of large trade show cities in North America (Bathelt and Spigel 2012), historical structures, investment decisions, and economic relationships have triggered different paths of trade show development that impact further investment decisions over time. The architecture of the respective facilities and the service economy are thus important building blocks that can be found in all world cities today. This contributes to processes that connect these cities to form global urban networks and allow them to generate economic growth (Derudder et al. 2012). But trade shows are not just crucial enablers in the global relational economy that establish trans-local and global economic pipelines (Bathelt and Glückler 2011); they are also crucial income generators for their host cities. According to a recent media report, it appears that in North America's most important trade show city, Las Vegas, revenues related to trade show and convention activities are larger than those due to the famous gambling centres in the city (Spillman 2007). This leads us to the next level of our discussion, which involves the capacity of trade shows to trigger regional and even national economic development.

5.4.2. Regional/National Economic Development

Trade show activities have substantial direct and indirect economic impacts on their host cities and the broader regional environment, which leads to distinct multiplier effects that feed into the regional economy and produce favourable conditions for growth (e.g. Sternberg and Kramer 1991; Schätzl et al. 1993). These economic impacts refer to the direct spending in the local economy by trade show organizers, exhibitors, and visitors (see also Chapter 2). Such expenditures typically include admission fees, exhibit set-up, and other exhibition-related services, as well as hotels, restaurants, and the leisure or entertainment activities of participants.[2] As reported in Bathelt and Spigel (2012), trade shows in Germany attract about 26.6 million visitors and 331,000 exhibitors per year (average over the period 2005–8). This generates more than €12.1 billion in direct economic effects (including the investments by trade show organizers), plus an additional €11.4 billion of indirect effects, creating a total of 226,300 jobs in the country (AUMA 2009b). The local economic impacts of trade shows are particularly felt at the city-region level. In Munich, one of Germany's large trade show cities, the overall effects of trade show participants are about €2.2 billion per year (on average over the period 2004–7) and result in about 22,000 additional jobs in the urban economy (Penzkofer 2008). In Vancouver, similarly, the direct and indirect effects of trade show and convention visitors create an additional regional income of over €1 billion per year (2007), generating 13,000 jobs (Tourism Vancouver 2007). At the national level, such economic impacts would be much diluted, as only the expenses of foreign participants should be taken into consideration. While important for the local economy, intra-national competition for the attraction of domestic exhibitors and visitors is a zero-sum game at the national level. National-level economic impacts remain significant only in the case of events that attract a significant foreign presence (particularly from the exhibitors' side, as the average local expense of exhibitors is greater than that of visitors).

Beyond the economic impacts on the local economy, trade shows (especially international events) establish connections between urban and national economies and the wider international industries and production chains that generate and maintain flows of goods, people, and knowledge, resulting in the establishment of knowledge pipelines to these places (Malecki and Poehling 1999; Bathelt et al. 2004). Such effects are so important that, in some cases, trade shows are purposively employed as part of regional or national development strategies. In South-East Asia, for instance, national governments have recognized this potential and use trade shows as a policy tool to support industrialization and national industry growth (Bathelt and Zeng 2014a; Li 2014b). Such support can encompass the establishment of world-class trade show/convention centres, the active establishment of international trade shows, as well as the subsidization of international trade show attendees (Weller 2014; Yokura 2014). In Taiwan, for instance, the government has actively supported the development of trade show activity for various reasons. Originally, it was seeking to drag the country out of political isolation by providing opportunities to generate wider international connections. Later, it actively supported trade show activity to drive the embeddedness of Taiwanese industries into global production networks. Meanwhile, the core agenda is to support the creative knowledge economy through large international get-togethers (Chang et al. 2014).

Li (2014a) demonstrates how trade show development supports industrialization processes in less developed and developing economies by providing crucial access to novel resources, technologies, and competencies. Beyond this aspect, he convincingly highlights the ways in which trade shows in developing contexts can provide a forum for industries to learn from international peers (i.e. suppliers and buyers) and acquire knowledge that enables upgrading and the development of new specializations. Li (2014a) argues that a specific type of middle-ground show is best equipped to enable such knowledge acquisition. Unlike ideal-type hub shows, import shows, or export shows, this type of show must be characterized by the right mix of substantial regional/national and international participation, including both visitors and exhibitors.

5.4.3. Reproduction of National Specialization Patterns

At a broader level, one would expect trade shows in the globalizing knowledge economy to spread news and information about new products and technologies—as well as about new market trends and regulatory changes in the technology field—quite widely across the globe and, thus, contribute to making this knowledge globally available or 'ubiquitous'. This is because firms are in an ideal position to use the knowledge acquired at trade shows in their own production contexts. Through their local, regional, or national production linkages, and through knowledge ecologies of production networks and clusters, this knowledge about global industrial trends from the trade shows' global buzz (Bathelt and Schuldt 2010) spreads spatially to become part of permanent local and/or relational buzz environments in a value chain (Bathelt et al. 2004).

As such, one might assume that trade shows are major events that trigger the diffusion of technologies, which then become available globally at the same time and price. As opposed to the framework suggested here, trade shows would become major players in diminishing national specialization patterns, actively contributing to convergence processes across national economies (Gibson and Bathelt 2010). This would pose a clear challenge to the varieties-of-capitalism approach (Soskice 1999; Hall and Soskice 2001), which suggests that countries develop distinct specialization patterns based on their specific national institutional configurations that lead to different economic development patterns. While convergence processes certainly exist to some degree, evidence presented by Bathelt and Gibson (2014) suggests that trade shows, in fact, serve to strengthen search patterns that are related to a firm's existing production context and pre-existing specializations. Even if new technologies become widely spread through these events, they are being adjusted to the different production contexts within which the firms operate, thereby furthering, rather than undermining, distinct economic specializations that exist in different industries and their territories.

Based on path-breaking work by Cohen et al. (1972), which captures the random and often non-linear dynamics of organizational choices, Bathelt and Gibson (2014) conceptualize international hub shows as so-called 'organized anarchies'. Featured in such organizational structures are (i) actors with unclear preferences, (ii) a multitude of technological opportunities that may be difficult to interpret, and (iii) fluidity or instability in terms of the time and energy participants spend searching for solutions (see also Cohen and March 1974).

Viewing trade shows as such 'organized anarchies', it is argued that the search processes of firms during these events tend to be guided by context-specific choices. In other words, the agents in such settings rarely rely on best-practices or optimal solutions when making decisions. Rather, they tend to adopt solutions that make the greatest sense within the context of their day-to-day practices. Bathelt and Gibson's (2014) work on the technological searches of exhibitors during international trade shows demonstrates that new products, components, and ideas that are adopted, or that 'catch an observer's eye', tend to be those which are closely or at least partially related to the established routines, practices, and production patterns of the firms. As such, firms simply try to make the most sense of new technological developments based on their existing capabilities and specializations. The cumulative consequences of such search patterns imply that firms tend to select technologies and solutions led by existing capabilities in products, strategies, and designs, rather than fundamentally changing them.

Gibson's (2015) study is the first analysis that aims to link these processes with the national institutional settings that shape the firms' structures and production contexts. Indeed, as already indicated, both the varieties of capitalism literature (Soskice 1999; Hall and Soskice 2001) and national systems of innovation approach (Lundvall 1988) suggest that the industrial practices and specialization patterns of firms are not independent from their national institutional contexts. The respective national specialization patterns in economic production within which the firms operate at their home bases lead to specific sets of problems and search patterns related to, for instance, specific bottlenecks (Lundvall and Maskell 2000). Institutional complementarities and co-evolutionary tendencies, as in the cases of the US, Germany, and China, result in distinct production environments for firms (Hall and Soskice 2001), which then guide the nature of their search processes at trade shows.

From this, we can be fairly confident that trade shows strengthen, rather than weaken, existing institutional structures. The effects of trade shows in terms of technological choice serve to reproduce the firms' specific contexts and strengthen their competitiveness (Gibson 2015). Indeed, based on a quantitative analysis of more than 450 firms from different trade show settings, Gibson (2015) finds significant differences in the nature of search patterns and inter-firm interaction between firms from different countries. While it is important to exercise care in interpreting these data, especially since there are no simple national stereotypes according to which firms operate (Faulconbridge 2008), this provides convincing arguments that link these patterns of behaviour to national institutional contexts of production.

In the end, inter-firm interaction at international trade shows encourages adjustments in production, strategies, and innovation that feed back into national production structures and serve to support continued specialization (Gibson and Bathelt 2010). These interaction processes do not simply promote 'ubiquitification' processes, as described by Maskell and Malmberg (1999a), or processes of convergence among distinct capitalist varieties but, in contrast, support ongoing processes of knowledge localization and contextualization (Storper 1997; Asheim 1999), through which the competitive capabilities of existing production environments are strengthened. Although further empirical work is needed to clarify these processes, these arguments suggest that, as firms in a specific production or innovation system come across particular day-to-day problems, their activities at international trade shows tend to revolve around those solutions which complement and strengthen their production contexts. In other words, the products, technologies, and knowledge pools that German, US, or Chinese firms find at international trade shows will, on average, be somewhat different and broadly feed into the respective reproduction processes that support territorial specialization patterns.

5.5. A DYNAMIC TWO-WAY INFLUENCE MODEL OF TRADE SHOW SPECIALIZATION AND TERRITORIAL SPECIALIZATION

Taken together, the previous two sections pave the way for a discussion of the mutual influences between trade show and territorial specialization at different spatial scales. Territories, including their image and cultural heritage, as well as the firms located in the respective local catchment basins, are the 'rich soil' from which trade shows have originated in many countries and from which they generate differentiating features in terms of the products showcased and markets served. At the same time, trade show specialization impacts economic territories by reinforcing existing economic specializations, boosting economic development, and, thus, affecting the host areas in multifaceted ways. Figure 5.2 shows, in a succinct and selective manner, some key constituting elements and main outcomes of the two-way influence between territorial specialization and trade show specialization.

It is clear, however, that this two-way influence model is best understood as a schematic description that requires adjustment to the specific context in question. From a dynamic perspective, for instance, the reciprocal influence between trade show and territorial specialization is stronger in certain phases

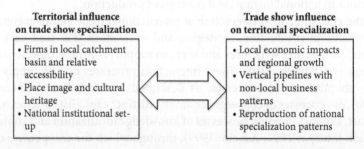

Figure 5.2. Two-way influence model between trade show and territorial specialization

of the trade show life-cycle than in others. Like products (Day 1981), events can sometimes be described in a cyclical way according to life-cycle phases (Getz 2000), ranging from introduction (i.e. foundation and early years) to growth (accelerated expansion) to maturity (characterized by extended periods of stability) and, eventually, decline (reduction of activities and importance).[3] In the case of trade shows, the transition from one phase to the next can be monitored by examining the evolution of key statistics (such as surfaces sold, number of exhibitors, or number of visitors; see Chapters 12 to 14 for empirical examples).

In the early introduction and growth phases of the trade show life-cycle, the link between trade show specialization and territorial specialization is at its peak. As anticipated, a trade show's exhibitor base is found first and foremost in the local area's catchment basin. To the extent that such areas are also hosts of a sufficient number of buying firms and, thus, become important initial markets, the trade show becomes increasingly attractive also for non-local firms that, through exhibiting, find opportunities to access the respective local markets. If external accessibility surpasses a certain threshold, a virtuous cycle is activated that can carry a trade show to the maturity phase. When the number of exhibitors increases, so too does the show's informational value for non-local visitors, which, in turn, feeds back into the trade show's attractiveness for non-local exhibitors. This is, of course, also linked to the number and purchase power of the potential customers at the show.

As the show progresses to national and international significance, it may turn into a hub event and enjoy many years of maturity, during which the link with the host area (at the local and national level) becomes weaker. In other words, due to their high level of internationalization, on both the exhibitor and visitor side, hub shows seem to lose their prior connection with the host areas. The maturity phase might end because of macroeconomic trends (for example, the decline of many European events is linked to the restructuring of European value chains and the growth experienced in other world regions) or because of rivalry between competing trade shows that aspire to become supranational reference events at the continental level (see Chapters 12 to 14). In the latter cases, less competitive and less successful trade shows tend to decline and find their most important market segments back in the local catchment basin.

From a structural perspective, the reflexive relationship between trade show specialization and territorial specialization also differs according to the type of trade show analysed. In the context of our knowledge-based, four-fold trade show typology (see Chapter 4), trade shows typically move from being local/domestic events (introduction phase) to export-oriented (growth) and, finally, to hub events (maturity) during their life-cycles. In the decline phase, if the local market is large enough to attract foreign exhibitors, they might become import-oriented or local events again before disappearing. In general, export-oriented events reflect territorial specialization on the exhibitor side, as the exhibitors selected (and products showcased) are of local origin and may reflect specific industry agglomerations. Comparatively speaking, import-oriented trade shows are less related to territorial specialization. They exist in areas where local suppliers are not sufficient to satisfy the demand for given products, thus providing market opportunities to non-local suppliers. In these cases, however, if the majority of exhibitors are not of local origin, the products showcased are adapted to local market needs, thus adjusting to and generally strengthening geographies of innovation and knowledge circulation that have distinct national specificities.

These comments clearly show that the interdependent relationship between trade show and territorial specialization, especially the effects of territorial specialization on trade show specialization, can vary widely according to the type of trade show and its particular stage in the life-cycle. The effects of trade shows on territories remain, to some extent, intact also for those events that appear to be more removed from their local territories. Local economic impacts/multiplier effects are even larger in the case of internationalized events that bring together economic actors beyond the hosting area. Similarly, regional growth and development effects might be of greater magnitude in the case of larger and internationalized events that enable local actors to establish long-range market relationships and knowledge pipelines with different types of business partners from abroad (Li 2014b). On the contrary, the reproduction of national specialization patterns is less marked when hub events are in their maturity phase. However, under the surface of cosmopolitanism, national differences still exist, related to the organizational cultures of organizers and the relative importance of local/national entrepreneurial associations in affecting the shows' knowledge-based strategies.

5.6. CONCLUSIONS

In this chapter, we suggest a model of reciprocal influences between trade shows and the territories that shape and define them. We propose an interdependent two-way influence model that extends existing literature. The chapter shows that even in the context of the globalizing knowledge economy, which is characterized by a decoupling and distanciation of cause-effect relations (Giddens 1990), we can identify substantial interdependencies and reciprocal relations between what we have coined 'trade show specialization' and 'territorial specialization'. Overall, the chapter attempts to answer two interrelated questions. To what extent do trade shows shape underlying economic and cultural-geographical factors and territories? And to what extent are trade shows conversely affected by these very same factors? In developing a theoretically robust answer to these questions, we emphasize that the nature of interdependent relations between trade show specialization and territorial specialization is not stable but subject to dynamic and structural contexts.

After reviewing theoretical positions that view trade shows either as mere reflections of underlying geographies, or as exerting a dominant influence over industries and markets, we illustrate the theoretical base of this book: the assumption of a two-way influence between trade shows and their territorial economic base. We demonstrate how trade show specialization depends on the characteristics of the firms located in the local catchment basin, on the host area's image and cultural heritage, and, more broadly, on the national institutional set-up. Turning to the issue of how trade shows, in turn, affect local areas, we discuss how trade shows generate local economic impacts and regional development, facilitate the establishment of pipelines with non-local business partners, and contribute to the reproduction of national specialization patterns. Finally, we discuss how the link between the trade show and the host area is stronger in some phases of the trade show life-cycle, and for certain types of trade shows as opposed to others.

The conceptualization developed in this chapter has important theoretical and methodological implications. First, our examination of the paradigmatic views on trade shows and underlying industries forms a useful basis for future research on trade shows and other temporary events across disciplinary borders. While the chapter stresses the reciprocal influence and co-evolution of trade shows and territories, there is certainly value in empirical studies stressing the impact of territorial (i.e. economic, social, cultural, and/or institutional) factors on trade show dynamics, or investigating the influence of trade shows on underlying industries and host areas. And, of course, empirical studies are always especially interesting if they find, or search for, deviations from the perceived regularities discussed in this chapter and look into the reasons and processes behind them (Becker 1998).

Second, the distinction made in this and the previous chapters between different types of trade shows and different phases of the trade show life-cycle can be usefully employed to assist in the purposive sampling of events to be investigated. Studies of either a comparative or longitudinal nature are needed that further our understanding of the nexus between trade show specialization and territorial specialization, and its dynamic changes. While much empirical work remains to be done, the chapters in Parts II and III represent a first step towards the development of such an ambitious research programme.

NOTES

1. Although it is difficult to compare the relationship of regional industry specialization and trade show development across countries and continents, even in the Chinese context, it can be found that trade show visitors associate trade shows with the regional industry foci (Jin et al. 2012).

2. The methodological literature evaluating the economic impacts of events (particularly mega-events such as the Olympic Games) warns us about exaggerated estimates linked to the fact that organizers often finance studies for self-promotional purposes (see Crompton and McKay 1994; Crompton 2006). Despite such methodological concerns, there is no doubt that the local economic impacts of international trade shows are substantial, given the recurring nature of these events and the higher expense patterns of participants (i.e. exhibitors and professional visitors), all of which sets these shows apart from one-off events and leisure initiatives which focus on consumers.

3. When proposing a trade show life-cycle model, we are aware that, despite its broad application, the product life-cycle model as a predictor or normative managerial device has long been subject to criticism (e.g. Day 1981; Storper 1985). Consequently, we view this concept as a useful heuristic device, rather than as a representation of typical trade show trends. Trajectories of trade show development can, in reality, be markedly different. For example, some events never reach the growth phase and are terminated a few editions after their introduction; other shows suddenly decline after years of sustained growth without enjoying a phase of maturity; and there are further cases of events revived after periods of maturity or even decline which enjoy a new growth phase (Allix 1922; Rinallo and Golfetto 2011). When referring to the life-cycle as one of many possible models, we aim to illustrate that the link between territorial specialization and trade show specialization is not fixated—but changes according to the stage process.

Part II

Trade Show Dynamics in Geographical Context

6

Trade Show Dynamics in Mature Markets 1: Europe

6.1. INTRODUCTION

Western Europe is the most highly developed trade show region in the world. Trade shows in Western Europe are on average larger than in other world regions. They can be distinguished according to their geographical reach (i.e. international, national, or regional/local), target visitors (firms or end consumers), and sector or industry compartment. Large international trade shows, in particular, tend to be located in the main manufacturing countries (Germany, France, Italy, and Spain) in highly accessible cities, often centred on traditional principal production cores. The main countries are also home to Europe's largest exhibition centres that are specifically built to host major collective events. In other European countries, trade show activity, in general, is much lower, and largely consists of national and regional events.

Between 1960 and 2000, the Western European trade show system underwent a major period of development and restructuring, though its roots go back even further (see Chapter 2). During this period, the number of trade shows multiplied, mainly related to specialized developments from the old generic sample fairs. Furthermore, many local shows that were initially held in industrial clusters moved location and gradually became concentrated in more accessible areas. This began at a national level, but later also extended to the international level. A significant boost to the internationalization of trade shows was provided by the construction and ongoing expansion of specialized exhibition venues, dominated, in particular, by a dozen very large facilities, almost all of which were built on the initiative of the local government bodies in the different countries.

The underlying objectives that led to the development of exhibition and trade show facilities in different countries and cities vary greatly. While investments in German venues, for example, have mainly been driven by the prospects of growth in the associated business tourism industry and the development of a regional trade show service economy, exhibition centres and events in Italy focused on supporting local/regional (and later also national) manufacturing industries. These varying goals of trade show development and the diverse composition of stakeholders have generated different types of events. In some cases, the events have been oriented towards the needs of European demand and import activities, while, in others, the focus has been on supporting national production and export activities.

In recent years, European trade show development has entered a phase of maturity. In the major Western European countries, in particular, this phase has been accompanied by a general stagnation or decrease in trade show activity. Reasonable growth is seen, however, in many Eastern European countries. Aside from the recessionary tendencies that have affected all economies in Europe, the stagnation in European trade shows is the result of the development of new manufacturing producers, particularly in Asia (see Chapter 8), which contest European leadership in the traditional manufacturing sectors. In these countries, new shows along with new venues are quickly being established. In addition to attracting an increasing number of European exhibitors to events in these newly developing markets, we have also witnessed a stagnation or decline in the attendance of non-European visitors at European trade shows. Altogether, this has resulted in intensified competition between similar trade shows at the European level. Increased worldwide trade show activity puts pressure on international events in Europe, encouraging a strict selection of events. This results in geographically significant concentration tendencies. In terms of long-term trends, it seems that each manufacturing industry develops one or two intercontinental trade shows that are able to attract non-European visitors to see the entire European product offering in that industry group. This means that other trade shows will be left to serve only local/national markets as import shows.

This chapter is largely based on data provided by the CERMES Trade Shows Observatory at Bocconi University, which has gathered information on Europe's leading trade shows for almost thirty years and analysed user behaviour during these events (CERMES 2012b, 2013). The next section traces the evolution of European trade shows in relation to the regional/national industrial structure, highlighting the main aspects of competition between events. This is followed by an analysis of trade show activities and their structure in the main European trade show countries. Finally, we explain observed differences in stakeholder and governance models with reference to historical specialties, and draw some general conclusions.

6.2. THE DEVELOPMENT OF AND COMPETITION BETWEEN EUROPEAN TRADE SHOWS

It is in European countries that we find the most developed and mature example of trade show activity. The exhibition capacity in Europe almost exclusively consists of specialized exhibition centres for collective trade events, which are, in many cases, very large. In 2011, Europe had a 48 per cent share of the world total exhibition capacity, representing twice the capacity available in North America, where exhibition venues are often multi-purpose facilities. All other world regions fall behind in terms of trade show activity. In the late 2000s, however, the European share of exhibition capacity decreased, despite the fact that exhibition venues have continued to expand (there was a 7 per cent increase in European capacity from 14.6 to 15.6 million square metres between 2006 and 2011). This is mainly the result of the rapid growth of trade show activity in the Asia/Pacific region, where exhibition capacity increased much faster, by 38 per cent, from 4.8 to 6.6 million square metres (UFI 2012a; see Chapter 8).

Thus, while the quantity of trade show activity in Europe is still the largest worldwide, with a 47 per cent share of global rented surfaces (CERMES 2013), we expect a reduction in this share in the future given current trends in the other world regions (UFI 2012a).

6.2.1. Trade Shows and European Industrial Organization

The unparalleled scope of trade show activity in Europe is linked to the leading countries' industrial organization, particularly the structure of traditional manufacturing industries, which are predominantly made up of small- and medium-sized enterprises with a high export orientation. The relatively small average firm size and large distances to final markets make it difficult and costly for firms to individually and directly reach potential customers in buying areas (Golfetto 1988, 2004; European Commission 2008). Additionally, firms tend to specialize in single production phases due to their limited size, and thus target intermediate markets or sell to wholesalers and distributers (European Commission 2008). Compared to large integrated US firms with complete in-house production cycles, the production of the same quantities in Europe often involves a larger number of small disintegrated firms that are specialized in a few production stages. This substantially increases the trade volume. As a result, the coordination between firms and between firms and markets is highly complex. This structure encourages collective organizations and means of communication, including industrial clusters, consortiums, trade associations, and trade shows, to become decisive tools in organizing trade flows (Pyke et al. 1990; Becattini and Rullani 1996; Golfetto 2000; Golfetto and Rinallo 2013).

With industrial development, trade shows have transformed from isolated events into specialized systems staged at regular intervals. Through this, the trade show business in Europe has become a specialized communication and exchange forum for business-to-business relations. Nearly all producers in manufacturing sectors take part in trade shows as exhibitors during the product renewal seasons,[1] where buyers evaluate the alternatives and decide their programmes. Industrial trade shows have thus become a 'periodical rite'—a temporary period of time when the entire industry group comes together (Borghini et al. 2006). European firms invest more in trade show participation than firms in other world regions. This is particularly true of the US, where firms operate more often in final consumer markets (Golfetto 2004; CEIR 2012). It is estimated that the share of European manufacturing firms' expenditures devoted to trade shows is between 23 and 33 per cent of their entire communication budget, with shares of 60 to 70 per cent for firms operating only in intermediate markets or with distributors (Golfetto 1988, 2004; AUMA 2012a). The large number of firms in the European production system also contributes to the high demand for exhibition space, as it translates into a higher number of booths and exhibitors at each event in relation to overall production levels.

In 2012, there were almost 8,000 international and national/regional trade shows in the European Union (excluding the local level), occupying a total of 45 million square metres of rented exhibition space. These shows hosted an aggregate 1.3 million exhibitors and approximately 140 million visitors (see Table 6.1). Of these events, only 900 were international shows; these were on average the largest, often involving thousands of exhibitors and sometimes hundreds of thousands of professional visitors. It must be noted, however, that these data include both business-to-business shows and business-to-consumer events. Of the international events, an estimated 85 to 90 per cent are business-to-business shows, while over 90 per cent of regional and national level events are business-to-consumer or mixed trade shows (CERMES 2012a). Business-to-business shows typically have greater value than business-to-consumer shows in terms of the trade that takes place at these events, business travel and the regional services they generate, and the degree of knowledge dissemination that occurs (see Chapter 2).

Table 6.1. Trade show activity in the European Union (EU-27) by geographical orientation, 2012

Indicator	International events	National/regional events	Total events
Events (number)	900	7,000	7,900
Stand space (net sq.m.)	17,000,000	28,000,000	45,000,000
Direct exhibitors (number of stands)	450,000	850,000	1,300,000
Visitors (number)	40,000,000	105,000,000	145,000,000

Source: CERMES 2013.

Note: sq.m. = square metres (1 square metre = 10.76 square feet).

6.2.2. Competition between Trade Shows and between Exhibition Centres

Since the late 1950s, trade show activity in Europe has been marked by continuous and intense growth in the wake of the rise of production and export capacities in its main manufacturing countries. The growth in trade show activity initially emerged from the transformation of the generic sample fair into many specialized sector shows (see Chapter 2). The specialization process continued uninterrupted in conjunction with a rise in the number of exhibitors and visitors, as well as an increase in the quantity of rented surface areas for booths. This has essentially lasted until the present day. Figure 6.1 highlights the sharp rise in activity in terms of the amount of surfaces rented (an indicator linked to the number of exhibitors) between 1975 and 2000 in the four major countries of trade show activity: Germany, Italy, France, and Spain. From 2000 onwards, however, trade show activity appears relatively stagnant, with a decrease in overall rented surfaces.

In many cases, the development of specialized trade shows has brought together producers belonging to different clusters and production regions in a single venue. This trend has offered national industries higher visibility and has attracted more visitors from abroad, due to the greater number and variety of products presented. With the availability of new, modern exhibition venues, created between 1980 and 2000, manufacturing firms from small local districts and large industrial regions across Europe often came together at the same international trade shows, aiming to attract potential buyers from European and, especially, non-European markets. In many cases, trade shows were related to specific national manufacturing

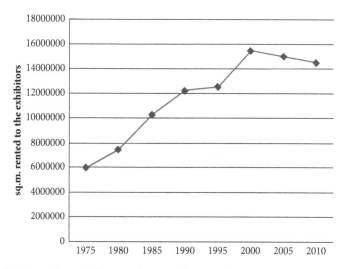

Figure 6.1. Rented trade show surfaces in the main European countries (Germany, Italy, France, and Spain), 1975–2010 (CERMES 2013)

traditions or strengths, as in the cases of Italian furniture, French fashion, and German machinery/machine tools. And on numerous occasions trade shows began to show signs of collaboration between national industries that were traditionally fragmented and in competition with each other. Such collaboration was due to the strong presence of trade associations as organizers.

This is not to suggest that competition between leading countries, and between clusters in the same country, stopped. Trade shows have sometimes been a forum for splinter events led by regional industries/associations. Rivalry has been particularly prevalent in countries where trade shows are viewed as a tool for the promotion of the local/national industry ('for-the-national-offer' events). Industry associations and/or trade show organizers sometimes prefer to hold separate events for each country, instead of coming together in the form of international collective events, which are perceived as a neutral marketing tool for individual enterprises (as suggested in the traditional marketing literature). In the case of textiles-clothing and fashion accessories, the highly fragmented Italian industries never fully took part in French trade shows, even though these were more accessible to intercontinental markets than Italian events. Rather, they preferred to host their own events and representations, which have long been divided among a large number of manufacturing clusters (see Chapter 12). The large number of international and national events that still exist in many industry groups is, therefore, only partially due to specialization by industry and end market; it often results from competition between different national industries and, in turn, between their local industries. The presence of an international event in a country should, however, be viewed favourably, as it would generate increased visibility and knowledge dissemination for the respective regional/national firms (see Chapter 4).

Competition also exists between the numerous exhibition complexes in major European countries (Rubalcaba-Bermejo and Cuadrado-Roura 1995). After a period of initial focus on international/intercontinental marketplaces, exhibition centres began to multiply. This building boom was largely driven by a desire to generate local/urban revenues from related business tourism and strengthen the production image of the host region (Golfetto 1991; Golfetto and Rinallo 2000; Chambre de Commerce et de l'Industrie de Paris 2001; Fondazione Fiera Milano 2001, 2006; AUMA 2012a; CCI Paris Ile-de-France 2012). As demonstrated by UFI (2012a), exhibition capacity in Europe has continued to grow significantly, with an increase of 7 per cent between 2006 and 2011, despite the fact that demand is basically saturated (AUMA 2012b; CERMES 2012a). This has generated a major drive for the creation of new shows and replication of existing shows in other exhibition centres—to the point where it goes against the interests of the producers, which feel forced to take part in more events than they would otherwise. Moreover, new exhibition centre activities have created splits and fragmentation within national industries, dividing existing shows into several splinter events.

Table 6.2. Exhibition capacity in Europe by country, 2012

Country	Cities (no.)	>200,000 sq.m.	Cities (no.)	100,000– 200,000 sq.m.	Cities (no.)	30,000– 100,000 sq.m.	Total no. of cities	Total sq.m.
Germany	5	1,584,814	7	890,014	7	440,860	19	2,915,688
Italy	2	609,500	5	666,904	9	559,860	16	1,836,264
France	1	647,243	1	139,119	14	621,622	16	1,407,984
Spain	3	808,242	2	230,100	6	205,813	11	1,244,155
Netherlands	–	–	2	227,956	9	415,706	11	643,662
United Kingdom	1	258,098	1	198,983	1	40,200	3	497,281
Russia	1	413,102	–	–	1	55,000	2	468,102
Switzerland	–	–	2	264,470	4	167,200	6	431,670
Belgium	–	–	1	153,310	4	180,089	5	333,399
Turkey	1	205,754	–	–	2	80,000	3	285,754
Austria	–	–	–	–	4	269,985	4	269,985
Czech Republic	–	–	1	120,300	1	95,200	2	215,500
Greece	–	–	1	129,250	1	60,000	2	189,250
Denmark	–	–	1	110,000	2	77,000	3	187,000
Poland	–	–	1	102,791	2	77,270	3	180,061
Sweden	–	–	–	–	3	155,000	3	155,000
Serbia	–	–	–	–	2	120,689	2	120,689
Hungary	–	–	1	113,000	–	–	1	113,000
Slovak Republic	–	–	–	–	2	100,906	2	100,906
Portugal	–	–	–	–	2	100,309	2	100,309
Bulgaria	–	–	–	–	2	96,500	2	96,500
Romania	–	–	–	–	2	92,195	2	92,195
Ukraine	–	–	–	–	1	86,018	1	86,018
Croatia	–	–	–	–	1	81,000	1	81,000
Norway	–	–	–	–	1	65,000	1	65,000
Finland	–	–	–	–	1	57,000	1	57,000
Luxembourg	–	–	–	–	1	31,135	1	31,135
Cyprus	–	–	–	–	1	31,000	1	31,000
Total	14	4,526,753	26	3,346,197	86	4,362,467	126	12,235,417

Source: Computed from UFI 2012.

Notes: : sq.m. = square metres (1 square metre = 10.76 square feet). Only cities with at least 30,000 square metres of indoor exhibition space and only facilities with at least 5,000 square metres are included.

As highlighted in Table 6.2, there are numerous trade show venues in Europe with facilities in 126 cities, offering an indoor exhibition space of over 30,000 square metres. More than 90 per cent of these venues are located in Western Europe, although we must keep in mind that exhibition centres with less than 5,000 square metres are not included. In recent years, however, new exhibition capacity has been created mainly in Eastern and Southern Europe, reflecting the recent growth of manufacturing activities in these countries.

More recently, the challenges facing European manufacturing together with increased intercontinental competition have stimulated new trends in the concentration of trade shows and exhibition venues in Europe. On the one hand, the economic recession associated with the global financial crisis has led to a selective drop in the number of exhibitors at trade shows of up to 20 or 25 per cent over the past three or four years, particularly in regions with more restricted intercontinental accessibility, such as some minor Italian, Spanish, and French cities. This tendency has been less visible, however, in central European countries such as Germany, which continue to appeal to intercontinental visitors (AUMA 2012a; CERMES 2013). On the other hand, the growth of manufacturing in other parts of the world, especially in Asia, has led to the development of new large trade show platforms in the respective countries (see Chapter 8). This has resulted in a decrease in the number of non-European visitors at many European shows, as well as cut-backs in the budgets of European exhibitors that now need to devote parts of their overall trade show budget to non-European shows. This makes it increasingly difficult for international visitors to attend more than one or two trade shows in each continent. Further geographical concentration of European international-level events will thus be necessary, generating more substantial competition between venues and events in the future (AUMA 2012a; Golfetto and Rinallo 2013). Along with increasing trade show market stagnation (see Figure 6.1), this leads to new rivalries between venues, cities, and countries, particularly with respect to hosting the dominant reference events or flagship fairs (see Chapter 4).

6.3. TRADE SHOWS AND EXHIBITION CENTRES IN THE MAIN COUNTRIES

6.3.1. Exhibition Centres and Main Cities

In the post-Second World War period, the countries with the largest number of international trade shows have also been those with the leading exhibition centres. These four countries—namely, Germany, Italy, France, and Spain—are among the leading manufacturing territories in Europe. Germany, for example, has created its most important exhibition centres since the 1950s and now has five major international venues in Hanover, Frankfurt, Düsseldorf, Cologne, and Munich, each with a size of over 200,000 square metres of net exhibition space (over 400,000 square metres of gross exhibition space) (AUMA 2012a; EMECA 2012; UFI 2012a). Much of this development was driven by local governments (Germany's Länder and cities). France has mainly concentrated its investments in two important exhibition centres in Paris, with Lyon clearly lagging behind, while Italy has focused on Milan—with Bologna, Verona, and Rimini centres being much smaller. Spain and the UK have also built major exhibition centres, but they are considerably smaller in size, with typical venues having between 100,000 and 200,000 square metres of net exhibition space (EMECA 2012; UFI 2012a). During the 1990s, many of these early trade show complexes were modernized, completely renovated, or expanded, which led to a further increase in Europe's overall exhibition centre capacity. These expansion activities have not affected the sequence of leading exhibiting countries in Europe, as Germany still leads the way in terms of exhibition capacity and trade show activity (see Table 6.2), followed by Italy, France, and Spain. The UK has lost much of its traditional trade show activity over the years, particularly following the widespread and severe deindustrialization processes of the 1960s through to the 1980s (Kitson and Michie 1996). In the 2000s, changes in the European trade show environment have primarily occurred in Eastern European countries, where numerous medium-sized and large exhibition centres were launched in, for instance, Moscow. Trade show activity in Eastern European countries is, nonetheless, still relatively limited compared to the main countries.

6.3.2. Trade Show Activity and Specialization

Within Europe, different countries occupy different positions in terms of the types of trade show activity. International events take place in the main manufacturing countries, while national and regional events (mostly catering to consumers) exist all over Europe (see Figure 6.2).

In the case of international trade shows, the country hosting the most events is Germany, with 38 per cent of activity in terms of rented exhibition space. Italy follows in second place with 24 per cent, France with 14 per cent, and Spain with 8 per cent. The remaining twenty-three European countries host just 16 per cent of events as measured by rented exhibition space. It is important to note that, while international events are limited in number (approximately 900 events out of a total of 6,900), they account for approximately 40 per cent of the total number of exhibitors at trade shows in Europe, 40 per cent of the total booth space, and 35 per cent of the total number of visitors (see Table 6.1). These are the shows with a high degree of international participation, during which many of the international trade linkages between European and non-European countries are initiated (Rosson and Seringhaus 1995; Golfetto

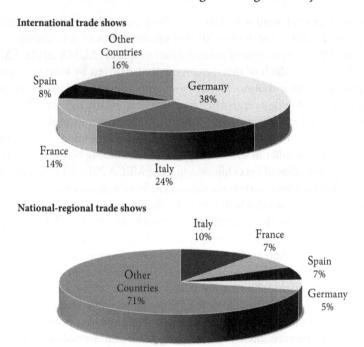

Figure 6.2. Market share of international and national/regional trade shows in the main European countries, 2010 (CERMES 2013)

2004). These are critical events through which competition between industries and cities unfolds and is generated. International hub trade shows in Europe are extremely large events, with up to 250,000 square metres of booth space, about 500,000 square metres of gross exhibition space, and 3,000 to 4,000 exhibitors (CERMES 2013). Such dimensions are rarely found in other world regions, with a few exceptions such as the International Consumer Electronics Show in Las Vegas or the China Import and Export Fair (former Canton Fair) in Guangzhou (see Chapters 7 and 8). Since the 1990s, there has been an increasing geographical concentration of international events in the four main trade show countries, most apparently in Germany. While trade show activity in Germany seems to be holding steady following the 2008 global financial crisis, the drop in activity in countries such as Spain and the UK reached 20 to 30 per cent in terms of rented exhibition space between 2008 and 2012 (CERMES 2013). Italy and France are trying to avoid a similar decline by reviewing and modifying the organizational structure of their events and venues. In some cases, organizers try to jointly promote events representing the same industry; in other cases, they move events to the same city, or try to transform national events into European ones (Golfetto and Rinallo 2013).

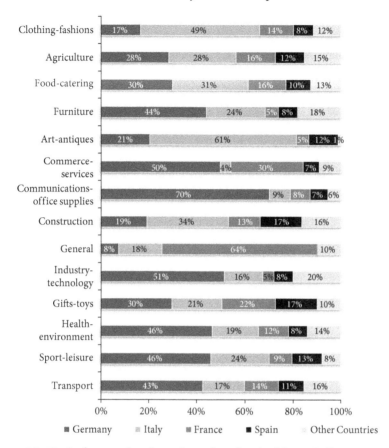

Figure 6.3. Trade show market shares (rented surfaces) of the main European countries by industry group, 2008/2009 (CERMES 2013)

With regards to the sectoral specialization of international shows, the main trade show countries lack a clear specialization model (see Figure 6.3). Yet, the importance of specific industry shows in each country roughly corresponds with the export capacity/strength of the respective country. It is difficult, however, to accurately grasp the locational logic behind all trade shows without going into the specific characteristics of each industry group. Overall, we find that Germany and Italy have the highest share of trade show activity (rented exhibition spaces) in the principal manufacturing sectors: Germany has the largest shares in industry-technology manufacturing, transportation (automotive), communications-office supplies, and furniture, while Italy boasts a larger share in clothing-fashion, art-antiques, and food events (see Figure 6.3).

National and regional shows differ from international events in that they are distributed throughout all countries in shares corresponding to their size. The main countries have shares ranging from 5 to 10 per cent, whereas a total of 71 per cent of activities take place in all remaining countries (see Table 6.2). These events are much smaller than international trade shows, with 8,000 through 10,000 square metres of net exhibition space in the main countries, and have fewer spillovers in terms of related service activity in the host regions. This is due not only to the smaller number of participants, but also related to the limited expenditures of participants (also Chapter 7). National and regional trade shows often target consumers as visitors and are focused on agricultural and consumer products. Some events are more diversified, however, combining different industries and including both consumers and professionals as visitors. In terms of their development, the shows are facing a phenomenon opposite to that seen in the context of international shows, since a growing dispersion of such activity can be observed. This is mainly due to the growing influence of Eastern European countries and other world regions.

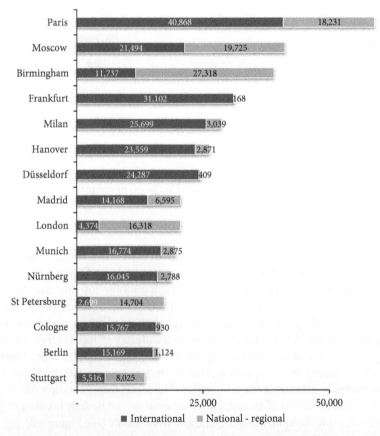

Figure 6.4. Top 15 European trade show cities by number of exhibitors at international, national, and regional events, 2008/2009 (CERMES 2013)

Another form of specialization can be seen in the distribution of trade show activity between the different cities. In fact, given the same volume of trade show activity as measured in terms of booth space and number of exhibitors, we find that some cities specialize in shows for professionals or business-to-business events, while others specialize in shows for consumers or business-to-consumer events. The cities of London, Birmingham, Stuttgart, and St Petersburg, for example, are mainly home to national/regional shows for consumers, while the other cities of the top fifteen in Europe, especially Paris, Frankfurt, Milan, Hanover, and other German cities, are primarily home to international business-to-business events (see Figure 6.4).

6.4. TRADE SHOW FUNCTIONS BY COUNTRY: STAKEHOLDERS AND GOVERNANCE MODELS

With respect to their governance, trade shows vary significantly across the different European countries. This is due to the different stakeholders involved with the exhibition centres and the combination of specific management activities

Table 6.3. Trade show stakeholders and governance models in leading European countries

Indicator	Germany	Italy	France	Spain	UK
Main facility owners					
Ownership	Local government	Local industry foundations and local government	Chamber of commerce and private investors	Local government	Private investors
Main objectives	Local services development	Local development	Local development and profit	Local services development	Profit
Main trade shows organizers					
Ownership	Facility owners (85–95%)	Producer associations	Private organizers	Facility owners (70–80%)	Private organizers
Main objectives	Local services development	National industry development	Profit	Local services development	Profit
Dominant type of trade shows	Intercontinental hubs	National export and import trade shows	National/ European export and import trade shows	National import trade shows	National import trade shows

Source: Golfetto 2004.

Table 6.4. Internationalization of trade shows in leading European countries by industry, 2009/2010

Industry group	Germany		Italy		France		Spain	
	{ % of foreign participants }							
	Exhibitors	Visitors	Exhibitors	Visitors	Exhibitors	Visitors	Exhibitors	Visitors
Clothing-fashions	52.7	34.5	36.6	36.3	66.2	48.0	25.0	3.8
Agriculture	53.1	15.3	19.7	10.1	22.8	3.7	25.7	8.1
Food-catering	61.5	33.1	9.2	7.7	41.8	19.6	24.7	11.7
Furniture	74.6	46.3	23.6	44.1	43.6	24.4	32.4	9.6
Art-antiques	23.9	1.6	25.2	0.6	56.3	0.0	56.5	0.7
Commerce-services	28.2	26.1	17.4	16.8	58.6	31.8	14.6	1.0
Communications-office supplies	49.6	9.4	35.6	6.3	84.8	71.3	55.7	0.9
Construction	43.1	25.8	31.0	17.4	37.7	17.3	34.4	9.0
General (mixed industries)	57.2	29.5	11.3	0.0	17.9	0.3	52.3	0.0
Industry-technology	43.5	26.5	31.8	15.7	34.4	13.6	45.9	8.6
Gifts-toys	68.2	37.9	25.6	13.2	38.8	41.4	32.8	2.2
Health-environment	51.9	21.7	40.4	19.4	42.5	28.2	51.0	2.9
Sport-leisure	67.0	21.8	37.8	3.7	31.9	1.0	27.1	3.6
Transport	53.8	17.9	28.9	7.9	44.1	6.1	28.9	0.3
Total	53.7	21.6	28.2	7.7	41.3	9.5	33.4	3.7

Source: CERMES 2013.

Note: Only international events are included.

associated with the organization of shows (see Chapter 4). Facility owners range from local governments to private investors with varying objectives (Hauswirth and Magri 2013; Nanetti 2013). Similarly, trade show organizers vary between countries from facility owners in Germany to producers' associations in Italy, to private organizers in the UK, all of which have different goals in holding their shows. As a result, the main European trade show countries have different dominant trade show types (see Table 6.3).

The international trade functions of shows also vary considerably. Table 6.4 summarizes these different positions for the four main countries and for different industry groups. The analysis reveals the general hub function of international shows in Germany, with international exhibitors mostly exceeding 50 per cent and international visitors ranging from 20 to 45 per cent. In the case of Italy, we find both international shows with a primary import function (e.g. in the industry groups communication-office supplies, construction, industry-technology, and health-environment) as well as shows that are mainly export-oriented (e.g. in the furniture industry group). In France, some industry groups focus on local demand shows (such as agricultural, sport, and general fairs), while others are characterized by hub events (e.g. communications-office supplies or clothing-fashion). In Spain, the emphasis is mostly on import fairs. The different trade show functions and specializations in the main European countries will now be discussed in more detail.

6.4.1. Germany

In Germany, trade shows are predominantly organized by the exhibition centres or their subsidiary organizations. In addition to managing the exhibition grounds (e.g. maintenance, installations, layout, and definition of the display areas) and providing basic services (e.g. logistics, clearing, utilities, and outfitting), these exhibition centres play a direct role in organizing many (or most) shows within their own facilities, and sometimes also events outside the centres themselves. The main show organizers in cities like Frankfurt, Düsseldorf, Cologne, Hanover, and Munich are large organizations that have often been in operation since the beginning of the twentieth century. These centres have thousands of employees and organize forty to seventy shows per year that occupy up to 90 per cent of the rental space within the centre (CERMES 2013). These exhibition centres mostly belong to the cities and Länder (federated states) in Germany, while trade associations participate in running the shows only through technical advisory committees (see, as an example, Messe Frankfurt GmbH 2012b). Trade show activity thus aims to generate growth within the local area/territory by offering a visibility platform for exports that, through the growth of trade show service activities, is demanded by exhibitors and visitors from other cities/regions and countries (e.g. exhibition services and business tourism services). The productivity of events is presented to stakeholders with the goal of maximizing the tax revenues produced for local government and the turnover created in the local/regional area (e.g. related to regional tourism services or local employment in trade-show-related activities), rather than with respect to an economic return on investments. In the case of exhibition centres with high international participation, the regional event impact in revenues has been estimated to be 15 to 20 times the revenue of the organizer (Golfetto 1991; Chambre de Commerce et d'Industrie de Paris 2001; AUMA 2006).

Because of this orientation, trade shows organized by German exhibition centres have always been open to international participation, particularly with respect to exhibitors. In short, the larger the number of international exhibitors there are, the larger the number of visitors. This, in turn, leads to a greater regional economic impact. This policy of openness is supported by the fact that Germany has always been both a major import market for manufacturing products, as well as an important exporter. Germany offers important visibility to exhibitors, regardless of foreign visitor attendance, and thus serves as an excellent base for trade shows across almost all manufacturing industries. The self-reinforcing relationship between foreign exhibitors and foreign visitors creates a virtuous cycle that leads these international shows to become hub events. Over the years, German trade shows have thus taken a lead in import and export activities in Europe, free from protectionist restrictions to exhibitor admittance. As illustrated in Table 6.4, international trade shows in Germany have a large share of foreign exhibitors with an average of 53.7 per cent of foreign exhibitors in 2009–10—with some sectors reaching 70 to 75 per cent. German shows also have the highest share of foreign visitors of all European countries with an average of 21.6 per cent. About 40 per cent of the foreign exhibitors and 20 per cent of the foreign visitors originate from non-European countries (AUMA 2012a). A map of the functions of German trade shows is presented in Figure 6.5, in which the different trade shows are placed according to their share of foreign visitors and exhibitors, differentiated by industry groups (see Chapter 4).

6.4.2. Italy

In the European context, Italy ranks second after Germany in terms of both manufacturing and trade show activity. Italy has a far greater number of firms in each industry than Germany (an estimated three times higher number), but these firms tend to be smaller in size and are lacking a specialized sales force and access to international markets because of limited resources (European Commission 2008, 2009; Golfetto and Rinallo 2013). This has generated a large demand for collective events and related exhibition facilities in Italy. The first international trade shows in Italy took place in the streets of Milan, long

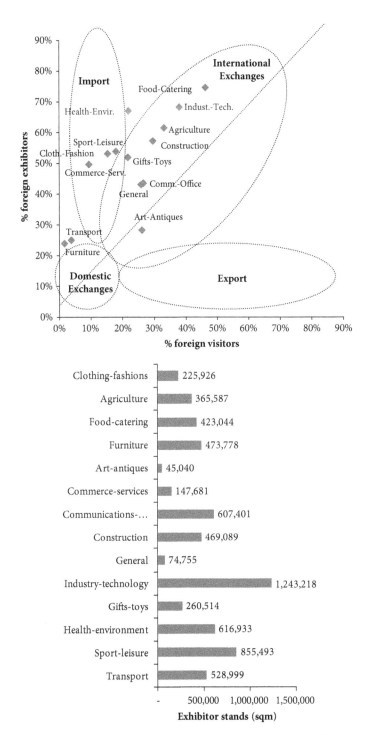

Figure 6.5. Internationalization, import-export function, and size of German trade shows by industry group, 2009/2010 (CERMES 2013)

before exhibition centres were constructed, and events were organized by local entrepreneurs and associations. In 1923, the first international exhibition centre was built in Milan, and many other smaller ones followed during subsequent years throughout the country. Of these, the main centres were established in Verona, Bologna, and Rimini. Until 2000, the country was unable to provide adequate exhibition facilities for international trade shows, however, after which major expansion activities were carried out in the main centres. This allowed exhibitors that were previously on waiting lists to participate in the trade shows. The exhibition centres outside of Milan have nonetheless remained characterized by restricted accessibility, which has made internationalization processes of Italian events difficult. Italian producers have, in turn, been among the largest group of foreign exhibitors at other main European shows, especially German events (AUMA 2012b; Unimev-Ojs 2013).

As a consequence, the orientation of international trade shows in Italy is, in many cases, very different from that in German shows (see Table 6.3). In Italy, exhibition centres were mostly built on the initiative of public local authorities, but the main international trade shows are controlled by strong national industry associations. The history of these events has often seen protectionist restrictions and a division between different manufacturing clusters—aspects, which have weakened their international position (Rinallo and Golfetto 2011; CERMES 2012b; Golfetto and Rinallo 2012). In the case of other shows, however, the determination and commitment of local entrepreneurs, particularly in supporting terms of innovation and collective visibility, have triggered the success and international recognition of entire industries. While the average share of international visitors in Italy is relatively low (see Table 6.4 and Figure 6.6), there are industries such as furniture-design and clothing-fashion, in which export trade shows play an important role. In these trade shows, many competence-release activities take place on the part of exhibitors (Golfetto and Mazursky 2004; Golfetto and Gibbert 2006; Zerbini et al. 2007), who try to compensate for the low geographical variety of exhibitors with presentations of highly sophisticated stands (including the presence of technical specialists and presentations of prototypes and products at work). Also visible are the activities of the organizers, which try to support knowledge enactment and dissemination processes in technological and consumer trends through the organization of trend sections, seminars, and so forth (see Chapter 4). However, due to their small size, the activities of trade show organizers are less well planned than in French shows (CERMES 2012b; CCI Paris Ile-de-France 2012). On the part of international visitors, due to the small size of the exhibiting enterprises, these events are mainly attended by wholesale distributors, which redistribute the semi-finished or finished products throughout non-European end markets—a function the small- and medium-sized exhibitors cannot perform themselves.

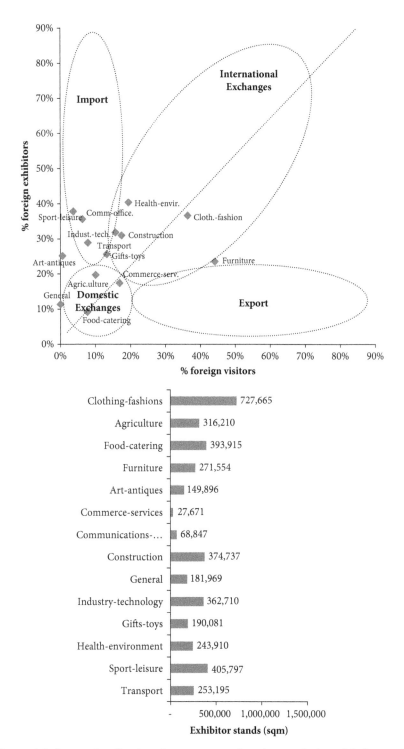

Figure 6.6. Internationalization, import-export function, and size of Italian trade shows by industry group, 2009/2010 (CERMES 2013)

6.4.3. France

In France, the main trade shows take place in Paris, where two large and several smaller exhibition centres are located. Some important shows are also held in Lyon. There are many other exhibition centres throughout the country, but these are small and mainly host business-to-consumer events, related to agricultural products and traditional local consumer goods (Economic Development Agency for the Paris Region 2013).

All of the centres in Paris are jointly owned by the local Chamber of Commerce (the majority shareholder) and a private real estate management firm (minority shareholder). International trade shows are predominantly organized by private firms (often profit-oriented multinationals) and, in a few cases, by trade associations (see Table 6.3). Many of the shows that take place in Paris are either international hub events or, in some cases (particularly in food and furnishings-accessories), export shows at the European level, with mainly European exhibitors and many visitors from non-European countries (CCI Paris Ile-de-France 2012; Unimev-Ojs 2013). Although France ranks only third in Europe in terms of the volume of trade show activity, some of its events are highly internationalized in terms of exhibitors and visitors. In fact, in some cases, the degree of internationalization is considerably higher than in Italian shows (see Table 6.4 and Figure 6.7). In the textile-clothing industry, Parisian shows share with Italian events the presentation of the highest quality of products in Europe (CERMES 2012b). In design-accessories, French events have even overtaken Italian ones in terms of international participation and product quality. The same goes for food/beverage shows, in which Italy has many fragmented events that compete with one another. More recently, Parisian exhibitions have also become the venue for shows that represent exhibitors from emerging non-European countries, especially from Asia (see Chapter 12).

6.4.4. Spain

The governance model of trade shows in Spain is similar to that of Germany in that the main exhibition centres sprang from the initiative of local governments (UFI 2012a; AFE 2013). Further, shows are mostly organized by the exhibition centres themselves (70–80 per cent of the total rented space). Nonetheless, trade shows in Spain, particularly international ones, are far fewer and smaller than in Germany, which corresponds to the country's comparatively limited manufacturing and export activities. Notwithstanding a few exceptions, trade shows are mainly devoted to import (see Figure 6.8). Shows in many industry groups display a fair degree of internationalization on the part of exhibitors, but have limited shares of international visitors, as illustrated in Table 6.4. The country's main exhibition centres are located in Barcelona and Madrid. Trade

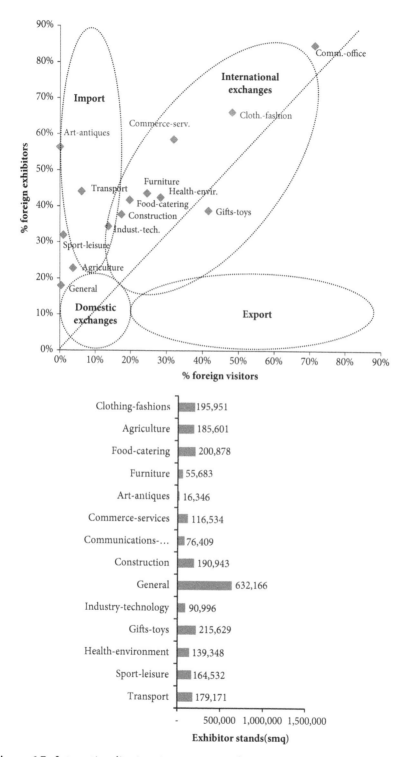

Figure 6.7. Internationalization, import-export function, and size of French trade shows by industry group, 2009/2010 (CERMES 2013)

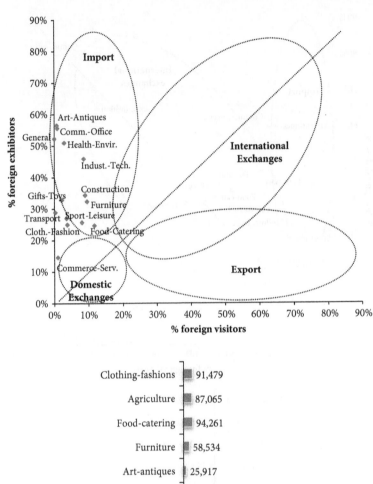

Figure 6.8. Internationalization, import-export function, and size of Spanish trade shows by industry group, 2009/2010 (CERMES 2013)

shows for professionals mainly take place in Barcelona, while Madrid is predominantly host to consumer shows.

6.4.5. United Kingdom

Exhibition centres in the UK are extremely varied in nature. In some cases, they are created on the initiative of local governments, while in other cases they are driven by the initiative of private entities. Organizers are mainly private, many of which operate on an international level. In terms of events, international shows that take place in the UK are not very common and have gradually disappeared over the years due to substantial deindustrialization and the downsizing of manufacturing in the post-Second World War period. The leading shows in the UK take place in Birmingham and London, and most of these events are targeted at consumers (UFI 2011).

6.4.6. Other European Countries

In the rest of Europe, trade show activity is much more limited than in the main event countries and is largely made up of local events that are oriented towards consumers or mixed. There are nonetheless some major exhibition centres with significant trade show activity, especially in the Netherlands, Switzerland, and Belgium. It is also important to note the recent growth of the trade show business in Eastern Europe, particularly Russia, as well as Southern Europe, including Turkey (UFI 2011, 2012a, 2012b).

6.5. DEVELOPMENT TRENDS

With the establishment and growth of new manufacturing and trade show activities in newly developed and developing countries, the world trade show system is being restructured and developing three or four major continental platforms (Europe; North and South America; China and East Asia; India and the Middle East). This marks a departure from the past, when the leading trade shows (those that revealed the trends of the entire industry) were mainly concentrated in Europe and, to a smaller extent, in the US. The world trade show system, in fact, follows the shifts in global industrial demand and, accordingly, exhibitors now regularly go to present their products and innovations in new and growing demand centres.[2] Earlier, many European trade shows (especially in Italy) were collective trade events that functioned in a different way, since local/regional firms presented their products to attract visitor-buyers from the rest of the world. As a consequence of a trade show system that is becoming increasingly polycentric, the appeal of the European 'for-the-export' trade shows is weakening, precisely because the different continental regions all create their own specific shows, suited to their own markets (Golfetto and Rinallo 2013).

Faced with these changes, many European trade show organizers are intensifying their activities and investments in non-European markets (AUMA 2012a). This serves the interests of the national exhibition centres and organizers by providing the conditions for exhibitors to swap between different world regions. It also helps organizers overcome economic difficulties linked to the maturity of the European trade show markets. Such activities meet the new needs of many European producers to approach emerging markets through trade show participation. They must choose events that best enable them to become familiar with a broadening set of economies around the world and that are suited to their commercial strategies. In such situations, trade shows become the preferable communication tools over other tools, since they offer multiple feedback and communication opportunities, as well as advantages in terms of evaluating the competitive environment, establishing local commercial networks, and so forth.

At first, important internationalization strategies were only exercised by German trade show organizers (i.e. the large exhibition centres), which have launched multinational trade show developments since the 1980s. While such multinational activities originally covered limited shares of total turnover for these organizers (5 to 15 per cent), more important involvement has occurred in Asian markets, in particular, since the 2000s (20 to 35 per cent of total turnover) (AUMA 2012a, 2012b). Contemporary activities and investments of European trade show organizers in new markets are different from the early ones made by German organizers. Today, trade show markets in emerging economies already have an abundant number of players, either competing for the same markets or having established permanent business bases there. As a result, new investments by European organizers (particularly smaller ones) aim to create joint ventures with local organizers, acquire exhibition areas, and rent them out to European enterprises.

Herein lies the threat of 'fragmented' competitive behaviour, which creates a 'battle' amongst trade shows driven by the local and national 'one-upmanship' of European exhibition centres. The drive for independence of some exhibition centres and organizers produces multiple joint-ventures and participation in non-European shows, with the outcome being that groups of European producers take part in different shows in the same sector and country, under the banner of a different exhibition organizer group. This feeds the 'battle of the venues' in that country and, in the best case scenario, producers achieve poor visibility and waste part of their efforts.

6.6. CONCLUSIONS

This chapter illustrates the features and recent trends of trade shows in Europe. First, it emphasizes the role of local/regional industry structure that has led to a high exhibition demand and, over the years, to the establishment of many major international shows. It also analyses the similarities and differences of exhibition facilities in the various countries, the type of trade show activity associated with these countries, and the development of this activity over time. We found that event specialization in the main European trade shows is largely a response to specialization processes in the countries' production systems.

Second, the chapter examines the different import-export functions of events in the main trade show countries in Europe. These functions are partially attributable to the different types of trade show stakeholders, in some cases more oriented towards the support of national/regional industries (and therefore more protectionist), while in other cases more focused on maximizing the related revenues/service employment of the host area (and thus more open to foreign exhibitors). Further, major trends in trade show activity are identified after the trade show business has entered a mature phase characterized by the geographical concentration of international and intercontinental shows to particular places and exhibition venues. The analysis also showcases the growing initiatives of European trade show organizers with regards to trade shows in emerging/developing countries, with the aim of accompanying European producers to these new events.

NOTES

1. The level of participation in trade shows stands at about 85 to 90 per cent of manufacturing firms in Europe (Golfetto 1988; AUMA 2012b).
2. In this sense, the shifts in markets continue to influence the locations of major trade show activity, as they did during the period of the early commodity fairs (Allix 1922).

7

Trade Show Dynamics in Mature Markets 2: North America

7.1. INTRODUCTION

While there is considerable information about the history and geography of European trade shows (see Chapter 6), North American shows developed much later and have not been studied as extensively as their European counterparts. Consequently, we know relatively little about the geography of trade show activity, the attendance by exhibitors and visitors, or the dynamic changes of the trade show business in the US and Canada (for an exception, see Zelinsky 1994). This chapter aims to address this gap in the literature by investigating the economic geography of North American trade shows, focusing on characteristics such as the number and size of trade shows in major US and Canadian cities. In doing so, it documents changes in the geography of these events over the past forty years, and identifies connections between trade shows and North America's broader economic geography.

Given the importance of trade shows in supporting knowledge flows and network building, as well as local economic development and job creation (see Chapters 3 and 5), it is surprising that so little is known about their size, structure, and development in North America. In order to study the current state of trade show activity, we draw on different datasets from the Center for Exhibition Industry Research (CEIR)–a US-based industry group that monitors North America's trade show business. The first data source used is the so-called CEIR Index (CEIR 2005, 2009), which provides information about trends in the number, attendance, size, and revenues of North American trade shows. This dataset presents estimates from a representative sample of trade shows—the so-called CEIR Index Events—consisting of 219 events in 2001 and 436 events in 2007. The second data source records events in the twenty-five largest North American trade show cities, broken down by industry group, size of trade show, and location. The detailed database from 2005, which is based on a census of the population of trade shows in that year, is used in conjunction with data from the CEIR Index Events from 2001 to 2007 to project the total number of shows each year by industry group (TSW and CEIR 2005; CEIR 2009).[1]

Taking this as a starting point, the chapter begins by providing a general discussion of the growth of trade shows in North America in the post-Second World War period. The next section focuses on recent structures and trends since the turn of the millennium. The analysis then pays attention to the rise of trade shows in Chicago, Las Vegas, and Toronto, to explore important trajectories in the development of major trade show cities. We demonstrate how these different trajectories were established over time in a relational manner through reflexive interrelationships between trade show development, historical structures, and infrastructure investments (Bathelt and Spigel 2012). From this, conclusions are drawn about the future geography of North American trade show activity.

7.2. POST-SECOND WORLD WAR TRADE SHOW GROWTH

In the post-Second World War period, shifts in the geography of North American trade shows were primarily driven by changes in economic development and associated infrastructure investments. In 1960, trade shows were heavily clustered in the manufacturing belt. The largest trade show cities were embedded in the existing road, rail, and air networks, and had large numbers of local industrial firms looking for opportunities to demonstrate their products. Events were clustered in cities like Chicago, New York, or Philadelphia. Other important trade show cities included Washington, DC, and Miami where capitol functions and leisure activities attracted shows and attendees (Zelinsky 1994).

By 1990, these patterns shifted substantially in response to changes in the industrial landscape. This shift reflected a dramatic shakeup resulting from the decline of the Fordist economy in traditional manufacturing centres and the rise of the 'sunbelt' (e.g. Perry and Watkins 1977). The most prominent change between the 1960s and 1990s was the movement of trade shows away from the industrial North-East and towards sunbelt and south-western cities like Las Vegas (which jumped in trade show ranking from 20th to 4th place) and New Orleans (from 16th to 2nd place). Some of the older industrial cities with ageing first generation trade show centres lost ground compared to the newer destinations in the sunbelt (Zelinsky 1994). An important factor influencing the locations of trade shows was variation in the costs associated with hosting trade shows in small versus large urban centres, and in places situated in the sunbelt versus the 'rustbelt' (AUMA 2009a). In terms of costs, for instance, unions had a strong impact on trade show activity, as most convention and exhibitions centres had contractual agreements with them. According to AUMA (2009a), a carpenter working at a trade show in Louisville, KY, earned about $45 per hour in the mid-2000s, while the hourly rate in New York was almost $150 (and $260 on weekends). Nonetheless, the shift of trade show activity to the South was gradual, and not abrupt. As a consequence, the mobility of trade shows generated gradual shifts in their spatial distribution, as events gravitated towards regions and cities that were growing and away from those that were shrinking. North-eastern and mid-Atlantic cities like Boston (10th in 1990) and New York City (11th place) thus remained important nodes in the trade show economy (Zelinsky 1994).

Geographical shifts in the North American trade show business continued after 1990, but they were not as strong as before and the mean centre[2] of trade show activity remained relatively stable.[3] Overall, the concentration of trade show activity in the US manufacturing belt largely dissipated by 2005, while prominent new clusters of trade show activity developed in the California/Nevada and Texas/Louisiana corridors, as well as in major Canadian cities.

Continuing shifts in the twenty-five largest North American trade show cities suggested that trade show activity was not locked into static geographies. As in Europe, the trade geographies were quite dynamic over time. While several large cities like New York and Chicago consistently retained their position in the rankings, the correlation between city population and number of trade shows declined from 0.76 in 1960 to 0.12 in 2005.[4] This demonstrates the success enjoyed by smaller cities like Orlando and Las Vegas in attracting a substantial number of trade shows as a consequence of large investments into the expansion of their infrastructure. As a result, the geography of trade shows was not a simple function of city size.

Despite the emergence of Toronto and Montreal as important trade show cites in the 1970s and 1980s, the US overshadowed the Canadian trade show business on the whole (AUMA 2002). Generally, Canadian cities are disadvantaged when competing for international trade shows because of the relatively small size of the Canadian market. Most international exhibitors focus on US trade shows, knowing that their Canadian clientele will likely attend these shows. The same cannot be said for American firms participating in Canadian shows. As a consequence, most Canadian shows have a primary regional/national focus, with only a few exceptions such as Calgary's Global Petroleum Show or Fort McMurray's Oil Sands Trade Show, which are international events.[5]

The post-Second World War shift in the North American economy and increased competition between North American cities contributed to image-making trends in urban centres. Selling the city as a trade show destination became a significant element of city branding and urban economic development (Bradley et al. 2002). Trade shows were valuable both for the employment and direct revenue they generated, but also because cities used trade shows to construct images of growth and modernization that encouraged future investments (Oppermann 1996; Oppermann and Chon 1997). While the immediate economic benefits of trade shows, such as direct and indirect job creation, were relatively localized, other benefits, especially the resulting knowledge flows and circulation, were broad and had a national (or even international) component.

In the next section, recent developments in the North American trade show business are discussed, suggesting that these structures and trends are evidence of continued growth, rather than stagnation or decline.

7.3. STRUCTURES AND TRENDS OF NORTH AMERICAN TRADE SHOWS IN THE 2000s

This section presents evidence of the continued growth of trade shows in major urban centres in the US and Canada during the 2000s. Overall, the number of events in the twenty-five largest North American trade show cities increased from 4,521 in 2001 to 7,753 in 2007. In the same time period, the average number of exhibitors and attendees per event increased by 31 per cent and 25 per cent, respectively (CEIR 2005, 2009). This growth is considerable given the high costs of trade show attendance, including extensive scheduling and the shipment of materials and people. The growth in the number of events seems clearly related to the high value attached to face-to-face encounters, as well as the multiple opportunities for strategy development and innovation that arise (see Chapter 3). This buzz generates opportunities for learning by interacting with partners, learning by observing competitors, and learning by inspecting other exhibits (Bathelt and Schuldt 2008, 2010).

While these data suggest that North American trade shows have increased in importance, one must be cautious in drawing conclusions about this growth. The trade show business as a whole initially experienced a decline in the wake of the 9/11 shock, resulting in a downturn that lasted at least until late 2002. Moreover, the number of trade shows in 2001 was depressed due to the collapse of the 'new economy' bubble and the IT shows associated with it (Breiter and Hahm 2006). The subsequent increase was due to both strong economic growth and a recovery from previous crises. Although some observers expected longer-term stagnation of trade show activities (AUMA 2004a, 2009a), many events and most sectors experienced substantial growth in the first decade of the new millennium.[6]

Depending upon which definition of trade shows (for instance, in terms of minimum size) is used, the US and Canada hosted between 5,000 and 13,000 events per year in the 2000s (AUMA 2009a). CEIR (2005) estimates that about 10,000 events in the mid-2000s were business-to-business (B2B) shows that attracted about 60 million attendees and 1.5 million exhibitors, generating direct revenues of $10.3 billion. This is an indication of the significance of trade shows to the overall North American economy and, more specifically, to the large urban trade show cities. In 2003, the economic impact of trade shows, derived from payments to direct and secondary employment and the local expenditures of delegates and exhibitors, was estimated to be as high as $140 billion (Lee and Back 2005).

Figure 7.1 illustrates the strong increase in both the number and size of trade shows between 2001 and 2007, with temporary interruptions in 2002 and 2005. Overall, the average size of events increased by 47 per cent, from 115,000 square feet in 2004 to over 165,000 square feet in 2007.[7] Although major US and European trade shows had, on average, a similar number of exhibitors, US shows fell far behind in terms of attendance (CERMES 2005). The 200 largest trade shows and exhibitions in the US had about 975 exhibitors per event in 2002, compared to about 1,130 and 610 exhibitors per international show in Germany and Italy, respectively, over the 2002–5 period. In terms of attendance, however, the 200 largest trade shows in the US had on average about 21,000 visitors, while international trade shows in Germany and Italy attracted about 65,000 to 70,000 visitors per event (Kresse 2003; Maskell et al. 2004; CERMES 2005).

In terms of sectoral breakdown, Figure 7.2 shows the steady growth of trade shows across most industry groups defined in the CEIR Index. Trade shows focusing on industry groups—such as government, public service, and non-profit services; professional business services; or construction, building, home, and

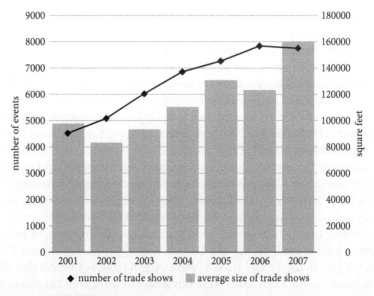

Figure 7.1. Total number and average square footage of North American trade shows, 2001–7 (CEIR 2005, 2009)

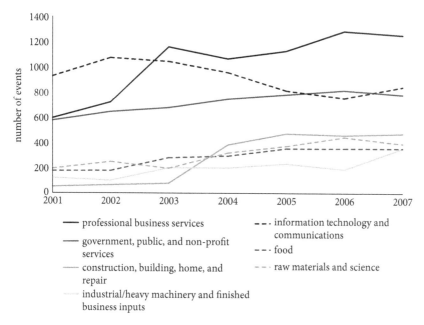

Figure 7.2. Number of trade shows in the top 25 North American trade show cities by selected industry groups, 2001–7 (CEIR 2005, 2009)

repair—saw consistent growth in the number of trade shows, exhibitors, and attendees over the time period from 2001 to 2007. There was, however, a noticeable drop in the number of information technology and communication shows, from 929 in 2001 to 842 in 2007. This is the only sector that saw a decline in the number of events, which appears to be related to the earlier 'dot-com boom-and-bust period'. The strongest growth in the number of shows can be found in industrial/heavy machinery and finished business inputs group (from 122 to 355), as well as in the professional business services group (from 596 to 1,254). While exhibitor growth was gradual and consistent across almost all industry groups (with the exception of food and raw materials/science where exhibitor growth was exponential after 2005), attendance levels grew in a relatively unequal manner across the different groups (CEIR 2009; Bathelt and Spigel 2012). From a knowledge-circulation perspective, this overall intensification of trade shows is an important trend as larger shows attract more exhibitors and attendees and provide a more fruitful environment for interaction and knowledge exchange among diverse participants (Borghini et al. 2006; Maskell et al. 2006).

While Figures 7.1 and 7.2 indicate considerable growth in the number of trade shows between 2001 and 2007, there was also substantial variation among industry groups in the development of event sizes/attendance levels. Average attendance per event, for instance, increased by 39 per cent in the construction, building, home, and repair industry group, but it decreased both in terms of

Table 7.1. Average number of exhibitors, attendees, and square footage of North American trade shows, 2001, 2004, and 2007

Industrial sector	Exhibitors per event			Attendees per event			Average square footage		
	2001	2004	2007	2001	2004	2007	2001	2004	2007
Professional business services (BZ)	308	408	461	5,623	6,350	6,586	61,324	81,761	104,670
Consumer goods and retail trade (CG)	776	706	720	16,156	14,502	15,210	220,531	177,117	355,082
Consumer services, sports, travel, entertainment, and art (CS)	397	438	520	9,726	11,402	16,171	123,308	131,705	180,620
Food (FD)	520	399	981	8,965	12,924	19,010	174,853	104,759	150,568
Government, public, and non-profit services (GV)	113	216	265	2,700	3,767	5,009	15,847	39,428	55,402
Construction, building, home, and repair (HM)	563	374	369	18,665	27,169	25,970	246,055	116,368	107,642
Industrial/heavy machinery and finished business inputs (ID)	639	712	495	7,837	12,069	8,098	125,393	176,935	165,002
Information technology and communications (IT)	189	178	226	6,353	5,259	6,489	61,828	54,308	66,606
Medical and health care (MD)	197	219	242	4,776	4,828	5,364	65,987	73,380	78,319
Raw materials and science (RM)	267	329	898	7,254	10,909	11,510	65,062	116,139	220,209
Transportation (TX)	199	234	249	20,714	20,173	16,229	89,239	120,176	104,696
Unweighted average	379	383	494	9,888	11,759	12,331	114,755	113,509	167,980

Source: CEIR 2005, 2009.

Note: 1 square metre = 10.76 square feet.

exhibitors per event and average exhibition space. This meant fewer opportunities for firms at individual events to observe the market and their competitors in this industry group. Table 7.1 also shows the effects of industry downturns in North America, as, for instance, the average square footage of information technology and communications shows declined by 12 per cent between 2001 and 2004, when the industry bottomed out. Industry groups which were relatively new to trade shows, such as professional business services, and more traditional segments, such as raw materials and science, both experienced strong growth in all size indicators, suggesting more and larger events were established across North America in these industry groups.

Table 7.2 suggests that major North American trade show cities have diverse sectoral specializations. The data, however, indicate few connections between the sectoral patterns of trade shows and the host cities' industrial specializations. This can be explained by two tendencies. First, over time trade shows have displayed strong growth across all industries. Second, North American trade shows are less place-bound than European shows. Many European trade show cities historically developed around specialized manufacturing regions (see Chapters 2 and 3) and, although changes in markets, technologies, and regulations led to relocations in the long term, these events often had stable locations over an extended period of time (Fuchslocher and Hochheimer 2000; Rodekamp 2003). As will be discussed, the development of trade shows in North America was different. Due to the importance of travelling salesmen in the industrial distribution system, and the significance of mobile conventions of technical communities that later attracted exhibits of products and technologies, trade shows in North America more often change their location from year to year (AUMA 2004a, 2009a). This suggests that the sectoral focus of trade shows is not necessarily related to strong regional/urban industry specialization.

In terms of the regional distribution of trade shows, Las Vegas stood out as North America's dominant trade show city with 780 events in 2005 (see Table 7.2). Its large-scale trade show infrastructure, based on large publicly owned convention centres and exhibition spaces, as well as hotel rooms and exhibition spaces in all the major casinos, gave the city the capacity needed to simultaneously host several major events (Jones 2006; Yang 2008). This highly developed infrastructure generated a competitive advantage in terms of contending for large international trade shows and is closely linked to the city's overall tourism business.

Toronto is North America's second largest trade show city, with 605 events in 2005 (see Table 7.2). It stands out not only for the large number of events it hosts per year, but also for its high proportion of business-to-consumer (B2C) shows (63 per cent of all shows). This indicates a structural difference between trade shows in American and Canadian cities (Bathelt and Spigel 2012). In 2005, all Canadian cities exhibited a high proportion of business-to-consumer shows: 44 per cent in Vancouver, 43 per cent in Ottawa, and 39 per cent in Montreal. In contrast, the average proportion of business-to-consumer shows in US cities was 15 per cent. It is, however, important not to interpret these numbers as a consequence of different demand- and supply-side patterns in the two economies. On the one hand, the large number of consumer-oriented shows in Canada reflects the difficulties associated with attracting overseas businesses to the relatively small Canadian market. A stronger focus on consumer-oriented shows thus appears to be a natural consequence. At the

Table 7.2. Number of trade shows and trade show location quotients by industry group in selected North American trade show cities, 2005

City	Number of trade shows (TFLQs) by industry groups											
	BZ	CG	CS	FD	GV	HM	ID	IT	MD	RM	TX	Total
Las Vegas, NV	127	114 (1.3)	80	46 (1.2)	42	53	28	111 (1.3)	86	26	51 (1.7)	780
Toronto, ON	80	92 (1.4)	132	36 (1.2)	42	38	16	48	60	28	21	605
Chicago, IL	75	25	37	25 (1.2)	45	20	21 (1.5)	58 (1.2)	81 (1.3)	19	12	431
Dallas, TX	54	66 (1.7)	40	17	24	32 (1.5)	10	22	32	10	20 (1.6)	344
San Diego, CA	61	21	23	11	52 (1.5)	5	7	47 (1.3)	75 (1.6)	19	12	338
Washington, DC	45	9	20	8	68 (2.2)	5	3	36	74 (1.8)	14	9	294
Houston, TX	35	20	34 (1.2)	11	29 (1.2)	24 (1.7)	13 (1.8)	11	15	18 (1.6)	11 (1.3)	229
San Antonio, TX	30	12	21	16 (1.5)	37 (1.6)	16	5	17	31 (2.1)	24	9	226
San Francisco, CA	35	15	16	7	29 (1.2)	6	4	54 (2.2)	38 (1.2)	13 (1.2)	3	222
Montreal, QC	16	24	56 (2.2)	11 (1.2)	7	13	10	15 (1.6)	23	10	9 (1.2)	198
Ottawa, ON	29	12	50 (2.2)	6	14	9	9	13 (1.6)	15	10	9 (1.3)	179
Vancouver, BC	24	26 (1.3)	46 (2.0)	11 (1.3)	6	8	1	17	22	11 (1.2)	5	177
Austin, TX	14	13	22	4	35 (2.0)	13 (1.2)	7 (1.3)	16	21	16 (1.9)	3	169
Minneapolis, MN	23	19	14	3	12	18 (1.9)	8 (1.7)	8	23	14 (1.9)	6 (1.1)	151
Phoenix, AZ	18	12	17	8	17 (1.2)	15 (1.2)	5 (1.7)	10 (1.2)	21	9 (1.3)	3	135
Total (top 25 cities)	1129	827	944	355	781	473	233	813	1054	374	281	7437

Source: CEIR 2005.

Notes: TFLQs = trade show location quotients; TFLQs ≥ 1.2 bolded (≥ 2.0 shaded); industry group abbreviations: BZ = Professional business services; CG = Consumer goods and retail trade; CS = Consumer services, sports, travel, entertainment, and art; FD = Food; GV = Government, public, and non-profit services; HM = Construction, building, home, and repair; ID = Industrial/heavy machinery and finished business inputs; IT = Information technology and communications; MD = Medical and health care; RM = Raw materials and science; TX = Transportation.

same time, this is also a reflection of trade show centre capacity exceeding demand for business-to-business shows—a gap which is filled by a large number of business-to-consumer shows. Differences in the structure of trade show activity, in turn, also affect the economic outcome in the respective cities. The large proportion of business-to-consumer shows in Canada suggests that Canadian cities derive fewer economic benefits (per attendee) from trade shows than US cities. This is true in terms of direct trade show-related revenues, as well as placing a city within global flows of industrial and commercial knowledge.

Of the twenty-one largest US trade show cities in 2005, thirteen were located in the southern and western regions of the sunbelt (e.g. Atlanta, Dallas, and Phoenix), while only four were situated in or close to the manufacturing belt (namely, New York, Chicago, Boston, and Minneapolis). Following Zelinsky's (1994) analysis, this finding indicates a continuation of the earlier movement away from manufacturing-dependent regions. The rise of southern and western cities as major trade show destinations is linked to their emergence as industrial and commercial hubs during the 1970s and 1980s. As the cities' economies and populations grew and became better integrated into national and international transportation networks, they developed into more popular destinations for trade shows. Because cities in the South and West were less densely built than those in the manufacturing belt, it was easier for them to establish new or expand existing trade show centres and hotel capacity. In the older cities in the North-East and Midwest, space for large-scale trade show centre development and expansion was more costly and sometimes harder to find.

In terms of the sectoral specialization of trade show cities, Table 7.2 provides additional information by presenting the trade show location quotients (TFLQs) for each sector in each city.[8] A TFLQ above 1.20 means that the respective city hosted over 20 per cent more trade shows in a sector than the average city in the dataset. TFLQs of 1.20 and higher are used as an indicator of sectoral specialization patterns in North American trade show cities. Although overall specialization patterns are not overly strong, some exceptions exist. San Francisco, for instance—adjacent to Silicon Valley and home of many high-technology firms—has a high TFLQ of 2.2 for information technology and communications trade shows. Chicago and Minneapolis—two cities in the Midwest—similarly have above average representations of industrial/machinery trade shows. And all Texas cities in the dataset (Houston, Austin, and San Antonio) have TFLQs between 1.6 and 2.2 in raw materials and science trade shows. This suggests that trade show organizers—at least in such prominent cases—have attempted to locate events in cities with a heavy concentration of their target industry. Washington, DC, has an equally high TFLQ for government and public sector trade shows, likely designed as export fairs in the first place (see Chapter 4). In contrast to Washington, DC, Ottawa reveals a relatively low proportion of government-related trade shows. This is, in part, due to the substantially lower aggregate number of government-oriented trade shows in Canada compared to the US. When recalculated only for Canadian cities, however, the TFLQ of government-related shows in Ottawa is 2.0, similar to that of Washington, DC. In sum, the TFLQs clearly reflect the importance of business-to-consumer shows in the Canadian trade show economy (see Table 7.2). Montreal, Vancouver, and Ottawa all have TFLQs between 2.0 and 2.2 in the consumer services, sports, travel, entertainment, and art group, while Toronto and Vancouver have TFLQs of 1.3 to 1.4 in the consumer goods and retail trade segment (see Table 7.2). In the case of Montreal, the high TFLQ in consumer services, sports, travel, entertainment, and art is clearly related to the city's arts and entertainment industries that are well-developed and are part of the city's vibrant cultural economy (Cohendet et al. 2010).

7.4. DEVELOPMENT PATHS OF TRADE SHOWS IN NORTH AMERICA

Both the data used and historical analysis suggest that the relational and material geographies of North American trade shows differ substantially from their European counterparts. Trade shows in Europe developed much earlier than in North America; and they more clearly reflect traditional trade and industry patterns, major trade routes, as well as governmental regulations, social struggles, and wars. This has resulted in segmented market patterns in Europe that gradually evolved over time, albeit that individual events sometimes changed location from one year to the next (Allix 1922). Shifts in trade show locations were influenced by political power, disparities in economic development, innovation cycles, and shifting markets (Bathelt 2012).

In contrast, North American trade shows emerged from the tradition of industrial exhibitions, conventions, and agricultural shows. One-time events, like the 1893 World's Columbian Exhibition in Chicago or the St Louis World's Show in 1904, and annual events, such as Toronto's Royal Agricultural Winter Show, brought together buyers and sellers and also served as platforms to present new inventions and products. The largest of these events helped local producers tap into global marketplaces, even before improvements in communication and shipping technologies spurred globalized commerce. While these events were extremely popular and critical to the development of the modern global economy, they were not trade shows in a modern sense (see Chapter 2). The historical world exhibitions were singular events designed to show off the achievements of industrial capitalism to the public without offering a formal occasion for industrial suppliers and customers to meet and conduct business. Agricultural and other periodic fairs served to compensate for the lack of central marketplaces in sparsely developed areas, such as many areas in Canada (Osborne 1980). Modern trade shows, in contrast, serve as regular meeting places for commercial buyers, users, suppliers, and related multipliers to present new products and processes, make deals, and observe the changing nature of the industry.

The development of major urban trade show centres in the US and Canada reveals different patterns than those found in Europe; they started later and took place in a largely homogeneous market. The following subsections illustrate three different growth trajectories of trade show development in Chicago, Las Vegas, and Toronto. These cases illustrate how reflexive relationships between urban planning, industrial needs, investment activities and strategies, and economic development gave rise to specific trajectories with varying material and relational geographies (Bathelt and Spigel 2012). Chicago's trade show business emerged in the 1950s out of its pre-existing manufacturing economy, while Las Vegas's trade show infrastructure emerged at the same time, but was based on a tourism strategy. Toronto's trade show economy grew strong in the late 1970s and early 1980s through explicit public-sector-related initiatives.

7.4.1. Chicago: From World Exhibitions to International Trade Shows

Like many other major industrial cities, Chicago has a long history of industrial exhibitions and trade shows, dating back to 1893 with the World's Columbian Exhibition—an international exhibition with 65,000 exhibits that attracted over 28 million visitors. The Century of Progress International Exhibition in 1933/4 similarly showcased major scientific, industrial, commercial, and cultural advances of the time (Findling and Pelle 2008). The city's industrial base took advantage of these exhibitions to demonstrate its products to the general public.

Chicago's role as a major trade show destination did not begin, however, until 1958 with the construction of McCormick Place (Metropolitan Pier and Exposition Authority 2011). Like most major trade show centres in North America, McCormick Place was built with government funds and was managed by a public corporation. Since its construction, McCormick Place has undergone several stages of restructuring and expansion. In 2008, it had over 2.6 million square feet of exhibition space, making it the largest such space in North America, and one of the ten largest in the world (AUMA 2004a, 2009c).

Despite its impressive size and ongoing investments, McCormick Place started to lose overall market share in the trade show business in the 1970s. As a consequence, the city's position in Zelinsky's (1994) rankings of trade show cities dropped from first in the US in 1964 to third in 1990, and further to fifth in 2005 (TSW and CEIR 2005). This is partially due to the growth of other trade show cities and increasing competition between them—a process also seen in Europe (Rinallo and Golfetto 2011; see also Part III). Chicago's standing in the North American trade show economy would likely have fallen even further had it not expanded and modernized its trade show centre to compete with newer facilities elsewhere (Holten and Draeger 1991).

The city is an example of a traditional industrial centre with trade show activities originally linked to its strong manufacturing base. It hosts large-scale national and international business-to-business shows that encourage important knowledge flows. Due to the transformation of the manufacturing belt and the rise of new trade show centres elsewhere in the US, it lost some of its former significance—yet, it is still an important trade show centre today. Chicago's experience illustrates the challenges that many cities in the Midwest face in maintaining their place as key nodes in the North American trade show business.

7.4.2. Las Vegas: From Leisure Capital to Trade Show Leader

Today, Las Vegas is the key location in the North American trade show business with about one-third more trade shows than the second-ranked city. Among others, Las Vegas hosts six out of the ten largest trade shows in North America (Fenich and Hashimoto 2004). The city's infrastructure is made up of trade show venues in many of the large hotel/casino complexes, as well as the Las Vegas Convention Center (LVCC). The LVCC is a large exhibition hall established in 1959 by the Las Vegas Convention and Visitors Authority (LVCVA)—a public organization funded through a hotel room tax (LVCVA 2011). The city's exceptional trade show infrastructure is marked by its vast capacity and resources (Velotta 1999; Jones 2006). It has more than 140,000 hotel rooms and over 43 million square feet of exhibition space (LVCVA 2009). With nearly 2 million square feet of exhibition space, the LVCC is not only the third largest trade show centre in North America (AUMA 2009a), it also has the largest amount of surface parking of any such centre. This allows it to host trade shows that no other city in North America can (e.g. large events with extra-large exhibits).

Originally, Las Vegas regarded trade shows as a way to increase casino revenue by funnelling business visitors into the city's gambling halls (Bergen 2003; Fenich and Hashimoto 2004). This was at a time when participation in trade shows was sometimes regarded as a reward for successful employees rather than a critical business function (Tanner 2002). Other cities, like Orlando and New Orleans, also pursued this strategy with success. Their cultural and leisure activities helped attract participants to not only attend trade shows, but also to engage in the broader tourism economy. Las Vegas's business tourism began to take off in 1959 with the establishment of the LVCVA, whose express purpose was to build the LVCC and promote trade show and convention tourism. Media reports suggest that revenues from trade show attendees may now be even larger than those from gambling (Spillman 2007). Moreover, employment effects of large international trade shows are substantial, directly contributing approximately 2,000 jobs to the regional economy—not including the indirect employment effects.

Until the early 1990s, the LVCC was the city's dominant trade show space. Yet, with the opening of the MGM Grand in 1993, which was the first hotel/casino to include substantial exhibition space, the LVCC began to compete with the local casinos for trade shows. Since then, multiple hotels/casinos have been built with extensive exhibition space, such as the Sands Expo and Convention Center and the Mandalay Bay Convention Center (Yang 2008; AUMA 2009a).

Las Vegas's trade show industry is unique in North America because of the simultaneous cooperation and competition between the public LVCVA and the privately run exhibition halls of the major hotels/casinos. The LVCVA is the main body responsible for promoting the city both as a tourist and trade show destination. Its work in selling and branding Las Vegas as a trade show destination supports the city's hospitality industry. But the LVCVA also operates the LVCC, putting it in direct competition with the large hotels/casinos for trade shows and exhibitions. While many other cities have a quasi-publicly operated trade show centre, no other city in North America has a similarly large concentration of major privately run trade show/exhibition centres. As a consequence of these influences, the city hosts a large number of major national and continental business-to-business trade shows.

7.4.3. Toronto: From Agricultural Marketplace to Trade Show Centre

Toronto is a relatively recent addition to the list of top North American trade show cities. Similar to other Canadian and US cities, it followed a traditional path in developing its trade show infrastructure, starting out as a temporary regional market in the area of agriculture and manufacturing in the nineteenth century, with events like the Canadian National Exhibition and the Royal Agricultural Winter Show (Osborne 1980; Walden 1997). Its transformation into a modern trade show city did not take place until the late 1970s to early 1980s. The Metro Toronto Convention Centre (MTCC)—the city's major downtown trade show facility with about 460,000 square feet of exhibition space plus an additional 180,000 square feet of meeting space—was created in 1984 as a partnership between the city, province, and federal government to boost tourism. Though funded as a partnership between all three levels of government, it is owned and managed by a provincial crown corporation (MTCC 2011). Initially, the MTCC was particularly oriented towards scientific and medical conferences; organizers saw this as a way of tapping into the city's strengths in biotechnological and medical research at local universities and firms.

In addition, the City of Toronto owns and operates the Direct Energy Centre—a trade show facility that opened in 1996 (renamed in 2006) on the exhibition grounds a few kilometres west of the MTCC. With 1.1 million square feet of exhibition space, the Direct Energy Centre is the largest such facility in Canada, substantially larger than the MTCC (Direct Energy Centre 2010). Due to its three large interconnected exhibition halls and its tradition as an agricultural fairground, this facility has been primarily used for larger business-to-consumer shows. In recent years, the facility was expanded and transformed to become more oriented towards business-to-business shows, as well as conventions and meetings.

Toronto is somewhat unusual in Canada, as well as in the North American context, in that it has two publicly owned convention centres. While there is some competition between the MTCC and the Direct Energy Centre, each has a different focus. The Direct Energy Centre has larger exhibit halls than the MTCC, making it a better venue for consumer-oriented shows, while the MTCC has a large number of smaller meeting rooms for conferences and trade shows with a distinct educational or instructional component. Thus, the two facilities rarely compete directly for events. Rather, they compete against centres in other cities to attract particular events. Moreover, Toronto has two privately run exhibition halls. The International Centre and Toronto Congress Centre were built in 1972 and 1995, respectively (International Centre 2011; Toronto Congress Centre 2011). Both are located close to Pearson International Airport, about 30 kilometres west of downtown Toronto. As these facilities are smaller than their publicly financed counterparts (together still over 1 million square feet), they focus more on local and regional trade shows as opposed to the larger, more nationally and internationally oriented events that take place in the downtown centres.

Overall, the trade show business in Toronto is not strongly linked to the specific regional industry base, although its events often have a large proportion of regional exhibitors and visitors. Toronto's trade show economy is marked by competition between the two public conference centres close to the downtown core and the two privately run centres in the suburbs. A similar structure of core–periphery competition can also be found in other North American trade show cities, such as Atlanta (Newman 2002). The suburban exhibition halls contribute to Toronto's high number of consumer-oriented

shows. While these are primarily regional events, they are important in advertising the trade show facilities and generating interest in future events. Such
consumer shows are, however, less important to the wider regional economy,
since the majority of people come from the near vicinity and do not add much
into the urban economy. Nevertheless, they still generate sizeable revenues
for the trade show centres.

7.5. CONCLUSIONS

This chapter provides evidence of the continued growth of North American
trade shows, despite changes in the capitalist system and various crises that
have occurred since the late 1990s. While trade shows in North America are
overwhelmingly local/domestic (or continental) exchange shows—sometimes
with a strong demand-driven import component—the trade show business has
experienced substantial changes during the post-Second World War period.
This chapter documents a geographical shift of trade shows from traditional
manufacturing cities to new trade show locations in the West and South of the
US, the rise of Canadian cities as important trade show locations, the continued importance of large metropolitan regions, as well as the impact of local and
regional policies on the trade show business through investments into new or
modernized world-scale facilities (Bathelt 2012). In terms of the latter form of
investments, Las Vegas was a first mover in North America's growing trade
show economy, but other cities followed. Major industrial cities, like New York,
Chicago, Boston, and Detroit, also extended and modernized exhibition halls.
These are the cities that dominated Zelinsky's (1994) account of the trade show
business during the 1960s. A second major wave of construction began in the
late 1970s, often as part of an urban revitalization campaign designed to attract
jobs and tourists to the declining downtown areas of major cities such as Balti-
more or Pittsburgh. Other cities which developed their trade show infrastructure in the mid-1990s, like Hartford, CT, and Columbus, OH, do not yet appear
among the top twenty-five trade show cities, but have certainly gained in
importance. While the latter cities have new state-of-the-art facilities, they are
still somewhat peripheral in the urban hierarchy and not well integrated into
international transportation systems (Bathelt and Spigel 2012).

　　If future shifts in the geography of trade shows are driven by increasing competition between cities/venues and a need to gain accessibility and visibility in
relation to global markets (Rinallo and Golfetto 2011), the leading metropolitan areas and transportation hubs with large international airports will likely
become even more dominant as trade show centres in the future. Following this
line of argument, we might expect these centres to attract trade shows from
other cities, thus moving up in the hierarchy of trade show locations. This

would also strengthen their position at the top of the urban hierarchy, while smaller and more remote cities fall behind.

Driven by the 2008 global financial crisis, we might expect a number of trends to influence the development of global trade show geographies in the future. These include further concentration of the trade show industry, relocations to new growth centres in Asia (see Chapter 8), experimentation with new trade show formats in niche markets, as well as merger activities in established market segments. However, major trade shows following a merger can only be held in cities with substantial trade show infrastructure and international air connections. While the trade show business has seemingly not been hit that hard by the global financial crisis, industry shifts will make it harder for second-tier cities in North America to become or remain important continental/international trade show locations in the future, requiring them to either significantly expand the size of their infrastructure or target a reduced market for more local shows.

NOTES

1. CEIR lists a total of eleven industry groups (CEIR 2005; see also Table 7.1 and 7.2). Although this classification differs from the fourteen industry groups distinguished by CERMES (2013), some basic categories are comparable (see Chapter 6 and Part III).
2. The mean centre represents a two-dimensional arithmetic mean in a geographical distribution (Bahrenberg et al. 1985: 70–6). It is here computed as a weighted average from the co-ordinates of the twenty-five largest trade show cities in North America within a spatial grid, using the number of trade shows per city as weights.
3. This was because substantial gains of states like California and Texas in the South were contrasted by the remarkable rise of the Canadian trade show cities Toronto, Ottawa, Montreal, and Vancouver in the North.
4. This is based on a correlation analysis between the number of trade shows and the population in each of the twenty-five largest trade show cities in North America for the years 1960 and 2005 (Bathelt and Spigel 2012).
5. In comparison, the trade show business in Mexico developed much later than in the US and Canada. It was triggered by globalization processes and the opening of the Mexican market starting in the 1980s. The respective events remained relatively small, typically having less than 50,000 square feet of exhibition space. According to AUMA (2004b), an average Mexican trade show had about 100 exhibitors and 7,500 attendees around the turn of the millennium.
6. It appears that this trend was not reversed during the 2008 global financial crisis. Although small and medium-sized regional events suffered, larger international trade shows were less affected, as exemplified by the Las Vegas example (Velotta 2009).
7. We measure the size of exhibition spaces in 'square feet' in North America and in 'square metres' elsewhere. Both can be easily converted by using a factor of '10' (precisely: 1 square metre = 10.76 square feet).

8. TFLQs are defined as ratios of the local importance of an industry group relative to its importance in the top twenty-five North American cities overall. These quotients for city j are calculated as $TFLQ_{ij} = (e_{ij}/e_j)/(E_i/E)$, where e_{ij} is a city's number of trade shows in industry group i; e is the total number of trade shows in the city; E_i is the total number of trade shows in sector i; and E is the total number of trade shows in the overall data set. It is important to note that this dataset only covers the top twenty-five trade show cities in North America, so the TFLQs are measured against those cities, and not the entire set of trade shows in North America.

8

Trade Show Dynamics in Emerging Markets:
The Asia-Pacific Region

8.1. INTRODUCTION

While there is a growing knowledge base about the development, structure, and economic geography of trade shows in Europe and North America (see Chapters 6 and 7; Allix 1922; Zelinsky 1994; CERMES 2005; Bathelt and Spigel 2012), relatively little is known about trade show ecologies in the Asia-Pacific region. Although it is generally difficult to obtain reliable trade show statistics, this is specifically true in the context of Asian economies. Since the 1990s, economic globalization processes have increasingly stretched out to include Asian countries, as several fast growing economies have successfully modernized their economic structure, attracted massive foreign-direct investments, and, at the same time, produced endogenous growth. Even the severe Asian financial crisis of the late 1990s did not act as a significant impediment to this growth, as the example of China illustrates (Zeng 2000). This generates hope that Asian economies might become future carriers and triggers of economic growth—even for the highly developed economies in North America and Europe. Since the onset of the global financial crisis in the late 2000s, such expectations have been regularly formulated in media reports.

Under the current growth conditions, we might expect increased trade show activity in Asia to become the trigger for accelerated economic growth; yet global developments in the trade show business do not clearly reflect this dynamic so far. In fact, data from the Global Association of the Exhibition Industry (UFI) suggest that the global distribution of trade show activity is fairly stable. In 2010, Europe and North America were clear leaders in terms of the projected number of exhibition centres and indoor exhibition space (see Table 8.1). The UFI database listed 477 facilities for Europe with an overall exhibition space of 16.2 million square metres, while North America had 370 exhibition centres with a total space of 7.7 million square metres (Beier and Damböck 2010). Asian trade show capacities were much smaller, with 143 exhibition centres in 2010, and an exhibition space of 4.6 million square metres.

In terms of leadership in trade show activity, however, China scored very high. It was the third largest country with respect to facility capacity, behind the USA and Germany, but ahead of other European countries such as Italy, France, and Spain (UFI 2007). The UFI's growth projection from 2006 to 2010 indicated some growth in Asian indicators, but not much stronger than that seen in Europe and North America. The UFI data showed an increase in the share of exhibition centres from 12 to 13 per cent of the world total (sixteen new centres), and growth in the share of exhibition space from 14 to 15 per cent of the total (an additional 700,000 square metres). However, since European and North American facilities were also expanded, their (projected) 2010 share was still dominant, with more than two-thirds of all centres and over three-quarters of the overall exhibition space (see Table 8.1).

This seeming stability in the global geography of trade show capacity is somewhat misleading, however, when we consider the rapid rate at which the Asian trade show business has developed over the past several years, especially in mainland China. This may pose a challenge to the leading role of European and North American exhibition centres in the future. First, the UFI database is incomplete as it is based on specifically approved facilities and does not include the myriad of other venues and events.[1] This is particularly significant with respect to China in terms of its overall capacity. Second, the 2010 projection was based on development patterns up until the mid-2000s and the designated expansion plans that existed at that time. As the case of China illustrates, the pace of development has increased since then, rather than decreased. Third, and most importantly, we must keep in mind that the Asia-Pacific region[2] cannot be

Table 8.1. Exhibition centres and indoor exhibition space by world region, 2006 and projection for 2010

World region	Exhibition centres 2006		Exhibition centres 2010		Indoor exhibition space 2006		Indoor exhibition space 2010	
	(no.)	(%)	(no.)	(%)	(million sq.m.)	(%)	(million sq.m.)	(%)
Europe	465	44	477	43	14.3	52	16.2	52
N. America	359	34	370	34	7.1	26	7.7	25
Asia	127	12	143	13	3.9	14	4.6	15
S. America	38	4	40	4	0.9	3	0.9	3
Middle East	32	3	33	3	0.6	2	0.9	3
Africa	25	2	24	2	0.5	2	0.6	2
Oceania	16	2	17	2	0.3	1	0.3	1
Total	1,062	101	1,104	101	27.6	100	31.2	101

Source: UFI 2007.

Notes: 1 square metre = 10.76 square feet; the data are based on UFI-approved exhibition centres and events and are thus very selective; care has to be exercised when interpreting absolute numbers; the data for 2010 are based on a projection of 2006 data.

treated as a homogeneous economic entity, exhibiting a homogeneous growth trajectory. The region is, in fact, highly diversified, with very different states of economic development and diverse, if not divergent, development paths.

The next section of this chapter describes the heterogeneous trade show business in the Asia-Pacific region, drawing on recent findings and discussions in the literature. We then turn to the case of China to illustrate the tremendous growth in trade show activity that has taken place since the mid-2000s. We present this case as an example of the dynamics that could also spill over to other Asian economies such as India in the short or medium term, or Thailand in the long term. Following this, two case studies of important national/international trade shows in Shanghai and Chengdu are investigated to demonstrate the rate at which Chinese trade shows can develop from an emergent stage into core places of knowledge circulation, network building, and idea generation. We conclude by suggesting that the initial focus of these events on imports, exports, and local/national trade direct sales may be quickly replaced as these trade shows become important focal points of the globalizing knowledge economy.

8.2. THE HETEROGENEOUS TRADE SHOW BUSINESS IN THE ASIA-PACIFIC REGION

This section illustrates the need to exercise care in making generalizations about the Asia-Pacific trade show business. Countries in the Asia-Pacific region represent very different stages of development and their trade shows reveal heterogeneous functions and opportunities. Although countries such as Japan and Australia are highly developed, and other countries such as Korea and Taiwan have caught up with the developed world, the overall Asian trade show business is clearly dominated by mainland China (see Table 8.2). Based on UFI data for 2008/9, China had eighty-seven exhibition centres with 3.6 million square metres of gross exhibition space and hosted 493 trade shows with an average size of over 15,000 square metres. According to all metrics, China was clearly ranked first within the Asia-Pacific region. It had more than half of all exhibition centres, two-thirds of the gross exhibition space, and one-third of the total number of trade shows in the Asia-Pacific region (UFI 2007). The average size of each show was twice as high as the Asian average and even larger than that in North America (Bathelt and Spigel 2012). Japan, Hong Kong, Korea, India, Australia, and Taiwan ranked far behind mainland China in these metrics. The discussion documents the enormous heterogeneity within the Asia-Pacific trade show business and briefly describes some of the reasons behind this diversity (see, for a detailed overview, Bathelt and Zeng 2014a).

Table 8.2. Number and size of trade shows and exhibition centres in the Asia-Pacific region by country, 2008/2009

Country	Exhibition centres	Total gross exhibition space	Trade shows identified	Average trade show size
	(no.)	(1000 sq.m.)	(no.)	(sq.m.)
China (mainland)	87	3,634.5	493	15,512
Japan	12	350.6	360	5,713
Hong Kong	3	151.9	85	9,676
Korea	12	223.3	146	5,108
India	12	257.5	131	5,294
Australia	8	115.2	165	3,092
Taiwan	4	105.4	62	7,395
Thailand	7	209.9	71	6,320
Singapore	4	203.6	69	3,322
Malaysia	4	71.3	47	4,750
Indonesia	3	31.7	41	3,927
Vietnam	4	33.8	47	2,995
Philippines	1	8.3	35	2,300
Macau	2	76.7	16	4,141
Pakistan	2	39.0	25	2,570
Total	165	551,2.7	1,793	8,003

Source: Beier and Damböck 2010: 40–1.

Notes: 1 square metre = 10.76 square feet; all data are estimated based on UFI data, as well as selected exhibition centres and events; care has to be exercised when interpreting absolute numbers.

8.2.1. Japan

Although Japan is the most highly developed economy in the Asia-Pacific region, its trade show business has remained relatively small. In 2008/9 it had a large number of events (360), but less than 10 per cent of the Asian indoor exhibition space (see Table 8.2). Trade shows in Japan are, on average, much smaller than those in China, which indicates that most Japanese events are not of international importance. In fact, despite a number of international trade shows, Japan has a strong tradition of local/regional shows in which regional policy plays an active role, to support regional industries and provide wider national market access for them (Yokura 2014). Trade shows in Japan are characterized as events that focus on intensive customer care, rather than places where sales are finalized or business is made (AUMA 2011). Although Japan is a leading industrial economy, it has remained somewhat difficult for foreign firms to access due to existing language barriers, as well as institutional and cultural specifics that are very different from Europe and North America. This is reflected in a relatively closed trade show business that shows signs of decline (UFI 2007).

8.2.2. Australia

Australia is also a highly developed economy in the Asia-Pacific region with limited trade show business (see Table 8.2). Most trade shows in 2008/9 were relatively small events with little international participation outside of industries where Australia's economy is strong, such as mining or pharmaceuticals. Australia's overall trade show business seemed to be stagnating and, to some degree, suffering from the rise of other Asia-Pacific economies. Although Australia benefits from its relative proximity to Asian economies and has become an important trading partner for China, the country may be in danger of losing its current position within the global economy, as European and North American multinationals and other firms are increasingly focusing on China and engaging less with the Australian market. As a consequence, Australia might develop into a 'new global periphery' that attracts little global attention in industries outside of its core economic areas.

Australia Fashion Week is a good example of this (Weller 2008) and demonstrates failed policy efforts to establish international market access. The Australian government unsuccessfully developed policies in the past to push Australia Fashion Week as a top export or international event. However, despite large government spending, international participation remained small and global attendees showed limited interest in the national fashion industry. While policy seemed to have overlooked supporting the development of national consumption and production, the case exemplifies the difficulties national industries have in gaining global market access. It appears that customer/user firms in Europe and North America have become more difficult to access for Australian industries, due to the latter's focus on other Asia-Pacific developments (Weller 2014).

8.2.3. Taiwan

Along with its impressive economic growth, Taiwan has developed a modern trade show business since the 1990s with some large well-known shows in areas such as computer/information technology, machine tools, and bicycles.[3] Although these do not have the character of flagship or leading-edge innovation shows, they play an important role in the Asian context and generate multiple learning opportunities for participating firms (Chen 2009). In the cases of computers, machine tools, and bicycles, they are linked to nearby production clusters that are embedded in global production chains (Dicken et al. 2001; Gereffi et al. 2005). State policies are designed to support trade shows that are related to strong value-chain contexts to stimulate learning and industrial upgrading in these chains (Chen 2011; Chang et al. 2014; Chen and Chu 2014). The goal is to utilize trade shows as a tool to support the transition from subcontract manufacturing to brand production.[4]

8.2.4. Singapore and Thailand

Singapore is a well-developed economy and an important hub for trade and corporate control functions for the entire South-East Asian market. Its economic growth is not based on endogenous industrial production functions, but rather relies on hub and gateway functions, with important harbour facilities and air transportation infrastructure. Because of its central location in South-East Asia, Singapore has become an important hub for trade shows that attracts attendees from neighbouring countries. Although not global in nature, these shows have a high degree of foreign participation, in terms of both visitors and exhibitors (Li 2014a). Yet, as other countries in the region, such as Thailand, are beginning to catch up in terms of economic development and establish their own national events, Singapore's role as a host for continental trade shows is increasingly challenged. Thailand, for instance, has the advantage of a stronger manufacturing base over Singapore and thus is a competitor in trade show activity for many industry groups (AUMA 2007).[5]

8.2.5. Other Developments in South and South-East Asia

Compared to Japan, Australia, Taiwan, and Korea, trade show development in South and South-East Asia is generally at an early stage. This includes trade show activity in countries such as Pakistan, Thailand, Indonesia, Malaysia, Vietnam, and the Philippines (AUMA 2007). Even India—another upcoming economic power in Asia—is lagging behind in terms of trade show activity (AUMA 2005). Although the country's trade show business is about the same size as that of Korea, Australia, and Taiwan (see Table 8.2), few events are truly international in character. Most trade shows in the 2000s were relatively small, with a largely regional/national orientation and a strong state influence (AUMA 2005). In many South and South-East Asian countries, the state plays an active role in the development of exhibition centres and in the trade show business in general.

In a comparative investigation of South and South-East Asian countries, Li's (2014) work provides important insights into the current and future trends of the trade show business. First, most trade shows in these countries are trade events that focus on actual selling activities and on negotiating contracts. In contrast, knowledge transfers are of lesser importance. Second, trade show specialization in the South and South-East Asian economies follows, to some degree, country-specific industrial specialization patterns. India, for instance, has a strong trade show presence in the food, textile, and metal/machinery industries, while Vietnam is strong in low-technology manufacturing, Thailand in metal/machinery, and Singapore in electronics (Li 2014a). Although many trade shows are regional or national in character, countries tend to develop a stronger presence in import fairs as their economies grow (e.g. Thailand and

Malaysia). This may indicate a development path from regional/national trade shows through a stage of import shows towards a stronger presence in international hub events, as the example of Singapore suggests (Li 2014a). Of course, such trends must be interpreted with caution as countries follow individual development paths, dependent on specific state influence and other contextual factors.

All of these developments are clearly outpaced by the exponential growth of trade show activity in mainland China since the 1990s—a topic which will be further explored in the next section.

8.3. RAPID TRADE SHOW DEVELOPMENT IN CHINA

Trade show growth in China has surpassed that in all other countries in the Asia-Pacific region. In 2008/9, exhibition centres in mainland China accounted for two-thirds of the Asia-Pacific region's total exhibition space, and trade shows were on average twice as large as in the Asia-Pacific region (see Table 8.2). This growth has largely occurred since the 1990s, because the establishment of China's trade show business began rather late.

The late start of trade show activity was due to the restrictive role of the state in organizing, controlling, and instrumentalizing trade shows. Prior to China's opening policy, the establishment of trade shows was driven by the goal of presenting the country favourably to the outside world and stimulating trade (Kay 2005). At that time, relatively small trade show centres with about 10,000 square metres of indoor exhibition space were built according to Russian conceptions and architecture. Such centres were established in Shanghai and Beijing, as well as in many other large Chinese cities. One exception to this was the establishment of the now famous Canton Fair or Export Commodities Trade Fair in Guangzhou in 1956 (known today as the China Import and Export Fair), in the south of China. The Canton Fair grew into one of the largest bi-annual trade shows worldwide, with about 10,000 exhibitors from China and 200,000 visitors from over 100 countries. Developed under the influence of close-by Hong Kong, it provided opportunities for Chinese producers to make contact with foreign buyers and for foreign buyers to order low-cost products in China (Powell 2007; Jin and Weber 2008). It was estimated that transactions during this event accounted for about one-quarter of China's overall exports in the early 2000s (Fu et al. 2007: 84).

Aside from the Canton Fair, trade show activity in China began to expand and develop further with Deng Xiaoping's opening policy in the 1980s. Trade shows were often jointly organized with organizers from Hong Kong or the USA, while larger ones were still under government control. In the period directly following the opening policy, foreign participation in Chinese trade shows grew rapidly. Firms from abroad attended trade shows as exhibitors to advertise and market their products in the country. It was not until Jiang Zemin's policies in the early 1990s, however, that large-scale convention/exhibition centres were systematically built. At this point, trade show centres were largely located in China's Coastal Special Economic Zones that had been established to attract foreign-direct investment. Shanghai, in particular, became an important centre of trade show activity in China (Kay 2005).

From the 1990s, trade and economic support policies at all levels of government led to a convention/exhibition centre building boom that continued into the late 2000s. While Hong Kong and relatively close-by Guangzhou were initially the dominating trade show locations, with a gateway function to connect foreign traders to Chinese producers (Powell 2007; Jin and Weber 2008), the trade show business quickly spread to other coastal cities and to Beijing. Shanghai, Beijing, and Guangzhou became the main cities of trade show activities. The combined number of trade shows in these three cities was 924 in 2007 and increased further to 1,204 in 2009 (AUMA 2008; Wang and Guo 2010). The overall number of trade shows in China, however, climbed even faster. Between 2009 and 2011 alone, the number of events grew from 4,600 to about 6,000 (Guo 2012).[6] Increasingly, events spread to inland and western Chinese cities, although Shanghai, Jiangsu, Beijing, Guangdong, and Zhejiang remained the core provinces of trade show activity. The results of this boom are shown in Table 8.3, which lists the Chinese cities with convention centres having at least 50,000 square metres of indoor exhibition space. Accordingly, the number of large facilities for trade shows, conventions, conferences, and exhibitions grew from thirty-one to thirty-eight between 2009 and 2011. This increase in the number of facilities went along with almost exponential growth in available exhibition space. The overall indoor exhibition space increased by more than a third (38.2 per cent) in these few years, from 2.5 to 3.4 million square metres.

In sum, the driving forces behind the exhibition/convention centre building boom in China included: (i) strong economic growth that led to a sharp increase in demand from the public and the private sector, (ii) state investments and tax incentives available for exhibition centre expansion, (iii) global mega events in China, such as the 2008 Beijing Olympic Games and the 2010 Shanghai World Expo (e.g. Nordin 2012), which directed additional state funds to the trade show business, and (iv) globalization and relocation processes of industries and trade shows from Europe to China (Kay 2005; Jin et al. 2010; Golfetto and Rinallo 2014).

All of these developments suggest that UFI data may overestimate the stability of global trade show geographies. The rapid development of trade show capacities in China during the 1990s and 2000s will undoubtedly have a strong impact on the global trade show business in the future, especially if other Asian economies follow China's lead. All of the large exhibition centres are easily accessible, have a modern infrastructure, and are well equipped, offering the necessary conditions to host sophisticated high-quality international events.

Table 8.3. Development of convention centres in China by location and size (indoor exhibition space ≥ 50,000 square metres), 2009–2011

City/province	Convention centres (no.)			Total indoor exhibition space (sq.m.)		
	2009	2010	2011	2009	2010	2011
Beijing[1]	3	2	2	236,600	173,000	173,000
Chengdu/Sichuan	1	2	2	55,000	165,000	143,000
Dalian/Liaoning[1]	1	–	–	79,300	–	–
Dongguan/Guangdong	1	1	1	100,000	100,000	100,000
Fuzhou/Fujian	–	1	1	–	80,000	80,000
Guangzhou/Guangdong	5	5	5	474,600	684,400	684,400
Guiyang/Guizhou	–	1	1	–	54,000	54,000
Hangzhou/Zhejiang	2	2	2	121,000	121,000	121,000
Harbin/Heilongjiang	–	1	1	–	56,500	56,500
Hefei/Anhui	–	1	1	–	120,000	120,000
Hohhot/Inner Mongolia[1]	1	–	–	57,000	–	–
Jinan/Shandong[1]	2	–	–	190,000	–	–
Jinhua/Zhejiang	1	2	2	100,000	193,200	193,200
Kunming/Yunnan[1]	1	–	–	70,000	–	–
Nanchang/Jiangxi[1]	1	–	–	75,000	–	–
Nanjing/Jiangsu	1	1	1	72,000	110,000	110,000
Nanning/Guangxi	1	1	1	80,000	65,800	65,800
Ningbo/Zhejiang	1	1	1	51,000	51,000	51,000
Qingdao/Shandong	–	1	2	–	59,000	179,000
Shanghai	1	3	3	126,500	271,800	345,500
Shenyang/Liaoning	–	1	1	–	105,200	105,200
Shenzhen/Guangdong	1	1	1	105,000	105,000	105,000
Shijiazhuang/Heibei	–	1	1	–	100,000	60,000
Suzhou/Jiangsu	–	2	2	–	131,000	131,000
Taizhou/Zhejiang[1]	1	–	–	65,100	–	–
Tianjin	–	–	1	–	–	56,200
Weifang/Shandong[1]	2	1	1	121,800	70,000	70,000
Weihai/Shandong[1]	1	–	–	80,000	–	–
Wuhan/Hubei	–	–	1	–	–	150,000
Xiamen/Fujian	1	1	1	80,000	60,000	60,000
Xi'an/Shaanxi	–	1	1	–	66,000	66,000
Xianyang/Shaanxi[1]	1	–	–	66,000	–	–
Zhengzhou/Henan	1	1	1	65,000	74,000	74,000
Zibo/Shandong	–	1	1	–	60,800	60,800
Total	31	35	38	2,470,900	3,076,700	3,414,600

Sources: Wang and Guo 2010; Guo 2011, 2012.

Notes: [1]The number of centres decreased in some cities between 2009 and 2011, as facilities were restructured for different uses; 1 square metre = 10.76 square feet.

The exhibition centre boom was particularly strong in the Shanghai region with the establishment of the Shanghai New International Expo Centre (SNIEC), which opened in 2001 (see Table 8.4). Between 2002 and 2011, the available indoor exhibition space of SNIEC almost tripled from 57,000 to over 150,000 square metres, while the turnover rate more than doubled. In 2011 the

Table 8.4. Number of trade shows, exhibitors and visitors, available exhibition space, and turnover rate of the Shanghai New International Expo Centre (SNIEC), 2002–2011

Year	Trade shows (no.)	Exhibitors (no.)	Visitors (millions)	Available exhibition space (sq.m.)	Turnover rate
2002	43	17,750	1.504	57,500	16
2003	45	22,350	1.641	57,500	18
2004	66	35,950	2.358	80,500	24
2005	67	46,400	2.547	80,500	29
2006	72	52,000	2.669	103,500	27
2007	78	58,750	3.102	103,500	30
2008	80	67,600	2,666	126,500	30
2009	78	61,750	2.838	126,500	28
2010	80	70,000	3,097	150,340	31
2011	94	81,700	4,047	150,340	32

Source: Geduhn 2012.

Notes: 1 square metre = 10.76 square feet; the turnover rate of a specific year measures the number of times the entire exhibition space is rented out in that year.

entire exhibition space was rented out thirty-two times. This is apparently one of the highest turnover rates in the world and more than twice as high as that of most European trade show centres (Bartsch 2012; Geduhn 2012). Along with this expansion, the number of annual trade shows increased from forty-three to ninety-four, while the number of visitors went from 1.5 to over 4 million (see Table 8.4).

Similar developments occurred in many other Chinese cities, generating a large number of new trade shows as well as attracting established trade show formats from older exhibition centres, for instance from Europe. Over time, cities in inland locations, such as Chengdu in Sichuan province, also developed a modern trade show infrastructure. Chengdu established a suburban exhibition centre that is connected to the city core through a new subway line. The Chengdu New International Exhibition & Convention Center consists of nine exhibition halls, covering 55,000 square metres of indoor exhibition space (Kay 2005; AUMA 2008). While media reports speculate about the need for consolidation as competition between different centres might increase, there is no indication of such developments at this point. In fact, expansion activities in trade show activity have continued in the early 2010s. In Shanghai, for instance, another (even larger) trade show centre is scheduled to be completed by 2015, close to Shanghai's former airport Hongqiao. With 400,000 square metres, the Hongqiao Convention and Exhibition Centre will have an indoor exhibition space larger than that of the SNIEC, elevating Shanghai to one of the world's top trade show locations in the future (Shi 2012).

8.4. EMERGENT CHINESE TRADE SHOW ECOLOGIES

Along with the exhibition/convention centre building boom,[7] the entire trade show business in China has changed. New, vibrant trade show ecologies have emerged and often challenge former trade show structures, which were characterized by inefficient organization and opportunistic management, as well as unprofessional participants (Skov 2006; Jin et al. 2010). Given the early stage of trade show development, one might expect regional/national sales events to dominate or strong import and export shows to develop in close connection to the wider industrial structure of the country. From this, it would appear that leading-edge innovation and knowledge creation processes only play only a minor role in the emergent trade show business in China (Young 2004; Jin et al. 2010). This would be very different from the large hub shows seen in Europe or North America (see Chapters 6 and 7).

As exemplified by the analysis of two important national/international events that follows (see Table 8.5), such expectations fail to appreciate the dynamic shifts in Chinese trade show activity. On the one hand, the fast growth of many consumer industries suggests that there is a need for modern trade shows that enable firms to connect with new markets, establish partnerships, and collect ideas for innovation. Due to this development, trade shows, such as 'Auto Shanghai', have become continental platforms in global industries for accessing Chinese and wider Asian markets (Bartsch 2011; Kong and Zhang 2014). On the other hand, economic growth in China generates a context within which trade shows play a key role to access new knowledge under conditions of high uncertainty regarding the type of knowledge needed and where to find it (Maskell 2014). The sales function of such events is no longer automatic or dominant, as trade shows are increasingly characterized by interaction patterns and knowledge circulation processes that are similar to leading events in Europe and North America.

Table 8.5. Number of exhibitors and visitors and exhibition space at case study trade shows in China, 2010

Trade show indicator	CIIF Shanghai	MWCS Shanghai	IG China Chengdu
Exhibition space (sq.m.)	103,500	34,500	12,000
Exhibitors (no.)	1,653	384	220
Overseas exhibitors (%)	34	35	9
Visitors (no.)	116,800	n.a.	10,000
Overseas visitors (%)	Small	Small	3

Sources: China International Exhibition 2010; China IIF 2011; Metalworking and CNC 2011.

Notes: CIIF = China International Industry Fair; MWCS = Metalworking and CNC Machine Tool Show; IG China = China International Exhibition on Gases Technology, Equipment and Application; 1 square metre = 10.76 square feet.

Both trade shows took place in November 2010: (i) the Metalworking and CNC Machine Tool Show (MWCS) in Shanghai and (ii) the China International Exhibition on Gases Technology, Equipment and Application (IG China) in Chengdu. MWCS was the key event of China's most important multi-sector industry trade show, the China International Industry Fair (CIIF), which took place in the SNIEC. As shown in Table 8.5, MWCS occupied a third of the exhibition space of CIIF with 34,000 square metres. The event was jointly organized by several national ministries and academies, as well as the city of Shanghai (China International Industry Fair 2011). IG China took place in the Chengdu New International Exhibition & Convention Center, and was organized by the national industry association of the gas industry (China International Exhibition 2010), with little state involvement. With an exhibition space of 12,000 square metres, the show was about a third of the size of MWCS. While MWCS had a very high proportion of overseas exhibitors (35 per cent), many of which originated from Europe, IG China had a much smaller share of foreign exhibitors at about 10 per cent. During the trade shows, an explorative study was conducted to characterize both events and analyse the nature of the interaction processes between different attendee groups. This involved systematic observation, as well as a total of seventy-eight semi-structured interviews, with a response rate of 93 per cent (Bathelt and Zeng 2014b).

8.4.1. Metalworking and CNC Machine Tool Show (MWCS), Shanghai

MWCS can be characterized as a machinery and manufacturing trade show, specializing in industrial machinery and equipment, CNC machine tools, plant engineering, and a wide range of metal-related and metal processing applications. The 2010 show was well organized and clearly not an event that focused on sales or trade activities. We found that the nature of knowledge exchange and interaction patterns was quite sophisticated and similar to comparable events in Europe. According to our interviews and observations, MWCS can be characterized as follows (Bathelt and Zeng 2014c).

1. The display of advanced technologies and presentation of latest innovations clearly played a smaller role at MWCS than in leading European events. During the interviews, foreign exhibitors mentioned that they did not show their most sophisticated innovations at MWCS and had smaller exhibits than in Europe or North America. Despite this, there was much discussion in the halls about new developments in the industry and innovation trends spotted by firms.

2. According to our interviews, direct sales activities did not stand out as the focal motivation behind trade show participation. Firms emphasized that MWCS was primarily an occasion to make direct customer contact with the Chinese market, from which sales could perhaps develop after the event. The

reasons to participate in the trade show were quite varied. About half of the exhibitors emphasized the desire to promote their brand in the Chinese market or strengthen their image. The other half were focused on establishing new customer contacts, instead of immediately selling their products.

3. Different from major exhibitions in Europe, the exhibition halls were not primarily set up for passive showcasing. Many firms had their equipment and machines in operation to demonstrate their performance. As a consequence, many parts of the exhibition halls were quite noisy and it was often difficult to understand what others were saying. The exhibition halls had the atmosphere of an actual workplace with the associated smells of oil and fumes and with heat development.

4. MWCS was not an export trade show. A large proportion of the visitors originated from the Yangtze Delta region, while exhibitors came from across China with a substantial proportion of international exhibitors (see Table 8.5). Yet, it would also be misleading to characterize MWCS as an import show. The participating firms insisted that the show was important because it provided them with an excellent overview of competition.

5. Aside from the official trade show schedule, another hidden, unofficial exhibition took place in the hallways. Here traders, representing Chinese firms from different parts of the country, were looking out for potential overseas customers. They were usually accompanied by employees with large bags or trollies, in which they carried sophisticated advertising materials and samples of the products they offered for sale on behalf of Chinese producers. They acted as knowledge brokers to catch the interest of international visitors and to connect with their clientele.

In sum, despite some differences, the nature of the conversations and interactions at MWCS was similar to that observed at European or North American trade shows. The classical roles of exhibitors and visitors were quite intermixed, however. On the one hand, many exhibitors spent a substantial amount of time looking through the exhibits in search of potential business or partners, and made direct contact with competitors. On the other hand, the exhibition hallways were used by traders who, disguised as visitors, represented producers from other Chinese regions to provide all sorts of information about their products to foreign visitors. The corresponding knowledge flows in either case were remarkably similar. This supports Maskell's (2014) implications, which would suggest strong knowledge exchange and knowledge creation processes at Chinese trade shows due to existing knowledge uncertainties.

8.4.2. China International Exhibition on Gases Technology, Equipment, and Application (IG China), Chengdu

IG China, which took place further inland in Chengdu, can be described as a specialized trade show for the gas industry, with a particular focus on the equipment side. Like MWCS, it was a well-organized professional event with little emphasis on actual trade or sales. In addition, neither exports nor imports played a significant role. Since the show was set in a mature industry context with many long-established firms that knew each other's product offerings well, innovation did not play a great role during the trade show. Three groups of exhibitors were identified that displayed different interaction patterns (Bathelt and Zeng 2014c):

The first group of exhibitors (half of the firms interviewed) were closely related to the core of the gas equipment business. They evaluated the show as a rare specialized event that enabled them to meet with their core customers. An important motivation for the firms was to reassure existing customers about their ongoing relationships. They also used the event to update their knowledge about direct competitors, systematically visit other exhibits, and talk to the corresponding personnel. As firms often had product portfolios that were partly overlapping, competitors were also important suppliers and/or customers. As a result, the exhibitors at IG China were, at the same time, visitors.

The second group of exhibitors (one-quarter of the firms) did not expect much from the event in terms of new business or knowledge about innovation; they were primarily there 'to show face'. Firms explained that IG China was helpful in developing and extending social relations with both existing customers and competitors. Relationship building was at the core of the agenda for these firms.

The third group of exhibitors (another quarter of the firms) were outside the main focus of the trade show and had come with different expectations. In contrast to what had been suggested by the show organizers, they did not meet large customer groups and had no business during the event. They thought IG China was not very helpful for them and questioned whether they would come again.

The findings about the different customer groups were supported by the fact that firms generally did not describe themselves as cost-oriented producers, but as quality/brand or performance-price ratio producers. The networking potential realized during IG China seemed to be particularly useful for small- and medium-sized firms, as it helped them stabilize their market position. Established firms enjoyed the specialized character of the show, which supported them in updating knowledge about the development of the Chinese market.

Overall, both trade shows support our hypothesis that modern trade show ecologies have emerged from within the fast growing Chinese economy that have developed structures similar to leading shows in Europe and North America. As suggested in the concluding section, these developments may pave the way for a vibrant and successful trade show business in other Chinese cities and across the Asia-Pacific region.

8.5. CONCLUSIONS

This chapter provides an overview of the Asia-Pacific trade show business, a topic which has, thus far, been largely neglected in the literature. The analysis shows that the Asia-Pacific region is the most dynamic contemporary global market region in terms of the trade show business. Despite the seeming stability in the global distribution of trade shows (UFI 2007), we observe strong growth processes related to both the establishment and expansion of convention/exhibition centres, as well as the number and size of events that take place. One must be careful in drawing general conclusions across the Asia-Pacific region, however, due to the large heterogeneity of economic structures and trade show developments across the various countries. Different trade show ecologies range from highly developed but stagnant activity in countries such as Japan and Australia to less-developed emergent shows in countries like India and Thailand. The most dynamic development can be observed in mainland China, which has become the leading trade show economy in the Asia-Pacific region.

The analysis reveals that trade shows in China are quickly developing into modern knowledge-intensive events with a similar structure to that at large shows in Europe and North America. The vertical, horizontal, and institutional cluster dimensions of these events enable an intensified circulation of information and knowledge, generating temporary global buzz (Bathelt and Schuldt 2010; see Chapter 3). Although sales activities and contract negotiations occur and are sometimes an important focus, as in the former Canton Fair, Chinese trade show ecologies are quickly changing. New modern exhibition facilities, such as those in Shanghai and Chengdu, host well-organized professional events. These develop into hotspots for knowledge exchange about new market and innovation trends in the industry, and are critical sites for relationship building. Although these events may not be focused on leading-edge innovation, processes such as knowledge transfers and circulation have gained substantial importance.

As economic development proceeds in the Asia-Pacific region, we can expect many trade show cities to emerge across several countries, with trade shows that develop from regional/national events into import or export shows, in which aspects of knowledge creation and circulation with respect to markets and technologies become increasingly significant. This brings forth a new era of polycentric and more localized knowledge circulation processes, characterized by a situation with key trade shows in each continent where manufacturers from different parts of the world present innovations that match specific local market needs (see Chapter 6). With continued growth, differentiated global trade show geographies will develop that are characterized by both increasing competition/rivalry between different exhibition centres and events, as well as an extended division of labour between global trade show locations.

NOTES

1. At present, however, there are no other databases that provide a complete overview of the Asian trade show business.
2. Here we include Australia and Oceania.
3. This is similar to some of the developments in Korea, where especially small- and medium-sized firms benefit from being visible to overseas visitors/exhibitors at international trade shows to strengthen their export performance (Kalafsky and Gress 2013a, 2014), albeit that these shows are primarily attended by a national/ East Asian audience (Kalafsky and Gress 2013b).
4. The goals of trade show-related policies changed over time, from ending the country's political and economic isolation to supporting industrial development, and finally creating incentives for the development of professional and 'creative services' (Chang et al. 2014).
5. The situation in Hong Kong is in many ways comparable with that in Singapore, as the city does not have a strong production base and loses some of its former functions as a gateway to mainland China. In China, different state levels from the central to municipal governments invest massively in the establishment of new and the expansion of established exhibition centres (Kay 2005). This seems to be partially driven by the political goal to draw away business from Hong Kong and to direct new business to major venues in Shanghai, Beijing, or Guangzhou.
6. The discrepancy between these numbers and the UFI statistics (see Table 8.1 and 8.2) suggests that it is necessary to exercise care in using these data.
7. This section is based on Bathelt and Zeng (2014c).

Part III

Specific Knowledge Generation Practices and Competition by Industry Group and Trade Show Type

9

Different Knowledge Practices in Hub Shows: The Cases of Lighting versus Meat Processing Technology

9.1. INTRODUCTION

In Part I we (i) developed a knowledge-based understanding of trade shows as temporary markets and temporary clusters and (ii) established a typology of trade shows that enables us to better understand the heterogeneity of knowledge flows during these events. Part II then applied these conceptions to investigate the global geographies of trade show ecologies and their dynamics. Part III builds on these discussions by analysing in more detail the different knowledge creation practices at trade shows and the competition between venues and events by effectively integrating Parts I and II.

As demonstrated in Chapter 2, trade shows have seen a dramatic change in focus over time, from places where products are traded to places where knowledge is exchanged. In this respect, the conceptions of the temporary cluster and the temporary market underscore two different perspectives (see Chapter 3), according to which knowledge circulation and transfer at trade shows are central to participating firms. The market perspective, on the one hand, focuses on how acquiring knowledge about consumer tastes and market changes brings firms together at these events. The technology or production perspective, on the other hand, is associated with knowledge that helps trade show participants find new partners, inquire about the latest innovation trends in products and production, and use other exhibits as benchmarks for self-evaluations. The leading international hub shows or flagship events are particularly significant in this respect because they generate, in the words of Rosson and Seringhaus (1995), a true microcosm of an industry and its most recent developments (Borghini et al. 2004).

This is especially important in the age of globalizing market structures, as such events localize the decentralized and varied product and technological developments within the closed temporal and material spaces of an exhibition, convention, or trade show venue. In doing so, leading international events have the capacity to generate decisive knowledge that may be used to establish, maintain, and govern new social and spatial divisions of labour across the globe. With intensified globalization processes, firms can no longer rely on traditional forms of geographical and socio-institutional proximity to generate decisive knowledge about markets and technologies (Bathelt and Glückler 2012); they also need to engage in major trade shows to determine long-term product and market strategies. Participation in these events also helps to organize and maintain widespread networks in innovation, production, and marketing, thereby reducing the necessity to be physically co-located with all the decentralized branches of the value chain.

As laid out in Chapter 4, hub shows create the primary temporary spaces of presentation and interaction of an entire industry or technology chain through the exhibition of global trends and developments (Rinallo and Golfetto 2011). They enable firms to engage in intense processes of interaction and observation over a few days to learn about industry and technology trends. These events become central meeting points for entire communities (Bathelt and Schuldt 2010) that help to maintain and reproduce these communities. Although they rarely have the character of field-configuring events in a more radical way as described by Lampel and Meyer (2008), they are nonetheless core events in the self-organization of technological fields and contribute to the reproduction and progression of these fields (Bathelt and Henn 2014).

This chapter presents empirical evidence of the various processes of knowledge dissemination and circulation during hub shows and suggests that these processes establish temporary clusters of knowledge circulation and generation. The processes are simultaneously decentralized and collective, and they have different structures depending on the type of event and industry group (Schuldt and Bathelt 2011). The next section introduces the two trade shows on which this chapter focuses: (i) Light and Building—International Trade Fair for Architecture and Technology (L + B), which has a strong design component, and (ii) the International Trade Fair for the Meat Industry (IFFA), which has a particular technology focus. The main section of this chapter analyses the different knowledge circulation and generation practices that result from the interactions of exhibitors with customers, competitors, suppliers, and other potential partners. Finally, some comments are made regarding the importance of global buzz and knowledge generation at hub shows.

9.2. L + B AND IFFA AS HUB SHOWS WITH A DIFFERENT DESIGN AND TECHNOLOGY FOCUS

Due to historical developments (see Chapter 2; Allix 1922), most hub shows take place in Europe, with a substantial number of them being located in Germany (see Chapter 6). The city of Frankfurt/Main, which hosts both events investigated in this chapter, is an important economic and financial centre in Germany and has become one of the most important locations for hub shows in the country. In 2003, Frankfurt/Main hosted twenty-four internationally leading trade shows, including the World Forum of the Process Industry (ACHEMA), the International Motor Show for Passenger Cars (IAA), and the Frankfurt Book Fair (Buchmesse). In 2003, for instance, a total of 40,295 exhibitors presented their products at these three shows alone, and more than 2.4 million visitors came to see and examine the exhibits (Messe Frankfurt GmbH 2003; AUMA 2004c). The two hub events, L + B and IFFA, are leading business-to-business trade shows in their respective industries, and are characterized by a high degree of internationalization. The majority of visitors and exhibitors at both shows are affiliated with international firms and organizations (see Table 9.1).

Although L + B and IFFA may not be representative of all hub shows, they are two major international flagship or reference events that mirror the breadth and dynamics of their respective industries, as well as the importance of localized processes of knowledge circulation and creation during such events.

Table 9.1. Number of exhibitors and visitors by origin and rented exhibition space at L + B and IFFA, 2004

Indicator	L + B	IFFA
Number of exhibitors	1,920 (100.0%)	852 (100.0%)
– German exhibitors	827 (43.1%)	433 (50.8%)
– Foreign exhibitors	1,093 (56.9%)	419 (49.2%)
– Important countries of origin of foreign exhibitors	Italy, Spain, France, Austria, Netherlands, as well as China, Taiwan	Italy, France, Spain, Netherlands, USA
Number of visitors	116,000 (100.0%)	57,000 (100.0%)
– German visitors	32,500 (28.0%)	22,000 (38.5%)
– Foreign visitors	83,500 (72.0%)	35,000 (61.5%)
– Important countries of origin of foreign visitors	Benelux, Italy, UK, Austria, France, Spain	Spain, Italy, Netherlands

Sources: Messe Frankfurt GmbH 2004a, 2004b, 2004d, 2004e.

Notes: L + B = Light and Building—International Trade Fair for Architecture and Technology; IFFA = International Trade Fair for the Meat Industry.

9.2.1. Light and Building—International Trade Fair
for Architecture and Technology (L + B)

L + B takes place every two years. In 2000, it spun off from the Hanover Industrial Fair, which is another hub show and one of the most important industry and technology trade shows worldwide. L + B brings together suppliers, producers, customers, and their respective competitors in the areas of lighting (technical and decorative lighting and accessories, as well as lamps), electrical engineering (cables and leads, electrical installation equipment, network technology, industrial controls and safety systems), and house and building automation. In 2004, 1,920 firms exhibited their products at L + B, 57 per cent of which were from other countries, such as Italy, Spain, France, the Netherlands, Austria, China, and Taiwan (see Table 9.1). A total of 116,000 people came as visitors. The fact that more than 70 per cent of the visitors came from outside of Germany, from countries such as Benelux, Italy, the UK, Austria, France, and Spain, exemplifies the global hub character of this event (Messe Frankfurt GmbH 2004a, 2004b, 2004c). Many of the products exhibited at L + B are design-intensive consumer goods directed towards particular aesthetic or symbolic needs. The discussion will focus on these product groups. Nevertheless, the show also includes product groups in which technological aspects dominate, as in the area of house and building automation.

9.2.2. International Trade Fair for the Meat Industry (IFFA)

IFFA was established as an international trade show in 1949 and takes place every three years. Although smaller than L + B, it is one of the world's leading trade shows in the area of meat production and processing. It shows products and technologies that cover all stages of the value chain, such as slaughtering and carving machines, processing equipment, boiling and smoking systems, packaging and transport technologies, as well as meat processing utilities. The show is centred on capital goods, in which Germany has particular strengths and large exports. Both shows, L + B and IFFA, developed out of the manufacturing strength of the German economy, although the respective industries are not especially concentrated in the Frankfurt region.[1] Design-related aspects of exhibits at IFFA are less important than technological features and aspects of practicality in handling them. In 2004, 852 firms exhibited their products at this hub event, almost half of which originated from foreign countries, such as Italy, France, the Netherlands, Spain, and the USA (see Table 9.1). Also, more than 60 per cent of the 57,000 visitors were from Spain, Italy, the Netherlands, and other countries (Messe Frankfurt GmbH 2004d, 2004e, 2004f).

Based on a random-sampling procedure that included some of the dominant key accounts in the industry, 142 interviews were conducted with owners, leading marketing managers, product developers, and engineers of exhibiting firms, accompanied by a questionnaire. The questions asked focused on the interaction practices of exhibitors with their customers, suppliers, competitors, and other firms. A comprehensive study of the two trade shows (see Bathelt and Schuldt 2008) indicates that the exhibitors at these events include a large variety of differently structured firms, such as large and small as well as mature and new firms. Both hub shows focus on traditional industries that have been established for a long time period, with market leaders being among the largest and oldest firms.

9.3. KNOWLEDGE CIRCULATION AND COMMUNICATION PRACTICES AT HUB SHOWS

In general, we observed a clear hierarchy of goals associated with participation in the two trade shows (see Table 9.2). As expected, interaction with customers was the most important incentive for firms to participate in L + B and IFFA. Over 60 per cent of the interviewees mentioned that the most important goals for participating in the events were related to (i) informing customers about their presence, (ii) making new customer contacts, and (iii) maintaining and intensifying contact with existing customers. These reasons were followed by the goal of presenting innovations: about 30 per cent of the firms at IFFA and over 40 per cent at L + B highlighted the innovation focus of the shows (also AUMA 1996, 1999). In contrast, the traditional sales function was seemingly

Table 9.2. Goals of trade show participation at L + B and IFFA, 2004

	Firm responses at L + B		Firm responses at IFFA	
Goal of trade show participation	No. ($n = 51$)	%	No. ($n = 51$)	%
Being there	33	64.7	34	66.7
Making new customer contact	31	60.8	32	62.7
Dealing with existing customers	31	60.8	25	49.0
Presentation of innovations	21	41.2	16	31.4
Sales and orders	4	7.8	1	2.0
Accessing new markets	–	–	4	7.8

Source: Survey results.

Notes: L + B = Light and Building—International Trade Fair for Architecture and Technology; IFFA = International Trade Fair for the Meat Industry.

Table 9.3. Importance of contact with customers, competitors, and suppliers at L + B and IFFA, 2004

Firm type	Median importance of contacts with other firms[1]	
	at L + B	at IFFA
Existing customer	1	1
Potential customer	1	1
Competitor	2	3
Existing supplier	3	5
Potential supplier	4	5

Source: Survey Results.

Notes: L + B = Light and Building—International Trade Fair for Architecture and Technology; IFFA = International Trade Fair for the Meat Industry.

[1] Measured at an ordinal scale from 1 (very important) to 6 (unimportant).

less important at these events. Although the large firms, in particular, indicated an interest in arranging sales and signing contracts while at the show, about 95 per cent of all firms interviewed mentioned that this was not the main reason for participating in the event.

Interaction with other firms, though characterized by a clear downstream focus, was widely split across different firms and actor groups (see Table 9.3). Customer interaction was clearly the most important type of interaction, but not the only one. Direct and indirect contact with competitors was also highly ranked, while contact with suppliers was deemed to be less important. This is not to suggest, however, that supplier and competitor interaction was of little or no value at the events. Despite the dominance of customer contacts, the following analysis shows that systematic interaction with competitors, suppliers, and complementary firms was also critical in obtaining an overview of the market, making comparisons, and gaining access to new materials.

9.3.1. Interaction with Customers

Customer contact was certainly the core focus of the exhibitors, and they typically contacted existing customers before the show to inform them about their presence and invite them to visit the exhibits. This was often done in a standardized way, in the form of a mass email for instance. But specific customers were also contacted individually and were invited to dinners or other events. While it was less common to make appointments with exhibitors at L + B, the situation at IFFA was different. Here, it was often necessary to make appointments in advance, as conversations about technical specifics required the presence of specialists during the show.

(i) Interaction with potential future customers

Meetings with potential customers were characterized by two different types of communication. In the first case, firms simply passed by other producers' exhibits to inquire in a general way about the production programme and its characteristics. At L + B, for instance, information about price and delivery conditions was typically circulated during such encounters and business cards were exchanged. The second, less frequent, type of communication style involved specific inquiries about possible solutions to the problems or specific needs firms had. This second type of meeting was more interesting and potentially valuable for exhibitors because it served as a basis for future interactions and transactions. This was especially important in technology contexts such as those found at IFFA. Such contacts serve as pre-conditions for and strong leads to the development of trans-local pipelines with new partners (Maskell et al. 2006; Bathelt and Schuldt 2008).

(ii) Interaction with existing customers

There were also two types of meetings that took place with existing customers: discussions of particular circumstances of business relations and exchanges of general information to intensify the relations. In the first case, the communication between firms assumed the character of negotiations and took place in a separate facility to create an atmosphere of privacy and intimacy, used, for instance, for contract negotiations. While the importance of capital goods shows as places where orders are made and contracts signed appears to be decreasing (Backhaus 1992; Meffert 1997), large firms and market leaders, in particular, reported substantial orders from their customers (also Power and Jansson 2008).

In the second case, general knowledge about markets and technological innovations within the industry was exchanged. Although mostly generic in character, such interaction enabled exhibitors to accumulate knowledge about customer needs and to detect market and technology trends. Sometimes, the firm representatives have known one another for many years and also exchanged private information. As trust developed over time in these relations, the corresponding knowledge flows were detailed and multiplex in nature (Uzzi 1997). Customer-specific adjustments, as well as other specific inquiries, were typically discussed at greater length after the show was finished.

(iii) Circumstances of getting together

Most of the producer–user interaction at L + B and IFFA occurred during the official trade show hours. Usually, initial contacts were made or meetings held at the producers' exhibits. In a few cases, where firms had introduced complex new machines and equipment to the market, customers were even invited to visit the producer's development centre to see how the machines operated under regular working conditions. At IFFA, one firm had organized helicopter flights to facilities in a neighbouring country for this purpose. This was not only preferable to having all the equipment transported to the exhibition hall, but it also created an initial pledge of commitment between the parties.

About 70 per cent of the exhibitors also wanted to meet with customers for dinners and other informal events in the evenings to discuss design variations and various technological aspects in a more relaxed atmosphere. Rather than focusing solely on business, such meetings were often intended as a more casual get-together. Not all exhibitors were interested, however, in meeting customers after trade show hours. Some looked forward to some time off at the end of a long trade show day. Those who did not recognize the value of informal meetings with customers did not view after-hours socializing as an opportunity to intensify existing contacts. Some firms at L + B aimed to meet foreign customers with whom contact was not as intensive throughout the year. Such meetings helped them to get to know one another on a personal basis. Interviewees indicated that they tested out how they fit with their business partners and whether they would 'share the same chemistry'.

There were substantial differences in how informal meetings with customers were structured. Large exhibitors typically organized evening events with customers, often including an artistic or musical programme. Small- and medium-sized firms (especially those at L + B) were more spontaneous in meeting with their customers and more interested in getting to know them on a personal basis. Large internationally organized firms also used trade shows to organize intra-firm meetings—as a forum to bring together personnel from different locations and countries. The idea was to engage managers in an exchange of experiences from different market contexts, support the formation of stronger bonds, and enable the development of solidarity (also Backhaus and Zydorek 1997; Kirchgeorg 2003). Through this, employees established personal networks within their corporate context that were later used when questions or problems arose.

About half of the respondents emphasized that they also had unexpected or accidental meetings with customers during important trade shows. Not surprisingly, the opportunity for unplanned meetings depended to some degree on how often firms participated in such events and how well networked they were. Overall, firms at L + B and IFFA indicated that 50 to 80 per cent of all customer contacts were with existing customers, the remaining being with potential future customers.

(iv) Customer information through third parties

Exhibitors also acquired information about potential customers through inter-action with third parties. Most firms noted that information flows through third parties occurred very regularly during the events. In order to make full sense of such information, firms needed to be experienced and know how to interpret the content of the respective conversations.

In addition, important information about customers was acquired through scanning the exhibits of other firms. This enabled firms to get ideas about trends in designs, innovation, and customer taste (e.g. AUMA 1999). Personal inspection of customers' exhibits allowed firms to gather experience that could not be acquired through conversations alone (Backhaus and Zydorek 1997; Goehrmann 2003a). Overall, the enormous amount of information, reports, opinions, and rumours during L + B and IFFA established a rich global buzz (Maskell et al. 2006; Bathelt and Schuldt 2010).

In earlier work, Prüser (1997) suggested that customer contacts during trade shows have potential long-term advantages for the exhibitors. Although our study confirms this argument, many firms did not openly acknowledge the importance of long-term effects. They pointed at another advantage of trade shows, however, in that firms were able to meet customer groups with whom direct contact was rare in day-to-day operations (e.g. Backhaus 1992; Prüser 2003). During L + B, for instance, producers of luminaires intensively exchanged ideas with architects, whom they would not normally meet. Others tried to get media coverage by actively making contact with representatives of national and international media.

Differences in the value of trade shows for the exhibitors seemed to be related to the character of customer communication in the respective indus-tries. While exhibitors at IFFA had frequent personal contact with their users throughout the year to guarantee smooth production, L + B exhibitors had fewer regular contacts and thus relied on the trade show as a forum for interaction.

9.3.2. Interaction with Competitors

Aside from customer interaction, trade shows provide unique opportunities to exchange knowledge with or acquire knowledge about competitors. Leading technology and innovation shows are, in fact, the most direct and fastest way to obtain an overview of the market and competitive environment (Rosson and Seringhaus 1995). Still, our analysis indicated that not all firms acquire such knowledge in the same systematic way. On the one hand, the small firms inter-viewed rarely had enough personnel at their exhibits to thoroughly scan and observe their competitors' products. On the other hand, some of the important market leaders had a great deal of self-confidence and thus did not spend much time observing peers. There seemed to be a tendency, particularly among the latter group of firms, to question the importance of trade shows in this respect. Our impression was that such firms could overlook less visible but significant trends or specific developments in the market, and thus miss market opportunities, by not spending more time on thoroughly analysing competition during the shows.

(i)   Direct competitor contact

Direct contact with competitors usually took place during trade show hours, as firm representatives visited the exhibits of their peers. Typically, such meetings involved short conversations about general business conditions and developments in the industry (also Dahl and Pedersen 2003). When approaching other exhibits, firm representatives had the choice of whether to introduce themselves or approach their competitors' exhibits incognito to 'spy out' certain information. While some firms said that the latter was common practice, others insisted that they would never conduct such business practices and would always wear visible firm tags. Among established small- and medium-sized firms, in particular, treating competitors in a fair manner seemed to be part of the code of conduct.[2]

The different types of interaction with competitors also depended on the specific industry context and the nature of competition. During IFFA, direct meetings with competitors were rare and information exchange was limited because of fierce competitive conditions in many industry segments. In contrast, information exchange with competitors seemed to be more open at L + B. Attendees were more relaxed and did not hesitate to talk to competitors, or share food and drinks with representatives from other firms on close-by exhibits. This openness was, in part, related to the fact that the lighting industry is highly segmented and differentiated. Especially small- and medium-sized firms often concentrate on particular market segments and have only partial market overlap. In such design-intensive industry groups, producer flexibility is also greater than, for instance, in the area of producing meat processing machines.

(ii)   Competitor information through third parties

Firms at both trade shows also received important information about the actions and strategies of their competitors by talking to customers and other firms (also Kirchgeorg 2003). Such knowledge flows did not necessarily have the character of passing on secrets. Rather, they were usually fairly general in nature, but served to round out the picture that firms already had of their competition. Comments made by third parties about the products of competitors, for instance, helped conclusions to be drawn about those firms' strengths or weaknesses.

(iii) Learning through observation and comparison

The most direct way to obtain information about competitors was simply to visit and inspect their exhibits. Through this, firms got to know about their competitors' products, modifications, input materials, as well as visions and future plans (also Strothmann 1992; Prüser 1997; Fuchslocher and Hochheimer 2000). This information provided firms with an opportunity to evaluate their own products and technological progress in relation to that of others through a benchmarking process. Because of the high density and omnipresence of multiple verbal and non-verbal cues at such events, hub shows play an important role in relation to and as a complement to other marketing instruments (also Backhaus and Zydorek 1997; Meffert 2003).

Some firms interviewed at L + B and IFFA viewed the opportunity to observe their rivals during trade shows as even more important than connecting with existing or new customers—although these might be extreme cases. Systematic scanning and analysis of other exhibits are generally important tasks because they enable firms to evaluate their own products better. From this, important conclusions on strategic decisions regarding future investments and product policies can be derived or supported. Unlike the exhibitors at IFFA, who had more regular contacts with competitors and their products during day-to-day operations, respondents at L + B mentioned that the trade show would be the only opportunity for them to get a full overview of their competition.

While some literature suggests that exhibitors keep new knowledge about technological developments secret prior to the show and then launch them during the show (Dahl and Pedersen 2003; Goehrmann 2003b), firms are usually well informed about the actions of their competitors and have some prior knowledge, even if this does not include all of the specific details. Of course, the most novel products and solutions are key issues of debate during a trade show. Such discussions are critical for firms to evaluate the importance of these innovations.

9.3.3. Interaction with Complementary Firms

In addition, firms at L + B and IFFA also acquired information about complementary firms operating in different countries and/or related market segments. Making contact with these firms was useful when looking for potential partners, for instance, in joint marketing campaigns or joint sales arrangements. To find an appropriate, capable, and reliable partner was especially important for firms who intended to enter new markets in a different country, especially a country with limited market transparency and uncertainty regarding the knowledge available and needed (Maskell 2014). Firms with limited experience in foreign markets were particularly likely to use trade shows as an opportunity to pre-select potential partners and make initial contact with them. The firms at L + B and IFFA often developed such contacts over several consecutive trade shows, using the sequence of such related events (Power and Jansson 2008) to get to know potential partners better over a longer time period. Through regular attendance at international trade shows, latent networks can develop, which can be activated and used when needed (Maskell et al. 2006).

9.3.4. Supplier Interaction

As opposed to customer and competitor interaction, contacts with suppliers were less important for exhibitors at L + B and IFFA (see Table 9.3). Consequently, they spent less time and effort dealing with existing and potential suppliers. This occurred despite the fact that the trade shows included firms in virtually all stages of the value chain, offering plenty of opportunities for interaction with relevant suppliers. The reason for the limited significance of supplier interaction was that the focus of the firms was primarily oriented downstream towards their customers.

Despite this, lots of direct contact occurred, as suppliers that were either exhibitors themselves or attended as visitors systematically visited the exhibits of existing and potential customers. Although this did not normally lead to in-depth discussions, it helped stabilize producer–user linkages and establish new ones. In fact, most firms at L + B and IFFA said that it was advantageous to also have personal contacts with suppliers during the show. Design-oriented small- and medium-sized firms, in particular, seemed to be interested in having access to innovative suppliers from different countries. Many interviewees mentioned that the high density of suppliers during the event would provide a multitude of opportunities to make such contacts. Through further scanning after the show, they would be able to identify appropriate potential partners for future collaboration.[3] It seems clear, however, that many firms did not fully exploit the potential to acquire knowledge about suppliers during the two trade shows.

9.4. CONCLUSIONS

This chapter provides evidence that hub trade shows are crucial temporary clusters that enable intensive processes of knowledge circulation and acquisition along several dimensions, involving customers, competitors, suppliers, complementary firms, multipliers, media, and third parties. Hub shows are reference events where firms intentionally present their new products, designs, and ideas and receive feedback for further improvements in return. Often research and development cycles are timed and scheduled in a way that allows producers to launch important innovations for the first time at these events. As such, these events function as predefined deadlines for the creation of new products, machines, or designs. Communication with specialists from the same or related technology fields during the shows helps to develop new ideas and strategies for production and innovation, identify specialists for the solution of particular problems, or find partners when expanding into new market regions. Flagship events, such as L + B and IFFA, thus provide opportunities to establish new and deepen existing networks. Intensive interaction and observation enable learning processes that stimulate knowledge generation. Through this, hub shows become catalysts for spotting, as well as setting, important trends.

With their focus on cutting-edge innovation, industrial leadership, and the presentation of global industry trends, the knowledge circulation practices and interaction patterns during hub shows are different from those at import, export, or regional shows—even though the general pattern of vertical and horizontal communication is similar (see Chapter 4). It is the hub show type that produces truly global buzz as discussed in Chapter 3. The multiplicity and intensity of meetings between firms with a similar technology focus is a direct consequence of the opportunities of geographical proximity and face-to-face interaction generated during the trade show. Firms do not need to make specific commitments or additional investments to initiate contacts with others. Yet they are unlikely to miss important developments if they pay attention and listen to the myriad of comments, evaluations, and gossip they hear during such hub shows.

This chapter indicates that hub shows as temporary clusters have become central nodes in the global political economy (Bathelt and Zakrzewski 2007). Their significance has increased with the progression of globalization processes. As discussed in the next chapter, different regional, national, and international trade shows occurring around the globe form a sequence of events and portray a catalogue of opportunities from which firms can select what best fits their business goals and strategies. Some, but not all, of these events are closely connected with one another. They are partially overlapping, yet at the same time serve different purposes within their technology field. Therefore, the goals of participation and the nature of the events differ from each other.

NOTES

1. This situation is similar to that of many other hub shows in Germany. While leading events like IAA, ACHEMA, and Buchmesse certainly have a strong regional industry base in the larger Frankfurt region, they are international or

      global in their orientation. They are not just events that showcase regional industry strengths and have not developed with this purpose (see Chapters 2 and 4).

2. Of course, the common observation of people illegally taking photos of other exhibits was another matter.

3. Many interviewees pointed out, however, that they would much prefer a separate trade show specialised in materials and supplies over a full-coverage show. This would allow them to dedicate more time to communicating with existing and potential new suppliers.

10

Cyclical Meetings or Field Reproduction? Knowledge Practices at International Lighting Shows

10.1. INTRODUCTION

Trade shows are important places for promoting, advertising, and selling products to wider markets (Skov 2006; Power and Jansson 2008). Yet they are also temporary places where important knowledge is exchanged about relevant industry or technology fields. This latter function is captured in the concepts of the temporary cluster and the temporary market (see Chapter 3), both of which develop a knowledge perspective in understanding the role of trade shows as catalysts for knowledge flows between distant firms (Borghini et al. 2004; Maskell et al. 2006; Bathelt and Schuldt 2010).

While the discussion of temporary clusters emphasizes the fact that agents of a particular value chain or technology field come together for a few days to engage in intensive communication and observation, it is important to keep in mind that the respective groups of firms, executives, managers, and technical specialists are involved in ongoing interaction processes that extend beyond the actual events and are connected through wider knowing communities (Cohendet et al. 2013). Aside from contacts through conferences and internet social networks, these agents attend multiple trade shows in different regions and countries on a regular basis—often many times per year (e.g. Norcliffe and Rendace 2003). The recurring character of such meetings is at the centre of the concept of 'cyclical clusters' (Power and Jansson 2008), which highlights the sequencing and connectedness of knowledge generation processes across trade shows in different places.

This chapter uses this conceptualization as a starting point to explore the relationships among trade shows in one specific technology field, namely, the lighting industry that was already part of the discussions in Chapter 9. At present, empirical evidence on the nature of knowledge flows across cyclical events is scarce (Schuldt and Bathelt 2011) and based on only a small number of observations.

Through a comparison of three important international business-to-business trade shows centred on the lighting and related industries, this chapter systematically analyses the goals and purposes of these events, the role and nature of knowledge exchanges, as well as dynamic changes of these events. The latter aspect is important as trade shows that were once complementary may, under different technological, economic, and regulatory conditions, begin to compete with one another (Rinallo and Golfetto 2011).

This chapter examines the following three trade shows: (i) Light and Building (L + B) 2004, Germany, (ii) IIDEX/NeoCon Canada 2008, Canada, and (iii) LightFair International 2009, US. The analysis is based on systematic observations and interviews conducted with exhibiting firms during these events.[1] Before presenting the results of the empirical analysis, the next section uses the literature on cyclical clusters and field-configuring events as a starting point to demonstrate the importance of defining trade shows as loosely connected events through which knowledge flows occur. In doing so, we suggest that these flows contribute to decentralized processes of ongoing field reproduction. The empirical results support this interpretation.[2]

10.2. FIELD REPRODUCTION IN TRADE SHOW SEQUENCES

While the definition of a temporary or 'periodic social economy' (e.g. Norcliffe and Rendace 2003) applies to almost every kind of trade show, investigations in management studies have recently referred to trade shows within the context of so-called 'field-configuring events' (FCEs) (Lampel and Meyer 2008). These are understood as events that have a substantial, sometimes radical impact on an entire industry and/or technology field. The term has been used to describe hierarchically organized events in periods of radical technological change, which serve to establish joint visions and understandings of a new technology and its future directions, as described, for example, by Garud (2008) and Möllering (2010). Lampel and Meyer's (2008) actual definition of such field-configuring events, however, is relatively vague and could be applied to almost all large trade shows in most industries.

In the case of some specific trade shows, the concept of 'field-configuring events' might prove more valuable, however. The literature on fabric/textile fashion shows (Entwistle and Rocamora 2006; Rinallo and Golfetto 2006), for instance, provides excellent case studies of how certain events not only impact, but even generate, entire fashion trends through a process that has been coined 'concertation' (Rinallo and Golfetto 2006). The functioning of concertation is related, in particular, to the role of powerful industry associations and trade show organizers that arrange, well in advance, a process of consensus-building about trends in materials, colours, and design schemes for the next fashion season (see Chapter 12). This consensus is later translated into code books that are widely distributed to the participants of the respective events. These code books become the basis for new fashion products that are developed by firms and are exhibited at upcoming fashion shows. What appears to be an emerging fashion trend is thus, in fact, the outcome of an organized, directed concertation process that configures the specific development of the future field of the industry.

Yet not all trade shows operate in such a manner. While organizers always have an impact on who is allowed to participate, how the exhibits are organized and presented, and which firms have a central or peripheral role at an event (see Chapter 5), they rarely control the knowledge circulation processes in such a substantial and planned manner. In many large industry shows, key knowledge flows occur in a decentralized fashion resulting from the myriad of interactions, observations, and discussions of the participants. In other words, they are not pre-structured in a hierarchical manner. In fact, few shows shape an industrial or technological field in the same path-breaking way that is implied by the concept of field-configuring events. Most trade shows impact their field in more decentralized, less predictable, and incremental ways; they are not associated with the same degree of technological uncertainty as is assumed in most research on field-configuring events. In addition, it is almost impossible to recognize an event as having field-configuring properties before it actually takes place and unravels its dynamics. Indeed, field-configuring events can only be identified after the fact, as the participants may or may not follow the suggestions and directions of the organizers. Möllering (2010) provides interesting insights into such processes in the case of a technology-focused engineering conference that developed quite differently from what was originally planned.

As Power and Jansson (2008) correctly point out, trade shows can hardly be viewed as singular events given that each industry has many different trade shows occurring in different countries and regions. This establishes a cycle of shows where overlapping technical communities meet and exchange knowledge about their industry/technology, its changes, and challenges. While Power and Jansson (2008) illustrate an interesting case of such interrelationships in the furniture industry, events in many other industries are, however, not necessarily connected in such a way. Many industry and technology fields are characterized by a myriad of trade shows, ranging from hub shows to import or export shows, and from global to national, regional, or local events (see Chapter 5). Even if we only take into account events with substantial international participation, there are comparable events in different places around the world that dramatically differ in terms of their focus and goals. It is hard to imagine that there would be much overlap, for instance, in terms of the individual participants who attend these events. Some small- and medium-sized firms attend only a few selected events centred on their home market. And while global players typically present at most of these major events, they often send different people with different specializations in order to match the shows' specific functions and needs. It is unlikely that all forms of trade show-related knowledge from all these events would be systematically collected by and fully exploited throughout a multinational corporation. While radically new knowledge is certainly transmitted through large corporate organizations, most forms of tacit and contextual knowledge do not easily spread through such channels.

This is clearly the situation found in the lighting industry to be described here; yet it is also typical for other industry settings. In these cases, it may be more appropriate to characterize trade shows as field-*reproducing*, instead of field-*configuring*, events because they shape and reshape the development of firm, industry, and technology fields in ongoing, often incremental ways. This occurs in a decentralized form from one event to the next, rather than through top–down agenda-setting. There is, of course, some degree of overlap with respect to the sets of firms and sometimes even the executives or technological specialists attending such events. This type of overlap is limited, however. Consequently, knowledge flows remain relatively localized and do not spread systematically. Nonetheless, they do contribute to ongoing field reproduction as important innovations, market trends, and regulatory changes are recurrent topics at all types of trade shows and spread to different corporate branches and localities around the world. These processes are important for the entire industry/ technology field and for large multinational corporations as they reduce the need for constant meetings and organized exchanges to keep everyone informed about the important developments in the technology field. The multiplicity of trade shows generates many opportunities for participants to be engaged in decentralized, yet consistent, forms of creating meaning, instead of merely following centralized interpretations.

While this chapter does not provide a detailed investigation of the latter aspects of sense-making processes, it compares the general nature of different trade shows, the goals of participation, the knowledge exchanges, and the dynamics of these events in the lighting industry. Based on this, we identify differences between the shows, highlighting the limited number of relationships and the lack of direct knowledge flows across the events. The results clearly show that these events should not be considered as *configuring* their respective fields in discontinuous ways; rather, they contribute to ongoing field *reproduction*.

10.3. LIGHTING SHOWS IN EUROPE AND NORTH AMERICA

In this analysis, we focus on the purposes and knowledge circulation practices of three international trade shows in the lighting industry. We also investigate linkages between the events that could be part of a wider trade show cycle in the lighting industry. The trade shows analysed are: (i) Light and Building 2004 in Frankfurt/Main (Germany), the global flagship show in the lighting industry, (ii) IIDEX/NeoCon Canada 2008 in Toronto (Canada), Canada's central lighting show, and (iii) LightFair International 2009 in New York (US), the leading lighting show in North America.

10.3.1. Light and Building—International Trade Fair for Architecture and Technology, Germany (L + B)

As opposed to the two North American shows, L + B is not an annual but a bi-annual event that takes place close to downtown Frankfurt/Main. It is a truly global show, attracting visitors and exhibitors from every continent. At the time of our study, L + B was clearly the largest of the three shows, with 1,920 exhibitors and about 116,000 visitors (Messe Frankfurt GmbH 2004a, 2004b, 2004c). The exhibition space was many times the size of that of the other shows. As discussed in Chapter 9 in more detail, the hub character of L + B and its importance as a key industry event becomes visible when looking at the geographical origins of attendees (see Table 10.1). As such, L + B clearly is the leading global show in the industry, mirroring global demand and supply changes (also Rosson and Seringhaus 1995), as well as showcasing the latest technological and design innovations (Bathelt and Schuldt 2005, 2008).

Table 10.1. Number of exhibitors and visitors at international lighting shows by origin, 2004–2009

Indicator	L + B	IIDEX	LightFair
Exhibitors (no.)	1,920	391	513
– Domestic exhibitors	43.1%	~ 75% (85% of these from southern Ontario)	76.6%
– Foreign exhibitors	56.9%	~ 25%	23.4%
Visitors (no.)	116,000	16,000	23,000
– Domestic visitors	28.0%	Predominantly Canadian visitors, mostly from southern Ontario	Predominantly US-wide visitors
– Foreign visitors	72.0%	Very few	Few

Sources: Messe Frankfurt GmbH 2004a, 2004b; IIDEX/NeoCon Canada 2008a, 2008b; LightFair International 2009a, 2009b, 2009c.

Notes: L + B = Light and Building—International Trade Fair for Architecture and Technology, Frankfurt 2004; IIDEX = IIDEX/NeoCon Canada, Toronto 2008; LightFair = LightFair International, New York, 2009.

10.3.2.　IIDEX/NeoCon Canada (IIDEX)

IIDEX is an annual trade show of the lighting industry that focuses on different aspects of the built environment, with a special focus on architectural, lighting, and interior design aspects (IIDEX/NeoCon Canada 2008b). As such, the event does not just focus on the field of lighting. It takes place at Toronto's Direct Energy Centre, which is located close to the city's centre, and is the largest show of this kind in Canada. In 2008, it had about 16,000 visitors and 391 exhibitors, with an overall exhibition space of 300,000 square feet (28,000 square metres) (see Table 10.1). Most of the visitors to IIDEX were from Canada, with a clear focus on southern Ontario. Similarly, the majority of the exhibiting firms also originated from Canada (about 75 per cent), while most foreign firms were from the US manufacturing belt. Despite featuring US and international firms on the exhibitor list, many non-Canadian firms were represented through Canadian-based branches, subsidiaries, or partners, with few representatives from the firms' home bases. There was also a lack of Asian participation, both in terms of exhibitors and visitors. Compared to L + B and LightFair, it would be misleading to classify IIDEX as an international or hub trade show; it clearly had a subcontinental focus. The show is better specified as a regional/national show, with neither a strong export nor import focus. Among other visitor groups, architects and students from local design and architectural pro-grammes at the universities were well-represented. Seen as potential future customers or multipliers, these visitor groups received considerable attention from exhibiting firms. Students were also viewed as potential future talent. At L + B, in comparison, such visitor groups were less important.

10.3.3.　LightFair International, US (LightFair)

LightFair is considered the largest annual trade show for the architectural and commercial lighting industries in North America (LightFair International 2009b, 2009c). The show is larger and more focused than IIDEX, but consider-ably smaller than L + B. It alternates its location on an annual basis between Las Vegas and New York. Like IIDEX, LightFair is a mid-sized trade show, which attracted 513 exhibitors and about 23,000 visitors in 2009 (see Table 10.1), while L + B had roughly four times as many exhibitors and five times as many visitors as LightFair or IIDEX. The event was held at the Jacob K. Javits Conven-tion Center in central Manhattan, which boasts over 675,000 square feet (about 63,000 square metres) of indoor exhibition space, though LightFair was not the only trade show being held at the facilities at that time. While respondents mentioned that New York tended to attract a more international audience than Las Vegas, the international character of the event was less pronounced than that of L + B. Three-quarters of the exhibitors (76.6 per cent) and an even higher proportion of the visitors were from the US. The second largest group of exhibitors and visitors originated from Canada, although the event also attracted exhibitors from countries such as China, Germany, Italy, Poland, Belgium, and the UK. Despite a substantial number of Chinese exhibitors, there were only a few Chinese visitors compared to L + B. LightFair was clearly directed towards the North American market and IIDEX more focused on the Canadian market, whereas L + B was a truly global event. Overall, the show was oriented towards large customers in the US market, including wholesale and retail traders, and innovation played a smaller role than at L + B.

In the discussion, the goals of participation, the nature of knowledge exchanges, and the dynamic changes of IIDEX and LightFair are characterized and compared with L + B.

10.4. PARTICIPANTS AND GOALS OF PARTICIPATION

The three trade shows investigated were very different in character and attracted a different audience. While L + B was clearly the global marketplace where firms introduced their latest innovations, made contact with global partners, and received an overview of world market trends, IIDEX was directed specifically towards the Canadian market. Participants emphasized the eclectic character of this show, which allowed them to connect with many different people primarily from within their southern Ontario neighbourhood (see Table 10.1). For many regional firms, this event was a natural outlet to make contact with existing customers and present their production programme. Not surprisingly, IIDEX mainly attracted small- and medium-sized firms that were often relatively young. These firms viewed the trade show as a test ground for their products and a possibility to connect with their home market. This was reflected in the size and age structure of the firms interviewed (see Tables 10.2 and 10.3).

Although many of the visitors were seen as multipliers through which future sales could be stimulated, sales and contract negotiations were clearly not the main focus at IIDEX. At the same time, however, the event was not an innovation hotspot, even though regional firms mentioned that the show offered opportunities to inspect some of the innovations from the past year. Instead, IIDEX was an event with a general networking and knowledge exchange character. Because of their relatively young age, a substantial proportion of the exhibiting firms (about 30 per cent) had only participated in the event in the past five years or less. The most established firms had attended for over ten years (35 per cent). Most participants saw IIDEX primarily in the context of the Canadian market and attended other trade shows throughout the year for their different perspectives, although only half went to LightFair and very few mentioned L + B. Even if they attended other events, the firms were typically not

Table 10.2. Firms interviewed at international lighting shows by size, 2004–2009

Employment class	L + B		IIDEX		LightFair	
	No.	%	No.	%	No.	%
1–20	12	23.5	14	48.3	5	13.2
21–50	5	9.8	3	10.3	12	31.6
51–100	6	11.8	4	13.8	5	13.2
101–500	14	27.5	2	6.9	7	18.4
≥ 501	14	27.5	6	20.7	9	23.7
Total	51	100.1	29	100.0	38	100.1

Source: Survey results

Notes: L + B = Light and Building—International Trade Fair for Architecture and Technology, Frankfurt 2004; IIDEX = IIDEX/NeoCon Canada, Toronto 2008; LightFair = LightFair International, New York, 2009.

Table 10.3. Firms interviewed at international lighting shows by age, 2004–2009

Age group (years)	L + B		IIDEX		LightFair	
	No.	%	No.	%	No.	%
< 10	5	9.8	11	36.7	6	11.3
10–< 20	11	21.6	3	10.0	15	28.3
20–< 50	10	19.6	11	36.7	19	35.8
50–< 100	19	37.2	3	10.0	10	18.9
≥ 100	6	11.8	2	6.7	3	5.7
Total	51	100.0	30	100.1	53	100.0

Source: Survey results.

Notes: L + B = Light and Building—International Trade Fair for Architecture and Technology, Frankfurt 2004; IIDEX = IIDEX/NeoCon Canada, Toronto 2008; LightFair = LightFair International, New York, 2009.

represented by the same people. Often local partners or local branches would organize the exhibits and present the firms' products. The different character of trade shows also required differently specialized attendees.

Compared to IIDEX, LightFair attracted an audience from a wider geographical range. Although the percentage of foreign exhibitors and visitors was similar to that of IIDEX, visitors originated from all over the US and many of the foreign exhibitors were from Europe or China (see Table 10.1). Like IIDEX, LightFair attracted a broad crowd of industry-related professionals, including architects, designers, engineers, urban planners, public utility representatives, and energy specialists (LightFair International 2009b). However, these people were not viewed as the core attendees. In terms of the target audience, most exhibitors pointed to the role of US distributors and retailers. LightFair had a stronger import and general sales focus than both the Canadian and the

German show. Overall, LightFair was characterized by a broader mix of small, medium-sized, and larger firms than IIDEX (see Table 10.2), and firms were on average older than those at IIDEX (see Table 10.3). LightFair can be characterized as an event where established firms create business and market their products, as opposed to being primarily a showroom for start-ups and small firms.

In terms of its main focus, LightFair is the key event that enables lighting firms to connect with the US market. Exhibitors at the show were interested in making direct customer contact and met with the marketing personnel of other firms, traders, consumer chain representatives, and large-scale buyers. While it was only slightly larger than IIDEX, there was a stronger market orientation. This was particularly true of foreign participants who tended to focus on establishing market access or broadening existing markets in North America, especially in the US. Many interviewees mentioned that their main reason for participating at the show was to engage in customer interaction, such as making contact with potential and existing customers from within the North American market. Others primarily wanted to promote their brand or product line and introduce new products. Access to or presence in the North American market was clearly the core focus of most exhibitors. Foreign firms were also actively looking for collaborators who could represent them in North America and help make contact with key customer groups.

At L + B, the situation was quite different, as it attracted a global audience (see Table 10.1), with German exhibitors and visitors representing only a minority of the attendants. L + B was viewed as the key event in the industry for inspecting and discussing developments in technologies, markets, and government regulations at a global level. As such, this was an event for national market leaders from around the world and for firms that target international markets. This event attracted the most internationalized and, on average, the largest, oldest, and most established firms (see Tables 10.2 and 10.3). Large established firms fully recognized the importance of this show and had sufficient financial resources to cover the high cost of participation.

Although overall sales and transactions were much higher than at IIDEX and LightFair due to the sheer size of the event, this was not the main focus: L + B was a global hub event where participants from around the globe came to look at recent developments and future trends in their technology field and discuss the dynamic changes taking place in their industry with global peers. Even firms without strong market shares in Germany or Europe attended the event to take part in this highly sophisticated buzz environment (also Bathelt and Schuldt 2010; Bathelt and Glückler 2011) and meet with customers and suppliers from North and South America or Asia. When comparing the event to IIDEX and LightFair, the atmosphere was more relaxed and less 'business-like'. Attendees took time to talk to others, had a snack at other booths, and even discussed with competitors their impressions about technologies, markets, industry rumours, and so on (Bathelt and Schuldt 2005, 2008).

In sum, the three events had a different focus and purpose, and thus attracted different sets of visitors. While there were clearly overlaps and cross-references between the three trade shows, fewer firms than expected regularly attended each of the different events. And when the firms did attend, they were often represented by different specialists. Few exhibiting firms were actually represented at all three trade shows. While there was some degree of overlap in terms of market leaders and large firms between L + B and LightFair, less than half of the firms interviewed at LightFair mentioned that they had attended L + B in the past; not unexpectedly, the share of firms that mentioned LightFair while interviewed at L + B was much lower. There was also some overlap between LightFair and IIDEX, but only a few interviewees at LightFair mentioned that IIDEX was relevant to them. Foreign firms, in particular, suggested that it was not necessary to participate in a Canadian trade show as the Canadian market was small and could easily be covered through attendance at LightFair.[3] When visiting the exhibits of the same firms during these shows, we rarely came across the same managers representing their firms. While based on anecdotal observations, it was obvious that the shows could not be viewed as cyclical events that were built on cumulative knowledge generation among the same groups of firms and attendees.

Although the events provided snapshots of the industry's product and technology structure, which were evolving over time, direct knowledge flows between the shows were limited. Instead, these trade shows were integral parts of the multi-layered knowledge flows within the lighting industry, complemented by industry reports, specialized publications, regular producer–user interaction, internet updates, and so on (also Borghini et al. 2006; Bathelt and Glückler 2011).

10.5. PRODUCER–USER INTERACTION
AND KNOWLEDGE CIRCULATION

Since the three trade shows serve different purposes, attract a different audience, and have a different focus, the knowledge exchange and circulation patterns are quite distinct from one another: L + B generates a temporary environment that allows participants to obtain a comprehensive overview of cutting-edge product and technology developments and the latest innovations; LightFair, in contrast, allows observers to receive a broad overview of market trends; and IIDEX provides a representation of limited market segments, as only a selection of product groups are shown and design innovations play a limited role.

In comparing the set-up of the events, it appeared that exhibitor booths differed markedly between the three trade shows. On average, L + B featured large, elaborate booths that were thoroughly designed and quite expensive. At IIDEX, the booths were substantially smaller, more crowded, and less complex than at the other events. The overall ensemble of exhibits was also somewhat eclectic and arbitrary. Furthermore, the trade show by-programmes were also quite different. While all three shows hosted a series of thematically related conference sessions, these were most comprehensive during L + B, with leading-edge talks, world-renowned industry specialists, and academics in sessions that covered a large variety of contemporary industry topics. Additional activities surrounding the trade shows were much more developed during L + B than at IIDEX and LightFair. During IIDEX, producer–user interaction was primarily focused on the exhibits themselves and discussions took place inside the exhibition halls. In contrast, L + B had a lot more show, dance, music, and arts entertainment elements that produced a spectacle of contemporary arts performances surrounding lighting applications (Bathelt and Schuldt 2005). These activities even extended beyond the trade show grounds into Frankfurt's downtown core (Messe Frankfurt GmbH 2004c).

In turn, the different contexts for meetings at these trade shows were associated with different communication patterns. In terms of the role of producer–user interaction, innovation, and the nature of knowledge exchange, there were distinct differences between the three lighting shows. L + B was an active driver of the industry's innovation dynamics, while LightFair and IIDEX were clearly not leaders in the introduction of new products and technologies.

At IIDEX, meetings with customers were rarely characterized by conversations about specific transaction procedures or new technological developments; they were often more generic in nature. Exhibitors presented the characteristics of their products and, in meeting with potential customers and third parties, got some ideas about market responses and trends. Exhibitors often knew visitors at their stands from former meetings and or existing customer interaction. Although this provided valuable feedback about the products, respondents were generally unable to describe specific examples of how such contacts had impacted innovation or problem solving in the past. Possibilities for accidental or off-site meetings at IIDEX were not extensive, although there were some informal organized get-togethers. Compared to L + B, the atmosphere at IIDEX was somewhat sterile and did not stimulate intensive producer–user interaction.

Although the presentation of the latest technological developments was not a major focus at IIDEX, participants still considered innovation to be an important aspect of the event. This was largely due to the fact that many interviewees only attended a limited number of trade shows every year and did not participate in global trade shows. As such, this regional/national event provided them with important updates regarding the technological dynamics in the lighting technology field. Participants used IIDEX as a benchmark to compare their products with those of other exhibitors. The number of direct competitors, however, was low due to the small scale and selective coverage of the show. The presentation of eco-friendly technologies and sustainable products and services was viewed as the most prominent example of innovation at the show; technological solutions surrounding light-emitting diodes—better known as LEDs—were also highlighted but were not as important as during LightFair.

At LightFair, the buzz of the industry clearly revolved around LEDs and other energy-saving lighting solutions able to replace the classical lightbulb. Although the European Union's decision to phase out the classical lightbulb in the European market by the end of 2012[4] was known long before IIDEX, it did not impact the show as much as it did LightFair. The shift in legislation spawned a new wave of technological innovation in the industry and even opened new opportunities for a wide range of design innovations. These innovations were related to the use of new materials and novel architectural opportunities in daylight applications, efficient lighting, decorative lighting fixtures, and interior and exterior luminaries, all of which were omnipresent during the exhibits in New York and became core elements of the event's buzz. Because of this innovation dynamic, respondents pointed out that attendance at LightFair was more important in 2009 than in previous years.

Compared to IIDEX, the atmosphere at LightFair was more conducive to inter-firm interaction and knowledge exchange as described by Maskell et al. (2006). The event was buzzing and people appeared busy going from one exhibit to the next or talking to the crowd of visitors at the booths and in the hallways. In contrast, IIDEX had a more sterile environment, attracted a smaller crowd, and had a slower pace. Exhibitors at IIDEX appeared nervous while looking around and actively talking to attendees passing their stands, whereas exhibitors at LightFair often offered free snacks and beverages to encourage people to stop for a few minutes. The attendees' agendas at LightFair were clearly more diverse than those at IIDEX. Most firms at LightFair indicated that they were searching for new partners during the event. Foreign firms, in particular, seemed to use the event to investigate potential avenues to enter the market or to expand in it. Interviewees mentioned that they would 'keep an open ear', as one interviewee phrased it, pay attention to social interaction, or collect business cards. Some said that they tried to talk to as many people as possible, always looking for the right potential partners to whom they could present their requests. Meetings at LightFair with existing and potential customers at the exhibits appeared more focused than at IIDEX and often involved specific information about products and prices. Most of the visitors at the exhibits were not known to the exhibitors, although they recognized existing customers and partners as important visitor groups. Discussions with suppliers were apparently more common during LightFair than IIDEX. This was due to the fact that more suppliers were represented with their own exhibits. In general, the focus of conversations was more market-driven. As a consequence, LightFair had a 'business-like' atmosphere, while L + B's strong design-focus made it appear, at least partially, like an exhibition.

Neither IIDEX nor LightFair were set up in a way that was comparable to the interactive, communicative environment at L + B, where visitors wandered around, talked to other visitors, directly approached exhibitors, returned to where they had spotted something interesting a few hours earlier, and discussed the details and properties of innovations that were specifically introduced at the show. Exhibitors often enjoyed a glass of wine with their competitors in the late afternoon at nearby stands and went out for dinner with interesting customers they met during trade show hours. L + B not only attracted a broad mix of leading managers, it also attracted a large group of engineers, designers, and the global press. These atypical visitors were not primarily interested in buying products (Borghini et al. 2006); rather, they played a decisive role in the collective sense-making processes that contribute to the field's technological development. They engaged in complex interactions with existing and potential future customers, partners, and suppliers, as well as competitors, media representatives, and industry observers (Bathelt and Schuldt 2005). As such, participation at L + B enabled firms to precisely evaluate their market and technology positions among global peers.

As summarized in Bathelt and Schuldt (2008: 864), L + B generates a complex knowledge ecology

> that is highly conducive for processes of pipeline formation and knowledge creation. The participants of these events are surrounded by a densely knit web of specialised information and knowledge flows that cannot be ignored. The multi-dimensional structure of this 'global buzz' enables firms to get an overview of what is going on and scrutinise the trends visible in the exhibits of competitors and complementary firms. Firms can evaluate their own activities and achievements by comparing themselves to others and make decisions about future strategies and products.

Attendees were not required to have direct contact with specific artefacts to become aware of new developments. The buzz during the event quickly led to the diffusion of news and gossip about innovations (also Maskell et al. 2006). It enabled both visitors and exhibitors to make informed choices about which exhibits to pay attention to and helped them evaluate these developments and make sense of them. This knowledge was crucial in revising and adjusting firm strategies and planning future innovation processes. At the same time, the generic exchange and market-related processes that existed at IIDEX and LightFair, respectively, also took place at L + B, albeit with a different orientation.

10.6.   CONCLUSIONS

This chapter systematically compares different trade shows in an industry/ technology field, suggesting that such temporary clusters are linked to one another. The events have overlapping agendas and some of the industry leaders attend all of them. At the same time, however, the trade shows have different functions, attract different sets of participants with diverse expectations, and demonstrate different goals of participation. Rarely do the same representatives participate in the same trade show, and direct knowledge transfers between these events are limited. This is simply because of the different purposes of the shows, which encourage different kinds of interactions. While L + B is the innovation leader in the lighting industry, establishing a crucial meeting point for global firms in the lighting field to discuss the latest technological, market, and regulatory developments, IIDEX is a regional/national event that brings together a limited market in the cross-border region between Canada and the US. In particular, it provides a platform for smaller and younger firms in the industry to explore their core markets and make new contacts. Interaction patterns at LightFair are broad in nature but focus on market access and sales-relevant contacts with wholesalers, retailers, and other customer groups. L + B, in contrast, attracts more owners, key decision-makers, and research and design specialists, as opposed to the sales and marketing personnel that are central figures at LightFair.

All of this suggests that these three trade shows are not part of a continuous integrated cycle of trade shows that leads to reflexive cumulative knowledge generation in the field. Moreover, these events should not be conceived of as field-configuring events that purposely shape and direct the development of the respective industry field. The processes identified in this chapter suggest that these events are partially overlapping, partially deviating projections of decentralized market and technology developments that are related to national and industry-wide regulations and norms, as well as technological discoveries.[5] While neither the layouts of these events, nor their outcomes are predictable, few participants are surprised about what they find and see (also Borghini et al. 2006; Bathelt and Gibson 2014). This is because they take part in the field's evolution and receive information about the field on a day-to-day basis through a variety of communication channels. As such, the trade shows contribute to and are vital parts of the field's ongoing reproduction.

Because of this role, the status of trade shows is not fixed and they often undergo dynamic changes involving growth, decline, or competition over time (Rinallo and Golfetto 2011). The lighting shows are embedded in the dynamic context of the industry and technology field. IIDEX, for instance, had clearly declined in importance and attendance during the 2000s. Participants pointed out that events such as the 9/11 terror attacks in New York and Toronto's severe SARS outbreak contributed to a drop in participation.[6] Exhibitors had also scaled back both their attendance and expenditures in terms of booth size and layout. While many felt that the trade show was on the decline, they still emphasized its unique character and substantial size within the Canadian context. In terms of size, LightFair also seemed to be smaller than in previous years. Regular participants of LightFair evaluated this show as a core, albeit somewhat stagnant, event in their industry in North America and most firms did not look beyond—for instance to Europe or Asia. The regained innovation dynamics with the perceived end of Edison's classical lightbulb was welcomed by most attendees. Unlike the other shows, and despite different expectations in the industry, L + B continued to grow during the 2000s and is still the undisputed innovation leader in the global lighting industry today. Between 2004 and 2012, the number of exhibitors grew by 20 per cent to 2,300 and the number of visitors by almost 70 per cent to 196,000. Still, 55.6 per cent of the visitors at L + B originated from outside of Germany (Messe Frankfurt GmbH 2012a).

NOTES

1. The empirical analysis presented is based on fifty-one interviews conducted at L + B, thirty-one interviews at IIDEX, and fifty-five interviews at LightFair. Firms were selected through a systematic random-sampling procedure stratified by exhibition areas and product groups. The response rate of firms was generally high compared to other studies, at 68, 78, and 82 per cent, respectively. The interviews focused on the characteristics of the trade shows, goals of participation, interaction with suppliers, customers, and competitors, and the effects and dynamics of the events.

2. While both North American trade shows were investigated using the same interview guide, the earlier interviews at L + B had a somewhat different focus, although the same areas of interest were covered. For this reason, L + B is compared with the other shows in a more aggregate fashion.

3. This is a typical problem of Canadian trade shows. Due to the relatively small size of the Canadian market and proximity to the US, many overseas exhibitors, as well as visitors, concentrate their trade show participation on US-based events to cover the entire North American continent. As a consequence, Canadian shows have a difficult time attracting an international audience (Bathelt and Spigel 2012).

4. This decision was made due to the large inefficiencies and the loss of energy in the use of classical bulbs (Frommberg 2009a, 2009b).

5. Of course, the specifics of knowledge circulation also depend on the actions of the respective trade show organizers.

6. In 2009, LightFair took place at the outset of what was portrayed in the media as a potential swine flu pandemic. While we expected this to have a substantial impact on the number of visitors and exhibitors, and on the nature of interaction patterns, this was actually not the case. The trade show was very busy and attendance was as high as had been announced months before its opening. Interestingly, the nature of interactions during the event also seemed unaffected. Visitors at the exhibits, for instance, were usually welcomed by a strong handshake that would signal exhibitor commitment.

11

Knowledge Practices and the Evolution of Export and Import Shows: The Case of Fabrics

11.1. INTRODUCTION

Textile-clothing trade shows are important and widespread events in Europe. They reflect the underlying industry, which consists of many small- and medium-sized firms and a supply chain that is divided into many subsectors of intermediate and final products. The industry is also strongly export-oriented in nature (EUROSTAT 2012). Textile-clothing trade shows allow small firms to reach out to overseas markets; they provide an important opportunity to align production know-how and liaise with downstream market trends among the various players and industry branches.

Trade shows focused on intermediate products, such as yarns and textiles, are mainly found in leading manufacturing countries, such as France and Italy, while those oriented towards finished products, such as clothing, are also held in other European countries. In the past, most of the international textile-clothing trade shows took place in Germany, which is where the first specialized trade shows emerged in large exhibition complexes created by local governments (CERMES 2012b; AUMA 2012b). Other leading manufacturing countries, such as Italy, only had local trade shows. This was partially due to the country's lack of accessibility and the existing exhibition infrastructure. Yet other European associations/groups of manufacturers also avoided competition with foreign exhibitors, and failed to explore the learning opportunities and broader exposure associated with such interactions. This changed, however, when formerly protectionist manufacturing groups decided to join a new exhibition in Paris—a decision which ultimately resulted in the decline of the main German textile-clothing trade show. The purposive concentration of various local exhibitions into one single venue also helped avoid a similar trend in Italian shows and, instead, improved the position of Italy.

This chapter presents findings from a longitudinal study of the characteristics and evolution of international textile and clothing trade shows in Europe between the end of the 1950s and 2010. This period captures the emergence of various 'wars' between European trade shows, reflecting the underlying rivalry between national industries (Rinallo and Golfetto 2006; Golfetto and Rinallo 2008). More recently, we find that competition has extended to Asian textile-clothing trade shows in remarkably similar ways.

In this chapter, we begin by summarizing the main characteristics of the European textile-clothing industry and its corresponding trade shows. We then provide an in-depth discussion of the features of fabrics trade shows, paying particular attention to differences in the import–export functions of the various events across countries. This is followed by tracing the sequence of rivalries between venues and events, referred to as a 'history of war', among the main fabric trade shows in Europe from the end of the 1950s to 2010. The discussion concludes by examining the nature and impact of the various strategies used by the different trade show organizers.

11.2. THE EUROPEAN TEXTILE INDUSTRY AND TRADE SHOW BUSINESS

The textile industry is an important manufacturing sector in Europe, comprising numerous branches, such as yarns, spinning, weaving, home-furnishing fabrics, and clothing. This industry is one of the oldest in Europe and continues to play an important, yet diminished, role. In 2010, for example, the European textile industry had a total of 191,000 firms that employed more than 1.7 million people and had total sales of about €153 billion (see Table 11.1). This accounted for about 3 per cent of the value added of the entire manufacturing sector in Europe (EUROSTAT 2012). Within Europe, the main manufacturing countries for the industry were Italy, Germany, France, Spain, and the UK.

Europe is the second most important player in the global marketplace, accounting for 29 per cent of worldwide exports. In recent years, China has been its leading competitor, with a 40 per cent share in 2010 (EUROSTAT 2012). But, along with the US, the European countries still represent the main consumer markets and importers worldwide and, therefore, attract considerable interest from major exporting countries—such as countries from South-East Asia. Since the 2000s, the competitive position of the European textile industry has experienced a strong decline due to the rise in imports of finished and semi-finished products from non-European countries (European Commission 2003a, 2003b). This brought about a reduction in production volumes and employment. This reduction in activity—by about one-third between 2002 and 2010 alone—has

Table 11.1. Economic structure and evolution of the textile-clothing industry in the European Union, 2002–2010

	Italy		France		Germany		UK		Spain		Total-5		Rest-10		Rest-22		EU-15		EU-27
	2002	2010	2002	2010	2002	2010	2002	2010	2002	2010	2002	2010	2002	2010	2002	2010	2002	2010	2010
Number of enterprises (thousands)																			
Textiles	28	16	5	5	4	4	5	4	10	6	52	35	18			27	70		62
Clothing	44	32	10	9	5	3	5	3	15	10	79	57	28			72	107		129
Total	72	48	15	14	9	7	10	7	25	16	131	92	45			99	177		191
Number of employees (thousands)																			
Textiles	312	150	109	50	116	80	120	60	113	46	770	386	322			276	1,092		622
Clothing	301	226	87	51	62	46	77	40	124	61	651	424	329			636	980		1,060
Total	613	376	196	101	177	126	198	100	237	107	1,421	810	651			912	2,072		1,722
Turnover (€ million)																			
Textiles	36,712	22,744	15,552	8,074	14,341	12,203	12,739	6,187	9,384	5,381	88,732	54,589	26,872			25,411	115,600		80,000
Clothing	41,591	31,414	10,569	8,718	8,984	8,115	7,458	3,308	5,891	5,997	74,493	57,549	13,590			15,451	88,083		73,000
Total	78,303	54,158	26,121	16,792	23,326	20,318	20,198	9,495	15,275	11,378	163,223	112,138	40,460			40,862	203,683		153,000
Value added at factor cost (€ million)																			
Textiles	10,801	5,932	4,130	2,228	4,633	3,608	4,697	2,200	2,880	1,547	24,171	15,515	8,376			6,485	35,517		22,000
Clothing	8,106	8,884	2,636	2,057	2,085	2,172	2,743	1,048	1,778	1,796	17,348	13,957	3,896			5,443	21,244		19,400
Total	18,907	14,816	6,767	4,285	6,718	5,770	7,440	3,248	4,658	4,475	44,490	29,472	12,271			11,928	56,761		41,400
Outside-EU exports (€ million)																			
Textiles	6,593	n.a.	3,073	n.a.	7,111	n.a.	2,338	n.a.	1,310	n.a.	20,425	n.a.	6,437			n.a.	26,862		17,772
Clothing	6,854	n.a.	2,372	n.a.	2,527	n.a.	1,332	n.a.	820	n.a.	13,905	n.a.	2,280			n.a.	16,185		15,146
Total	13,447	n.a.	5,445	n.a.	9,638	n.a.	3,670	n.a.	2,130	n.a.	34,330	n.a.	8,718			n.a.	43,047		32,919
Outside-EU imports (€ million)																			
Textiles	3,690	n.a.	1,770	n.a.	4,409	n.a.	3,071	n.a.	1,243	n.a.	14,183	n.a.	4,739			n.a.	18,922		21,833
Clothing	5,711	n.a.	6,837	n.a.	13,873	n.a.	10,906	n.a.	2,278	n.a.	39,605	n.a.	10,680			n.a.	50,285		62,103
Total	9,401	n.a.	8,607	n.a.	18,282	n.a.	13,977	n.a.	3,521	n.a.	53,788	n.a.	15,419			n.a.	69,207		83,936

Source: EUROSTAT 2012.

greatly impacted the leading manufacturing countries, especially Italy and the UK (see Table 11.1).

The importance and complexity of the European textile-clothing industry is reflected in the respective trade shows. In 2009, the European textile-clothing industry staged a total of seventy-five international trade shows (150 events per year, as they were held every six months) exclusively for professional buyers. These events attracted 24,000 exhibitors and almost 900,000 visitors, about 700,000 square metres (see Table 11.2). These exhibitions account for 70 to 75 per cent of all trade exhibitions in the industry (in terms of exhibitors and surface area), and are largely concentrated in France, Germany, Italy, and Spain. Other trade shows tend to be national or regional in character and can be found in almost all European countries. In terms of the event structure, the European textile-clothing industry does not have significant consumer shows (Rinallo et al. 2006; Golfetto and Rinallo 2008).

Textile-clothing trade shows typically operate on a semi-annual basis due to seasonal changes in fashion. The events tend to be highly specialized according to the various stages in the intermediate product chain (e.g. yarns and fabrics). They also specialize on the basis of user types and the nature of the end product (e.g. womenswear, menswear, childrenswear, underwear, casual wear, etc.). European trade shows in this sector are widely regarded as the most important in the world due to their large size and ability to attract international visitors. Exhibitors, many of whom are non-European, tend to invest heavily in these exhibitions, often devoting more than 50 per cent of their total promotional budget to participation in such events (Golfetto 2004). European shows in this industry—especially yarn and fabric trade shows— are considered important because of their ability to establish fashion trends and influence the purchase decisions of international buyers (CERMES 1994, 2012b). In contrast, the ability to launch new global trends in the clothing industry is mainly attributed to the more publicized Fashion Weeks, especially the 'primary circuit' of such events in Paris, Milan, London, and New York (Rinallo 2011b).

Prior to 2000, international trade shows in the entire textile-clothing value chain enjoyed substantial growth; but more recent data indicate a general decline (see Table 11.2). While the downturn in the 2000s is partly due to a drop in European consumption, there are also signs of major structural changes underlying this trend. The demise of clothing exhibitions appears to be linked to the concentration of retail, distribution, and production, which has led to a decline in the number of visitors and producers-exhibitors. In comparison, the reduction in the number of intermediate products trade shows seems primarily related to the contraction of the European manufacturing industry, caused by the growth of newly industrialized countries (European Commission 2003b; EUROSTAT 2012). All branches of the industry group have documented an

Table 11.2. International trade shows in the textile-clothing industry in Europe, 1990–2009

	1990	2000	2005	2009
Yarns				
Events	4	8	10	9
Rented surfaces (sq.m.)	27,825	44,713	45,788	30,884
Exhibitors	933	1,440	1,313	876
Foreign exhibitors	409	757	728	482
Visitors	39,458	133,096	94,668	37,998
Foreign visitors	6,762	56,709	55,675	20,066
Fabrics				
Events	10	14	20	17
Rented surfaces (sq.m.)	168,471	170,966	177,888	136,277
Exhibitors	4,249	4,071	5,395	4,204
Foreign exhibitors	2,239	1,974	3,269	2,957
Visitors	120,229	169,841	199,932	163,940
Foreign visitors	35,421	93,369	109,788	86,508
Clothing				
Events	46	57	41	49
Rented surfaces (sq.m.)	570,393	786,496	594,851	539,574
Exhibitors	16,680	26,431	20,330	18,905
Foreign exhibitors	4,898	7,500	6,839	6,755
Visitors	737,417	614,560	815,196	659,884
Foreign visitors	199,784	197,426	175,602	187,534
Total				
Events	60	79	71	75
Rented surfaces (sq.m.)	766,689	1,002,175	818,527	706,735
Exhibitors	21,862	31,942	27,038	23,985
Foreign exhibitors	7,546	10,231	10,836	10,194
Visitors	897,104	917,497	1,109,796	861,822
Foreign visitors	241,967	347,504	341,065	294,108

Source: CERMES 2012a.

increase in overseas exhibitors in the 2000s, which is linked to the increasing import function of these shows.

A change that is worth noting is the geographical shift of trade shows within Europe. From 1990 to 2009, France and Italy increased their market share of international trade shows over Germany (see Figure 11.1)—a shift that relates to active competition among the main events for intermediate products. In 1990, the situation was very different: Germany was the clear trade show leader, with Italy and France following behind.[1]

European textile-clothing exhibitions are currently threatened by the growth of trade shows in newly developed Asian countries, most notably China. A growing number of European manufacturers are now exhibiting at non-European events to gain direct access to the respective export markets

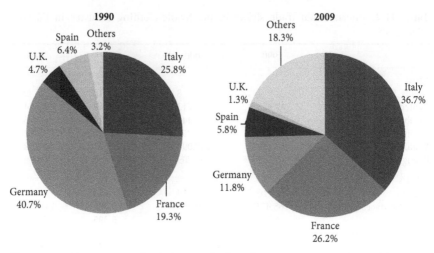

Figure 11.1. European textile-clothing trade shows by country, 1990 and 2009 (CERMES 2012a)

(AUMA 2012b; CERMES 2013). Simultaneously, buyers from these economies reduce or limit their visits to European trade shows because of geographical proximity of the new Asian trade shows (Rinallo and Golfetto 2014). As a consequence, concerns are widespread that these processes could diminish Europe's leadership in international exhibitions. In addition to significantly reducing business tourism, such a decline might lead to less visibility for European products, as well as fewer knowledge exchanges and networking opportunities. In many cases, a decline in European leadership could also mean losing control of the collective marketing and communication processes that have allowed European firms to build market development strategies (see Chapter 12).

11.3. INTERNATIONAL TRADE SHOWS FOR THE FABRIC INDUSTRY: IMPORT–EXPORT FUNCTIONS

The clothing-fabrics industry branch is the main sector for intermediate products in the European textile production chain, with ten international trade shows (twenty events per year) in 2010. The major events of this branch are located in France and Italy. One key aspect distinguishing international trade shows in this sector is their import–export function; international reach may be oriented more towards exhibitors or visitors, resulting in a different import–export function (see Chapter 4). Table 11.3 highlights three types of events.

Table 11.3. International fabric trade shows in Europe

Trade show, city (period)	Organizer	Product range/exhibitor country of origin		Trade show statistics (spring editions) 1986	1999	2009	Date 2009
Park Lane Collections, London (1993)	British National Wool Textile Export Corp. (NWTEC); same dates as Fabrex	Wools, mainly UK	Sq.m.	900[1]	//	//	//
			Exhibitors	29[1]			
			(% foreign)	n.a.			
			Visitors	n.a.			
Fabrex, London (1979–92)	Philbeach Events, supported by NWTEC; same dates as Park Lane	Mainly wools/ initially only UK exhibitors; subsequently open to other Europeans	Sq.m.	8,000[1]	//	//	//
			Exhibitors	447			
			(% foreign)	(53%)[1]			
			Visitors	10,400			
			(% foreign)	(6%)[1]			
Interstoff, Frankfurt (1959–99)	Messe Frankfurt GmbH; controlled by local authorities.	Wide range/ open to exhibitors from across the world	Sq.m.	40,512	4,367	//	//
			Exhibitors	1,044	270		
			(% foreign)	(78%)	(90%)		
			Visitors	23,248	10,773		
			(% foreign)	(45%)	(44%)		
Première Vision, Lyon (1972–8) Paris (since 1979)	Première Vision le Salon S.A.; launched by French Textile Associations	Top quality innovative firms/mainly from western Europe	Sq.m.	17,851	41,708	31,171	10–13 February
			Exhibitors	471	822	693	
			(% foreign)	(55%)	(73%)	(84%)	
			Visitors	27,609	39,346	38,869	
			(% foreign)	(57%)	(76%)	(81%)	

continued

Table 11.3. (Continued)

Trade show, city (period)	Organizer	Product range/ exhibitor country of origin	Trade show statistics (spring editions)			
Prato Expo, Florence/ later: Milano Unica (since 1979)	Pratotrade; initiative launched by the Prato Textile Association	Mainly wool, high and medium-high quality fabrics/Tuscany	Sq.m.	n.a.	6,248	//
			Exhibitors		101	
			(% foreign)		(1%)	
			Visitors		5,911	
			(% foreign)		(33%)	3–6 February
IdeaComo, Cernobbio-CO /later: Milano Unica (since 1975)	E.F. IdeaComo; founded by a group of silk manufacturers from Como	Mainly silk fabrics, medium-high quality fabrics/ mainly Italy	Sq.m.	9,550	2,423	1,031
			Exhibitors	90	69	28
			(% foreign)	(18%)	(20%)	(4%)
			Visitors	3,871	717	19,719
			(% foreign)	(31%)	(26%)	(27%)²
IdeaBiella, Cernobbio-CO/ later: Milano Unica (since 1978)	Associazione IdeaBiella; founded by manufacturers from the Biella area	Medium-high quality wool fabrics/ northern Italy	Sq.m.	6,110	5,250	5,090
			Exhibitors	50	61	65
			(% foreign)	(0%)	(0%)	(23%)
			Visitors	2,150	739	19,719
			(% foreign)	(60%)	(65%)	(27%)²
Moda In, Milan/ later: Milano Unica (since 1984)	S.I.Tex S.P.A.; founded by Italian Textile Associations	Quality, innovative firms/ Italy and western Europe	Sq.m.	10,680	22,737	12,220
			Exhibitors	279	582	364
			(% foreign)	(25%)	(25%)	(21%)
			Visitors	13,525	22,042	19,719
			(% foreign)	(16%)	(24%)	(27%)²
Shirt Avenue, Cernobbio-CO/ later: Milano Unica (since 1999)	Consortium of Italian Producers	Shirting/ mainly northern Italy	Sq.m.	//	//	2,264
			Exhibitors			38
			(% foreign)			(32%)
			Visitors			19,719
			(% foreign)			(27%)²

Show	Organizer	Products/Provenance	Metric				Dates
Tissu Premier, Lille (since 1985)	Eurovet; controlled by Fédération de la Maille	High cost products/ mainly Turkey, France, and Italy	Sq.m. Exhibitors (% foreign) Visitors (% foreign)	n.a.	5,589 322 (49%) 7,771 (47%)	2,692 147 (43%) 4,533 (36%)	21–22 January
Texworld, Paris (since 1998)	Messe Frankfurt France SA; purchased in December 2001	Medium-low cost products/ worldwide, mainly Asia	Sq.m. Exhibitors (% foreign) Visitors (% foreign)	//	//	11,557 656 (100%) 13,244 (85%)	9–12 February
TextilModa, Madrid (since 2001)	IFEMA, Feria de Madrid	Wide range/ Worldwide	Sq.m. Exhibitors (% foreign) Visitors (% foreign)	//	//	2,043[3] 88 (39%)[3] 2,897[3] (3%)[3]	28 February –2 March 2007[3]

Source: Adapted from Rinallo and Golfetto 2011: 8.

Notes: // = no trade show.

[1] Data refer to 1989.

[2] Co-located trade shows with joint visitors.

[3] Data refer to 1998.

Textilmoda in Madrid belongs to the group of import trade shows, with 50 per cent of its exhibitors originating from other countries, while its visitors are mainly national in character (3 to 5 per cent international visitors). The second group of trade shows includes all of the Italian events: IdeaBiella, IdeaComo, PratoExpo, Shirt Avenue, and Moda In. In 2005, these five events were grouped together in Milan. Three of the shows (IdeaBiella, IdeaComo, and PratoExpo) had previously been staged in venues near the manufacturing districts where they were originally established. All of these exhibitions have a small share of international exhibitors (5 to 20 per cent), but a high proportion of international visitors (30 to 40 per cent). The French show Première Vision in Paris can be considered a hub event, as 84 per cent of the exhibitors and 81 per cent of the visitors originate from other countries. The same applies to Texworld in Paris, which has almost 100 per cent international exhibitors and 85 per cent international visitors. As will be described, the difference between the two events lies mainly in the quality of the products exhibited. If we take into account the distinction between European and non-European exhibitors, however, Première Vision may be better characterized as a trade show of European offerings (for-export show), whereas Texworld focuses on European demand (for-import show). Tissue Premier (Lille) is a smaller event for fabrics and accessories, but has also become a hub trade show, despite its more difficult-to-reach location.

11.4. COMPETITION AMONG EUROPEAN FABRIC TRADE SHOWS: A 'HISTORY OF WAR'

European trade shows for clothing fabrics have been engaged in an interesting competition with each other since the 1980s, when event leadership began to move from Germany to France and Italy (see Figure 11.2). Italy hosted three small exhibitions, which were spin-offs from the textile districts of Como (Idea Como), Biella (IdeaBiella), and Prato (PratoExpo), and one larger event (Moda In), which took place in the Milan exhibition complex. Frankfurt was the location of the industry's leading trade show Interstoff, which was also the industry's oldest show that had existed for almost thirty years. France had a young, but rapidly growing trade show, Première Vision, which moved from Lyon to Paris in 1979.

By the late 2000s, this landscape had changed dramatically (see Figure 11.2 and Table 11.3). At the end of the 1990s, Fabrex and Park Lane had closed, and the UK no longer had important trade shows for clothing fabrics. These closures followed the restructuring of the UK's manufacturing industry, which led to a major reduction in the number of textile firms in the country. Italian trade shows joined together in a single location, Milan, under the joint umbrella of Milano Unica. Spain had a small import event in Madrid that was established

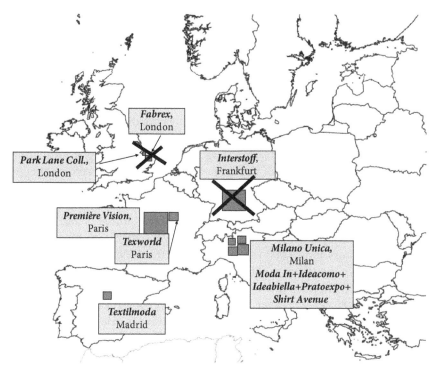

Figure 11.2. Spatial dynamics of fabric trade shows in Europe, 1986 and 2010 (CERMES 2012b)

in 2001; and France hosted Première Vision, the industry group's main event, as well as Texworld, which primarily focused on imported products from Asia. The German giant Interstoff completely lost its former importance and, finally, closed its doors in 1999.

These twenty years represented a period of tremendous turmoil and confrontation among the main trade shows, as each competed to become the mainstay event for the entire European clothing-textile industry. This occurred in several 'stages of war'.

11.4.1. The Undisputed Leadership of Interstoff (1959–1989)

From 1959 to 1979, Interstoff was widely regarded as the leading trade show in the industry. Established towards the end of 1959 by Messe Frankfurt GmbH, the first Interstoff edition had sixty exhibitors and 2,600 visitors. From the very beginning, Interstoff encouraged German exhibitors to interact with other European and non-European exhibitors—a practice in line with most international German trade shows (Golfetto 2004; CERMES 2013). Despite the backing of the German association of fabric manufacturers, the organizers did not adopt a protectionist approach to safeguard German exhibitors from international competition. Instead, Messe Frankfurt focused on the benefits offered to the city and region (which together represent the shareholders of the exhibition centre) through increased demand for trade show-related services and higher tax revenues. This created a large-scale trade show and meeting place for non-German exhibitors, which was supported by Frankfurt's central geographical location and international accessibility. Over time, proximity to the industrial and consumer markets attracted a large number of international exhibitors, as well as a growing number of European and non-European visitors (Rinallo and Golfetto 2011). Interstoff became the main stage for European producers to present their products to non-European markets, as the large number and variety of exhibitors provided a good overview of the industry's international offerings. At the height of its success in the early 1990s, Interstoff attracted close to 1,200 exhibitors and 24,000 visitors twice a year, with exhibits occupying a surface area of more than 40,000 square metres (Golfetto and Rinallo 2012; CERMES 2013). The show did not have strong links with the regional industry base, as almost 80 per cent of the exhibitors and over 60 per cent of the visitors came from other countries. Attendance by non-European exhibitors represented about 20 to 25 per cent of the total, while non-European visitors accounted for 15 to 18 per cent. The show featured a very broad range of fabrics, with different materials for different uses. Until the late 1980s, Interstoff remained the undisputed trade show leader in the industry by participation and size indicators, as well as trade publications. At the time, it was widely viewed as the most important clothing-textiles event in the world (CERMES 1994).

Although various initiatives had been launched to copy Interstoff, there were no real rivals in the European context. One such attempt started in Paris, at the beginning of the 1960s, but the trade show only lasted a few sessions. Another attempt was launched in Milan in 1963, with the establishment of Mitam. Yet Mitam also closed after a few sessions, giving rise to a number of smaller trade shows located in different manufacturing regions that specialized according to their surrounding industrial districts.

Interstoff encountered a number of challenges in the 1990s, however, when visitors began to question its trade show model (CERMES 1994; Golfetto and Rinallo 2012). Visitors found it increasingly difficult to navigate the sprawling trade show, which was packed with seasonal proposals of fabrics in a rather unorganized manner.[2] The trade show layout did not follow any specific knowledge strategy and most exhibitors requested the same booth locations they had in previous years to make it easier to meet with visitors. Only during the last sessions of Interstoff were European exhibitors spatially separated from non-European exhibitors in an attempt to create some semblance of order. Furthermore, each exhibitor had their own fashion proposals, making it difficult for buyers to grasp any major industry trends. As noted by one buyer who regularly attended the show, 'Interstoff was really a giant . . . from year to year, it became more time-consuming and tiring to visit all the exhibitors . . . Moreover, people went home confused because they could not grasp the direction fashion was taking.'

Dissatisfaction also spread to a number of European manufacturers, which felt that their visibility as exhibitors was compromised due to Interstoff's size and organization—both of which made it difficult to draw meaningful quality/ style comparisons among exhibitors. Exhibitors maintained that the event did not allow them to easily meet with leading customers, which impaired their ability to grasp important trends in demand. Many European manufacturers, consequently, moved to a new, more focused trade show, Première Vision, in Paris. According to one of our interviewees, those that continued to attend Interstoff felt that the show 'no longer represented the real trends of the sector and visitors were increasingly less representative of high-end purchase markets' (Rinallo and Golfetto 2011).[3]

11.4.2. The Irresistible Ascent of Première Vision and the 'Concertation Process' (1989–1999)

Following the Interstoff crisis, Première Vision became the leading European trade show for the clothing-fabrics industry—a position it maintained throughout the 1990s. The trade show's standing was recognized not because of its size, but because of its ability to give attendees a feeling for the main trends in the industry and future fashion.

Première Vision was originally established in 1973 by a group of high-quality weavers from Lyon, who felt that their products would have gone unnoticed at Interstoff. At first, the weavers decided to present their collections separately in Lyon, and then, from 1979 onwards, they presented their collections in Paris. Like Frankfurt, the Paris venue assured intercontinental access through its airports. It was also widely considered to be the fashion capital of the world—the home of many designers and other purchase influencers. The trade show and the city allowed people to grasp the most sophisticated, fashion-conscious market trends, as well as engage in the types of knowledge exchange needed to design products. In 1977, other French textile companies were invited to join the initiative and, in 1980, the organizers extended their invitation to a group of carefully selected exhibitors from Western Europe, particularly from Italy. As this was positively received, the trade show took off quickly. The organizing activity remained basically under the control of the French trade associations of textile manufacturers. However, given its strong ties with other European industry associations, the trade show aimed to promote the image of European manufacturing more broadly, working primarily with the leading Italian trade shows (Rinallo et al. 2006; Rinallo and Golfetto 2011).

Exhibitors were admitted to Première Vision based on the quality and creativity of their products and the financial stability of their firms (Golfetto and Rinallo 2012). Despite continued pressure to admit exhibitors from all over the world, Première Vision maintained a relatively strict exhibitor screening policy that privileged high-quality European producers. It was not until 2002 that the trade show accepted a small number of selected non-European producers, all of which were industry leaders in their respective countries. The exhibition was also demanding for exhibitors because it required attendance by producers and did not allow distributors to exhibit fabrics. The organizers believed that producers, as opposed to distributors, could best express their commitment to innovation and bring with them product developers and designers to explain their new developments. The latter were particularly appreciated by visitors (often designers and other experts from buyer companies) because they were able to acquire useful know-how and exchange views about the future of their activity (CERMES 1994; Golfetto 2000; Rinallo and Golfetto 2011).

With respect to the trade show layout, exhibitors were originally grouped by country of origin. But after a visitor survey revealed a preference for a layout based on material types, the exhibition format was changed. Categories for styles and consumer markets were subsequently introduced, and other reorganizing work was done to make it easier for visitors to understand changes in supply and market trends. The trade show was highly visitor oriented, to help visitors find what they were looking for as quickly as possible. According to an interview with the managing director Daniel Fauré in 2005, '[t]he market has become more difficult, with buyers having to work faster ... Buyers need to find specific products that fit into their business. This new segmentation will help buyers find what they need more quickly' (*Drapers Record* 2005).

As far as timing is concerned, Première Vision put into place a strategy that was consistent with its desire to position itself as the presenter of innovation in the fabric industry. The dates for the semi-annual event were set three to four weeks before the traditional dates of Interstoff, offering designers and buyers a 'first look' at the new collections. As a result of their respective strategies, Première Vision and Interstoff began to satisfy different needs. The French exhibition was viewed as the key event presenting international innovation that was critical for learning about new trends in the sector, while its German rival was considered to be a commercial event, which was useful for finding suppliers that offered good value for money, often from developing countries (Golfetto 2004).

The enormous success of Première Vision was, however, mainly linked to the introduction of an important innovation in organization called 'trend concertation', which refers to a process of understanding consumer trends, involving the key players in the industry (Rinallo and Golfetto 2006). It was through this process that the exhibition started to simultaneously 'design and present' fashion trends for the following years. This innovation made the trade show remarkably influential not only in terms of the choices made by buyers of fabrics, but also in terms of the choices made regarding downstream markets and collateral industries. As demonstrated in Chapter 12, this process is similar to the process of technological standard affirmation (Tushman and Rosenkopf 1992; Rosenkopf and Tushman 1998; Rinallo et al. 2006; Golfetto and Rinallo 2008).

Other fabrics trade shows in Europe, especially Interstoff, did not passively sit by and watch the success of Première Vision. In fact, Interstoff was the first of many trade shows that tried to copy the trend concertation mechanism. They were too late, however; Première Vision was considered the leading exhibition and its trends remained the most influential in the sector. As one interviewee stated, 'the Germans did not have the standing to be perceived as leaders in style' (CERMES 1994). The leading manufacturers had already gone to Première Vision.

Messe Frankfurt also began to aggressively promote itself as the gateway to the European market for US and Asian textile manufacturers. But, in 1999, a private organizer opened a new trade show in Paris called Texworld, heralding the end of the Interstoff monopoly for non-European textile exhibitors. A mere shadow of its glorious past, Interstoff gave up competing with Première Vision and attempted to refocus on fabrics for sportswear by launching the new parallel trade show Techtextil, which was dedicated to technical and high-performance textiles. The new concept was not able to turn the event around. After the fall/winter show of 1999, with only 2,600 visitors, Messe Frankfurt officially closed down Interstoff, putting an end to one of the main events in the history of the Frankfurt exhibition complex (see Figure 11.3).

11.4.3. The Union of Italian Trade Shows (2000–2005)

After the closure of Interstoff, Première Vision went through a period of undisputed leadership in Europe, much like its predecessor. After some years, however, a new threat emerged when Italian trade shows were grouped into a single event in Milan, known as Milano Unica.

Prior to this, Italian manufacturers had already become the largest group of exhibitors at Première Vision, accounting for at least twice as many exhibitors as the French. This was cause for some concern among Italian producers as it seemed to strengthen the visibility of French competitors. At the same time, Italian fabric trade shows did not have a central meeting point, but were staged in different regions at different times of the year. Because of this fragmentation, many overseas buyers stopped attending. As a consequence, some important customers could only be met in Paris. At that time, however,

(i) Exhibitors

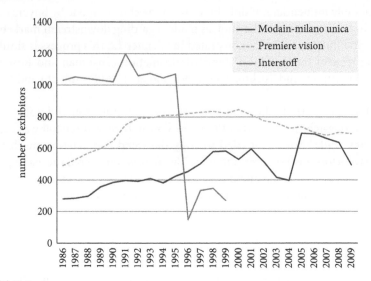

(ii) Visitors

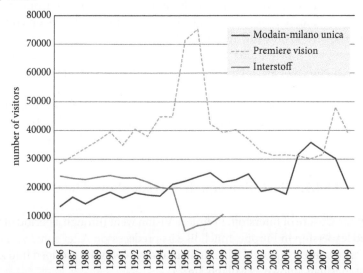

Figure 11.3. Exhibitors and visitors at Interstoff, Première Vision, and Milano Unica, 1986–2009 (CERMES 2012a) (*Notes:* Fall/winter editions are of similar size and have a similar trend; starting from 2005, data for Milano Unica are computed as the sum of Moda In, IdeaBiella, IdeaComo, Shirt A, and Prato Expo; PratoExpo has been cancelled since 2009)

the clothing-fabrics sector was about to face new challenges associated with the SARS epidemic in Asia, the terrorist attacks on the World Trade Center in New York (both of which reduced the willingness of firms to travel to such events), the ongoing trade liberalization, and the potential invasion of trade shows by new Asian competitors. As a response, the smaller regional/national Italian fabric shows joined forces in 2003, and launched Milano Unica, 'the Italian trade show of European textiles' in 2005 (Golfetto and Rinallo 2012; CERMES 2012b). The primary objective of Milano Unica was to overcome the fragmented nature of Italian shows and one day, perhaps, overtake Première Vision.

Until then, Italian trade shows in the clothing-fabrics sector had been complex and difficult for overseas observers to understand. The three small international exhibitions in Italy—IdeaComo, IdeaBiella, and PratoExpo—were established towards the end of the 1960s by their respective regional producer associations. They were held in prestigious locations, such as Villa Erba on Lake Como and Fortezza da Basso in Florence, which were close to the manufacturing districts they represented. The events were highly specialized, as were the respective manufacturing districts: IdeaBiella specialized in classic woollen fabrics for menswear, IdeaComo in silk fabrics for womenswear, and Prato Expo in wool fabrics with high-fashion content. A fourth national event, Shirt Avenue, was created in 1999 and displayed mainly shirting fabrics. The fifth trade show Moda In was based in Milan, founded by the cotton association in 1984. Although established later than the other shows, the accessibility of its venue and its ability to attract many producers from across Italy helped make it the biggest Italian exhibition in the industry. Moda In, like Interstoff before, also tried to follow the example of Première Vision by introducing important innovations during the event. Exhibitors were carefully selected from Western Europe on the basis of the quality, creativity, and innovative nature of their collections. Moda In also implemented a styling trend concertation mechanism with exhibitors, the results of which were displayed during the event inside the so-called trends area. Additionally, Moda In introduced a new layout, organizing the exhibits on the basis of the intended use of the fabrics (e.g. shirting, womenswear, and sportswear), while the other trade shows, including Première Vision, organized them primarily according to geographical origin. Despite these efforts, the innovations and trends presented at Moda In were often overshadowed by Première Vision, which was still larger and better known. To overcome this competition, Moda In decided to cooperate with Première Vision, contributing its own ideas (and those of its key exhibitors) to the success of the French trade show.

With respect to the originally smaller Italian events, many exhibitors described the atmosphere as similar to that in a private club (Rinallo and Golfetto 2011; Golfetto and Rinallo 2012). This was quite different from the larger trade shows in other countries, which seemed crowded and anonymous in comparison. For instance, visitors were personally invited by exhibitors to meet during event hours. And such meetings would often be continued later on at a firm's premises, as visitors were invited to learn more about the technical aspects of the products on display at the show. The strong presence of overseas buyers, who were drawn to the show by the specialized range and manufacturing excellence of the exhibitors, made these events typical export trade shows.

When the announcement was made in March 2005 that Italian fabric shows were to join forces, many observers asked themselves whether Milano Unica would mark the beginning of a new 'war' among trade shows. Some Italian manufacturers announced that they would stop attending Première Vision to concentrate on Milan. This represented a substantial threat to Première Vision, as approximately 330 out of 700 exhibitors at Première Vision originated from Italy. Milano Unica also moved the dates forward for both of its sessions in order to present its novelties before Première Vision. In 2006, exhibitor and visitor attendance for the spring session (see Figure 11.3) were similar for the two trade shows. Attendees even maintained that the trends presented at Milano Unica were more useful than those at Première Vision because they appeared to have more concrete applications, such as more specific colours and fabric samples.

A major difference between the two events involved the extent of their international reach. In 2005, 82 and 80 per cent of the exhibitors and visitors at Première Vision, respectively, were international, compared to only 18 per cent of the exhibitors and 35 per cent of the visitors at Milano Unica (see Table 11.3). This was not a major concern, however. It was linked to how the market was structured, as Italy had become the centre for both the supply and demand of clothing fabric in Europe, with 2006 sales almost twice as high as those in countries such as Germany or France (see Table 11.1). This simply resulted in higher national participation.

The Italian trade show alliance Milano Unica was not without challenges, however. A key problem was the strong cultural identity linking the firms from each industrial district and separating them from others. Interview data suggest that the organizers of the various trade shows found it difficult to agree on location, dates, and, according to one journalist, on 'which region the food and drinks to be served at the event would come from'. The fear of losing their original identity in a large-scale event prompted the former Moda In, Prato Expo, IdeaComo, IdeaBiella, and Shirt Avenue trade shows to remain visibly separate. Although these shows were hosted in the same exhibition centre in Milan, they held their own event with a separate organization and entrance. Not surprisingly, this combined Italian trade show lasted only three years. Many small Italian firms felt the effects of the economic downturn in the late 2000s, and, after some disagreement over organization, some of the Prato Expo exhibitors returned to Florence taking with them part of the visitors.

Première Vision's response to the new Italian threat began to take shape even before Milano Unica was officially established. Through a number of alliances and acquisitions, Première Vision started to coordinate the various Paris trade shows of intermediate products (i.e. textiles, yarns, accessories, and textile design). With the establishment of the new firm PVE S.A. in 2004, the organizers of Première Vision and Expofil (a yarn trade show) merged in order to better exploit synergies between their events. In May 2005, Expofil and Première Vision created an alliance with the other important fashion exhibitions in Paris: Le Cuir à Paris (a semi-processed leather products show), Indigo (a textile design show), and Mod' Amont (a trade show for buttons, embroidery, zippers, and other accessories). All of these events have since been jointly promoted under the umbrella of Première Vision Pluriel. Indigo was also purchased by PVE S.A. As a result, the trend concertation activities at the various trade shows are now coordinated (see Chapter 12). In 2007, PVE S.A. was partially sold to two multinational firms that operate in the exhibition and events industry—namely, Eurovet and GL Events—to further improve its international reach. The Première Vision Association, representing the French textile industry, still maintained majority control of the new group. It remains unclear at this point, however, whether it will continue its protectionist policy regarding the European industry in the future. The results of these steps towards reorganization appear to have paid off for Première Vision at the moment. Despite the difficulties that have faced the entire European trade show business in the 2000s, Première Vision has re-established its lead ahead of Italian trade shows.

11.4.4. Europeans in Asia and Asians in Europe (2006–2010): The Future of Collective Marketing

Since the beginning of the new millennium, new textile trade shows have begun to make their appearance in Asia and Europe. Initially, Asian exhibitions played a marginal role since their respective industries were unable to reach European and North American markets due to export restrictions established by the GATT Multifibre Arrangement. Once these restrictions were removed in 2005, however, international markets were flooded with Asian products (EURO-STAT 2012). These products enjoy significant comparative advantages in terms of labour costs compared to products from Europe and North America. Many European and non-European producers have thus started to exhibit at Asian trade shows, at least to monitor the movements of their new competitors (Golfetto and Rinallo 2013; Rinallo and Golfetto 2014).

Import trade shows are also gaining a foothold in Europe and, instead of focusing on high-quality, high-fashion products, offer an overview of lower quality fabrics. Such events, especially Texworld in Paris, feature supplier-exhibitors who primarily originate from Asia, and buyer-visitors from Western Europe. After the closure of Interstoff, Texworld was purchased by Messe Frankfurt in 2001 to continue—this time, in Paris—its policy of reaching out to Asian markets. In 2010, the trade show rented out approximately 16,000 square metres of exhibition space and hosted about 850 exhibitors (especially from China, Korea, Taiwan, India, and Turkey) and almost 15,000 visitors. It now acts as the main entry point to the European market for non-European manufacturers. Other fabric import shows of a smaller size are being held in other European countries as well. In Milan, for example, Intertex has about 100 exhibitors, mainly from China and India.

For European trade shows, competition has thus become progressively larger in scale, both in terms of geography as well as in relation to the types of offerings on display (Rinallo and Golfetto 2014). Confronted with these challenges, some organizers—especially German ones—have established new trade shows in Asian markets, often in partnership with local partners and governments. By 1987, Messe Frankfurt had already established its first trade show in Asia using the Interstoff trademark. Although Interstoff closed down in Germany, it continues to live on through its Asian spin-offs and, more recently, also in Russia. Messe Frankfurt also currently organizes Intertextile in Shanghai and Beijing, as well as Texworld India in Mumbai.

Similarly, Première Vision works outside its national borders. However, these are mainly small initiatives to promote the Paris event. One of the longest running initiatives exists in New York: European Preview. This is a workshop that presents the season's trends and colours, along with a small section with exhibitors from Première Vision. The most recent overseas initiatives in Shanghai, Moscow, and Tokyo seem to share the same goal as the New York event, which is to promote exports by European exhibitors (mainly from Italy and France) and to get local buyers interested in viewing the complete range in Paris.

11.5. CONCLUSIONS

This chapter has investigated international trade shows for the textile-clothing-fabric industry in Europe and provides a number of important insights. First, it highlights close links between trade shows and local clusters. Trade shows are an important tool for local clusters, as they allow them to collectively promote and develop their industry base. This relationship mainly exists in industries that are comprised of small- and medium-sized enterprises, whereas trade show attendance for larger exhibiting firms remains a more individualistic endeavour (Golfetto and Rinallo 2012). On the other hand, small companies seem to suffer from the competitive dynamic and practice of comparison found at trade shows, even if they acknowledge that competitors represent an important learning opportunity.

Second, the chapter shows how competition among trade shows generates competition among hosting regions/cities, on the one hand, and among groups of producers through their trade associations on the other. Hosting regions benefit from exhibitions in terms of business tourism and related service growth, while local industries gain exposure and strengthen their identity (see Chapter 5). Nevertheless, the goals of hosting regions and national industries often collide and give rise to conflicts. In any case, trade show organizers differ with respect to the types of stakeholders they address. When strategies are targeted at national industries, trade shows become a means of collective promotion; when strategies are focused on maximizing attendance to increase regional service/tax impacts, trade shows become neutral stages for anyone in search of exposure. Moreover, organizers may develop policies/solutions that significantly intervene in the learning and knowledge exchange processes at trade shows (Rinallo and Golfetto 2011). This may be related to exhibitor selection, the reorganization of exhibition layouts, the timing of events, the selection and exposure of innovations, and trend concertation (see Chapter 4). Our analysis suggests that such policies/solutions should be especially well developed in the case of trade shows that promote national production, given their need to compensate for a limited national variety of exhibitors.

Third, our findings support the view that the spatial distribution of trade show activity reflects structural aspects, such as the consistency of demand and supply markets for a given industry in the catchment basin. However, these influences interact with the strategic actions of trade show organizers. In the clothing-fabric industry, these actions have a substantial impact on promoting or controlling knowledge exchange, and overcoming some of the structural restrictions leading to limited visibility of regional industries (see Chapter 5).

Finally, the chapter outlines the role of leading European trade show organizers in developing multinational structures and operating in non-European markets. In some cases, this involves developing protectionist marketing strategies for European producers at non-European trade shows while, in others, it involves active measures to reverse the slowdown of trade show activity in Europe.

NOTES

1. In the clothing sector, alone, exhibition activity has always been more evenly distributed among the main trade show countries.

2. Similar complaints were more recently voiced at CeBit—the world's leading trade show in the area of information and communication technology (Bathelt and Zakrzewksi 2007). Because of the sheer size of the event and the lack of order in the exhibits, even long-time visitors found it difficult to grasp the trends in the field and get an overview of new developments. This led to a decline in participation, including some key accounts such as Nokia (*Frankfurter Rundschau* 2006).

3. Of course, we must keep in mind that Interstoff's gradual demise was also related to the drastic decline of the German clothing-textile-fabrics industry (see Table 11.1). And due to its small regional production basis, industry support for the trade show was also not as strong.

12

The Impact of Trade Show Organizers on Industry Innovation: 'Concertation' Processes in Fashion

12.1. INTRODUCTION

Already in Chapter 4, we emphasized the role of event organizers in influencing and even actively shaping the knowledge flows during trade shows. While there are many events where the role of trade show organizers is less direct and less visible (see Chapter 10), this chapter presents the case of fashion fabrics, where so-called 'concertation' or 'trend concertation' has a direct impact on the products developed and shown and on the knowledge flows that occur during trade shows—as well as on the entire wave of fashion products that follow from this. As such, Première Vision and similar trade shows are prime examples of field-configuring events, in the terminology of Lampel and Meyer (2008).

Concertation is a process used by French and Italian producers of high-quality fabrics to build and affirm their innovations in relation to others in the 'high fashion' industry. This takes place under the conditions of growing competition from emerging countries in the fabric industry field, as the industry has partially relocated to developing economies, particularly in Asia. At the centre of the concertation process are efforts to activate and coordinate key agents in the industry (and their corresponding knowledge inputs) by the organizer of Première Vision in Paris—the industry's main trade show for clothing fabrics. Originally organized by a French manufacturers' association, Première Vision is now managed together with other European associations in the industry to address the seasonal proposals and innovations developed by producers of high-quality fabrics. The organizer's coordinating work is mainly carried out during the months leading up to the trade show. This is done by supporting research into future consumer behaviour, organizing meetings among experts to discuss trends, building agreements among the players regarding which trends to select, and engaging exhibitors in the trends that have been selected for the new collections. The process is completed during the trade show where trends are exposed through the layouts, special trends areas, communications to visitors, and relations with the press.

Central to the concertation process is the creation and exchange of knowledge about fashion trends in clothing fabrics, which eventually leads to the affirmation of specific innovations and styles proposed by European manufacturers-exhibitors as parts of the dominant trends in fashion. This also helps generate the image of certain manufacturers as the important leaders and innovators in the industry at an international level (Rinallo et al. 2006; Rinallo and Golfetto 2006; Golfetto and Rinallo 2008, 2012).

The next section describes the main characteristics of innovation processes in the textile-clothing sectors, followed by a brief description of the organizer of Première Vision. The core of the chapter involves an in-depth analysis of the different stages of the concertation process. We conclude with a discussion of the impact of trade show organizers' practices on the industry.

12.2. INNOVATION IN THE FINE FASHION APPAREL INDUSTRY

In the fashion apparel industry, innovation processes are mainly about style. Style means creativity in cut, colour, and relative combinations, patterns, fabrics, and their processing and finishing. When embodied in clothing, these elements of style satisfy symbolic functions that allow consumers to express their individual identity, and may also signal social status. Contrary to the widespread belief that innovation in fashion style is mainly created by a limited set of celebrity designers (e.g. Armani or Dolce & Gabbana) who work in relative isolation on the fashion pipeline, the entire fabric industry, which supplies materials and fabrics, is also a central hub for innovation. In most cases, designers would not be able to provide clothes that consumers associate with dominant fashion trends if their suppliers did not have the technical ability and end-market knowledge to produce yarns and fabrics that incorporate the creative solutions aligned with those trends. In other words, designers are inspired by upstream creativity that is aligned with what consumers value and what they want their clothes to express. This means that fabric producers must anticipate consumer needs in order to develop solutions that complement the core competence of designers and apparel producers in creating fashionable end products (Golfetto and Mazursky 2004; Zerbini et al. 2007).

As suppliers of the apparel industry, fabric producers provide both technical and creative content. Technical content is mostly provided by upstream actors (e.g. textile machinery or chemical component producers) and is equally available to most competitors. Consequently, it cannot be a source of competitive advantage. To differentiate their goods, fabric producers must, therefore, vary their bi-annual collections in terms of colour (e.g. ruby or clay furrow), structure (e.g. for jacquard fabrics, satin, or chiffon), aspect (e.g. structured, light, washed-out, or opaque), touch (e.g. soft, warm, fluid, or compact), decoration (e.g. arabesque, cashmere, or irregular stripes), and treatment (e.g. burnt-out, washed, or gummy coating). These highly differentiated elements are deliberately designed to be invested in finished goods with symbolic and expressive properties that will be valued by consumers (Entwistle and Rocamora 2006; Rinallo et al. 2006). In the development of their new collections, however, fabric producers face serious problems of modularity tied to consumer behaviour (clothes and accessories are bought and used by consumers, yet not necessarily at the same time), as well as the fragmented, non-integrated nature of the fashion industry supply chain. Innovation in the high fashion industry cannot occur in a vacuum but has to address the context of the consumer and consumption side.

To avoid the risk of innovations that do not fit with prevailing trends, firms must consider consumers' future tastes along with the innovation efforts of upstream and downstream partners and producers of complementary products when preparing their own collections. A fabric firm must decide, for example, whether its range of colours will correspond with that produced by knitwear, velvet, and other semi-finished textile manufacturers, as well as by its competitors. Furthermore, all semi-finished textile products must fit with the dominant apparel styles and cuts. Finally, from the purchaser's point of view, it is important to consider the issue of compatibility, as consumers will combine apparel with accessories (e.g. clothes with shoes or bags) to express their identity and, at the same time, signal membership in specific reference groups (Cappetta et al. 2006). Standards are thus needed to reduce uncertainty in innovation.[1]

Although issues of modularity and compatibility are not unique to this setting, fabric producers face additional threats to their survival. First, the fabric industry is highly fragmented in the sense that it includes many firms within each specialized stage of the value chain. Most of these firms are small and medium-sized enterprises, and even the market leaders lack the resources and skills needed to establish their own innovative solutions as the 'dominant design' (Cappetta et al. 2006). Second, because it is linked to the fashion system, the innovation cycle for fabrics is extremely short, with seasonal collections launched at least once every six months. Third, the fragmented nature of the manufacturing and retail system in the industry means that new fabric products must be presented far in advance of consumer purchases. In September 2013, for instance, fabric producers needed to present to their customers (the apparel producers) their proposals for the spring/summer 2015 apparel collections—i.e. eighteen months before the end products were available in retail stores. Thus, since consumer tastes are ever-changing, new product development is inherently risky and requires some form of fashion forecast to reduce uncertainty.

12.3. PREMIÈRE VISION AS ORGANIZER OF THE MAIN CONCERTATION PROCESS

The challenges of the industry field serve as a strong incentive for French and Italian fabric producers (which are international industry leaders) to cooperate with each other in order to reduce risks in innovation. The idea of a 'trend concertation' was first launched by the organizers of Première Vision in Paris, in 1976, just a few sessions after the first show. Its founding members recognized the advantages of coordinating the exhibitors' seasonal efforts in fabric innovation. A similar process was introduced a few years later by Milan's Moda In, and various other trade shows soon followed suit in industry groups, such as yarns, leather goods, bags and shoes, and eyewear. In most cases, however, trade shows did not establish a complete concertation process, but only displayed fashion and style trends, coordinated jointly with the main exhibitors (CERMES 2012b).The initial organizers were only a small group of weavers in Lyons, but Première Vision quickly earned the support of leading associations of French textile manufacturers. The organization, referred to as Première Vision Le Salon S.A.,[2] remained under the control of the associations of fabric manufacturers for many years. Its sole focus during this period was on staging the French event. In 2004, Première Vision Le Salon S.A. merged with the organizers of the Expofil yarns exhibition in Paris, which was also controlled by the manufacturer associations and, like Première Vision, was committed to forecasting industry trends. Since 2005, the newly merged company—PVE S.A.— has been involved in promoting various clothing exhibitions in Paris under the collective name of Première Vision Pluriel. Such exhibitions include Le Cuir à Paris (semi-processed leather goods), Indigo (textile design), and Mod'Amont (buttons, embroidery, and accessories). Trend forecasting for the various trade shows has since been coordinated and jointly carried out. In 2007, two international event organizers—i.e. Eurovet and GL Event—became part of the PVE S.A. corporate structure. PVE also began staging a number of trade shows outside of Europe. While these events are attended by some European exhibitors, the primary goal is to promote the European event abroad (see Chapter 11).

12.4. CONCERTATION: HOW TO SELECT THE FUTURE IN FASHION

The concertation process of fashion trends was introduced by Première Vision to address two distinct sets of needs, which involved both exhibitor-manufacturers and visitor-buyers. As already noted, the main challenge for fabric manufacturers is to predict shifts in demand and fashion trends.

Customers have generally become more demanding and expect a significant amount of creativity from suppliers. Yet, due to the highly fragmented textile and supply chains, fabric manufacturers are required to develop collections almost two years before the clothes incorporating those same fabrics are presented by retailers and made available to end consumers. As a result, the innovations presented by fabric manufacturers in the past rarely followed specific fashion trends (which could have emerged after the product presentations), and many of these innovative efforts were subsequently rejected or poorly received by the market.

In addition to the needs of manufacturers are the needs of buyers. More specifically, buyers expressed a growing dissatisfaction with their visits to fabric trade shows (such as the sprawling Interstoff in Frankfurt), often returning confused and bewildered by the vast array of offerings in different styles and qualities (see Chapter 11). Their complaints were initially dealt with by the organizer of Première Vision through the accommodation of a number of meetings among manufacturers with the goal to agree on future innovation trajectories. This process became increasingly sophisticated over time and was eventually supported by special investments in research into consumption, as well as the active participation of clothing manufacturers and retailers. Within a few years, this process succeeded in defining future product ranges that were more consistent and that could be easily communicated to buyers. Over time, the concertation process became a fundamental driver in fashion trends, taking root throughout the textile-clothing chain, and even beyond, for instance, in the automotive and furniture industries (Rinallo and Golfetto 2006).

Concertation in the fabric industry occurs twice per year and begins at least five to six months before the opening of Première Vision. It comprises four fundamental stages in which a growing number of players are involved (see Figure 12.1).

12.4.1. Forecasting and Selecting Consumption Trends

The first stage in the concertation process is to select the fashion trends to be supported through the event. At this stage, the agents involved initially identify a broad number of scenarios and emerging trends in consumption. These trends are the result of ad hoc research and meetings among experts, including panels of sociologists, cool hunters, bureaux de style (Guercini and Ranfagni 2012), designers, associations in the textile chain, and representatives from the most innovative fabric producers. Over the years, the French trade show also set up an international observatory of trends, which acts as a global socio-cultural surveillance unit that aims to identify the trends that are most likely to influence the textile and fashion industries (Rinallo and Golfetto 2006).

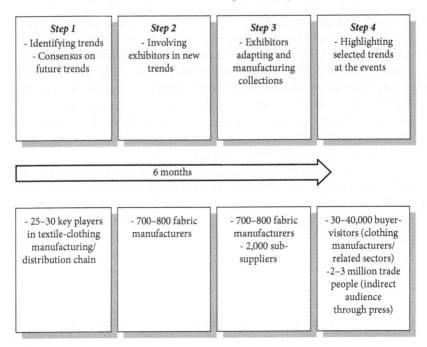

Figure 12.1. The trend concertation mechanism at Première Vision and the players involved

The observatory's analyses in Europe, North and South America, and Asia are carried out by a broad network of specialists, including architects, designers, trend forecasters, experts in new technologies, sociologists, and anthropologists. These specialists identify consumption patterns in specific subcultures that aim to anticipate the direction in which society as a whole will move. These patterns inform new fashion products and fabrics. At this stage, emerging trends in society are 'translated' into new ideas in fabrics and clothing. Increasing environmental awareness, for example, has encouraged products, colours, and designs that respect or reflect such principles—such as raw materials that do not harm the environment, natural colours, simple clothing styles, and so on. Similarly, in the aftermath of 9/11, the world became a less secure place for many consumers and conspicuous consumption was no longer considered appropriate. Apparel and fabrics were thus required to fit with the consumer's desire for safety, which led to less blatantly luxurious designs.

True concertation takes place in the next step, however, when a relatively small group of fashion trends is selected (Rinallo et al. 2006). These trends are subsequently translated into instructions for the development of new textiles, which are then passed on to the fabric exhibitors. This critical step occurs during so-called 'concertation meetings', which bring together representatives from all stages of the textile-apparel value chain. At the 'concertation tables', representatives and members of the fabric industry trade associations, in upstream and downstream markets, and in complementary products, have an opportunity to express their opinions regarding future trends. Leading producers (those that are able to launch their own trends), distributors, and bureaux de style may also be involved and offer a specific contribution to the concertation process.

During the concertation meetings, decisions tend to be more 'politically motivated' than technically induced and generally involve no more than thirty to forty leading firms from the industry group. During the meetings, trends identified by the trade show organizer are compared with those forecasted by the invited parties. The meetings then create a consensus among the relevant actors regarding future common trends (Golfetto and Rinallo 2008). Extreme ideas with little support are abandoned in favour of ideas with widespread appeal. Finally, syntheses are reached through negotiations among representatives from the main exhibitor countries, who often have quite different requests they wish to support. In 1992, for example, 'Germany insisted on nature-inspired colours, whereas Austria suggested rediscovering the five continents and their colours. France firmly backed melancholy to evoke energy, harmony, and light in a simple, well-motivated message about yellow' (Mazzaraco 1993: 23).

Concertation meetings thus reduce variety in new collections and increase compatibility on the purchasing side. Moreover, although important differences exist between the trends identified at Première Vision and those identified at other trade shows, they are similar in many ways and are largely compatible, as most of the interested parties are involved in different concertation tables and provide similar input.

12.4.2. Involving Exhibitors in Concerted Trends

Once consensus has been reached, the information on selected trends becomes the content the exhibitors at Première Vision are informed about through special workshops. The purpose of these workshops is to be inspirational for the development of the season's new collections. The trends are given evocative metaphors and labels (e.g. 'search for equilibrium', 'urban soul', or 'cyber culture'); colour tones are precisely specified according to the Pantone colour system, which allows a colour to be selected and specified by assembling creative palettes and conceptual colour schemes; and, presentations are given by distributing special material (such as colour cards, trends notebooks, CD-ROMs, etc.), which also become work tools for the firms operating downstream in the fashion industry. One concertation expert interviewed referred to the presentation of trends by emphasizing that 'we make a lot of poetry, here'. This hints at the inspirational nature and aesthetic quality of the materials that serve as an aesthetic trigger for the development of new fabric collections. For example, the directions for future fashion innovation portrayed at Première Vision for the autumn/winter 2009/2010 collection included the following: 'Electric shocks' was described as a direction by participants, involving 'deeply coloured darks contrast in a binary and high-voltage cadence with subversive and grating brights'; 'flamboyant resonance' was described to be similar to when 'volcanic condensations intersect, in an undulating and explosive harmony, with voluptuous incandescence'. The visual descriptions of these fashion innovations are similarly evocative (Première Vision 2008).

The process of affirming the selected trends begins at this stage, involving all exhibitors who have been admitted to display at the trade show. A total of 700 to 800 exhibitors are involved in each edition. Although they are not required to adopt the proposed trends, they are certainly influenced by the forecasts made and the trends selected by the organizers (Rinallo and Golfetto 2006).

12.4.3. Developing Collections on the Basis of Concerted Trends

In the months that follow, exhibitors develop new fabric collections, incorporating—albeit with individual adaptations—the guidelines about the fashion trends that they have received from the trade show organizers. At this stage, differences can be detected in how trends are employed by exhibitors, depending on their size and innovation competences.

A large share of Première Vision's exhibitors are small- and medium-sized enterprises with limited consumer-oriented design and research capabilities. For these firms, the information materials on trends distributed at the Première Vision workshops are especially valuable because they make it unnecessary to carry out market research on their own and, at the same time, offer the opportunity to decide whether and to what extent to deviate from the main trends. Large firms, which often have their own style ranges, are another matter because of their large resources—although they often consider the guidelines they receive from the organizers' concertation workshops. The comments of exhibitors are interesting in this respect. As one Italian firm interviewed explained, 'our style director goes to the workshop [where trends are presented], takes notes, and when she comes back to the factory, she discusses with the production and marketing guys. It's very useful for us to have the trend books and the colour cards; it would be tough otherwise' (Italian exhibitor at Moda In, sixteen employees). Another Italian exhibitor put it like this: 'We follow the trends, but not always. We have our own brand image, and sometimes we propose new fabrics that aren't entirely compatible with the trends. But customers won't care, they'll follow us' (Italian exhibitor at Première Vision, 120 employees) (Rinallo et al. 2006).

It is at this stage that the process of adopting the selected trends is extended from the exhibitors at trade show to their suppliers, sub-suppliers, and collateral manufacturers who become involved in the production in various ways. It has been estimated that at least another 1,500 to 2,000 firms become involved in the process at this stage (Rinallo et al. 2006).

12.4.4. Highlighting Selected Trends at Première Vision

The last stage of the concertation process occurs when the collections developed by the exhibitors are presented at the trade show. This is when forecasts are transformed into realities. During the trade show, the offerings of exhibitors become visibly synchronized with the seasonal trends decided on beforehand, minimizing the risk that the collections are unsuccessful or 'out'. Trends areas, exhibitor layouts, and materials for visitors highlight all the trends that have been selected, as well as variations on these trends. The trends are explicitly visible in the so-called trends areas, which artistically display the most representative swatches for each trend. These areas, with their strong visual impact, make it possible to grasp 'at a glance' what is new, often allowing associations to be made with new products developed by specific manufacturers. Additionally, the trend documents, which are distributed to the exhibitors beforehand, are also made available to the visitors during the trade show in order to make the trends easier to understand. Finally, the exhibition layout further highlights the fashion trends in the various product categories and for the various markets. The designs above the stands often show the same fabric colours and styles, which generates a very effective visual ensemble. This is also highlighted by the basic styles the organizers require for the fittings of exhibitor stands, which are pre-fitted with pre-set modules. Buyers and designers from clothing firms (the visitors) can thus quickly identify the main trends. These trends are portrayed by the media as ways in which exhibitor firms respond to emerging seasonal trends.

At this last stage, the concertation process becomes a flow of communication that involves all visitors at Première Vision, representing some 30,000 to 40,000 firms. Furthermore, since media reports circulate the fashion trend information to millions of readers, the communication process is expanded towards a huge audience of potential buyers, which helps affirm the selected trends. The trade show is also visited by manufacturers from industry groups other than clothing, typically those seeking to source information that will help them better align their production with fashion trends. This applies both to related products, such as knitwear, bags, shoes, or accessories, as well as other products, such as furniture or cars. Even manufacturers of clothing fabrics who are not among the exhibitors at Première Vision tend to employ or even imitate the selected trends, thus contributing to their dissemination.

The final result of the concertation process is that the forecasts made at the beginning of the process are put into practice and thus confirmed. This benefits all trade show exhibitors, who, in addition to not getting their collections 'wrong', also reap obvious rewards in terms of their image as innovators. In other words, manufacturers outside the trade show tend to be seen as imitators, not innovators (Golfetto and Rinallo 2008).

12.5. CONCLUSIONS

This chapter examines a sophisticated process called trend concertation by fashion industry members. French and Italian weavers in the fine fashion apparel industry introduced this process in the trade shows they controlled in order to support their position as world leaders in the industry, against strong competition from emerging countries. The process involves forecasting future developments in social and consumer values with the goal to guide style innovation in a way that does not disperse individual efforts. By developing new knowledge about downstream markets, Première Vision—the first trade show to employ concertation processes—soon became a key site for learning and knowledge exchange in the global fashion business. Most trade shows in the clothing fabric industry have since adopted Première Vision's formula and their business now involves the provision of relevant and timely information to industrial buyers, rather than the mere renting of space to exhibitors.

As a consequence, the network of producers represented by the organizers of Première Vision (and recently other trade shows) affirms the standardization of products and styles in ways that are similar to those found in high-technology industries—although arranged through a different process (Tushman and Rosenkopf 1992; Rosenkopf and Tushman 1998). In sum, the concertation process accomplishes the following goals: (i) it provides a competitive advantage to the group of firms that display what will become the winning standard (dominant design); (ii) it unites competitors to create a 'critical mass'—large enough to accelerate the adoption of the concerted standards; (iii) concertation constructs a favourable competitive environment, since season forecasts become reality in the manner of a self-fulfilling prophecy; and (iv) it broadcasts the new trend very broadly (Rinallo et al. 2006). Another outcome of the concertation mechanism is the social stratification of the marketplace—there is a differentiation between leaders and followers and between innovators and imitators. This has important implications in terms of marketplace status and premium prices.

Beyond the case of the fabric and clothing industry, this chapter emphasizes the role of trade shows as platforms that stabilize cooperation among competitors. The strategic management literature suggests that cooperation among competing actors, otherwise known as coopetition (Brandenburger and Nalebuff 1996; Bengtsson and Kock 2000), is often unstable. Trade shows tie together competing firms that serve the same market by defining a common place and time for their promotional activities. In doing so, they create a critical mass that attracts visitor-buyers for the benefit of all competitors. Beyond the promotional element, trade shows also give rhythm to the innovation cycle of suppliers (Golfetto 2004; Power and Jansson 2008). In this chapter, we demonstrate that trade shows can, in some circumstances, affect not only the timing but also the content of innovation, thus becoming true field-configuring events (Lampel and Meyer 2008) that shape the evolution of their underlying industries.

The clothing fabric industry might constitute an extreme field, in which trade show organizers can intervene in the firms' innovation processes in stronger ways than in most other fields. Indeed, in other industries studied (also Chapter 10), we did not find similarly 'invasive' organizers whose activities influence exhibitors' inner processes. Nevertheless, the interactions between trade show organizers and exhibitors, along with their impacts on industry developments and knowledge dynamics, remains poorly understood and requires further attention across a variety of empirical contexts (see Chapter 4).

Regarding the issue of instability and conflicts among cooperating competitors, this chapter views the concertation process as intrinsically harmonious, where exhibitors come together as a community of actors to cooperate for the common good. Community, of course, also entails conflict (Anand and Watson 2004), and such tensions are particularly apparent among the larger exhibitors with structured research and development processes and more consolidated brand images. These exhibitors sometimes propose fabric collections that are not entirely compatible with the concerted trends, or purposely deviate from them. In the initial stages of the concertation process, when a common future is enacted, cooperation entails value creation for all intervening actors; yet, in later stages, competitive differentiation pressures emerge as individual exhibitors fight to capture greater shares of the jointly created value. Overall, the literature on trade shows, exhibitions, and field-configuring events is silent on the issue of competitive tensions among exhibitors, on the one hand, and among exhibitors and organizers on the other. Future research on this topic needs to engage more deeply in empirical analyses of these tensions and how they affect knowledge dynamics at trade shows.

NOTES

1. Cappetta et al. (2006) have highlighted the similarity between style innovation in fashion and the patterns of technological innovation described by Abernathy and Utterback (1978) and Anderson and Tushman (1990). As in other industry groups, innovation cycles in fashion include processes of radical and incremental innovation, with ferment phases (where many new styles are proposed) followed

by the selection of dominant designs. However, because of the symbolic properties of fashion goods with respect to consumers' needs for distinction, the dominant design coexists with market niches for products which are radically different—but nevertheless highly appreciated by some consumers. Chanel tailleurs or Armani tuxedos, for instance, are classics that do not vary with seasonal fashions.

2. The abbreviation 'S.A.' stands for 'Société anonyme' (in French) and is similar to the designation of a 'public limited company'.

13

Territorial Specialization and Trade Show Competition: The Case of Italian Marble and Ceramic Technologies

13.1. INTRODUCTION

From the perspective of trade show organizers, this chapter reconstructs the competitive dynamics of two Italian events in stone and ceramic technologies: Marmomacc and Tecnargilla, respectively. We adopt a longitudinal approach based on a variety of secondary and primary data, including trade show statistics, news sources, internal documents, as well as interviews with organizers, trade associations, exhibitors, and visitors. Based on these data, we examine how the two events have faced competitive pressures from both domestic and foreign rival trade shows. We use these case histories to exemplify some of the theoretical claims made in Part I. In particular, we demonstrate the following: how trade shows can be employed by networks of firms for collective marketing and competition purposes; how trade show development reflects territorial specialization and macroeconomic trends in the underlying industries; and how the adoption of knowledge-based strategies can affect the life-cycles of these events, while at the same time shaping the evolutionary patterns and innovation trajectories of underlying industries (see Chapters 3 to 5).

We investigate the cases of Marmomacc and Tecnargilla, from their early struggles to their development as leading events in Europe. The chapter pays particular attention to the role of these events in the promotion of Italian technology abroad, which is strongly related to the rich heritage and competencies of Italian firms. We conclude with a discussion of the two cases in light of the theoretical themes highlighted.

13.2. MARMOMACC AND THE STONE TECHNOLOGY INDUSTRY

Italy has a long tradition in marble and natural stone extraction and processing. While extraction takes place throughout the country, stone processing is geographically concentrated in two industrial districts: one located between Tuscany and Liguria in the regions of Massa Carrara, Lucca, and La Spezia, and the other located in the Verona region (Laboratorio delle Imprese 2008, 2010). In this industry, trade shows are typically organized along the vertical dimension; that is, they showcase the entire supply chain from semi-finished products to tooling machines, equipment, and processing materials. In the early 1990s, two of the industry's most important European trade shows took place in Italy (Marmomacc in Verona and Carrara Marmotec in Massa Carrara), with another major event in Germany (Stone + Tec in Nürnberg) (see Table 13.1). Outside of Europe, trade show activities in the marble and natural stone industry were still in their infancy. Today, Europe hosts at least two other established trade shows at an international level in Spain. There are also six other important events that take place outside of Europe's core, in Turkey, India, the United States, Brazil, and China (see Table 13.2).

13.2.1. The Birth and Development of Marmomacc (1961–1990)

Marmomacc was the first international trade show dedicated to the marble sector and, for almost twenty years, it served as the primary reference point for the stone industry worldwide. Founded in 1961 by a group of local firms specializing in the extraction and processing of marble (most notably, Verona's red marble), the event was initially conceived as a festival. It took place at the end of the summer in Sant'Ambrogio di Valpolicella, a small city in the centre of the Veronese extractive basin, and was organized by the municipality of Sant'Ambrogio in cooperation with the local industrial district (La Repubblica 1998; *L'Arena* 2008).

The Sant'Ambrogio location provided the event with several advantages, at least during the show's initial phases of development. First, it was situated in close geographical proximity to the extraction areas and to a critical mass of producers of machines for the extraction and processing of marble. It was also reasonably close to Germany, which, at the time, represented one of the largest markets in Europe for marble products. Second, the area was easily accessible and enjoyed a well-developed infrastructure for shipping goods abroad. Finally, the Veronese region was well-known as a tourism destination, thanks to its proximity to Lake Garda and the Italian Alps. These factors were instrumental in Marmomacc's initial success, as the event became a convenient meeting spot for the entire marble supply chain. As described by our interviewees, its relaxed

Table 13.1. Main international marble and natural stone trade shows in Europe, 1990–2010

Trade show, city year established	Month/ frequency	Products showcased	Organizer	Trade show statistics		
				1990	2000	2010
Marmomacc, Verona (Italy), 1961	October/ annual	Marble and stones (raw materials, finished products, and technology)	Veronafiere—Ente Autonomo per le Fiere di Verona	Sq.m.: 28,930 Exh. (% foreign): 1,165 (18%) Vis. (% foreign): 47,664 (20%)	Sq.m.: 57,149 Exh. (% foreign): 1,145 (31%) Vis. (% foreign): 51,746 (38%)	Sq.m.: 75,251 Exh. (% foreign): 1,530 (55%) Vis. (% foreign): 56,024 (47%)
Stone + Tec, Nürnberg (Germany), 1979	November/ bi-annual (odd years)	Marble and stones (raw materials, finished products, and technology)	Nürnberg Messe GmbH	Sq.m.: 21,060[1] Exh. (% foreign): 482 (38%) Vis. (% foreign): 31,518 (15%)	Sq.m.: 50,357[1] Exh. (% foreign): 1,251 (66%) Vis. (% foreign): 46,102 (24%)	Sq.m.: 30,303[1] Exh. (% foreign): 770 (61%) Vis. (% foreign): 34,458 (30%)
Piedra, Madrid (Spain), 1996	May/ bi-annual (even years)	Marble and stones (raw materials, finished products, and technology)	IFEMA—Feria de Madrid	//	Sq.m.: 18,589 Exh. (% foreign): 369 (37%) Vis. (% foreign): 19,936 (8%)	Sq.m.: 22,631[3] Exh. (% foreign): 415 (44%) Vis. (% foreign): 28,025 (6%)
Carrara Marmotec, Carrara (Italy), 1980	May/ bi-annual (even years)	Marble and stones (raw materials, finished products, and technology)	Internazionale Marmi e Macchine Carrara spa	Sq.m.: 26,902 Exh. (% foreign): 600 (17%) Vis. (% foreign): 36,824 (20%)	Sq.m.: 30,638 Exh. (% foreign): 551 (20%) Vis. (% foreign): 39,836 (43%)	Sq.m.: 18,924 Exh. (% foreign): 315 (21%) Vis. (% foreign): 16,740 (23%)

Table 13.1. (Continued)

Trade show, city year established	Month/ frequency	Products showcased	Organizer	Trade show statistics		
				1990	2000	2010
Expostone, Moscow (Russia), 1999	June/ Annual	Marble and stones (raw materials, finished products, and technology)	EXPOSTROY na Nakhimovskom	//	n.a.	Sq.m.: 10,270 Exh. (% foreign): 308 (60%) Vis. (% foreign): 5,000 (n.a.)
Marmol (inside Cevisama), Valencia (Spain), 1995	February/ Annual	One exhibition hall dedicated to marble and stones (raw materials, finished products, and technology) inside a trade show dedicated to ceramics	Feria Valencia	//	Sq.m.: 2,495[2] Exh. (% foreign): 62 (30%) Vis. (% foreign): 50,686 (17%) (Cevisama visitors)	Sq.m.: 2,045[2] Exh. (% foreign): 67 (52%) Vis. (% foreign): 79,421 (29%) (Cevisama visitors)

Source: CERMES 2013.

Notes: sq.m. = square metres; // = no trade show; exh. = number of exhibitors; vis. = number of visitors; % foreign = share of foreign exhibitors or visitors.

[1] Data refer to 1991, 2001, and 2009.

[2] Data refer to 2001 and 2009.

[3] Data refer to 2008.

Table 13.2. Main international marble and natural stone trade shows outside of Europe, 1990–2010

Trade show, city, year established	Month/ frequency	Products showcased	Organizer	Trade show statistics		
				1990	2000	2010
China Xiamen International Stone Fair, Xiamen (China), 2001	March/ annual	Marble and stones (raw materials, finished products, and technology)	Xiamen Jinhongxin Exhibition Co., Ltd.	//	//	Sq.m.: 95,000 Exh. (% foreign): 1,300 (n.a.) Vis. (% foreign): 101,526 (20 %)
Stonetech, Shanghai (China), 1994	April/ annual	Marble and stones (raw materials, finished products, and technology)	CCPIT Building Materials Sub-Council (in cooperation with CIEC Exhibition Co. (HK) Ltd.)	//	n.a.	Sq.m.: 65,000 Exh. (% foreign): 769 (19%) Vis. (% foreign): 46,962 (n.a.)
Marble, Izmir (Turkey), 1995	March/ annual	Marble and stones (raw materials, finished products, and technology)	IZFAS—Izmir Fair Services	//	n.a.	Sq.m.: 43,625 Exh. (% foreign): 1,146 (n.a.) Vis. (% foreign): 54,227 (n.a.)
Vitoria Stone Fair, Vitoria (Brazil), 1989	February/ Annual	Marble and stones (raw materials, finished products and technology)	Milanez & Milaneze S/S Ltda	n.a.	n.a.	Sq.m.: 35,000[2] Exh. (% foreign): 450 (n.a.) Vis. (% foreign): 22,911 (n.a.)

continued

Table 13.2. (Continued)

Trade show, city, year established	Month/ frequency	Products showcased	Organizer	Trade show statistics		
				1990	2000	2010
Natural Stone, Istanbul (Turkey), 2004	November annual	Marble and stones (raw materials, finished products and technology)	CNR Expo Trade Fairs, Inc.	//	//	Sq.m.: 22,700 Exh. (% foreign): 459 (10%)[4] Vis. (% foreign): 26,000 (9%)
Stona, Bangalore (India), 1987	February/ bi-annual (even years)	Marble and stones (raw materials, finished products and technology)	AIGSA—All India Granites and Stone Association (in cooperation with Veronafiere since 2011)	Sq.m.: n.a. Exh. (% foreign): 70 (n.a.)[3] Vis. (% foreign): n.a. (n.a.)	Sq.m.: n.a. Exh. (% foreign): 320 (20%)[3] Vis. (% foreign): 15,000 (n.a.)	Sq.m.: 16,000 Exh. (% foreign): 390 (13%) Vis. (% foreign): 50,000 (20%)
Stonexpo/Marmomacc Americas, Las Vegas (USA), 1987	October/ Annual	Marble and stones (raw materials, finished products, and technology)	Hanley Wood Exhibitions	n.a.	n.a.	Sq.m.: 10,497[1] Exh. (% foreign): 276 (n.a.) Vis. (% foreign): 6,000 (n.a.)

Source: CERMES 2013.

Notes: sq.m. = square metres; // = no trade show; exh. = number of exhibitors; vis. = number of visitors; % foreign = share of foreign exhibitors or visitors
[1] Data refer to 2008.
[2] Data refer to 2009.
[3] Data refer to 1992 and 2002.
[4] Data refer to 2009.

atmosphere was also conducive to business and enabled multiple opportunities for observing key developments in the industry and interacting with leading agents.

After a few years, the show had already reached a remarkable size in terms of the number of visitors and exhibitors it attracted. Yet, the exhibition's success and the larger scale of operations posed organizational difficulties for the municipality of Sant'Ambrogio, which lacked a sufficiently large staff and the competencies needed to run the increasingly complex event. As a result, the exhibition was entrusted to Veronafiere in 1979—an organization that owned and managed the Verona trade show venue. While the trade show remained in Sant'Ambrogio until 1991, Veronafiere began to open the event to foreign exhibitors. Although it was still predominantly an export trade show, our interviewees stressed that some of the privileges granted to local producers (e.g. having booths in the most desirable positions) were gradually eliminated in order to give equal treatment to all exhibitors.

Under the new management, the exhibition enjoyed further growth and drew increasing foreign attendance. In 1985, Marmomacc attracted almost 800 exhibitors and approximately 33,000 visitors in a hall spanning 22,000 square metres (CERMES 2013). In 1990, the number of exhibitors was already 1,165 (18 per cent being foreign exhibitors) and the number of visitors about 48,000 in an exhibition area of almost 29,000 square metres. Foreign visitors represented approximately 20 per cent of total attendance (see Table 13.1), with a significant presence from Germany and South America. Our interviewees explained that the latter was a result of the diversification of the regional industry's export flows. In 1991, the exhibition had reached full capacity and there was a long waiting list of hopeful exhibitors.

13.2.2. Local Conflicts and the Development of Rival Events (1990–2000)

In 1992, Marmomacc moved to the Verona trade show venue because of challenges associated with satisfying space requests from the exhibitors. The relocation was also motivated by issues with public transportation services from Sant' Ambrogio to train stations, airports, and the hotel areas. These problems were not an issue in Verona due to improved accessibility and the venue's greater capacity. At the same time, Veronafiere acquired full control of the exhibition and Marmomacc fully opened its doors to non-local exhibitors, domestic and foreign alike.

These changes caused some discontent, however. Many local producers resented the fact that the municipality of Sant'Ambrogio consented to the relocation, as they feared a loss of identity in a larger exhibition that could potentially loosen its historical link with the local marble industrial district.

These producers did not support the newly relocated show and some preferred to exhibit at foreign trade shows. Others created a competing event in Sant'Ambrogio and even started legal action against Veronafiere. In 1992, this resulted in two competing events being held in the Veronese area at about the same time: one in Sant'Ambrogio, named Marmomacc, which was organized by local marble producers; the other in Verona, named Intermarmomacch, which was organized by Veronafiere (*L' Arena* 2008). This coexistence of events, which lasted until 1994, created much confusion among exhibitors and visitors who initially split themselves roughly equally between the two shows (some also decided to attend both events). Intermarmomacch eventually became the preferred event with the more sustainable strategy, and the competing show in Sant'Ambrogio closed down. During this period of confusion, two competing events—Stone + Tec (Nürnberg) and Carrara Marmotec (Marina di Carrara)—grew very quickly. Soon both events, but particularly Stone + Tec, had reached a position that challenged the leadership of Marmomacc. In 1993, for instance, Marmomacc registered a significantly lower number of exhibitors and visitors than these two competitors (see Table 13.1).

(i) Carrara Marmotec

Carrara Marmotec was created in 1980 by Carrara Fiere—the owner of the local trade show venue—with the support of the Tuscany region. The immediate success of the show was due to its link with Carrara's white marble, which is world-renowned for its quality and aesthetic value. Because of this, the Carrara event initially attracted different visitors than the Verona show. It was more oriented towards the US and Middle East markets which, as emphasized in our interviews, were important users of Carrara white marble during the 1980s. These differences, which were related to the specialization of the underlying local industrial districts, initially made the two Italian shows complementary. This was true despite the lack of coordination between their respective organizers.

By 1985, Carrara Marmotec had already reached a considerable size, with approximately 600 exhibitors and more than 35,000 visitors in an exhibition space of 25,000 square metres (CERMES 2013). Taking advantage of the conflict between the two Veronese events, the show reached its peak in 2000, but started to decline thereafter. Our interviews revealed that, since the early 1990s and particularly following the Gulf War, the local industrial district had difficulty exporting to the Middle East. Carrara Marmotec responded by introducing a greater number of foreign exhibitors. Yet this was not enough to compensate for the decline in the number and rented surfaces of local producers. Over the course of only a few years, Marmomacc was able to re-establish its leadership over the domestic competitor, largely because it focused on a diversified exhibitor basis and varied markets.

(ii) Stone + Tec

Stone + Tec was established as a trade show in 1979 on the initiative of Nürnberg Messe GmbH, the organizer and owner of the Nürnberg trade fair venue. Unlike Marmomacc, Stone + Tec was not conceived as an export event. Its strategy was to attract foreign producers to penetrate the large market represented by Germany and its neighbouring countries. In 1990, though still significantly smaller than Marmomacc, Stone + Tec had already achieved an impressive size, with 482 exhibitors and 31,000 visitors in an exhibition space of 21,000 square metres (see Table 13.1). But the conflict between the events in Italy led to a rapid increase in the presence of Italian exhibitors, who were considered market leaders. Between 1991 and 1993, the number of Italian exhibitors at Stone + Tec increased by almost 400 per cent from 55 to 273 (CERMES 2013). Producers from other countries soon followed and, as a consequence, Stone + Tec developed a strong international dimension. By 2001, the show had doubled in size, with 1,251 exhibitors and 46,000 visitors on a surface of more than 50,000 square metres (CERMES 2013). The international press, at the time, viewed Stone + Tec as the main European show for the natural stone industry. While it did not surpass Marmomacc in terms of size (as Marmomacc attracted more visitors), the German event reached a higher level of internationalization among exhibitors. In 2001, foreign exhibitors represented 66 per cent of the total at Stone + Tec, compared to 31 per cent at Marmomacc (CERMES 2013). This was largely due to Stone + Tec's policy of welcoming all producers, irrespective of quality levels and geographical origin.

13.2.3. Marmomacc's Recovery and Market Development Activities

Despite this new competition, Marmomacc began to show signs of recovery in 1994. This was largely due to the presence of buyers from target markets, particularly South America, the US, and Northern Europe. After the Sant'Ambrogio show closed its doors, the exhibiting firms that had previously been divided between the two events joined together in Marmomacc. This was an important pre-condition underlying Marmomacc's rapid growth and ability to surpass Stone + Tec, in terms of both exhibitors and visitors (see Table 13.1). At this time, Stone + Tec had also started to attract an increasing number of manufacturers from developing countries exhibiting low-cost products. High-quality producers consequently favoured the Verona event where quality differences appeared better defended. Parallel to this, the Veronese industrial district performed better than its Tuscan–Ligurian rival, thanks to the local firms' increased professionalism and internationalization.

Although our interviews suggest that Italy had lost its position as the world's main producer and exporter of natural stone materials by that time, it maintained its traditional importance in stone-processing technology. China was the first to surpass Italy, followed by India and Turkey, despite the fact that these countries delivered stones of different quality. Asian competitors were also increasingly supplying marble-processing technology. Although European (particularly Italian) tooling machines and related equipment had originally contributed to quality improvements in local marble products, these were now imitated by producers from other countries and produced at a lower cost. Also, the new international trade shows that had become established reflected the global restructuring of the natural stone industry (see Table 13.2). As a result, Marmomacc needed to further open itself to foreign exhibitors, especially those from new production countries. Based on our interviews, this did indeed occur, but under the following specific conditions: (i) Italian producers-exhibitors had to maintain a central role in the show, in terms of visibility inside the exhibition layout; (ii) only high-quality producers were selected as exhibitors; and (iii) there was to be a continued focus on marble and natural stone, thus barring admission to imitations of such products, regardless of quality. Taken together, these measures strongly supported Marmomacc's leadership in the field despite changes in the production environment. On the one hand, foreign exhibitors increased the size of the show and its attractiveness to foreign visitors; on the other hand, the focus on high-quality marble and natural stones protected exhibitors from undesired comparisons with low-quality products or lower-cost substitutes.

One of the main challenges facing Italian producers at the time was the need to increase the perceived value of their products in order to compete with lower priced alternatives offered by foreign competitors. To address this challenge, Marmomacc attempted to position marble and stone materials as fashion/design products, thus building on Italy's reputation in aesthetic and symbolic industries (Il Sole 24 Ore 2002). This strategy was hindered, however, by the limited market orientation and weak marketing and communication competencies of Italian firms. While having strong technical skills in treating materials, they tended to be small in size and had limited knowledge of end markets and buyer behaviours. Moreover, as indicated by the interviewees, the sales channels of stone products, particularly in Europe, were mediated by wholesalers who treated large volumes of various materials in a standardized manner. In the final markets, product differences were difficult to perceive by consumers, given the absence of branded products. The only way to overcome this was through geographical origin qualifications (i.e. 'Italian marble'). According to our interviewees, another problem was that consumers primarily associated marble with tombstones and church floors, and even architects and interior designers had limited knowledge of the differences among various marble varieties.

In response to these challenges, the organizers of Marmomacc adopted various knowledge-based strategies aimed at building a specific 'industry culture' and educating the market about the broader applicability of the products. As our interviews suggest, Marmomacc's strategies focused, in particular, on the differences between the quality of its exhibitors' products and that of non-exhibitors. The trade show thus became a platform for mobilizing entrepreneurial associations, market leaders, as well as partner-ships between firms targeted at collective promotional projects. It was important to promote marble as a design-oriented product with a large vari-ety of different applications (both in interior and exterior decorations) that could be viewed as both a design furnishing accessory and a surface. To accomplish this, the show conducted advertising and public relations cam-paigns in Italy and elsewhere, focusing in particular on architectural maga-zines that targeted both architects and consumers. During the event itself, architectural experiments were launched featuring the use of marble in a variety of different settings, such as hotel halls, spas, and public spaces. To support this, various installations were realized at the Triennale Design Museum in Milan, Salone del Mobile (see Chapter 14), and other important international furniture and design trade shows. Such activities yielded high visibility in the international press, thus fostering knowledge flows about the industry, its products, their applicability, and their status as design products.

Marmomacc targeted much of its promotional activities at purchase influ-encers and decision-makers for decoration materials (i.e. architects and designers) and opinion leaders (i.e. star architects and specialized journal-ists). An important goal was to help these professionals discern differences among stone materials and communicate the competencies of marble tech-nology producers, to assist decision-makers in finding high-end technical and aesthetic solutions to increase the value of their realizations. Mar-momacc had already involved architects since 1987, with the institution of a biennial international award for Architecture in Stone (Marmomacc 2013a) supported by a prestigious international jury of historians, critics, and pro-fessors of architecture. Winning projects aimed to highlight new trends and innovative experiences in the architectural use of natural stone and were displayed at highly attended exhibitions and award ceremonies. Marmomacc also adopted another design initiative, Marmomacc Meets Design, which involved the selection of innovative examples of marble and stone-based furnishing accessories by well-known designers and firms; it showcased these applications in special areas inside the show (Gulf Construction 2008).

Marmomacc's attempt to build a culture of marble and natural stone technology and design led to a series of educational initiatives targeting architects, product designers, and other opinion leaders. Such initiatives included courses, workshops, and presentations during architectural associations' meetings and recognized continuing education programmes. For instance, Marmomacc became the continuing education provider at the American Institute of Architects in 1998. In this role, it organized a four-day workshop on design surrounding natural stone, which was eventually recognized by professional architectural associations in the UK, Canada, South Africa, and elsewhere. Marmomacc also collaborated with Italian universities and sponsors in the design of a specialized Master of Science in building, architecture, and contemporary stone design at Milan's polytechnic school for architects, engineers, and industrial designers. It also offered specialized courses at various other Italian universities (Marmomacc 2013b).

Since the 1990s, the organizers of Marmomacc attempted to promote the image of marble and natural stone as 'made in Italy' to an international audience. It did so by bringing together a selection of producers and their products at important trade shows worldwide. Though traditionally regarded as being inferior to individual marketing activities in terms of return on investments (Seringhaus and Rosson 1998), this new generation of collective participation was characterized by the goal of building a coherent image in key export markets. These joint exhibits basically functioned as a brand extension of Marmomacc, providing a guarantee to visitors that they would find well-selected exhibitors and multiple learning opportunities, similar to those they would find at the Verona exhibition. Beyond organizing collective exhibits, Marmomacc also entered into commercial partnerships with some foreign trade show organizers in strategic markets (e.g. US, India, and Saudi Arabia). These partnerships involved the co-organization of shows and, in some cases, the creation of common brands (Marmomacc 2013c).

Today, Marmomacc is considered the leading international trade show in the natural stone products and technologies industry; it has become a mandatory stopover in the industry's global trade show circuit. In 2010, despite the global economic crisis, Marmomacc attracted 1,530 direct exhibitors (55 per cent of which were of foreign origin) and more than 56,000 visitors (47 per cent foreign visitors) in an exhibition hall spanning more than 75,000 square metres (see Table 13.1). More importantly, by linking marble and natural stone to the design system, and supporting cooperation between leading firms and world-renowned architects, Marmomacc established a visible example for smaller, less market-oriented firms to imitate. While our data do not allow us to conduct a complete analysis of the cultural impact of the show, it seems clear that the event plays an important role in shaping the innovation trajectories of exhibitors and the behaviours of downstream markets.

13.3. TECNARGILLA AND THE PROMOTION OF ITALIAN CERAMIC TECHNOLOGY

Ceramic production technologies consist of various specialized industries that produce building bricks, sanitary ware, tableware, and ceramic tiles. The origins of the ceramic tile industry, in which Italy is considered to be a world leader, are intertwined with the history of production in Italy. This history dates back to the earthenware and crockery craftsmanship of the thirteenth century, as well as early twentieth-century manufacturing (Porter 1990; Abruzzese et al. 2004; Russo 2004). The industry took off and developed an international profile in the 1950s during Italy's post-war reconstruction, when all types of building and interior decoration materials were in high demand. During this period, there were only a handful of ceramic tile producers in Italy, geographically concentrated in and around Sassuolo, a small city near Modena in the Emilia Romagna region. Due to high domestic demand and low investment costs, the number of ceramic producers grew almost exponentially in the years that followed. While there were only fourteen ceramic producers in 1955, that number reached 102 by 1962 (Porter 1990; Russo 2004). Originally carried out as quasi-artisanal production, the activities of tile firms benefited from the availability of engineers working in other industries located nearby. These engineers contributed to the mechanization of production in the industry.

Initially, Sassuolo tile producers relied on foreign exports for both their technology and raw materials. Despite the presence of nearby red clay deposits, the technology for ceramic production was imported from Germany, France, and the US during the 1950s and relied on white clays that were imported from the UK. Over time, however, local producers increasingly learned to adapt foreign technology to process locally available red clays. Eventually, technicians working for tile producers started their own tile equipment and technology firms (Porter 1990; Russo 2004), which became internationally competitive during the 1970s. Faced with growing internal competition and the effects of the 1973 energy crises, the Sassuolo tile technology district eventually developed process innovations that significantly decreased labour and energy costs, as well as production time. As a consequence, it became a world leader in the industry. By the 1980s, Italy was home to approximately 200 tile technology producers, 60 per cent of which were located in the Sassuolo area (Porter 1990; Russo 2004). While these producers initially focused their attention exclusively on the domestic market, they later began to export their products to other European countries (particularly Spain), South America (mostly Brazil), and Asia.

13.3.1. Cooperation and Competition among the Main Trade Shows (1980–1999)

The most important European trade shows dedicated to ceramic production and processing equipment emerged in the late 1970s and early 1980s (see Table 13.3). The industry's first specialized trade show, CERAMITEC, was founded in 1979 in Munich, Germany, by Messe München GmbH—the organization that manages the local exhibition venue. Our interviews suggest that, at this time, Italian producers of ceramic technology typically exhibited their exhibits at SAIE, an international building exhibition established in Bologna in 1965 that is dedicated to a wide range of industries surrounding the construction industry. When voices from within the industry increasingly began to call for a promotional event specialized in ceramic technologies, some of the leading producers of ceramic and building brick equipment, along with the trade show organizers Fiera Bologna and Fiera di Rimini, developed and established a new event: Tecnargilla.[1] Organized by Fiera di Rimini, the show was launched in 1980 in Rimini. Later, the newly constituted Association of Italian Manufacturers of Machinery and Equipment for Ceramics (ACIMAC) also became involved in the show's organization. Initially operating on an annual basis, Tecnargilla took place at the same time as Bologna's SAIE. With 140 exhibitors (thirty of foreign origin) and 7,500 visitors attending its inaugural edition (CERMES 2013), Tecnargilla represented a potential threat to its German competitor CERAMITEC. Instead of engaging in a direct competition, however, the organizers of Tecnargilla and CER-AMITEC entered into the so-called 'Munich Agreement', which defined the frequency and conditions of each show. According to this agreement, CER-AMITEC would be held as a tri-annual event, while Tecnargilla would follow a yearly cycle. During the years of overlap, Tecnargilla would assume a national focus. Generally, however, German firms also committed to attending Tecnargilla and exhibiting full showcases of their machinery and technology in its international editions.

In terms of the industry's international events, another, smaller show[2] existed in the city of Stoke-on-Trent in England—an area known since the seventeenth century for tableware manufacturing. During the 1990s, this show moved to the more accessible Birmingham exhibition venue. The three events showcased a somewhat different product mix due to the specialized demand of ceramic technology buyers in their respective catchment basins. Whereas Tecnargilla focused on tile production, CERAMITEC was devoted to technology

Table 13.3. Main international ceramic technology trade shows in Europe, 1990–2010

Trade show, city, year established	Month/ frequency	Products showcased	Organizer	Trade show statistics		
				1990	2000	2010
Ceramitec, Munich (Germany), 1979	May/ tri-annual	Machinery, plants, equipment, materials, and additives for ceramics, clay ceramics, technical ceramics, and powder metallurgy	Messe München GmbH	Sq.m.: 28,859[1] Exh. (% foreign): 582 (48%) Vis. (% foreign): 25,254 (47%)	Sq.m.: 44,509 Exh. (% foreign): 830 (63%) Vis. (% foreign): 28,660 (51%)	Sq.m.: 19,887[1] Exh. (% foreign): 656 (51%) Vis. (% foreign): 14,601 (57%)
Tecnargilla, Rimini (Italy), 1980	September/ bi-annual (since 2002), tri-annual (1989–1999), annual (1980–1988)	Machinery, plants, equipment, materials, and additives for ceramics, clay ceramics, technical ceramics, and powder metallurgy	Rimini Fiera spa and ACIMAC	Sq.m.: 16,265[2] Exh. (% foreign): 300 (34%) Vis. (% foreign): 14,775 (27%)	Sq.m.: 38,312[2] Exh. (% foreign): 505 (22%) Vis. (% foreign): 27,747 (40%)	Sq.m.: 30,732 Exh. (% foreign): 302 (22%) Vis. (% foreign): 31,599 (46%)

Source: CERMES 2013.

Notes: sq.m. = square metres; exh. = number of exhibitors; vis. = number of visitors; % foreign = share of foreign exhibitors or visitors

[1] Data refer to 1991 and 2009.

[2] Data refer to 1989 and 1999.

for building bricks and sanitary ware. And the Birmingham show specialized in machines for tableware production.

CERAMITEC was initially at the top of the hierarchy of ceramic technology trade shows. One of its key strengths was its geographical position in the centre of the supply and demand of different industry segments. In 1991, CERAMITEC had a size of almost 29,000 square metres, with 582 exhibitors (48 per cent of whom were foreign) and more than 25,000 visitors (47 per cent international visitors) (see Table 13.3). At about the same time, Tecnargilla had a surface space of about 16,000 square metres (1989), with 300 exhibitors (34 per cent of foreign origin) and almost 15,000 visitors (27 per cent foreign visitors). While reliable data on the Birmingham trade show are hard to find, our interviews with trade show organizers and exhibitors suggest that it was significantly smaller than the other events, with less than 5,000 square metres of exhibition space during the early 1990s (CERMES 2013).

The year 1992 represented a major turning point in Tecnargilla's development. At this point, the association of Italian ceramic technology producers decided not to renew their commitment to the collective participation of Italian exhibitors at the Birmingham event—an event focused on tableware technology that had decreased in market importance. It no longer seemed justified to make the promotional investments to participate in this show. According to our interviewees, the decision to discontinue collective participation encouraged other exhibitors to withdraw as well. The Birmingham event consequently declined and ultimately closed down. In the aftermath of this experience, Italian producers began to recognize their collective importance and considered the possibility of entering into direct competition with CERAMITEC. Yet, in 1994 and 1997, CERAMITEC saw a dramatic increase in size. While this increase in size was partially due to the Italian exhibitor contingent, Tecnargilla remained a follower at this point—albeit a relatively large one (CERMES 2013).

Due to the continued strength of Italian ceramic technology in the global marketplace, Tecnargilla continued to grow and soon began to challenge CERAMITEC. This was made possible by an expansion of the exhibition space. Previously, the Rimini venue was completely saturated by Tecnargilla, making further increases in rented space effectively impossible. During the renovations to Rimini's exhibition venue during the second half of the 1990s, however, the organizers of Tecnargilla decided to temporarily move the event to the trade show venue in Verona, which was considerably larger than the one in Rimini. In 1996 and 1999, Tecnargilla thus experienced a considerable increase in the number of exhibitors and essentially doubled its rented surface space (CERMES 2013). In 1999, the organizers further improved learning opportunities at the event through the establishment of a series of collateral events, including the Ceramic Technology Transfer Day, which was devoted to applications of scientific research to ceramic materials, processes, and plants (personal interviews). Because of this experience, observers in the industry and the organizers of the show were convinced that the Italian show would overtake CERAMITEC.

Another important aspect contributing to Tecnargilla's growth was the decision to change the frequency of the events. After the termination of the Birmingham event, the trade show cycle favoured CERAMITEC, since there was a vacant year before the German show would take place, with Tecnargilla taking place the following year. In an effort to compromise on this front, our interviewees informed us that the Italian trade show organization proposed a simpler bi-annual alternation between the two events. But CERAMITEC refused. In 2002, when Tecnargilla returned to Rimini, the show decided to adopt a bi-annual rhythm. Since CERAMITEC's rhythm remained a tri-annual one, this meant that once every six years the two events took place during the same year. These decisions signalled the end of cooperation between the two organizations and the beginning of a more conflictual relationship.

13.3.2. Leadership of Tecnargilla (2000–2009)

CERAMITEC responded to the growing success of its Italian rival by strengthening its 2000 edition with the inclusion of conferences and technical seminars, which aimed to enhance the show's media visibility and increase its overall impact on the field. The event programme was eventually organized in cooperation with the German ceramic industry association. The show also benefited from the renovation and extension of the Munich trade show venue, which enabled an increase in CERAMITEC's exhibition space and in the number of exhibitors. The number of visitors remained the same as before (CERMES 2003).

Meanwhile, Tecnargilla continued to follow the development path initiated in the previous decade. In 2002, it returned to the Rimini venue, which had been entirely rebuilt, tripling its exhibition capacity. The reconstructed venue also allowed for some innovations. First, it introduced a new exhibition area, Kromatech, which was dedicated to aesthetics, colours, and raw materials in the ceramics field. By linking technology to product design, Tecnargilla was able to build on Italian capabilities and the country's reputation in aesthetic and lifestyle domains. Second, it installed a series of cultural events and parallel activities, such as ceramics workshops, to support the show's visibility and attractiveness. For the first time in Tecnargilla's history, as emphasized by our interviewees, there was a waiting list of exhibitors, which underlined the growing importance of the show.

In the early 2000s, CERAMITEC and Tecnargilla were evenly matched in terms of rented exhibition space and number of visitors (44,000 square metres and 29,000 visitors for CERAMITEC; 38,000 square metres and 28,000 visitors for Tecnargilla; see Table 13.3). In terms of the number of exhibitors, however, CERAMITEC was still in the lead. By the mid-2000s, however, Tecnargilla surpassed CERAMITEC in rented exhibition space. A key factor in this advancement was the decision of the Association of Italian Manufacturers of Machinery and Equipment for Ceramics to stop organizing Italian collective exhibits at CERAMITEC. The final collective participation, in 2003, was particularly rich and well-organized; it occupied over 15,000 square metres (one-third of the overall exhibition space), and coined a new brand, Tech Gate, which highlighted Italian leadership in ceramic production technology. From that point on, Italian exhibitors interested in participating in the German event did so individually. Based on our interviews, the decision to terminate collective participation at CERAMITEC had two motivations: first, the attractiveness of the German market had declined for many Italian producers, as the demand for ceramic tiles had decreased; second, Italian industry representatives believed that the image of Italian producers would be better promoted in the context of an Italian show.

Consequently, the number of Italian exhibitors attending CERAMITEC drastically declined, from 176 in 2003 to sixty-one in 2006 and thirteen in 2009 (CERMES 2013). The vast majority of Italian exhibitors concentrated on participating at Tecnargilla. Moreover, foreign customers who met with Italian producers in Munich followed the Italian exhibitors to Rimini. As a result, CERAMITEC experienced a decrease, most notably in the number of visitors, which fell by 16 per cent between 2000 and 2003 (CERMES 2013). In 2006, when Tecnargilla and CERAMITEC occurred at the same time (and also in 2009), the German event further declined with respect to total rented exhibition space and the number of visitors. The number of exhibitors remained quite stable, however, as CERAMITEC extended trade show participation to previously untapped industry segments, such as advanced ceramics (i.e. ceramics with special properties for specific uses). According to our interviews with trade show organizers and exhibitors, these changes reduced CERAMITEC's reputation as a showcase of tile production technology and limited its importance in the areas of sanitary ware and building bricks. This latter development was also due to the acquisition of some of the largest German firms by former Italian rivals.

In 2004, Tecnargilla's visitors surpassed those of CERAMITEC for the first time since direct competition between the two shows started (CERMES 2013). With respect to exhibitors, Tecnargilla introduced a new section called Claytech, which was dedicated to brick building technologies that had previously been shown primarily at CERAMITEC. This consolidated the show's leadership (Tecnargilla 2013).[3] Despite the temporal overlap between the two shows in 2006, Tecnargilla's visitor base continued to grow, due in part to the invitation of qualified buyer delegations from the main ceramic-producing countries.

13.3.3. Collective Participation at Foreign Shows

Thanks to its traditional leadership in ceramic tile technology and the new sections devoted to previously neglected industry branches, Tecnargilla positioned itself as the European meeting place for the entire industry—a place where exhibitors presented their innovations for the first time and where visitors learned about key trends in the ceramic technology field. The industry association supported the use of the event as a promotional platform for Italian ceramic technology. In the new millennium, the industry association decided to strengthen international promotional activities through collective exhibits at trade shows outside of Europe. Three events became the focus of these activities:

(i) Ceramics China (Guangzhou, May)

This annual trade show is exclusively dedicated to ceramic production technology (Ceramics China 2013). The industry association's presence in China originally started in the late 1980s. Faced with a growing number of competing trade shows, the association selected this show to become a reference event abroad for the Italian industry.

(ii) Mosbuild (Moscow, April)

Mosbuild is a general construction trade show held annually (Mosbuild 2013). Since it was selected by the industry association, Italian producers have occupied an entire exhibition hall dedicated to ceramic technology.

(iii) Expo Revestir (São Paulo, March)

This annual trade show is dedicated to finished products (covering materials) (Expo Revestir 2013). The association decided to participate in this event under the brand name 'Tecnargilla Brazil' to emphasize the collective participation of Italian producers. The association also contributes to the event by sponsoring a ceramic technology conference.

In the view of the Association of Italian Manufacturers of Machinery and Equipment for Ceramics, collective exhibits are particularly important in establishing a national production system's presence in overseas markets. Unlike individual exhibits, a collective presentation supports an image of solidarity, stability, and variety, all of which help to convey the culture of

Italian producers and their role in ceramic tile technology. Once they become successful, collective exhibits become less important, as individual producers extend their market search on their own, based on existing customers.

In the early 2000s, Tecnargilla's organizers adopted a calendarization strategy in partial overlap with two finished products trade shows: Cersaie, a Bologna show dedicated to ceramic tiles, and Marmomacc. As indicated in our interviews, the goals behind this strategy are two-fold. On the one hand, this approach appeals to international visitors who now have the option of attending different trade shows during a single trip to Italy and thus gain a better view of the entire production chain. On the other hand, the overlap between Cersaie and Tecnargilla strengthens the image of the Sassuolo industrial district whose producers are central to both events. Innovation is clearly the key message emphasized in Tecnargilla's marketing communications. In 2010, the event was named 'The Future of Ceramics', and the communication campaign aimed to explain the reasons for the event's leadership in the ceramics technology field. As indicated through personal interviews, this suggested that 60 per cent of the world's ceramic technology turnover is represented at the show and that its exhibitors are the most innovative firms in the field.

13.4. CONCLUSIONS

This chapter analyses the history and development of two leading European trade shows in the marble and ceramics technology industries. These export-oriented events highlight the role of trade shows in the collective marketing of industrial districts and their respective national industries. In the case of the marble and natural stone technology industry, the presence of two rival industrial districts in Tuscany and Veneto hindered the establishment of a national-level trade show for many years, enabling the expansion of foreign events. The concentration of leading producers in one industrial district instead helped facilitate the international recognition and expansion of Tecnargilla in the ceramic technology industry. Compared to Marmomacc, it was easier to mobilize the domestic exhibitor base in the case of Tecnargilla. Eventually, however, both shows became leading events in the global trade show circuit, providing a promotional platform for domestic producers to showcase their commercial offerings and innovations. Protectionist attitudes softened over time as organizers recognized the value of including well-selected foreign competitors: indeed, their presence contributed to the international visibility of the shows in general and their attractiveness to international visitors/buyers.

The shows and industries investigated in this chapter clearly reflect the conceptualizations developed in Part I of this book regarding the interrelationships and reflexive dynamics between industry agglomerations in an urban/regional/national context and their respective trade shows (see Chapter 5). In particular, three conclusions can be drawn from this analysis.

First, the cases of Marmomacc and Tecnargilla illustrate how territorial specialization affects trade show specialization and, more generally, competition among events. In the case of ceramic technology, the specializations of trade shows in Italy, Germany, and the UK were based on the different product specializations of firms in the respective regional/national catchment basins. In the case of marble, the trade shows in Carrara and Sant'Ambrogio/Verona were strongly influenced by the specific natural resources found in these regions and the competencies of firms. Through showcasing these product specializations, the trade shows attracted buyers interested in such products, thereby encouraging the further specialization of local firms. As a consequence, these export events were strongly linked to overseas demand trends in product groups that were central to the underlying industry agglomerations.

Second, as the most successful shows progressed through their life-cycle to growth and maturity, the dependence on the local industry basis weakened. The presence of international buyers attracted further exhibitors from different branches of the industry, making the show attractive to more buyers, thus creating a virtuous circle. In the case of Tecnargilla, the organizers accelerated the virtuous cycle by constructing specialized exhibition areas dedicated to other industry branches. By attracting non-local producers with heterogeneous specializations, the event was no longer a simple reflection of the underlying Sassuolo industrial district. Still, the trade show remained distinct from its German competitor by maintaining a specific 'Italian flavour'. Trade show life-cycles can differ, however; they do not follow a deterministic sequence. Some of the events never reach international recognition, nor are they able to diversify beyond the specialization of the underlying local/regional firms. Such variations in trade show dynamics depend on macroeconomic trends favouring certain productions over others, on the organizers' reactions to changes in the global supply chains, and on the action taken by the organizers of rival events.

Third, the cases described in this chapter emphasize the role of trade show organizers (and their supporting stakeholders) in strengthening the competitiveness of their events by adopting knowledge-based strategies that multiply the learning opportunities for visitors and exhibitors alike (see Chapter 4). In the case of Marmomacc, for instance, the organizers were instrumental in promoting the culture of Italian marble as a brand, which was otherwise hard to differentiate from lower-priced substitutes.

NOTES

1. In Italian, the term 'argilla' refers to clay.
2. Despite our best efforts, we were unable to identify the name of this show; it has long ceased to exist. Data on this event (i.e. rented surfaces, exhibitors, visitors, dates) are not included in the CERMES Trade Fair Observatory database for the period under consideration. Information provided in the text is, thus, based on personal interviews with Italian ceramic producers and Tecnargilla organizers.
3. Additionally, the new exhibition section 'Kermat' was introduced, dedicated to advanced ceramic products and corresponding production technologies.

14

Knowledge Dynamics in Export Shows: The Affirmation of the Italian Furniture Industry

14.1. INTRODUCTION

Export trade shows are aimed at supporting regional/national manufacturers and, therefore, include a reduced number of foreign exhibitors. Conversely, visitors to these events usually include a high number of potential buyers from other regions and countries who expect to examine a wide range of products and buying alternatives in a short period of time. Such shows are somewhat restricted in their potential for knowledge exchanges, as the products exhibited are only partially representative of what is available at a broader international scale in the industry. Horizontal learning processes between exhibitors are thus focused on local knowledge. Vertical relations between participants allow visitors to acquire in-depth knowledge from regional manufacturers; yet such relations require substantial time and are associated with high costs, because it is necessary to visit several shows in different countries in order to gain full information about market trends. For this reason, export trade shows tend to be abandoned by visitors over time in favour of hub events that provide a global overview of the market (see Chapter 4; Rinallo and Golfetto 2011).

The trade show Salone Internazionale del Mobile in Milan, or simply Salone del Mobile (SMM), represents an exception to this trend. This event has succeeded not only in promoting the once-fragmented Italian furniture industry at a global level, but also in establishing and maintaining its role as a leading world event. This is true despite its focus on Italian products and despite competition from international hub events.

This chapter outlines the history of Salone del Mobile and its development into a leading world event for the furniture industry. Behind its particular growth process is the strong guiding hand of the organizers of Salone del Mobile, the national association of manufacturers in the industry. Central to the show's success was the adoption of practices to foster knowledge exchanges between exhibitors, as well as efforts to strengthen the visitors' learning experiences. These initiatives have, in turn, triggered other parallel 'fringe events' that were spontaneously launched by firms. These parallel events have enhanced the learning experience of all participants. As a result, Salone del Mobile has remained a strong contender in the context of competing international trade shows in the furniture industry.

The history of Salone del Mobile depicted here is based on a wide range of primary and secondary sources. These include: interviews with exhibitors, visitors, and the organizers of Salone del Mobile as well as other events; documents from the organizers' archives; articles in the international press; and statistical data regarding the number and origin of exhibitors and visitors at European furniture trade shows. The next section describes the industrial context of Salone del Mobile and the characteristics of important competing events. This is followed by an outline of the history of the event and of the organizers' main initiatives. We conclude by summarizing the chapter, focusing in particular on the organizers' efforts to encourage knowledge exchanges.

14.2. FURNITURE TRADE SHOWS IN EUROPE

The European furniture industry is one of the main players in the global furniture market, with a share of almost 19 per cent of global exports (EUROSTAT 2011). In recent years, imports have also been high, leading to a deficit in the trade balance of many European countries. A large share of the imports originates from China, which has become a strong competitor for European manufacturers. The main manufacturing countries in Europe are Italy and Germany, followed by the UK, France, Spain, and Poland. With the exception of a few large manufacturing firms, the industry is generally dominated by small enterprises, as 86 per cent of furniture makers in the European Union have fewer than ten employees (EUROSTAT 2011).

In addition to being the leader in the European furniture sector, Italy is also the third largest European consumer market after Germany and the UK. In terms of overseas trade, Italy is the largest exporter in the European Union. Germany is the second largest furniture producer in Europe and also the second largest exporter. While both countries differ in terms of industrial structure, Germany has long been Italy's most important rival in the industry. Despite considerable variation in the total number of firms, the furniture industry in each country is about the same size in terms of value added. There are about ten times more firms in Italy compared to Germany, but German firms are on average ten times larger (Eurostat 2011).

Furniture trade shows have a strong historical basis in Europe. Between the 1950s and late 1970s, most of the main manufacturing countries hosted their own trade shows, aimed at promoting their respective national industries. The first broader European event was the International Möbelmesse Köln (known today as 'imm cologne—the international furnishing show'), which was founded in 1949. By 2010, there were thirteen European furniture trade shows operating on an international scale (CERMES 2012b). There were also numerous specialized events dedicated to lighting, kitchens, and office furniture. International events are usually business-to-business shows, although the public is often allowed access for one or two days. Visitors include wholesale distributors, export-importers, mass retail buyers, traditional retailers, and contractors for hotels, offices, and municipalities. There are also many architects and decorators, many of which act as purchase influencers for large buyers and final consumers. Aside from these international events, there are many furniture shows on the national and regional scale that are directed towards consumers. At these events, furniture is often showcased together with other consumer goods or in general showrooms (CERMES 2013).

The 2000s have seen a substantial reduction in the number of European trade shows at an international level and a growing focus on a few main events with intercontinental appeal. This is partly due to a reorganization of the furniture industry and the resulting concentration of manufacturing and distribution firms (CERMES 2012b). It also relates to an increase in promotional investments by European exhibitor-producers in non-European events (CERMES 2012b).

The most influential events are those located in the main furniture manufacturing countries: Italy, Germany, and France. It is important to note, however, that the ranking of these events has undergone some changes in recent years (see Figure 14.1). In fact, until the late 1990s, Cologne's Möbelmesse was the clear leader in terms of size, number of exhibitors, visitors, and international participation. Since 2000, however, this position has been challenged by Salone del Mobile of Milan, not so much in terms of size, but in terms of its reputation for innovation and trend-setting. In contrast, Salon du Meuble in Paris has experienced a sharp decline.

As discussed, these events operate according to different internationalization strategies. Möbelmesse Köln has always had a larger number of foreign exhibitors (on average almost 60 per cent of the total in the 2000s) than foreign visitors, especially from countries outside Europe. It can thus be characterized as a traditional import trade show. Over time, however, Möbelmesse Köln has also increased its share of international visitors and has become a hub event. Salone del Mobile is clearly oriented towards exports, with more than 50 per cent of its visitors from overseas and a limited number of overseas exhibitors (between 15 and 18 per cent). The Salon du Meuble in Paris is primarily an

(i) Visitors

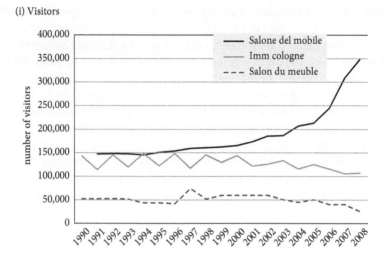

(ii) Exhibitors

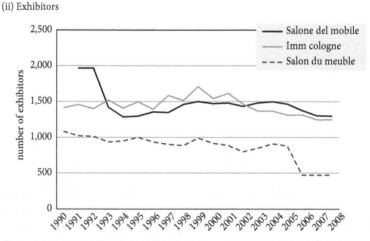

Figure 14.1. Evolution of the number of visitors and exhibitors at Salone del Mobile and major competing trade shows (CERMES 2013)

import trade show. It has suffered a significant reduction in internationalization in the period 2000–8 compared to 1990–9 (see Table 14.1).

14.3. SALONE DEL MOBILE: ORGANIZERS' STRATEGIES FOR INDUSTRY VISIBILITY

This section relates the recent success of Salone del Mobile in Milan to the development of competing furniture trade shows and the organizers' efforts to support knowledge circulation.

Table 14.1. Evolution of main furniture shows in Europe, 1990, 2000, and 2008

Trade show, city, start date	Month	Organizer	Trade show statistics		
			1990	2000	2008
Internationale Möbelmesse, Köln, 1949	January	KölnMesse	Sq.m.: 174,883 Exh. (% foreign): 1,416 (58%) Vis. (% foreign): 142,926 (27%)	Sq.m.: 185,494 Exh. (% foreign): 1,453 (66%) Vis. (% foreign): 143,851 (27%)	Sq.m.: 151,490 Exh. (% foreign): 1,068 (65%) Vis. (% foreign): 106,677 (33%)
Salon du Meuble, Paris, 1960	January	COSP—Compagnie d'Organization des Salons Professions SAFI – since 2006	Sq.m.: 76,877 Exh. (% foreign): 1,082 (44%) Vis. (% foreign): 52,534 (21%)	Sq.m.: 79,130 Exh. (% foreign): 804 (37%) Vis. (% foreign): 60,002 (13%)[2]	Sq.m.: 43,695 Exh. (% foreign): 368 (40%) Vis. (% foreign): 33,341 (33%)
Salone del Mobile, Milan, 1961	April (September until 1989; April since 1991)	COSMIT, controlled by Federlegno-Arredo	Sq.m.: 144,302[1] Exh. (% foreign): 1,968 (13%) Vis. (% foreign): 147,321 (64%)	Sq.m.: 144,506 Exh. (% foreign): 1,471 (15%) Vis. (% foreign): 165,253 (46%)	Sq.m.: 152,207 Exh. (% foreign): 1,298 (18%) Vis. (% foreign): 378,825 (56%)

Source: CERMES 2013.

Notes: sq.m. = square metres; exh. = number of exhibitors; vis. = number of visitors; % foreign = share of foreign exhibitors or visitors.

[1] Data refer to 1991.

[2] Visitors refer to 1999.

14.3.1. Salone del Mobile as a Collective Project

Salone del Mobile was established in Milan in 1961 by Cosmit, an organizing committee representing leading Italian furniture makers. At the time, the reference event for the industry was Möbelmesse Köln, which attracted many foreign exhibitors. These were grouped together by the organizer in separate pavilions according to their nationality. Among them, Scandinavian exhibitors enjoyed particular commercial success thanks to international recognition achieved by the Nordic design initiative, which started in the 1950s. Our interviews suggest that the capability of German and Scandinavian producers to present themselves in a joint and consistent manner to overseas buyers inspired the creation of a similar initiative in Italy.

In Italy, numerous events were traditionally held in the main manufacturing districts, including Brianza in Lombardia, and the Veneto and Pesaro regions. According to one industry expert, Italy had too many local/regional trade shows that were of little value in promoting exports, despite considerable investment. Unlike those established in other countries, the Italian initiatives were often characterized by 'a pinch of parochial jealousy and envy' (Brivio 1958: 12). They featured styles that were not highly recognizable and included many imitations. Italian furniture makers were primarily oriented towards local/regional markets and continued to produce classical furniture, while new forms of production and styles found in Northern Europe were rapidly taking hold on international markets (and in Italy as well). It was widely understood, however, that export markets offered significant development opportunities, particularly if the domestic market became saturated. The Italian firms were artisan-based producers; their skills involved working with wood rather than understanding the demands of consumer markets or international distribution. Our interviews suggest, however, that they were able to obtain some knowledge regarding these market-related aspects by participating in the international trade shows in their districts.

Salone del Mobile, which was held for the first time in September 1961 at the Milan trade show venue, was a collective project organized by the association of furniture manufacturers to attract overseas visitors. The organizers stated in interviews that its overarching goal was to boost the Italian industry by accelerating competition between firms, disseminating technological know-how, and promoting a distinct Italian furniture style.

Using these strategies, Salone del Mobile began to challenge the furniture trade shows in Cologne and Paris, as well as the broader furniture industries in these countries. Salone del Mobile followed an annual rhythm, a format that was immediately copied by the previously bi-annual events Möbelmesse and Salon du Meuble. On its first occasion, Salone del Mobile attracted 328 exhibitors and 11,300 visitors (800 of whom were foreign) in an exhibition space spanning 11,860 square metres. Only three years later, in 1964, Salone del Mobile had almost tripled in size, with overseas visitors exceeding 10 per cent (CERMES 2011a, 2012). Between 1960 and 1964, exports also tripled and the Italian furniture industry began its transformation from artisan-based to industrial-production-based. According to our interviewees, Italian firms were extremely curious and excited about what they might see and experience at Salone del Mobile. They apparently returned home after each event full of plans and innovative ideas for their future production activities. They were particularly interested in meeting with foreign buyers who explained the specific tastes of their home countries and introduced Italian producers to different distribution systems.

14.3.2. Visibility of Stylistic Innovation and Design Culture

In the years that followed, Salone del Mobile opened a new pavilion during the event that highlighted collaborations between designers and manufacturers. Prior to this, only highly sophisticated manufacturers that made design furniture presented their innovations at the Triennale (Milan's museum for design, architecture, and decorative art). This symbolic distinction between art-oriented design in a 'high-brow' cultural organization and practical commercial work was subsequently blurred by Salone del Mobile. While Salone's new pavilion for design furniture featured only thirty exhibitors out of a total of 1,073 in its inaugural year, it received substantial international press coverage. It is this event that marked the beginning of a new, unique design line that was perceived as fundamentally Italian in nature. As one interviewee explained, it was 'continually seeking change and perfection . . . which does not stop at the function of a table, a chair, a bed, or a wardrobe but penetrates deeper into forms which respond to new lifestyles and new needs'. Even in mass-produced furniture, one could appreciate the 'meticulous care and permanent refinement which made Italian craftsmanship synonymous with quality' (Lazzaroni 1996: 23). The Italian furniture industry was at the core of this new style. On the one hand, it involved a close relationship between industrial firms and leading designers (e.g. Castiglioni, Magistretti, etc.); on the other hand, Italian firms, characterized by a strong artisanal tradition and organizational flexibility, had a talent for transforming the designers' rough ideas and sketches into real products.

A first parallel event to Salone del Mobile was organized in 1965, again by Cosmit. Defined as the 'Retrospective exhibition for a documentation of furniture design in Italy from 1945 to today', it spoke to the unusual engagement of a trade show within the cultural sphere (personal interviews). The organizers' belief that cultural development would permeate the entire sector was realized in subsequent years. In the late 1980s, parallel events relating to the history and culture of furniture and design became a fixture of the show. Some examples of such parallel events included: 'Giuseppe Maggiolini, Marquetry-maker' (1987); 'Pieces of furniture as aphorisms: Thirty-five pieces of furniture of the Italian rationalism' (1988); and 'Neoliberty and surroundings' (1989). These events mainly took place inside the trade show district. In 1987, Cosmit's efforts on this front received formal recognition with the Compasso d'Oro, the highest Italian award in design. Our interviewees viewed this as a clear acknowledgement of Salone del Mobile's contribution to the promotion and dissemination of a design-oriented manufacturing sector. Salone del Mobile was awarded the prize again in 1998. Behind all of this was Cosmit's desire to create a trade show that would offer a complete experience and a place where participants had an opportunity to preview future trends. Coupling industrial designs and products with the arts was seen as a meaningful way to accomplish such goals.

As a result of this initiative, and the various forms of imitation and competition it inspired, the products showcased at Salone del Mobile soon took on a style that was perceived as distinctively 'Italian'. Foreign buyers began to recognize and appreciate Italian style, and the international press acknowledged Salone del Mobile's role in enhancing the visibility of Italian design around the world (Lazzaroni 1996).

14.3.3. Emergence of Sub-Sectors

After the early years, the organizers of Salone del Mobile began reorganizing the exhibition floor to assign specific show areas to different sub-sectors of the Italian furniture production chain. Wood-working machines were taken out of the show and transferred to a new event at a different time of the year, where furniture makers, as visitors only, could browse at a more leisurely pace. The same occurred to accessories and parts, which were moved to another show (Sasmil) in 1969.

New events and parallel trade shows were launched by Cosmit, with the aim of offering increased visibility to specific sub-sectors associated with interior furnishing. This was a response to the significant differences that existed in the innovation cycles and distribution channels of different product groups. While chairs and tables were designed on an annual basis, for example, kitchens with domestic appliances were characterized by slower innovation cycles. Furthermore, some sectors, such as lighting and office furniture, demanded greater visibility to showcase their range of products and to optimize promotion through special sales channels. As revealed in personal interviews, this led organizers to separate and promote some sectors by displaying them at the same time in special pavilions.

Some products were assigned a bi-annual schedule, which encouraged alternation. The show Eurocucina (a kitchen and domestic appliance show), for instance, was launched in 1974 as a bi-annual event occurring in even years, whereas Euroluce (a lighting show since 1965) and EIMU (an office furniture show since 1982) were held during odd years. In 1988 and 1989, two other events were created: Salone Satellite (a pavilion entirely assigned to young creators) and Salone del Complemento d'Arredo (a trade show specializing in furnishing accessories, as an annual event alongside Salone del Mobile). The latest event in this segmentation—Salone Bagno Arredo—was launched in 2003 for bathroom furnishings. Subsequently, Salone del Mobile and its parallel events were given a new trademark that seemed more fitting for the whole group: I Saloni.

According to interviews with firms that participated in these events, the creation of specific trade shows strengthened the firms' competitiveness in international markets. The sub-sector events were viewed as particularly valuable in this respect.

Over the years, Cosmit also introduced changes to the exhibition layout of each trade show in order to enhance the visitors' perceptions of products. Initially, exhibitors were grouped together based on product similarity or complementarity, rather than nationality (which was the key layout criterion followed by competing trade shows). Specifically, larger and more innovative firms were positioned at the centre of exhibition areas, surrounded by smaller and emerging firms. This layout favoured the latter types of firms, which benefited from the larger visitor flows generated by market leaders. This format was ultimately changed, however, as the organizers' arranged exhibitors by style according to three product clusters: classic furniture, design furniture (the most appealing to visitors and the most in demand by exhibitors), and modern furniture (a hybrid incorporating classic and design).

14.3.4. Position in the International Cycle of European Trade Shows

In 1991, Salone del Mobile's position in the annual trade show cycle was moved forward from September to April. This was considered in interviews with observers a more favourable month for buyers because it was closer to the stock renewal cycle at sales outlets. There had originally been an unspoken agreement between Salone del Mobile and Möbelmesse Köln regarding the month during which each event would take place. The events in Paris and Cologne both took place in January. Salone del Mobile and the Cologne trade show also cooperated by hosting the Office Design Forum and the Office Design Competition (a showcase of selected products and designs and an international competition for designers and architects) in alternate years. This method of coordinating events was extended to other types of products in order to avoid presenting both lighting goods and kitchens in the same year. Beyond this, the objective of such coordination decisions was to keep new and emerging competitors out of the main event circuit.

Salone del Mobile played an important role in the furniture industry as new items were always previewed in Milan, even though the show was held last in the annual trade show cycle. From the perspective of the international press, Salone del Mobile was crucial in presenting and ensuring the success of new innovations. As described in the *New York Times* in 1987, '[t]he Salone del Mobile di Milano is the most prestigious forum for contemporary furniture. Although few of the designs presented here will end up in American living rooms, they will be as influential in the world market of design ideas as the French couture showings are in fashion' (Slesin 1987: para. 1). In 1989, the same newspaper assigned an even greater significance to the show: 'Visitors who went to the fair looking for new practical ideas were in the wrong place. But those who responded to the new openness, the eclectic attitudes and the wealth of creativity that keep this annual event at the top of the international design calendar were not disappointed' (Slesin 1989: para. 6). And in 1991, the same newspaper referred to Salone del Mobile as 'indisputably the world's most influential furniture fair' and 'a furniture Mecca' (Vogel 1991: para. 2). Quoting a prominent buyer, the newspaper further suggested that '[t]here's no question Milan is the most exciting; it always is' (Vogel 1991: para. 2). By comparison, Salone del Mobile's international competitors were viewed as far less oriented towards the presentation of innovation and emerging trends. According to personal interviews, the competitors were more market-oriented, each targeting specific national markets in Europe. The Paris event, for instance, was focused on the French and Belgium markets, while Cologne was oriented towards Germany and countries in Northern and Eastern Europe. In terms of non-European visitors, Milan maintained its first place.

14.3.5. Development of Spontaneous Off-Site Events: The 'Fuori Salone'

Starting in the early 1990s with the 'Fuori Salone', we saw a new way of organizing off-site or fringe events. Salone del Mobile's policy of selecting exhibitors and the lack of additional exhibiting space for others led some firms to organize independent shows in other parts of Milan. These fringe events were a great success right from the start, and were seen as part of the innovation atmosphere surrounding the Milan event. As labelled in an editorial on this new phenomenon, 'At Milan fair, there's vitality if not practicality'. It was also noted that '[f]or many of the most avant-garde manufacturers the traditional locale of the fair was not suitable. Many followed a growing exodus to the centre of the town. Involved in a game of serious one-upmanship, they captured such incongruous ad-hoc spaces as a cloister, a gas station, a castle and a parked truck as noteworthy locations to showcase their new products' (Slesin 1989:

paras. 9–10). This new development created a vibrant atmosphere and multiple meeting opportunities for international visitors, both at the shows and at private parties in the centre of the city.

Many exhibitors soon realized the advantages of showcasing their goods away from the fairgrounds, enabling them to continue their relations with clients after hours. This custom became increasingly popular, involving not only firms that were left out of Salone del Mobile, but also many that were part of the trade show. The latter firms began to organize their own events to meet clients and show their products in more spacious and private locations. The venues ranged from shops and showrooms to museums, old factories, and theatres. Some exhibitors even chose off-site events over the traditional show.

Despite some initial reluctance to accept phenomena beyond their own control, the organizers of Salone del Mobile—with the support of the municipal council—also began contributing to off-site events by bolstering the city's cultural programme. The themes were different from the typical furniture and design areas at the show because they were aimed not just at buyers, but also at the broader public. They included a series on the great design masters, inaugurated in 1996 with the monographs of Achille Castiglioni and Joe Colombo, and followed in later years by the expositions dedicated to Giò Ponti and Vico Magistretti in 1997, Alvar Aalto in 1998, and Bruno Munari and Ettore Sottsass Jr. in 1999. The events organized in the late 1990s enhanced the cultural flavour of the entire trade show. From 2000 onwards, cultural projects with even wider appeal were organized in the most prestigious areas of the city. According to our interviews, these events attracted renewed attention from the press, encouraging journalists, art critics, and opinion leaders to attend Salone del Mobile and its off-site events.[1]

Over time, the cultural programme attracted more and more off-site events, organized not only by furniture producers, but also by designers, artists, collectors, trade magazines, educational establishments, and museums, as well as firms from industries associated with Italian creativity, such as fashion and cuisine. It seemed that visitors to Salone del Mobile, and specifically the communities of professionals and consumers interested in design, had become a coveted target audience for anyone with something to present. An additional advantage was that these so-called 'design people' were perceived as trend-setters. By observing them interact with products and services at events, it seemed possible to learn about emerging consumer trends.

In some quarters of the city, the off-site events were also coordinated to some extent by agencies which rented available space to exhibitors and organized a programme. The Fuori Salone was eventually promoted and 'catalogued' for visitors by the magazine *Interni*. 'Foreigners were asking me if there was something else to see besides the fair,' explained the editor of the guide in a personal interview in 2010, 'and so we began with a map of Milan, folded into four, where the furniture stores were marked.' The map soon became a useful guide, continually getting bigger to contain more and more events that were quite heterogeneous, located in a growing number of places throughout the city. Between 2002 and 2008, the number of off-site events increased from 250 to 570 (CERMES 2011b).

Visitors to Salone del Mobile increasingly enjoyed this carnival-like atmosphere. In addition to providing a clear picture of the industry and emerging trends, the ability to immerse oneself for a few days in the flurry of events, excitement, and objects often stimulated the kinds of feelings and emotions that fertilize new ideas. This sentiment was well confirmed in our interviews. According to some participants, the environment was particularly favourable because it offered a close-up look at the highly sophisticated Italian furniture and surrounding design market (CERMES 2011b).

14.3.6. Impact of Visibility on the Italian Furniture Industry

Since 2000, Salone del Mobile has surpassed other European furniture and design trade shows; it is now recognized as the largest event in the industry in terms of rented floor space, exhibitors, and visitors (see Figure 14.1), as well as the most prestigious one. In the eyes of industry operators it is at the top of the league. Salone del Mobile differs from other trade shows that focus on marketing-related exchanges, because it allows participants to learn about design trends as they actually happen (CERMES 2012b; also Power and Jansson 2008). Along with the success of the fringe events, as reported in the international press, this has strengthened the Italian furniture industry's reputation for innovation, spreading it far beyond the industry.

As noted in tourism studies (Rinallo 2011a), such events create images that can benefit entire countries. These events can transmit 'messages' about a host country to those actually taking part in the events (direct audience), as well as those informed through the media (indirect audience). More specifically, trade shows (especially export shows) provide a platform for local firms to display their skills and products, and help them become more widely recognized. Thus, they contribute to the creation of what the marketing literature calls 'country of origin effects'—that is, the impact of a product's geographical origin on the perceived quality of that product, as well as the consumer's willingness to pay a premium price for it (Peterson and Jolibert 1995; Khalid and Baker 1998; Verlegh and Steenkamp 1999; Pharr 2005).

Research on national and international media coverage of Salone del Mobile in the period from 1981 to 2009 (CERMES 2011a) allows us to get an impression of the potential impact of the event's image on the Italian furniture industry.[2] The analysis shows a sharp rise in the number of articles

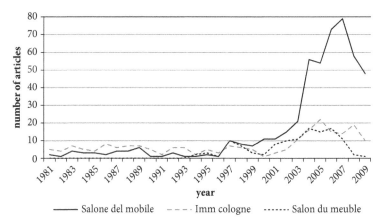

Figure 14.2 Number of articles per year about main furniture trade shows published in international press releases, 1981–2009 (CERMES 2013) (*Note:* Data based on 1,384 and 826 articles from the Factiva and LexisNexis databases, respectively, and from websites of international newspapers, both general and design-oriented)

featuring Salone del Mobile compared to furniture shows in Cologne and Paris (see Figure 14.2). This is not surprising, as this captures the periods when off-site events took off. Generally, national newspapers tend to focus more on the events in their own country (hence, *La Repubblica* dedicates more space to Salone del Mobile, while *Die Welt* devotes more to Möbelmesse). Yet, in non-European or 'non-partisan' magazines, greater space is given to Salone del Mobile than to the other main furniture shows. In terms of content, Salone del Mobile is clearly the industry's main international event for displaying cutting edge designs and setting new fashion trends. It is a place where visitors from all over the world come to 'breathe' creativity and innovation (CERMES 2012b). Salone del Mobile's reputation reverberates through the image of Milan, known as the international capital of design. It also feeds into the reputation of Italian firms, underlining their focus on quality, craftsmanship, and aesthetics.

By and large, Salone del Mobile generates a publicity spin-off for Italian products and Italian producers. This is largely due to the off-site events, which attract considerable media interest aimed at final consumers. The popularity of Salone del Mobile is also due to the fact that it is the largest trade show dedicated to design in Europe, in terms of the number of exhibitors and visitors (see Figure 14.1). This critical mass has much to do with the presence of foreign exhibitors benefiting from the prestige of being selected to exhibit at Salone del Mobile, while at the same time contributing to the greater visibility of Italian design.

14.4. CONCLUSIONS

This chapter investigates the history of Salone del Mobile from its origins as a local trade show to its present role as a critical site for knowledge exchange regarding emerging trends in the furniture and design industry at an international level. Our discussion pays particular attention to the practices of organizers in the development of the event. Leaving aside the specific learning and knowledge exchange processes of exhibitors and visitors (see Chapters 9 and 10), we focus on the role of trade show organizers in the management of physical and relational proximity.

In this sense, the case of Salone del Mobile provides further empirical evidence of some of the key points addressed in previous chapters. In the first place, the story of Salone del Mobile confirms that there is great potential in organizing events that unite national manufacturers from different industrial clusters. This is true in terms of both international competitiveness and opportunities for learning and sharing knowledge. The strong local identity of industrial clusters, along with their spirit of competition with other manufacturers in the same country, often makes it difficult for them to join in a common project (see Chapter 12). This seems to be particularly true in Italy, which, unlike other European countries, is characterized by many regional industrial districts. Yet, in the context of the Italian furniture industry, organizers represent strong business associations. This has been instrumental in overcoming the challenges of regionalism, as we have seen through the creation of a trade show that is supported by a critical mass of exhibitors which would otherwise focus on smaller events with less international visibility.

Secondly, we found that the success of Salone del Mobile was largely determined by a number of knowledge-generating mechanisms. These include: the selection of innovative design-oriented exhibitors; the organization of market-sensitive exhibition layout solutions, resulting in separate bi-annual events for sub-sectors; and the promotion of key innovations through special exhibition areas.

It is important to note, however, that the organizers of Salone del Mobile had access to knowledge-generating mechanisms that are rarely available at other trade shows. In part, such mechanisms are easier to realize at trade shows that promote consumer products with a high symbolic value and that attract considerable interest from the media and general public. The case of Salone del Mobile highlights the potential effects of creating a particular 'product culture'—or more specifically, facilitating a better understanding of the industry's products among gatekeepers and opinion leaders, aside from the pursuit of short-term commercial aims. It involves complementary initiatives beyond the main trade show venue, which include different regional players in manufacturing and knowledge services, universities and higher learning organizations, and the cultural and entertainment sectors. These initiatives offer participants a 'full immersion' or complete social experience that combines learning with entertainment; yet they are all related to the future development of the industry. Such experiences are of great value for business visitors who take part in what may be viewed as real 'learning expeditions' (Borghini et al. 2006; Rinallo et al. 2010) that go beyond the simple acquisition of knowledge about products and prices.

NOTES

1. Examples of these types of events include 'Rooms and Secrets' in 2000; '1951–2001 Made in Italy?' in 2001; 'Imagining Prometheus' in 2003; 'The Devil of the Hearth' in 2006; 'Room with a View: Art and Interior Design in Italy 1900–2000' in 2007; 'Leonardo's Last Supper: A Vision by Peter Greenaway' in 2008; and 'Magnificence and Design – Five Hundred Years of Great Italian Furniture in Comparison' in 2009.
2. Studies on country-of-origin effects are often based on experimental research designs, testing the impact of geographical provenance on the image of certain products and the consumers' willingness to pay. Here we follow a different approach, drawing on a media content analysis. This allows us to both quantify and qualify the effects of being exposed to publicity with respect to the Italian furniture/ design industry and international audiences.

Part IV

Theory, Policy, and Management Implications

15

Implications of a Knowledge-Based Understanding of Trade Shows

15.1. MAIN FINDINGS

In this book, we propose a conceptualization of the nature, extent, and structure of interaction and learning processes at trade shows that draws on a knowledge-based understanding of these events. The book sheds light on how trade shows operate in the knowledge economy, how they have become major building blocks in innovation and globalization processes, and yet how they differ from country to country, from industry to industry, from venue to venue, and even from event to event. Based on empirical evidence from numerous trade shows in different industries and geographical contexts, we highlight (i) the knowledge acquisition and release processes carried out by trade show exhibitors and visitors, (ii) the nature and content of the knowledge circulated and co-produced by actors involved in trade show activities, and (iii) the strategies through which trade show organizers, exhibitors, and visitors shape learning at these events.

The book has developed a consistent argument regarding the role of trade shows in the globalizing knowledge economy. Part I laid out the conceptual foundations of the knowledge-based perspective, documenting the early development of trade shows and how they have changed over time. Influenced by changing economic and political conditions related to the supply and demand of products and technologies, as well as the policies governing trade restrictions, trade shows developed from places where goods from distant regions/countries were brought by the local population into places where only samples of goods are provided (especially in business-to-business events, which are at the focus of this book; see Chapter 1). Over time, they have become essential places for knowledge exchange and circulation with respect to products, innovations, markets, technologies, potential transaction partners, and general production conditions (see Chapter 2). In the eighteenth and nineteenth centuries, the evolution of such events was often linked to the development of a strong or specialized manufacturing base, as in the cases of Italy and Germany, for instance. While trade shows have always had the character of temporary markets with a focus on vertical value-chain-related linkages, increasingly broader knowledge flows surrounding the conditions for production and innovation became crucial elements over time. In the twentieth century, these events developed into temporary clusters with complex horizontal, vertical, and institutional dimensions and sophisticated communication and knowledge ecologies (see Chapter 3). However, the knowledge flows that occur during trade shows are not homogeneous. This is illustrated in a knowledge-based typology that demonstrates how the nature and internal dynamics of trade shows are crucially linked to the geographical origins of both the exhibitors and visitors. From this, we distinguish four types of trade shows: national/regional shows, import shows, exports shows, and international hub shows (see Chapter 4). Within this context, trade show organizers (exhibition facility owners, public authorities, industry associations, or private firms) play an important role in determining the focus and goals of trade shows, selecting participant groups, and sometimes in shaping the nature or substance of knowledge flows. Beyond these forces, it is important to keep in mind the persistent two-way influence between trade show specialization (and the corresponding interaction and knowledge exchange patterns) and territorial economic specialization (see Chapter 5). The structure of the local/regional/national economy impacts the establishment and nature of trade shows, while these events simultaneously impact their surrounding urban/regional/national environments through economic multiplier effects and knowledge spillovers. While the link between trade show development and territorial economic development is not always obvious, and may have weakened over time, it is omnipresent and partially explains the differences in trade show activities between different countries. It also sheds light on how the nature of knowledge flows changes during the trade show life-cycle.

Part II applied this knowledge-based conceptualization of trade shows to specific global developments, focusing on the formation of continental platforms in Europe, North America, and the Asia-Pacific region. In Europe, we argue that the large share of small- and medium-sized firms in manufacturing industries and the proximity of many different economies have given rise to highly international events, particularly in the form of export and hub shows (see Chapter 6). Over time, Europe's growth in trade show activity has stimulated increasing competition between venues, cities, and even countries, sometimes resulting in 'trade show battles'. In the North American context, the nature and specialization of trade shows is impacted by differences in the manufacturing and distribution system (see Chapter 7). This has resulted in the development of large consumer shows and industry demand-driven events, instead of the international hub events that developed in Europe. Yet, there is considerable variation in terms of individual events and trade show trajectories found in different US cities. In contrast to the stagnation tendencies associated with some European events, trade show developments in the Asia-Pacific region have been remarkably dynamic (see Chapter 8). Driven by economic growth and specific support policies for trade show development, there has been a considerable increase in the number, size, and variety of trade shows—from import shows and regional/national shows to continental hub events. While such growth has been particularly evident in Singapore and increasingly in China trade show activities and development trajectories differ substantially across the region. In recent years, we have also seen a number of trade shows in mature industries relocate from Europe to Asia, while European trade show organizers increasingly export event formats to the Asia-Pacific region and organize events in countries such as China. This has led to increased trade show-related competition between events, venues, and countries, especially with respect to flagship events—a trend that will likely continue in the future. In sum, we are witnessing the development of a polycentric trade show system, with the establishment of continental trade show platforms in each of the world regions, where international exhibitors showcase products/solutions targeted to the specific continental/national clientele.

Part III used these insights as a starting point to investigate differences in the nature of knowledge generation practices across different types of events (i.e. international hub shows, exports shows, and import shows) and different industry groups. While international hub events or flagship fairs are probably the most important type of events in terms of producing global knowledge flows about an industry or technology field, the nature of knowledge circulation and exchange is highly complex and differs according to product and industry characteristics. This is illustrated using the cases of the lighting and meat processing industries (see Chapter 9). Even within a single industry group, such as lighting, international events in different countries and cities serve different purposes and are consequently characterized by a different structure of participants and knowledge flows. Although trade shows belonging to the same industry or technology field may have overlapping agendas and knowledge bases, resulting in specific trade show cycles, their direct interrelationships are often limited. Such events generate the conditions for ongoing gradual knowledge generation within their field (see Chapter 10). In other words, these shows normally have the nature of field-reproducing events in the globalizing knowledge economy. The fabrics industry is used to study knowledge circulation processes at import and export trade shows (see Chapter 11). It also illustrates how competition between events and venues has developed over time and how active trade show organizers have helped to overcome the structural constraints of their events. The case of fashion fabrics represents a type of trade show where field configuration, rather than field reproduction (see Chapter 10), dominates and where trade show organizers play a crucial role in planning and directing this configuration process (see Chapter 12). In this context, the process referred to as 'concertation' suggests that what appears to be an emerging fashion trend during a trade show has actually been purposely organized and orchestrated long in advance. The cases of ceramics and marble technologies are used to illustrate how globalization processes create dynamic fields leading to increased competition between events, venues, and even countries (see Chapter 13). While trade show geographies are thus highly dynamic and constantly adjust to new environmental conditions in production, demand, and political regulation, structural changes from one event to the next are still more incremental than radical. The case of furniture shows further demonstrates how knowledge practices are in a constant state of emergence and reconstruction due to geographical competition between different exhibition centres and how this generates a fundamentally dynamic trade show business (see Chapter 14).

In this concluding chapter, the theoretical and practical implications of the knowledge-based understanding of trade shows are further discussed. The scope of our book is one that intersects with many disciplines interested in understanding globalization, innovation, local economic development, and competitiveness. Because of these multidisciplinary influences, we describe the theoretical implications of our approach for economic geography, management/ marketing, and other disciplines that have substantive interests in trade shows or can use empirical investigations of these events to deal with issues of broader theoretical interest. While the book is mainly directed to researchers and students in the social sciences, these issues are also of interest to policy-makers, regional planners, public managers, local governments, as well as operators in the trade fair industry. Accordingly, we derive policy and managerial implications for these groups of actors. We also discuss some implications of our findings that are relevant to the participants at these events, the exhibitors and visitors who observe and interact with one another during trade shows. Finally, we look to the future.

15.2. THEORETICAL IMPLICATIONS

The findings and explanations presented in this book have important theoretical implications for a wide range of disciplines and scholarly debates. In the discussion that follows, we highlight our contribution to some of these academic conversations. In our own research, trade shows have never been the sole focus of investigation, but rather useful empirical contexts for making sense of various aspects of the knowledge economy. It is through our collective efforts in this book that we are able to draw conclusions regarding the significance of such events for firms, industry actors, local governments, and other stakeholders. As part of this process, we found conventional approaches to the study of trade shows to be limited in understanding their importance and role in the knowledge creation processes they enable and support. A new generation of studies on trade shows and other events in the late 2000s, conducted by researchers from different disciplines, suggests that we are not alone in our belief that these events need to be better understood.

15.2.1. Implications for Economic Geography

In conventional studies in economic geography, trade shows have primarily been dealt with by analysing the spatial distribution of these events and changes in this distribution, often related to the localized effects of trade show activity for their surrounding urban and regional, and sometimes even national, economies. The focus has been on the material manifestations of economic activity, as expressed in studies investigating the geography of the firm, urban industry agglomerations, industrial milieux, clusters, regional and national innovations system, and so on (e.g. Cooke and Morgan 1998; Goodman et al. 1989; Porter 1990; Camagni 1991). This research focuses on ongoing economic activities that can easily be identified and studied in permanent entities. Although such research has been interested in understanding the underlying causes of agglomeration and changes in agglomeration processes over time, knowledge flows and the linkages between permanent industry sites have often been downplayed in the mainstream literature. It is through a transfer in the analytical focus from structures to flows, from material characteristics to knowledge, and from permanent to temporary settings that new perspectives have developed (i.e. Bathelt et al. 2002; Borghini et al. 2004; Maskell et al. 2004). The work on temporary clusters and temporary markets, in particular, has led to new perspectives on trade shows and similar temporary settings, viewing such events as places that connect permanently separated production spaces and support, initiate, or shape global connections between these spaces (Norcliffe and Rendace 2003; Power and Jansson 2008; Ramírez-Pasillas 2008; 2010). This work has stimulated interest in investigating the role of trade shows in the knowledge economy and opened up new avenues of enquiry for future research. We offer a brief summary of four of these perspectives here.

First, trade shows and their underlying infrastructure are important elements in the urban landscape and have become drivers of the development of creative economies and creative cities (Florida 2005). Many of world's leading cities have exhibition, convention, and/or trade show centres in or near some of their most valuable downtown spaces. These are often associated with architectural innovations, spectacles, and sophisticated arts and entertainment elements that spill over into the neighbouring downtown areas, and, in fact, the entire urban field (e.g. Bathelt 2012). The connection between such events and urban development, creativity, and innovation is, however, still under-researched.

Second, trade shows can be viewed as an integral element in the development of global economic geographies of knowledge transfer over distance (Bathelt and Henn 2014). There are multiple configurations of economic knowledge exchange that link and enable ongoing communication between different cultural, political, and institutional spheres, sometimes over very large distances worldwide. Existing research on economic interaction has generally viewed temporary get-togethers of communities, ongoing business travel, or transnational network relations separately, however, instead of viewing them as vital elements of global architectures of economic knowledge flows and communication.

Third, trade shows, conferences, and other get-togethers are beneficial not only for leading clusters and global centres of control; they also enable remote firms and peripheral regions to create linkages to the global economy and acquire knowledge that is not readily available within these regional environments or existing networks. Temporary clustering encourages distributed communities to meet, discuss, and negotiate their different institutional and cultural contexts, supporting the formation of wider communities of practice that can easily collaborate, instead of operating in isolation. Cole and Barbera (2014) provide an insightful example of how international events and regular meetings have fostered the formation of a cross-national European community in the animation industry. This has enabled small national industries to collaborate and collectively survive in the face of the large dominant US animation industry.

Fourth, while much research has viewed trade shows as elements of economic trade and exchange that are fundamentally grounded in the past, the knowledge perspective opens up a different outlook on such events, especially considering future challenges and associated changes in the global economy. In the new shortage economy (i.e. Giddens 1990), for example, which is characterized by the dramatic effects of global climate change and 'peak oil' on individual mobility and overall transportation costs, periodic international meetings, such as trade shows and conventions, may become increasingly important in maintaining global contact, communication, and knowledge flows.

15.2.2. Implications for Marketing

In the field of marketing, trade shows are mainly regarded as promotional instruments that are particularly relevant for producers operating as suppliers in business-to-business markets (i.e. trade show exhibitors). Indeed, trade shows establish temporary markets that relate to the exhibitors' marketing efforts, aiming to advertise their products, strengthen their brands, and eventually stimulate sales. The importance of trade shows in circulating, exchanging, and generating knowledge is, however, largely downplayed and understudied in the marketing literature. Empirical work in the industrial marketing scholarship has only recently started to unpack marketing-related learning processes at these events (Golfetto et al. 2004; Borghini et al. 2006; Li 2006, 2007; Zerbini et al. 2006; Rinallo et al. 2010; Zerbini and Borghini 2012). While this work initially developed independently from the economic geography research on trade shows as learning places, this book suggests that the two perspectives are complementary in developing advanced conceptualizations of how trade shows and similar types of events shape knowledge creation, innovation processes, and, more generally, the evolution of markets and industries. This knowledge-based perspective of trade shows contributes to ongoing conversations in the marketing literature in a number of ways.

First, our work contributes to a micro-level perspective on trade shows. While marketing research mostly focuses on exhibitors and returns on trade show investments, the micro-perspective presented in this book suggests that learning should be viewed as a key driver and outcome of trade show performance. As demonstrated in the conceptualization of trade shows as temporary clusters (see Chapters 3 and 4), exhibiting firms at trade shows obtain crucial 'experiential knowledge' about how to adapt their core productive competencies to the heterogeneous needs of customers in different industries and geographical markets. This is particularly true for small- and medium-sized enterprises operating in business markets that lack access to more sophisticated market research. As such, the learning opportunities provided by trade shows can have an important impact on market-led innovation, export development, and internationalization.

Second, the marketing literature on visitor behaviour tends to be preoccupied with the role of trade shows as information sources employed by industrial buyers in their purchasing processes (for a review and critique, see Borghini et al. 2006). Business-to-business marketing scholarship rests on the idea that new purchases are decided collectively by a group of people inside the buying organization that have different functional backgrounds and varying degrees of influence—the so-called buying centre (Johnston and Bonomia 1981; Jackson et al. 1984; Lilien and Wong 1984; Kohli 1989). However, this literature downplays the fact that members of the buying centre belong to different occupational communities that gather at trade shows (e.g. designers and architects at furniture or lighting trade shows; see Chapters 10 and 14) for a variety of different purposes other than buying (Rinallo et al. 2007, 2008). Consumer researchers have long investigated how such events can provide geographically dispersed communities of consumers with a platform for interaction (McAlexander and Schouten 1998; Fournier and Lee 2009; Rinallo 2011a). As indicated in this book, it appears useful to follow this line of research also in the context of business-to-business marketing research on trade shows.

Third, future studies could employ the typology of trade shows suggested in this book (local/national, import, export, and hub events) for purposes of 'theoretical sampling' of events to be investigated in empirical research (Glaser and Strauss 1967; Yin 1994). Trade shows embody a variety of goals and thus most firms adopt a balanced trade show portfolio based on the exploitation/defence of current market positions and the exploration of new opportunities. The findings of most marketing studies arguably depend on the specificities of the trade shows examined; yet, to date, little attention has been paid to this factor. Treating trade shows as if they were homogeneous events, however, makes it difficult to accurately interpret empirical evidence and generalize findings across industries and events.

Fourth, beyond the micro-level perspective presented in this book, we espouse a view of trade shows as macro-marketing instruments that operate at a scale larger than that of the individual firm (Bartels and Jenkins 1977; Hunt 1981; Fisk 1981; Shultz 2007). As highlighted in Chapter 4, trade show organizers play an important role in creating the context within which the individual behaviours of marketplace actors take place. The micro-level marketing scholarship on trade shows is largely silent about the role of organizers and how their activities can positively or negatively affect the individual exhibitors' value creation and profit maximization (for exceptions, see Munuera and Ruiz 1999; Borghini et al. 2006; Rinallo and Golfetto 2006; Rinallo et al. 2006, 2012; Golfetto and Rinallo 2008; Gopalakrishna et al. 2010; Geigenmüller and Bettis-Outland 2012). In this book, we highlight the strategies organizers employ to make their events knowledge-rich spaces that contribute to increased competitiveness of exhibitors and enhanced learning capabilities of visitors (see Parts I and III). In our view, this constitutes an important point of departure from previous work. We hope that future studies in marketing will utilize this approach by examining how organizers can work together with exhibitors to boost competitiveness.

Fifth, remaining at this macro-level perspective, trade shows (particularly export-oriented events) are sometimes employed by entrepreneurial associations and other industry actors as promotional platforms to achieve collective marketing goals (see Part III). From a cultural perspective, some of these events can be viewed as rich empirical settings where industries legitimize themselves, where memories about their past are re-enacted (Peñaloza 2000, 2001), and where commercial mythmaking can occur (Rinallo and Pinchera 2013; also Thompson and Tian 2008). This book supports this body of work by conceptualizing how trade shows 'build their own culture' around a particular industry. They do this by presenting the historical roots of the sector and educating other market agents about differences in the functional and symbolic qualities of products—or, in other words, by contributing to the transfer of meaning (McCracken 1986) from the culturally constituted world to intermediate and consumer goods. Our agenda is to inform future explorations with respect to the linkages between collective events, markets, and culture.

15.2.3. Implications for Other Disciplines

Economic geography and marketing are the core disciplines from which the arguments in this book develop; yet several other bodies of work are related to a knowledge-based view of trade shows that may benefit from the insights emerging based on this perspective. Here, we provide two examples of such research relating to organization studies and political science.

(i) Organization studies

In management and organization studies there is an ongoing debate on field-configuring events, or events that shape the emergence and development of markets, industries, professions, and technologies (Lampel and Meyer 2008). It is interesting to note that, while trade shows are considered as an important example of a field-configuring event (Lampel and Meyer 2008), empirical work applying this concept has thus far largely neglected this event type (for an exception regarding cultural fairs, see Moeran and Pedersen 2011). As a whole, our book contributes to the field-configuring events literature by demonstrating that trade shows can, and occasionally do, have profound consequences for industries, markets, and organizational fields—albeit not in the discontinuous and sometimes radical ways that are the focus of Lampel and Meyer's (2008) conceptualization of field-configuring events.

There are, however, elements of knowledge-based strategies that can be thought of as forms of field-configuring mechanisms that are specific to trade shows. An extreme version of a field-configuring strategy is the 'concertation' process in fashion fabrics (see Chapter 12), which shows how the main themes of the next fashion cycles are not self-emerging, but rather result from a thoroughly planned process. Few trade shows possess this capacity, however; in most cases, trade shows affect fields in subtler, more decentralized, and incremental ways. The discussion of lighting industry trade shows in Chapter 10 suggests that most manufacturing trade shows lack the planned and consciously directed structure needed to shape an entire industry or technology field. Many of the interactions between the participants at global flagship or reference events occur in a largely decentralized fashion, following the general changes in economic, technological, institutional, and political conditions. As such, trade shows do not easily fit the description of field-configuring events in the discontinuous sense of the term; rather, they reflect elements of the ongoing reproduction of fields (Gibson and Bathelt 2014) or their maintenance (Schuessler et al. 2013).

Since numerous trade shows exist for every industry, adopting a focus on individual events downplays the system of concurrent impacts—sometimes converging, sometimes diverging—caused by the events that compete for attention and resources from constituencies in the same field. The literature on field-configuring events could, therefore, go beyond its current emphasis on singular events with an almost revolutionary nature, to include a broader conceptualization of field-reproducing capacity. This should be treated as a dependent variable (rather than an a priori defining characteristic of these events) that is susceptible to change across events and their life-cycles.

(ii)   Political science

In the field of political science, trade shows have received very little attention. In the political economy literature, for instance, they are only mentioned in passing, usually as expressions of increasing globalization trends (Bathelt and Gibson 2009). In recent work, however, there is evidence to suggest that trade shows should be given more careful consideration, particularly within the context of comparative political economy studies. On the one hand, the vivid debates during the 2000s regarding why different modes of capitalism continue to exist in different national contexts and how they change over time have not been resolved (e.g. Hall and Soskice 2001; Crouch 2005; Haddow 2008). In particular, explanations about how dynamic adjustments of political economies occur in response to changes in global economic, ecological, and political conditions are still in their infancy (e.g. Hall and Thelen 2009). In this context, Gibson's (2015) work provides first insights into how the search and interaction processes of firms at international trade shows contribute to ongoing patterns of economic specialization, as opposed to convergence in the application and production of technologies.

On the other hand, trade shows could play an important role in economic development processes and the transition of less-developed economies, as demonstrated in recent studies about trade show ecologies in the Asia-Pacific region (Bathelt and Zeng 2014a). Trade shows seem to be an important tool in how countries position themselves and their industries within the context of global competition and which strategies and policies they use to support economic development. As such, they act as critical 'glue in the global political economy' (Bathelt and Gibson 2009).

15.3.   POLICY AND MANAGERIAL IMPLICATIONS

In similar ways, these disciplinary perspectives aim to derive improved conceptualizations and empirical studies that help to understand the phenomenon of trade shows in the globalizing knowledge economy. An incentive of this academic work is to draw conclusions for policy-makers, trade show organizers, and participating firms to develop strategies and policies to more effectively use these events to stimulate economic growth and development. In this context, this section formulates implications for export promotion policy, innovation policy, local/regional governments, trade show organizers, as well as exhibiting and visiting firms.

15.3.1. Implications for Export Promotion Policy

When thought of as public policy instruments, trade shows are usually considered as export promotion tools in a broad sense, designed to stimulate sales to other regions or other countries. The underlying rationale is based on implications from conventional export-base theory (e.g. Richardson 1973; Lloyd and Dicken 1977), which suggests that exports of regional products to other regions/countries lead to financial flows into that region that will trigger a local/regional multiplier process. As a consequence, a variety of public or quasi-public organizations (e.g. central and local governments, export promotion organizations, chambers of commerce, and industry associations) financially support the trade show business. In many countries, organizers of export-oriented trade shows that attract foreign buyers receive financial support from different levels of government. Sometimes, programmes exist that even provide financial support for firms to participate, individually and/or collectively, in foreign trade shows. The organization of collective participation is another instrument considered necessary in early stages of the internationalization process of firms when they lack the organizational skills and financial resources to attend foreign trade shows (Seringhaus and Rosson 1998; Skallerud 2010). The empirical findings presented in this book support the view that trade shows are powerful and flexible export promotion tools, but suggest that knowledge flows about foreign markets and related opportunities may be (or will become) more important than directly stimulated sales.

(i) Local trade show support

Our analysis in Parts I and III suggests that local trade shows and their organizers should be supported if they are able to bring together a substantial number of local suppliers as exhibitors with non-local buyers as visitors. With respect to the trade show typology developed in Chapter 4, export-oriented and hub events would be the main recipients of such support, whereas local/national shows and import or demand trade shows would not be considered. In order to differentiate events along such lines, the use of certified data on trade show attendance, especially with respect to visitors, becomes a key issue, as supporting organizations need reliable figures in their decision-making processes. This is not a trivial request as many venues, cities, and countries do not have processes in place that provide reliable statistics.

With respect to export promotion, the discussions in Part III suggest that it may be useful to develop policies that provide incentives to organizers to adopt knowledge-based strategies to bolster the competitiveness of events. In particular, such policies could encourage the development of practices that build upon the history and culture of the local industry and educate non-local visitors about functional and symbolic differences between local and non-local products.

Such export promotion policies may, however, be mainly relevant to developed regional and national economies, such as those in Western Europe. In the context of less-developed and developing economies that do not have a well-developed industry base or are focused on raw material processing and lack extended value chains, economic development may benefit more from import trade shows (Bathelt and Zeng 2014a). Such events can provide crucial linkages to upstream or downstream producers from other regions and possibly stimulate future investments, such as foreign-direct investments or collaborations. Any policy implications, of course, must be adjusted to the specific regional and national economic and political context.

(ii) Collective participation in non-local trade shows

Support for the collective participation of firms from a particular region (or national state) in non-local trade shows particularly makes sense in the case of hub and import-oriented events. From a collective marketing perspective, local exhibitors could be requested to concentrate their promotional presence jointly at one or a few competing trade shows in a given country or subcontinental market area because a fragmented presence across many events may not convey the image of a consistent local economic system. Knowledge-based strategies that highlight the history and culture of a region and its core competencies can increase awareness and improve the image of local producers. Yet this requires a change in the organizational mode of collective participation—from one based on renting larger exhibition areas to be split between local exhibitors (collective stand logic) to one that aims to design persuasive experiences for visitors by means of specific stand-designs, the selection of specific exhibitors (especially market leaders), and the organization of leisure and cultural events. The goal of such design elements would be to create a specific image of the region, its producers, and their competencies.

It can be assumed that such collective participation in a given country will, over time, have some life-cycle characteristics. More specifically, collective participation will likely develop from an introductory stage to maturity and, possibly, decline. The role of collective participation initiatives is to accompany regional firms in the process of familiarizing themselves with distant markets. Once this goal has been achieved, collective presentations become less important and collective stands will be replaced by individual stands. At this stage, regional governments and industry associations would shift to more generic, 'softer ways' of promoting their local industries.

(iii) Support for individual trade show participation

Even support for individual trade show participation may be useful if based on a knowledge-based perspective. Many of the considerations about collective participation are also valid in the case of individual exhibitors and their exhibits. One could, for instance, imagine establishing policies to provide support for small- and medium-sized enterprises if they exhibit their products at hub trade shows or import-oriented events in other countries. Such policies could have a specific learning focus, accompanied by some kind of training on what can be learned and how, with respect to market-sensing and market-scanning, when participating in such events.

15.3.2. Implications for Innovation Policy

Beyond export promotion, trade shows can serve as useful policy instruments to support or stimulate innovation. The research presented in this book strongly suggests that trade shows are important learning platforms that can assist firms in developing the technological and market-related knowledge necessary to innovate based on observing and interacting with non-local partners, competitors, and customers. Consequently, trade shows can be used as tools for innovation policies that particularly target small and medium-sized enterprises, which lack the formalized new product development routines of their larger counterparts. More specifically, trade shows are instrumental in helping firms to match their technological core competencies with customer needs, which vary across geographical markets and sectors (see Chapter 3). They form important benchmarks for the development of products and technologies, and provide stimuli for firms to innovate along certain trajectories. By planning trade show participation at events located in different countries or focused on different sectors, firms directly influence their ability to learn and to innovate. This function of trade shows is still little-understood, however, and often challenged in academic debates.

One policy approach could be to offer specific training to firms regarding the utilization of trade shows to support technology- and product-related learning and innovation. Policy-makers could also financially support firms' visits to trade shows that enable access to complementary producers, new markets, or technology leaders. It would also be useful to implement policies that support the learning processes of firms at major non-local trade shows, with the goal of identifying suitable partners for research and innovation along the value chain. This would target both the vertical level (customers or suppliers) and the horizontal level (complementary producers).

Trade show organizers could also be the starting point of innovation-related policies that provide incentives to develop knowledge-based strategies (see Chapter 4). Such policies could involve, for example, market research activities targeted at the exhibitors' product development needs, assistance in the establishment of technological or aesthetic standards during trade shows, or support in the organization of side events or special exhibition areas that drive technology transfer.

But it is important to keep in mind that not all trade shows are equally suitable as starting points for innovation policies. Consumer shows or local/national events, for instance, might not have the necessary prerequisites to establish support policies. Instead, innovation-related policies would focus on a limited number of leading business shows, often those that also qualify for export promotion policies. In every industry, a limited number of flagship shows and reference events have emerged as the key sites for exhibitors to showcase their new products and for visitors to learn about key developments in the industry. Others, such as the smaller events that have emerged from local industrial districts, are less relevant in the context of innovation policies. To the extent that these export-oriented events do not allow access to exhibitors from other regions and countries, they risk reproducing the institutional lock-in of permanent industrial clusters (e.g. Hassink and Shin 2005; Visser and Boschma 2006). Public authorities should therefore support trade shows where local firms can learn from observing and interacting with non-local competitors, develop marketing competencies and market-based innovations, and ultimately foster the competitive advantage of their home region/nation.

15.3.3. Implications for Local/Regional Governments

Trade shows are often supported by local/regional governments because they generate local economic impacts linked to the business tourism and service economy these events generate (see Chapters 2 and 5). Local/regional trade shows with international participation could help—if well linked to the local economy—to generate greater visibility and external linkages for the respective producers. While this may be an important anchor to develop a local/regional trade show business, not all regions have the economic structure to support such developments. Whereas large diversified metropolitan centres have advantages in stimulating events that positively impact their regional economy, only selected communities in non-metropolitan contexts may have similar opportunities. And only a few cities, such as Las Vegas and Orlando, in the US, may be capable of establishing a successful trade show business without such regional linkages (Bathelt and Spigel 2012).

In many cases, trade shows that are supported or organized by local/regional governments tend to privilege the organization of large events with limited exhibitor selection in order to maximize injections into local economic multiplier processes. However, such policies may, at times, neglect the specific needs of local industry actors that may prefer smaller, more selective export-oriented trade shows. In tourism studies, scholars have long questioned the narrow focus on economic aspects, encouraging a deeper investigation into the broader impact of trade shows on host areas and communities, including their psychological, socio-cultural, environmental, and political effects (e.g. Ritchie 1984; Syme et al. 1989; Hall 1992). As suggested by Cuadrado-Roura and Rubalcaba-Bermejo (1998), focusing solely on the local economic impact of events may result in 'clone trade shows', which are organized to fill exhibition venues but may lack a clear link to a region's economic specialization. This emphasis on fiscal returns may be short-sighted, particularly from a regional policy perspective. Indeed, it may simply create events that, from the very beginning, are in direct competition with established shows and have little chances of triggering regional industry development. Local/regional governments in developing and less-developed contexts are particularly vulnerable and, in fact, need to avoid such narrow perspectives.

Even in developed contexts, such events might confuse foreign exhibitors and visitors, weakening established trade shows in the same country and benefiting foreign competitors (see Chapters 11 and 13). From this perspective, sustainable trade show business models need to be based on event concepts that contribute to the strengthening of local/regional/national economic systems and their respective economic specializations (see Chapter 5). In other words, care should be exercised not to set up local/regional venues and events in unnecessary competition with other venues and events that could be potentially damaging.

15.3.4. Implications for Trade Show Organizers

From the perspective of trade show organizers, there are several tasks that can be conducted to transform events into leading knowledge-intensive spaces that foster the competitiveness of their regional/national exhibitor and visitor base. Trade show organizers can select specific target exhibitors and visitors, improve knowledge release and acquisition processes regarding the industry or technology field, take steps to curb undesired knowledge spillovers, invest in knowledge creation processes, and, finally, put energy into 'building culture' around a regional/national industry. Under conditions of intensified competition between organizers around the globe, such strategies can help organizers build a competitive advantage. This can become an important foundation for success in the case of 'trade show wars' between organizers.

Our case studies of trade shows in Part III also suggest that the adoption of knowledge-based strategies requires industry-specific competencies. Organizers have different supporting stakeholders and histories that affect their core competencies and strategic decision-making. To be successful in the increasingly competitive and globalizing trade show business, they need to utilize the specific knowledge of an industry group's top players and influencers, its core cluster locations, key market segments, as well as its technological and market developments. Empirical evidence suggests that not all organizers are similarly endowed with such industry-specific knowledge of exhibitors' marketing problems, visitors' learning needs, and an industry's specific structure and history. In fact, this becomes a major challenge when organizers are responsible for many different trade shows across a wide range of industries. This suggests that smaller, more focused organizers may have advantages in pursuing knowledge-based strategies and that large organizers with a diversified trade show portfolio might do better in collaborating with industry associations that can compensate for their lack of specific industry knowledge. To become true knowledge centres, trade show organizers must build specific knowledge for each of the industry groups they intend to operate in. This involves hiring dedicated staff and engaging in partnerships with competent partners.

15.3.5. Implications for Exhibitors and Visitors

A knowledge-based view of trade shows also has important practical implications for the firms participating in these events. Our analysis, for instance, suggests that firms should aim to participate in international trade shows to acquire knowledge about their markets and technologies, learn about market opportunities in other regions and countries, explore potentially new technical knowledge and innovations in their industry, and compare themselves with other firms and competitors in the industry.

(i) Exhibitors

Exhibitors often view trade shows mainly as sales promotion and image-building instruments, with the expectation that returns on investments can be measured through short-term impacts on sales or brand image. The marketing literature has recently started to examine the role of trade shows in disseminating knowledge for promotional reasons (competence release), and in learning from competitors and market developments (see Chapter 3). Yet such processes are still under-researched and have, thus far, had little impact on the nature of trade show participation and broader trade show practices. In our view, a knowledge perspective can strongly influence how firms choose events, where they exhibit their products, how they design their participation, and how they evaluate it. For example, firms may decide to plan to engage in exploratory modes of participation at selected events, with the several goals in mind. They may gauge whether a geographical market is promising or not, whether product development and engineering staff (as opposed to sales personnel) should be present at the exhibits, how interaction with current and potential customers should be structured to obtain ideas for innovation, and whether trade show evaluation models could include knowledge development (Bettis-Outland et al. 2010, 2012).

In addition, our analysis indicates that trade shows can be utilized as collective marketing instruments that encourage firms to cooperate with rivals and complementary producers in achieving common overarching goals. Executive training programmes that target exhibitors typically suffer from an individualistic bias, which originates from viewing other exhibitors as competitors in gaining the limited time and attention of visitor-buyers. While this book does not downplay the omnipresent horizontal competition among exhibitors, trade shows can also be employed for collective promotional projects designed for networks of firms—be they related to local industrial clusters, national industries, or non-geographical networks (see Chapter 2). Exhibitors might find ways to team up with other firms and organize collective participation at domestic and foreign trade shows. These types of collective participation, which can be mediated by industry associations, require the adoption of a strategic partnership approach with trade show organizers. This goes beyond a simple collective stand approach; it requires that firms design and manage such participations as collective events, aiming to present the strengths and distinctive features of the entire network of firms for the target markets.

(ii) Visitors

With respect to visitors, empirical research demonstrates that trade shows are attended by heterogeneous groups of firms, organizations, and participants (see Chapter 2). The increasing presence of 'atypical' visitors (firms not engaged in buying processes) is one of the most obvious examples of the current role of trade shows as key nodes in the globalizing knowledge economy. Our analysis strongly supports the view of trade shows as priceless knowledge resources for visiting firms. The value of their participation does not only derive from conventional sales-related vertical interactions with exhibitors, but also from horizontal learning experiences alongside other visitors—i.e. members of the same or complementary knowing communities. Of course, full exploitation of the insights gained during trade shows requires that the respective knowledge is systematically shared and discussed with other firm representatives that are not present at these events.

In times of economic slowdowns, firms might be tempted to limit their staff at international trade shows and participate in fewer events, for a shorter time period, and with fewer representatives from buying departments. The discussions in this book, however, suggest that such decisions may have negative consequences in terms of missed learning opportunities. To avoid this, firms could adopt countermeasures to at least partially compensate for missed learning opportunities. One way of doing this may be to use internet and social media applications to connect with trade show portals, exhibitor search engines, and the like. Active review of the media coverage of trade shows can provide a basis for virtual explorations of knowledge acquisition opportunities, although such activities can hardly be viewed as equivalent substitutes.

15.4. OUTLOOK

This book advances a novel conceptualization of trade shows and their role in the globalizing learning economy that opens up new perspectives on a phenomenon that has been fundamentally undertheorized and understudied in the past. Our knowledge-based conceptualization sheds new light on trade-related events that have been crucial in regional growth, industrial development, and trade patterns since at least medieval times. We view these events not merely as by-products of globalization processes, but rather as fundamental drivers and enablers of such processes. This book has attempted to investigate trade shows without preconceived ideas about their role in contemporary economic systems. Our agenda is to hint at research gaps that exist and provide conceptual and empirical insights in order to stimulate a new generation of cross-disciplinary debates and academic studies. This, in turn, may lead to innovative ways of organizing trade shows and strategically employing these events in areas such as export promotion, innovation, local economic development, marketing, and as learning instruments.

We conclude by highlighting two drivers of change that currently shape the trade show business (Golfetto and Rinallo 2013). The first concerns a trend in exhibitor behaviour and exhibitor needs, as large firms and market leaders, in particular, begin to shift their promotional efforts from trade shows towards individual firm-specific events. Investments in the latter type of events are growing quickly and have sometimes led to a reduction of the budgets allocated to trade show participation (Event View 2010; Rinallo 2011a; Event Marketing Institute 2012). Such types of events include open houses or private conventions that are sometimes held by firms during the trade show days. Contributing to this behaviour is the supposed need of some large firms to be at the centre of attention. While such counter-events are highly dependent on the existence and attractiveness of trade shows in the first place, they pose a challenge to trade show organizers who are in danger of losing revenues. The respective trade shows may also become less attractive to visitors, as opportunities for knowledge acquisition begin to stagnate. In line with arguments regarding the difficulty of transforming temporary clusters into permanent clusters (Maskell et al. 2004; Bathelt 2012), it seems that individual firm-specific events can only work in the long term if backed up by a vibrant trade show business that generates effective knowledge hot spots. Events such as the Salone del Mobile (see Chapter 14) demonstrate, however, that the lively atmosphere created by individual events can sometimes extend learning opportunities beyond the exhibition venues to involve entire cities—instead of merely disrupting and threating the sustainability of trade shows. Further research is needed to fully understand the tensions and interrelationships between individual and collective events, such as trade shows, and the resulting learning implications for participants.

The second driver concerns the role of technology in the creation of trade shows. In the past, trade show organizers have been reluctant to employ new developments in digital technology in their events. As a consequence, many events today make conservative use of new technologies that are designed to provide information and basic services to exhibitors and visitors. These technologies are often employed to facilitate booking services, stand design, and visualization during the interaction phase with exhibitors, or for mapping visitor pathways. In more innovative events, trade show organizers extend shows through websites about the exhibitors and their exhibits that are open to selected visitor-buyers, which are given access by the exhibitor firms. This allows for greater, yet still limited, visibility of the most innovative products presented during the show. Initiatives of this kind extend the scope of trade show activities temporarily and geographically. They also serve to blur the line between physical and virtual representation. At the very least, they constitute novel phenomena which require careful investigation in the future.

Like the proverbial 'phoenix rising from the ashes', trade shows have proven to be highly resilient temporary and periodic forms of social organization in a particular industry or technology field; indeed, they have constantly renewed themselves and adjusted to changing economic, political, cultural, social, and technological conditions, despite repeated challenges and various periods of decline. The advent of experiential forms of individual and virtual events, which enable individuals to interact in unprecedented manners, will undoubtedly affect the way trade shows are organized and utilized in the future. Past experiences suggest, however, that trade shows will continue to adapt and maintain a crucial role in the learning economy. As mass mobility and mass transport will become increasingly expensive in the future, these occasional opportunities for business communities to get together may, in fact, become more indispensable in sustaining global knowledge circulation processes.

Bibliography

Abernathy, W. J., and Utterback, J. M. (1978), 'Patterns of Industrial Innovation', *Technology Review*, 80 (June–July), 40–7.

Abruzzese, A., Lupi, I., Vergani, G., and Zavoli, S. (2004), *Forme del tempo: Viaggio nei quarant'anni of Assopiastrelle (Shapes of Time: Journey into the Forty Years of Assopiastrelle)* (Milan: Lupetti).

AFE—Asociación de Ferias Españolas (2013), *Presentaciones Congreso AFE* (Madrid: AFE): <http://www.afe.es/> accessed Oct. 2013.

Allix, A. (1922), 'The Geography of Fairs: Illustrated by Old–World Examples', *Geographical Review*, 12, 532–69.

Amin, A., and Cohendet, P. (2004), *Architectures of Knowledge: Firms, Capabilities, and Communities* (Oxford: Oxford University Press).

Amin, A., and Thrift, N. (1992), 'Neo-Marshallian Nodes in Global Networks', *International Journal of Urban and Regional Research*, 16, 571–87.

Anand, N., and Watson, M. R. (2004), 'Tournament Rituals in the Evolution of Fields: The Case of the Grammy Awards', *Academy of Management Journal*, 47, 59–80.

Anderson, P., and Tushman, M. L. (1990), 'Technological Discontinuities and Dominant Designs: Cyclical Model of Technological Change', *Administrative Science Quarterly*, 35, 604–33.

Asheim, B. T. (1999), 'Interactive Learning and Localised Knowledge in Globalising Learning Economies', *GeoJournal*, 49, 345–52.

Asheim, B., Coenen, L., and Vang, J. (2007), 'Face-to-Face, Buzz, and Knowledge Bases: Socio-Spatial Implications for Learning, Innovation, and Innovation Policy', *Environment and Planning C*, 25, 655–70.

AUMA—Ausstellungs- und Messeausschuss der deutschen Wirtschaft (1996), *Ziele und Nutzen von Messebeteiligungen (Goals and Uses of Trade Show Participation)*. AUMA edition, 4 (Berlin: AUMA).

AUMA (1999), *Messefunktions- und Potentialanalyse (Goals and Potentials of Trade Show Participation)*. AUMA edition, 9 (Berlin: AUMA).

AUMA (2002), *Messemärkte Ausland—Kanada (Foreign Trade Show Markets—Canada)* (Berlin: AUMA): <http://www.auma.de/_pages/d/04_MessemaerkteAusland/0402_Laenderprofile/040215_Kanada/04021501_Uebersicht.aspx> accessed Aug. 2012.

AUMA (2004a), *Messemarkt USA (Trade Show Market USA)*. AUMA Compact, 5, 10 Mar. (Berlin: AUMA).

AUMA (2004b), *Messemarkt Mexiko (Trade Show Market Mexico)* (Berlin: AUMA): <http://www.auma.de/_pages/d/04_MessemaerkteAusland/0402_Laenderprofile/040218_Mexiko/download/MessemarktMexiko.pdf> accessed Aug. 2012.

AUMA (2004c), *AUMA Messe Guide Deutschland (AUMA Trade Show Guide for Germany)* (Berlin: AUMA).

AUMA (2005), *Messemarkt Indien (Trade Show Market India)* (Berlin: AUMA): <http://www.auma.de/_pages/d/04_MessemaerkteAusland/0402_Laenderprofile/040212_Indien/download/Messemarkt%20Indien.pdf> accessed June 2012.

AUMA (2006), *German Trade Fair Industry: Key Figures 2006* (Berlin: AUMA).

AUMA (2007), *Messemarkt Südostasien (Trade Show Market Southeast Asia)* (Berlin: AUMA): <http://www.auma.de/_pages/d/04_MessemaerkteAusland/0402_Laenderprofile/040224_Suedostasien/download/Suedostasien.pdf> accessed June 2012.

AUMA (2008), *Messemarkt China (Trade Show Market China)* (Berlin: AUMA): <http://www.auma.de/_pages/d/04_MessemaerkteAusland/0402_Laenderprofile/040208_China/download/Messemarkt_China.pdf> accessed June 2012.

AUMA (2009a), *Messemarkt USA (Trade Show Market USA)* (Berlin: AUMA): <http://www.auma.de/_pages/d/04_MessemaerkteAusland/0402_Laenderprofile/040226_USA/download/Messemarkt_USA.pdf> accessed June 2013.

AUMA (2009b), *Die gesamtwirtschaftliche Bedeutung von Messen und Ausstellungen in Deutschland: Ergebnisse für ein durchschnittliches Messejahr des Zeitraums 2005–2008 (Annual Economic Effects of Trade Shows and Exhibitions in Germany: Average of the Years 2005–2008)* (Berlin: AUMA).

AUMA (2009c), *Die Messewirtschaft: Bilanz 2008 (The Trade Show Economy: 2008 Balance)* (Berlin: AUMA).

AUMA (2011), *Messemarkt Japan (Trade Fair Market Japan)* (Berlin: AUMA): <http://www.auma.de/_pages/d/04_MessemaerkteAusland/0402_Laenderprofile/040214_Japan/download/Messemarkt_Japan.pdf> accessed June 2012.

AUMA (2012a), *German Trade Fair Industry: Key Figures 2012* (Berlin: AUMA).

AUMA (2012b), *German Trade Fair Industry: Review 2012* (Berlin: AUMA).

Backhaus, H. (1992), *Investitionsgütermarketing (Investment Goods Marketing)* (Munich: Vahlen).

Backhaus, H., and Zydorek, C. (1997), 'Von der Mustermesse zur ubiquitären Messe' (From Sample Fairs to Ubiquitous Trade Fairs), in H. Meffert, T. Necker, and H. Sihler (eds), *Märkte im Dialog: Die Messen der dritten Generation (Markets in Dialogue: Trade Shows of the Third Generation)* (Wiesbaden: Gabler), 134–58.

Bahrenberg, G., Giese, E., and Nipper, J. (1985), *Statistische Methoden in der Geographie, 1. Uni- und bivariate Statistik (Statistical Methods in Geography, 1. Uni- and Bivariate Statistics)*, 2nd edn (Stuttgart: Teubner).

Barney, J. B. (1991), 'Firm Resources and Sustained Competitive Advantage', *Journal of Management*, 17, 99–120.

Bartels, R., and Jenkins, R. J. (1977), 'Macromarketing', *Journal of Marketing*, 41 (4), 17–20.

Bartsch, B. (2011), 'Vorfahrt für China' (Right of Way for China), *Frankfurter Rundschau*, 20 Apr., 15.

Bartsch, B. (2012), 'Marktplatz China' (Marketplace China), *Frankfurter Rundschau*, 23 Apr., 12.

Bathelt, H. (1998), 'Regionales Wachstum in vernetzten Strukturen: Konzeptioneller Überblick und kritische Bewertung des Phänomens "Drittes Italien"' (Regional Growth in Networked Structures: Conceptual Review and Critical Evaluation of the Phenomenon of the 'Third Italy'), *Die Erde*, 129, 247–71.

Bathelt, H. (2005), 'Geographies of Production: Growth Regimes in Spatial Perspective 2 – Knowledge Creation and Growth in Clusters', *Progress in Human Geography*, 29, 204–16.

Bathelt, H. (2006), 'Geographies of Production: Growth Regimes in Spatial Perspective 3 – Toward a Relational View of Economic Action and Policy', *Progress in Human Geography*, 30, 223–36.

Bathelt, H. (2007), 'Buzz–and–Pipeline Dynamics: Toward a Knowledge–Based Multiplier Model of Clusters', *Geography Compass*, 1, 1282–98.

Bathelt, H. (2012), 'International Trade Fairs and World Cities: Temporary vs. Permanent Clusters', in B. Derudder, M. Hoyler, P. Taylor, and F. Witlox (eds), *International Handbook of Globalization and World Cities* (Cheltenham and Northampton, MA: Edward Elgar), 177–88.

Bathelt, H., and Gibson, R. (2009), 'Global Buzz and Global Pipelines: International Fairs as the Glue of the Global Political Economy', *Discourse*, 18 (3), 6–7.

Bathelt, H., and Gibson, R. (2014), 'Learning in "Organized Anarchies": Technological Search Processes and Knowledge Flows at International Trade Fairs', *Regional Studies*, 48, doi: 10.1080/00343404.2013.782591, forthcoming.

Bathelt, H., and Glückler, J. (2003), 'Toward a Relational Economic Geography', *Journal of Economic Geography*, 3, 117–44.

Bathelt, H., and Glückler, J. (2011), *The Relational Economy: Geographies of Knowing and Learning* (Oxford: Oxford University Press).

Bathelt, H., and Glückler, J. (2012), *Wirtschaftsgeographie. Ökonomische Beziehungen in räumlicher Perspektive (Economic Geography. Economic Relations in Spatial Perspective)*, 3rd edn (Stuttgart: UTB–Ulmer).

Bathelt, H., and Henn, S. (2014), 'The Geographies of Knowledge Transfers: Toward a Typology', *Environment and Planning A*, 46, forthcoming.

Bathelt, H., Malmberg, A., and Maskell, P. (2002), *Clusters and Knowledge: Local Buzz, Global Pipelines and the Process of Knowledge Creation*. DRUID Working Paper 2002–12 (Copenhagen: www.druid.dk/wp/wp.html).

Bathelt, H., Malmberg, A., and Maskell, P. (2004), 'Clusters and Knowledge: Local Buzz, Global Pipelines and the Process of Knowledge Creation', *Progress in Human Geography*, 28, 31–56.

Bathelt, H., and Schuldt, N. A. (2005), *Between Luminaries and Meat Grinders: International Trade Fairs as Temporary Clusters*. SPACES, 2005–06 (Toronto and Heidelberg: www.spaces-online.com).

Bathelt, H., and Schuldt, N. (2008), 'Between Luminaires and Meat Grinders: International Trade Fairs as Temporary Clusters', *Regional Studies*, 42, 853–68.

Bathelt, H., and Schuldt, N. (2010), 'International Trade Fairs and Global Buzz, Part I: Ecology of Global Buzz', *European Planning Studies*, 18, 1957–74.

Bathelt, H., and Spigel, B. (2012), 'The Spatial Economy of North American Trade Fairs', *Canadian Geographer*, 56, 18–38.

Bathelt, H., and Taylor, M. (2002), 'Clusters, Power and Place: Inequality and Local Growth in Time-Space', *Geografiska Annaler*, 84B, 93–109.

Bathelt, H., and Zakrzewski, G. (2007), 'Messeveranstaltungen als fokale Schnittstellen der globalen Ökonomie' (Trade Fairs as Focal Intersections in the Global Economy), *Zeitschrift für Wirtschaftsgeographie*, 51, 14–30.

Bathelt, H., and Zeng, G. (eds) (2014a), *Temporary Knowledge Ecologies: The Rise and Evolution of Trade Fairs in the Asia-Pacific Region* (Cheltenham and Northampton, MA: Edward Elgar).

Bathelt, H., and Zeng, G. (2014b), 'Trade, Knowledge Circulation and Diverse Trade Fair Ecologies in China', in H. Bathelt and G. Zeng (eds), *Temporary Knowledge Ecologies:*

The Rise and Evolution of Trade Fairs in the Asia-Pacific Region (Cheltenham and Northampton, MA: Edward Elgar), forthcoming.

Bathelt, H., and Zeng, G. (2014c), 'The Development of Trade Fair Ecologies in China: Case Studies from Chengdu and Shanghai', *Environment and Planning A*, 46, forthcoming.

Bautier, R.-H. (1970), 'The Fairs of Champagne', in R. Cameron (ed.), *Essays in French Economic History* (Homewood, IL: Richard D. Irwin), 42–63.

Becattini, G. (1990), 'The Marshallian Industrial District as a Socio–Economic Notion', in F. Pyke, G. Becattini, and W. Sengenberger (eds), *Industrial Districts and Inter-Firm Co-operation in Italy* (Geneva: International Institute for Labour Studies), 37–51.

Becattini, G., and Coltori, F. (2006), 'Areas of Large Enterprise and Industrial Districts in the Development of Post–War Italy: A Preliminary Study', *European Planning Studies*, 14, 1105–38.

Becattini, G., and Rullani, E. (1996), 'Local Systems and Global Connections: The Role of Knowledge', in International Institute for Labour Studies (ed.), *Research Series*, 103 (Geneva: International Institute for Labour Studies), 159–74.

Bechky, B. A. (2003a), 'Sharing Meaning across Occupational Communities: The Transformation of Understanding on a Production Floor', *Organization Science*, 14, 312–30.

Bechky, B. A. (2003b), 'Object Lessons: Workplace Artefacts as Representations of Occupational Jurisdiction', *American Journal of Sociology*, 109, 720–52.

Beck, U. (2005), *Power in the Global Age: A New Global Political Economy* (Malden, MA: Polity).

Becker, H. S. (1998), *Tricks of the Trade: How to Think about your Research While You're Doing it* (Chicago: University of Chicago Press).

Beier, J., and Damböck, S. (2010), *The Role of Exhibitions in the Marketing Mix*, 2nd edn (Paris: UFI; Ravensburg: Baden-Wuerttemberg Cooperative State University).

Bello, D. C., and Barksdale, H. C. Jr (1986), 'Exporting at Industrial Trade Shows', *Industrial Marketing Management*, 15, 197–206.

Bello, D. C., and Lohtia, R. (1993), 'Improving Trade Show Effectiveness by Analyzing Attendees', *Industrial Marketing Management*, 22, 311–18.

Belussi, F. (2003), 'The Changing Governance of IDs: The Entry of Multinationals in Local Nets—The Case of Montebelluna', in B. T. Asheim, and Å. Mariussen (eds), *Innovations, Regions and Projects: Studies in New Forms of Knowledge Governance* (Stockholm: Nordregio), 317–47.

Belussi, F., and Pilotti, L. (2002), 'Knowledge Creation, Learning and Innovation in Italian Industrial Districts', *Geografiska Annaler B*, 84, 125–39.

Bengtsson, M., and Kock, S. (2000), ' "Coopetition" in business networks', *Industrial Marketing Management*, 29, 411–26.

Benner, C. (2003), 'Learning Communities in a Learning Region: The Soft Infrastructure of Cross–Firm Learning Networks in Silicon Valley', *Environment and Planning A*, 35, 1809–30.

Bergen, K. (2003), 'Las Vegas and Orlando Bruising Chicago's Trade Show Business', *Chicago Tribune*, 11 Sept.

Bettis-Outland, H., Cromartie, J. S., Johnston, W. J., and Borders, A. L. (2010), 'The Return on Trade Show Information (RTSI): A Conceptual Analysis', *Journal of Business and Industrial Marketing*, 25, 268–71.

Bettis-Outland, H., Johnston, W. J., and Wilson, R. D. (2012), 'Using Trade Show Information to Enhance Company Success: An Empirical Investigation', *Journal of Business and Industrial Marketing*, 27, 384–91.

Black, R. (1986), *The Trade Show Industry: Management and Marketing Career Opportunities* (East Orleans: Trade Show Bureau).

Blythe, J. (2002), 'Using Trade Fairs in Key Account Management', *Industrial Marketing Management*, 31, 627–35.

Boggs, J. S., and Rantisi, N. M. (2003), 'The "Relational Turn" in Economic Geography', *Journal of Economic Geography*, 3, 109–16.

Bonoma, T. V. (1983), 'Get More out of your Trade Shows', *Harvard Business Review*, 61 (Jan.–Feb.), 75–83.

Bordley, R. (2003), 'Determining the Appropriate Depth and Breadth of a Firm's Product Portfolio', *Journal of Marketing Research*, 40 (1), 39–53.

Borghini, S., Golfetto, F., and Rinallo, D. (2004), 'Using Anthropological Methods to Study Industrial Marketing and Purchasing: An Exploration of Professional Trade Shows', paper presented at the Industrial Marketing and Purchasing Conference (Copenhagen): <http://www.impgroup.org/paper_view.php?viewPaper=4505> accessed Dec. 2013.

Borghini, S., Golfetto, F., and Rinallo, D. (2006), 'Ongoing Search among Industrial Buyers', *Journal of Business Research*, 59, 1151–9.

Boschma, R. A. (2005), 'Proximity and Innovation: A Critical Assessment', *Regional Studies*, 39, 61–74.

Bradley, A., Hall, T., and Harrison, M. (2002), 'Selling Cities: Promoting New Images for Meetings Tourism', *Cities*, 19, 61–70.

Brandenburger, A. M., and Nalebuff, B. J. (1996), *Co-opetition* (New York: Double day).

Braudel, F. (1979), *Le jeux de l'exchange: Civilisation matérielle, économie et capitalisme, xv–xviii siècle* (Paris: Colin).

Braun, B. M. (1992), 'The Economic Contribution of Conventions: The Case of Orlando, Florida', *Journal of Travel Research*, 30, 32–7.

Breiter, D., and Hahm, J. (2006), International Participation at Association Meetings and Conventions Report, report to the National Convention Management Association—Industry Issues Committee (Chicago).

Britton, J. N. H. (2004), 'High Technology Localization and Extra-Regional Networks', *Entrepreneurship and Regional Development*, 16, 369–90.

Brivio, D. (1958), *Il mobile italiano* (Milan: Cosmit).

Brown, J. S., and Duguid, P. (1991), 'Organizational Learning and Communities of Practice: Toward a Unified View of Working, Learning, and Innovation', *Organization Science*, 2, 40–57.

Brusco, S. (1982), 'The Emilian Model: Productive Decentralisation and Social Integration', *Cambridge Journal of Economics*, 6, 167–84.

Callinicos, A. (2004), *Making History: Agency, Structure and Change in Social Theory* (Leiden: Brill).

Camagni, R. (ed.) (1991), *Innovation Networks: Spatial Perspectives* (London and New York: Belhaven).

Cappetta, R., Cillo, P., and Ponti, A. (2006), 'Convergent Designs in Fine Fashion: An Evolutionary Model for Stylistic Innovation', *Research Policy*, 35, 1273–90.

Carman, J. M. (1968), 'Evaluation of Trade Show Exhibitions', *California Management Review*, 10 (Winter), 35–44.

Carreras, A., and Torra, L. (2005), *Why did Modern Trade Fairs Appear?* Working Paper, 874 (Barcelona: Department of Economics and Business, Universitat Pompeu Fabra): <http://www.econ.upf.edu/docs/papers/downloads/874.pdf> accessed Sept. 2013.

Cavanaugh, S. (1976), 'Setting Objectives and Evaluating the Effectiveness of Trade Show Exhibits', *Journal of Marketing*, 40 (4), 100–3.

Caves, R. E. (2000), *Creative Industries: Contracts between Arts and Commerce* (Cambridge, MA: Harvard University Press).

CCI Paris Ile-de-France (2012), *Tourisme d'affaire à Paris-Ile-de France* (Paris: CCI Paris Ile-de-France): <http://www.etudes.cci-paris-idf.fr/telecharger?lien=sites%2Fwww.etudes.cci-paris-idf.fr%2Ffiles%2Fupload%2Fpublications%2Fetudes-salons-1303.pdf> accessed Oct. 2013.

CEIR—Center for Exhibition Industry Research (2005), *2nd Annual CEIR Index: 2005 Edition* (Chicago: CEIR).

CEIR (2009), *CEIR Index Events: 2001–2007 Aggregate Totals*. Unpublished data provided from the Center for Exhibition Industry Research (Chicago: CEIR).

CEIR (2012), *Trends in Use of Exhibitions*. Unpublished report (Dallas: CEIR).

Ceramics China (2013), *Exhibitors* (Guangzhou: Ceramics China): <http://www.ceramicschina.com.cn/EN/main/Exhibitiors.asp> accessed Sept. 2013.

CERMES—Research Centre on Markets and Industrial Sectors (1994), *Tendenze nella Domanda di Servizi Fieristici: Rapporto Moda-Persona (Trends in the Demand of Trade Fair Services: Report on the Fashion Industry)*. Unpublished research report (Milan: Bocconi University).

CERMES (2003a), *Prospettive di Xylexpo nella Competizione Fieristica Internationale (Prospects of Xylexpo in the International Trade Fair Competition)*. Unpublished research report (Milan: Bocconi University).

CERMES (2003b), *Prospettive di ITMA: Le percezioni degli espositori italiani (ITMA's Prospects: Italian Exhibitors' Perceptions)*. Unpublished research report (Milan: Bocconi University).

CERMES (2005), *Trade Fair Observatory—International Trade Fair Report on Leading 5 European Countries (2005): Statistical Appendix* (Milan: Bocconi University).

CERMES (2011a), *Annual Report on the European Trade Shows Industry, 1990–2010*. Unpublished research report (Milan: Bocconi University).

CERMES (2011b), *Annual Report on the European Trade Shows Industry, 1990–2010*. Unpublished research report (Milan: Bocconi University).

CERMES (2012a), *Annual Report on the European Trade Fair Industry, 1996–2010* (Milan: Bocconi University).

CERMES (2012b), *Fiere e marketing collettivo: Mezzo secolo di storie tra distretti industriali e distretti commerciali' (Trade Shows and Collective Marketing: Half a Century of Histories about Industrial and Commercial Clusters)*. Unpublished research report (Milan: Bocconi University).

CERMES (2013), *Trade Show Observatory*. Database of European trade show activity (Milan: Bocconi University).

Chambre de Commerce et d'Industrie de Paris (2001), *Activité 2000 des Centres d'Expositions de Paris Ile-de-France* (Paris: CCIP).

Chang, J.-Y., Hsu, J.-Y., and Chou, T.-L. (2014), 'State Strategy and Industrial Socio-Economic Practices in Taipei's International Trade Fairs', in H. Bathelt and G. Zeng (eds), *Temporary Knowledge Ecologies: The Rise and Evolution of Trade Fairs in the Asia-Pacific Region* (Cheltenham and Northampton, MA: Edward Elgar), forthcoming.

Chen, L.-C. (2009), 'Learning through Informal Local and Global Linkages: The Case of Taiwan's Machine Tool Industry', *Research Policy*, 38, 527–35.

Chen, L.-C. (2011), 'The Governance and Evolution of Local Production Networks in a Cluster: The Case of Taiwan's Machine Tool Industry', *GeoJournal*, 76, 605–22.

Chen, L.-C., and Chu, L.-I. (2014), 'Upgrading of Latecomer Industries in Taiwan and the Case of the Taipei International Machine Tool Show', in H. Bathelt and G. Zeng (eds), *Temporary Knowledge Ecologies: The Rise and Evolution of Trade Fairs in the Asia-Pacific Region* (Cheltenham and Northampton, MA: Edward Elgar), forthcoming.

Child, J. (1997), 'Strategic Choice in the Analysis of Action, Structure, Organizations and Environment: Retrospect and Prospect', *Organization Studies*, 18, 43–76.

China International Exhibition on Gases Technology, Equipment and Application (2010), *IG China 2010* (Chengdu: IG China): <http://www.igchina-expo.com/home.php?> accessed Nov. 2010.

China International Industry Fair (2011), *After Show Report 2010* (Shanghai: CIIF): <http://www.ciif-expo.com/uploadfile/article/uploadfile/201012/20101231092500457.pdf> accessed Jan. 2012.

Clark, G. L., and Tracey, P. (2004), *Global Competitiveness and Innovation: An Agent-Centred Perspective* (Houndsmill and New York: Palgrave Macmillan).

Clausen, E., and Schreiber, P. (2000), *Messen optimal nutzen: Ziele definieren und Erfolge programmieren (How to Optimise the Use of Trade Fairs: Defining Goals and Planning Success)* (Würzburg: Schimmel).

Cohen, M. D., and March, J. G. (1974), *Leadership and Ambiguity: The American College President* (New York: McGraw-Hill).

Cohen, M. D., March, J. G., and Olsen, J. P. (1972), 'A Garbage Can Model of Organizational Choice', *Administrative Science Quarterly*, 17, 1–25.

Cohen, W. M., and Levinthal, D. A. (1990), 'Absorptive Capacity: A New Perspective on Learning and Innovation', *Administrative Science Quarterly*, 35, 128–52.

Cohendet, P., Grandadam, D., and Simon, L. (2010), 'The Anatomy of the Creative City', *Industry and Innovation*, 17, 91–111.

Cohendet, P., Héraud, J.-A., and Llerena, P. (2013), 'A Microeconomic Approach of the Dynamics of Creation', in P. Meusburger, J. Glückler, and M. el Meskioui (eds), *Knowledge and Economy*. Klaus Tschira Symposia: Knowledge and Space, 5 (Berlin and Heidelberg: Springer), 43–59.

Cole, A., and Barbera, D. (2014), 'Negotiating Conventions and Creating Community: The Case of Cartoon and European Animation', *Journal of Economic Geography*, 14, forthcoming.

Cooke, P., and Morgan, K. (1998), *The Associational Economy: Firms, Regions, and Innovation* (Oxford: Oxford University Press).

Cornish, S. (1997), 'Product Innovation and the Spatial Dynamics of Market Intelligence: Does Proximity to Markets Matter?', *Economic Geography*, 73, 143–65.

Cox, K. R., and Mair, A. (1988), 'Locality and Community in the Politics of Local Economic Development', *Annals of the Association of American Geographers*, 78, 307–25.

Crevoisier, O., and Maillat, D. (1991), 'Milieu, Industrial Organization and Territorial Production System: Towards a New Theory of Spatial Development', in R. Camagni (ed.), *Innovation Networks: Spatial Perspectives* (London and New York: Belhaven Press), 13–34.

Crompton, J. L. (2006), 'Economic Impact Studies: Instruments for Political Shenanigans?', *Journal of Travel Research*, 45, 67–82.

Crompton, J. L., and McKay, S. L. (1994), 'Measuring the Economic Impacts of Festivals and Events: Some Myths, Misapplications and Ethical Dilemmas', *Festival Management and Event Tourism*, 2, 33–43.

Crouch, C. (2005), *Capitalist Diversity and Change: Recombinant Governance and Institutional Entrepreneurs* (Oxford: Oxford University Press).

Cuadrado-Roura, J. R., and Rubalcaba-Bermejo, L. (1998), 'Specialization and Competition amongst European Cities: A New Approach through Fair and Exhibition Activities', *Regional Studies*, 32, 133–47.

Dahl, M. S., and Pedersen, C. O. R. (2003), *Knowledge Flows through Informal Contacts in Industrial Clusters: Myths or Realities?* DRUID Working Paper, 03–01 (Copenhagen): <www.druid.dk/wp/wp.html> accessed Apr. 2005.

Damer, B., Gold, S., de Bruin, J., and de Bruin, D.-J. (2000), 'Conferences and Trade Shows in Inhabited Virtual Worlds: A Case Study of Avatars 98 and 99', in J. C. Heudin (ed.), *Second International Conference, Virtual World 2000, Paris, France, July 5–7, Proceedings*. Lecture Notes in Computer Science, 1834 (Berlin and Heidelberg: Springer), 1–11.

Day, G. S. (1981), 'The Product Life Cycle: Analysis and Application Issues', *Journal of Marketing*, 45 (Autumn), 60–7.

Day, G. S. (1993), *The Capabilities of Market-Driven Organizations* (Cambridge, MA: Marketing Science Institute).

Day, G. S. (1994), 'The Capabilities of Market-Driven Organizations', *Journal of Marketing*, 58 (October), 37–51.

De Roover, R. (1942), 'The Commercial Revolution of the Thirteenth Century', *Bulletin of the Business Historical Society*, 16, 34–9.

Derudder, B., Hoyler, M., Taylor, P., and Witlox, F. (eds) (2012), *International Handbook of Globalization and World Cities* (Cheltenham and Northampton, MA: Edward Elgar).

Dicken, P., and Malmberg, A. (2001), 'Firms in Territories: A Relational Perspective', *Economic Geography*, 77, 345–63.

Dicken, P., Kelly, P. F., Olds, K., and Yeung, H. W.-C. (2001), 'Chains and Networks, Territories and Scales: Towards a Relational Framework for Analysing the Global Economy', *Global Networks*, 1, 89–112.

Direct Energy Centre (2010), *About Direct Energy Centre* (Toronto: Direct Energy Centre): <http://www.directenergycentre.com/database/rte/files/AboutDirect%20Energy%20Centre.pdf> accessed Aug. 2010.

Drapers Record (2005), 'Première Vision to Reveal Revolutionary New Layout', *Drapers Record*, 10 Dec., 4.

Dudley, J. (1990), *Successful Exhibiting* (London: Kogan-Page).

Dwyer, L., Foryth, P., and Spurr, R. (2005), 'Estimating the Impacts of Special Events on an Economy', *Journal of Travel Research*, 43, 351–9.

Economic Development Agency for the Paris Region (2013), *Paris Region Tradeshows* (Paris: Paris-Region): <http://www.parisregion-tradeshows.com/index.php4?coe_i_id=172> accessed Oct. 2013.

EMECA—European Major Exhibition Centres Association (2012), *Facilities* (Brussels: EMECA): <http://www.emeca.com/> accessed Oct. 2013.

Entwistle, J., and Rocamora, A. (2006), 'The Field of Fashion Materialized: A Study of London Fashion Week', *Sociology*, 40, 735–51.

Epstein, S. R. (1994), 'Regional Fairs, Institutional Innovation, and Economic Growth in Late Medieval Europe', *Economic History Review*, 47, 459–82.

European Commission (2003a), *The Future of the Textile and Clothing Sector in the Enlarged Europe* (Brussels: European Commission): <http://ec.europa.eu/enterprise/sectors/textiles/documents/communication-2003_en.htm> accessed Oct. 2013.

European Commission (2003b), *Evolution of Trade in Textile and Clothing Worldwide* (Brussels: European Commission): <http://ec.europa.eu/enterprise/sectors/textiles/documents/communication-2003_en.htm> accessed Oct. 2013.

European Commission (2008), *Small Business Act for Europe (SBA)* (Brussels: European Commission): <http://ec.europa.eu/enterprise/policies/sme/documents/sba/index_en.htm#h2-1> accessed Oct. 2013.

European Commission (2009), *European Business: Fact and Figures, 2009* (Brussels: European Commission): <http://epp.eurostat.ec.europa.eu/cache/ITY_OFFPUB/KS-BW-09-001-01/EN/KS-BW-09-001-01-EN.PDF> accessed Oct. 2013.

EUROSTAT (2011), *Manufacture of Furniture Statistics—NACE Rev. 2* (Luxembourg: European Commission): <http://epp.eurostat.ec.europa.eu/statistics_explained/index.php/Manufacture_of_furniture_statistics_-_NACE_Rev._2> accessed Apr. 2012.

EUROSTAT (2012), *Manufacture of Textiles Statistics—NACE Rev. 2* (Luxembourg: European Commission): <http://epp.eurostat.ec.europa.eu/statistics_explained/index.php/Manufacture_of_textiles_statistics_-_NACE_Rev._2> accessed Apr. 2013.

Event Marketing Institute (2012), *Event Track 2012: Event and Experiential Marketing Industry Forecast and Best Practices Study* (Norwalk: Event Marketing Institute).

Event View (2010), *Global Report* (Norwalk: Event Marketing Institute).

Evers, N., and Knight, J. (2008), 'Role of International Trade Shows in Small Firm Internationalization: A Network Perspective', *International Marketing Review*, 25, 544–62.

Expo Revestir (2013), *Presentation* (Sao Paulo: Expo Revestir): <http://www.exporevestir.com.br> accessed Sept. 2013.

Faulconbridge, J. R. (2007a), 'Exploring the Role of Professional Associations in Collective Learning in London and New York's Advertising and Law Professional-Service-Firm Clusters', *Environment and Planning A*, 39, 965–84.

Faulconbridge, J. R. (2007b), 'London's and New York's Advertising and Law Clusters and their Networks of Learning: Relational Analyses with a Politics of Scale?' *Urban Studies*, 44, 1635–56.

Faulconbridge, J. R. (2008), 'Managing the Transnational Law Firm: A Relational Analysis of Professional Systems, Embedded Actors, and Time-Space-Sensitive Governance', *Economic Geography*, 84, 185–210.

Fenich, G. G., and Hashimoto, K. (2004), 'Casinos and Conventions: Strange Bedfellows', in R. R. Nelson (ed.), *Current Issues in Convention and Exhibition Facility Development* (Binghamton, NY: Haworth Hospitality), 63–80.

Filippi, M., and Torre, A. (2003), 'Local Organizations and Institutions: How can Geographical Proximity be Activated by Collective Projects?', *International Journal of Technology Management*, 26, 386–400.

Findling, J. E., and Pelle, K. D. (2008), *Encyclopedia of World's Fairs and Expositions* (Jefferson, NC: McFarland & Co.).

Fisk, G. (1981), 'An Invitation to Participate in Affairs of the Journal of Macromarketing', *Journal of Macromarketing*, 1, 3.

Florida, R. (2005), *Cities and the Creative Class* (New York and London: Routledge).

Florio, M. (1994), 'Fair Trades by Trade Fairs: Information Providing Institutions under Monopolistic Competition', *Small Business Economics*, 6, 267–81.

Fondazione Fiera Milano (2001), *Le ricadute economiche dell'attività di Fiera Milano sul territorio (The Economic Spin-off of Fiera Milano on the Territory)* (Milan: Guerini).

Fondazione Fiera Milano (2006), *Impatto Fiera: Imprese e professioni intorno al polo espositivo di Rho-Pero (The Fair Impact: Firms and Professions on the Exhibition Centre of Rho-Pero Neighbour)* (Milan: Fiera Milano Edizioni).

Fournier, S., and Lee, L. (2009), 'Getting Brand Communities Right', *Harvard Business Review*, 56 (Apr.), 105–11.

Frankfurter Rundschau (2006), 'CeBit droht Umsatzeinbruch' (CeBit Threatened by Sales Collapse), *Frankfurter Rundschau*, 20 Dec.

Frommberg, L. (2009a), 'Birnen–Problem' (Bulb Problem), *Frankfurter Rundschau*, 28 Aug., 18.

Frommberg, L. (2009b), 'Licht aus' (Lights off), *Frankfurter Rundschau*, 28 Aug., 18–9.

Fu, H., Yang, G., and Qi, Y. (2007), 'Factors Affecting Trade Show Effectiveness for Chinese Small and Medium-Sized Exporters', *International Management Review*, 3 (3), 84–96.

Fuchslocher, H., and Hochheimer, H. (2000), *Messen im Wandel: Messemarketing im 21. Jahrhundert (Trade Shows in Transition: Trade Show Marketing in the 21st Century)* (Wiesbaden: Gabler).

Garud, R. (2008), 'Conferences as Venues for the Configuration of Emerging Organizational Fields: The Case of Cochlear Implants', *Journal of Management Studies*, 45, 1061–88.

Geduhn, H.-J. (2012), 'Shanghai New International Expo Centre', paper presented at the Shanghai New International Expo Centre, 25 May (Shanghai).

Geigenmüller, A. (2010), 'The Role of Virtual Trade Fairs in Relationship Value Creation', *Journal of Business and Industrial Marketing*, 25, 284–92.

Geigenmüller, A., and Bettis-Outland, H. (2012), 'Brand Equity in B2B Services and Consequences for the Trade Show Industry', *Journal of Business and Industrial Marketing*, 27 (6), 428–35.

Gereffi, G., Humphrey, J., and Sturgeon, T. (2005), 'The Governance of Global Value Chains', *Review of International Political Economy*, 12, 78–104.

Gertler, M. S. (2004), *Manufacturing Culture: The Institutional Geography of Industrial Practice* (Oxford: Oxford University Press).

Getz, D. (1997), *Event Management and Event Tourism* (New York: Cognizant Communications).

Getz, D. (2000), 'Festival and Special Events: Life Cycle and Saturation Issues', in W. Garter and D. Lime (eds), *Trends in Outdoor Recreation, Leisure and Tourism* (Wallingford: CABI), 175–85.

Gibson, R. (2015), *Dynamic Capitalisms? Understanding National Specialization Patterns through Inter-Firm Interaction at International Trade Fairs.* Ph.D. thesis (Toronto: Department of Political Science: University of Toronto).

Gibson, R., and Bathelt, H. (2010), *Understanding the Dynamics of Specialization and Diffusion Processes across Capitalist Varieties: A Conceptual Intervention Regarding the Role of International Trade Fairs.* SPACES, 2010–04 (Toronto and Heidelberg: http://www.spaces-online.com).

Gibson, R., and Bathelt, H. (2014), 'Field Configuration or Field Reproduction? The Dynamics of Global Trade Fair Cycles', *Zeitschrift für Wirtschaftsgeographie*, 58, forthcoming.

Giddens, A. (1984), *The Constitution of Society: Outline of the Theory of Structuration* (Cambridge: Polity Press).

Giddens, A. (1990), *Consequences of Modernity* (Stanford, CA: Stanford University Press).

Gingold, M., and Wilson, D. (1998), 'Buying Center Research and Marketing Practice: Meeting the Challenge of Dynamic Marketing', *Journal of Business and Industrial Marketing*, 13, 96–108.

Glaser, B. G., and Strauss, A. L. (1967), *The Discovery of Grounded Theory: Strategies for Qualitative Research* (Chicago: Aldine).

Glückler, J. (2007), 'Geography of Reputation: The City as the Locus of Business Opportunity', *Regional Studies*, 41, 949–62.

Godar, S. H., and O'Connor, P. L. (2001), 'Same Time Next Year – Buyer Trade Show Motives', *Industrial Marketing Management*, 30, 77–86.

Goehrmann, K. E. (2003a), 'Die Nutzung der IT auf der Messe steht erst am Anfang' (The Application of IT During Trade Shows is Only Just Beginning), *WirtschaftsKurier*, Nov., 24.

Goehrmann, K. E. (2003b), 'Messen als Instrument des Regionen– und Politmarketings' (Trade Shows as an Instrument of Regional and Policy Marketing), in M. Kirchgeorg, W. M. Dornscheidt, W. Giese, and N. Stoeck (eds), *Handbuch Messemanagement: Planung, Durchführung und Kontrolle von Messen, Kongressen und Events (Handbook of Trade Show Management: Planning, Execution and Control of Trade Shows, Conventions and Events)* (Wiesbaden: Gabler), 87–96.

Golfetto, F. (1988), *Il sistema fieristico internazionale (The International Trade Fair Industry)* (Milan: Angeli).

Golfetto, F. (1991), *L'impatto economico delle manifestazioni fieristiche (The Economic Impact of Trade Shows)* (Milan: EGEA).

Golfetto, F. (2000), 'Reti di imprese e meta-organizzatori: Il ruolo delle fiere' (Firm Networks and Meta-Organizers: The Trade Shows' Role), *Sinergie*, 18, 189–211.

Golfetto, F. (2004), *Fiere e comunicazione: Strumenti per le imprese e il territorio (Trade Fairs and Communication: Tools for Firms and the Territory)* (Milan: EGEA).

Golfetto, F., and Gibbert, M. (2006), 'Marketing Competencies and the Sources of Customer Value in Business Markets', *Industrial Marketing Management*, 35, 904–12.

Golfetto, F., and Mazursky, D. (2004), 'Competence-Based Marketing', *Harvard Business Review*, 51 (Nov.), 26.

Golfetto, F., and Rinallo, D. (2000), 'L'immagine del territorio e le manifestazioni fieristiche: Una verifica empirica' (Trade Fairs and Host Areas' Image: An Empirical Test), in E. Valdani and F. Ancarani (eds), *Strategie di Marketing del Territorio (Place Marketing Strategies)* (Milan: EGEA), 311–21.

Golfetto, F., and Rinallo, D. (2008), 'Reshaping Markets through Collective Marketing Strategies: Lessons from the Textile Industry', in K. Tollin and A. Carù (eds), *Strategic Market Creation: Realizing Radical Innovation from a Marketing Perspective* (Chichester: John Wiley & Sons), 97–123.

Golfetto, F., and Rinallo, D. (2012), 'Competition and Collective Marketing: A History of the European Textile Industry Trade Shows', in S. Borghini, A. Carù, F. Golfetto, S. Pace, D. Rinallo, L. Visconti, and F. Zerbini (eds), *Prodotto, consumatore e politiche di mercato quarant'anni dopo: Scritti in onore di Stefano Podestà (Product, Consumer and Market Policies After Forty Years: Writings in Honour of Stefano Podestà)* (Milan: EGEA Online), 369–94.

Golfetto, F., and Rinallo, D. (2013), 'Trade Show Events, from Live to Digital: Towards the Development of New Competencies', in Fondazione Fiera Milano (ed.), *Exhibitions in Years 2.0: Between Internalization and Local Development* (Milan: EGEA), 119–53.

Golfetto, F., and Rinallo, D. (2014), 'The Evolution of Trade Show Systems: Lessons from Europe', in H. Bathelt and G. Zeng (eds), *Temporary Knowledge Ecologies: The Rise and Evolution of Trade Fairs in the Asia-Pacific Region* (Cheltenham and Northampton, MA: Edward Elgar), forthcoming.

Golfetto, F., Gibbert, M., and Zerbini, F. (2004), 'Impartive Capacity: Towards a View of the Supplier as a Competence Provider', paper presented at the Strategic Management Society Conference (San Juan, Puerto Rico).

Goodman, E., Bamford, J., and Saynor, P. (eds) (1989), *Small Firms and Industrial Districts in Italy* (London and New York: Routledge).

Gopalakrishna, S., and Lilien, G. L. (1995), 'A Three Stage Model of Industrial Trade Show Performance', *Marketing Science*, 14 (Winter), 22–42.

Gopalakrishna, S., Roster, C. A., and Sridhar, S. (2010), 'An Exploratory Study of Attendee Activities at a Business Trade Show', *Journal of Business and Industrial Marketing*, 25, 241–8.

Gospodini, A. (2002), 'European Cities in Competition and the New "Uses" of Urban Design', *Journal of Urban Design*, 7, 59–73.

Grabher, G. (1993), Rediscovering the Social in the Economies of Interfirm Relations', in G. Grabher (ed.), *The Embedded Firm: On the Socioeconomics of Industrial Networks* (London and New York: Routledge), 1–31.

Grabher, G., Ibert, O., and Flohr, S. (2008), 'The Neglected King: The Customer in the New Knowledge Ecology of Innovation', *Economic Geography*, 84, 253–80.

Grant, R. M. (1996), 'Toward a Knowledge-Based Theory of the Firm', *Strategic Management Journal*, 17, 109–22.

Guercini, S., and Ranfagni, S. (2012), 'Creation of Fashion Trends and Role of the Bureau de Style for Textile Innovation', *Journal of Global Fashion Marketing*, 3, 12–21.

Gulf Construction (2008), 'All Eyes on Verona as Marmomacc Opens', *Gulf Construction*, 1 Oct., 23.

Guo, J.-R. (2011), *Blue Book of Convention and Exhibition Economy: Annual Report on China's Convention and Exhibition Economy 2011* (Beijing: Social Sciences Academic Press, in Chinese).

Guo, J.-R. (2012), *Blue Book of Convention and Exhibition Economy. Annual Report on China's Convention and Exhibition Economy 2012* (Beijing: Social Sciences Academic Press, in Chinese).

Haddow, R. (2008), 'How Can Comparative Political Economy Explain Variable Change? Lessons for, and from, Canada', in L. A. White, R. Simeon, R. Vipond, and J. Wallner (eds), *The Comparative Turn in Canadian Political Science* (Vancouver: UBC Press), 221–37.

Hall, C. M. (1992), *Hallmark Tourist Events: Impacts, Management and Planning* (London: Belhaven Press).

Hall, P. A., and Soskice, D. (2001), 'An Introduction to Varieties of Capitalism', in P. A. Hall and D. Soskice (eds), *Varieties of Capitalism: The Institutional Foundations of Comparative Advantage* (Oxford: Oxford University Press), 1–68.

Hall, P. A., and Thelen, K. (2009), 'Institutional Change in Varieties of Capitalism', *Socio-Economic Review*, 7, 7–34.

Hamel, G., and Prahalad, C. K. (1994), *Competing for the Future* (Cambridge, MA: Harvard Business School Press).

Hardy, C., and Maguire, S. (2010), 'Discourse, Field-Configuring Events, and Change in Organizations and Institutional Fields: Narratives of DDT and the Stockholm Convention', *Academy of Management Journal*, 53, 1365–92.

Harrison, B. (1992), 'Industrial Districts: Old Wine in New Bottles?', *Regional Studies*, 26, 469–83.

Hassink, R., and Shin, D.-H. (2005), 'Guest Editorial: The Restructuring of Old Industrial Areas in Europe and Asia', *Environment and Planning A*, 37, 571–80.

Hauswirth, I., and Magri, P. (2013), 'Exhibitions as a Tool for Industrial Policy to Promote Export', in Fondazione Fiera Milano (ed.), *Exhibitions in Years 2.0: Between Internalization and Local Development* (Milan: EGEA), 17–44.

Hay, C. (1995), 'Structure and Agency', in D. Marsh and G. Stoker (eds), *Theory and Methods in Political Science* (Basingstoke: Macmillan), 189–208.

Held, D., McGrew, A., Goldblatt, D., and Perraton, J. (1999), *Global Transformations: Politics, Economics and Culture* (Cambridge: Polity Press).

Hodur, N. M., and Leistritz, F. L. (2006), 'Estimating the Economic Impact of Event Tourism: A Review of Issues and Methods', *Journal of Convention and Event Tourism*, 8, 63–79.

Holten, L., and Draeger, H. (1991), 'Is the City Losing its Convention Pull? Bustling, Lucrative Trade Show Business at a Crossroads', *Chicago Sun-Times*, 2 June.

Hubbard, P. (1995), 'Urban Design and Local Economic Development: A Case Study of Birmingham', *Cities*, 12, 243–51.

Hunt, S. (1981), 'Macromarketing as a Multidimensional Concept', *Journal of Macromarketing*, 1, 7–8.

IIDEX/NeoCon Canada (2008a), *IIDEX Mediaflash.* Press release (Toronto: IIDEX/NeoCon Canada): <http://www.iidexneocon.com/2008/index.php/newsletter/> accessed Sept. 2008.

IIDEX/NeoCon Canada (2008b), *2008 IIDEX/NeoCon Canada Official Show Guide* (Toronto: IIDEX/NeoCon).

Il Sole 24 Ore (2002), 'Oggi apre il Marmomacc' (Today Marmomacc Opens), *Il Sole 24 Ore*, 3 Oct., 19.

International Centre (2011), *International Centre: History* (Toronto: International Centre): <http://www.internationalcentre.com/history> accessed Aug. 2011.

Jackson, D. W., Keith, J. E., and Burdick, R. K. (1984), 'Purchasing Agents' Perceptions of Industrial Buying Center Influence: A Situational Approach', *Journal of Marketing*, 48 (4), 75–83.

Jeppesen, L. B., and Molin, J. M. (2003), 'Consumers as Co-Developers: Learning and Innovation outside the Firm', *Technology Analysis and Strategic Management*, 15, 363–83.

Jin, X., and Weber, K. (2008), 'The China Import and Export (Canton) Fair: Past, Present, and Future', *Journal of Convention and Event Tourism*, 9, 221–34.

Jin, X., Weber, K., and Bauer, T. (2010), 'The State of the Exhibition Industry in China', *Journal of Convention and Event Tourism*, 11, 2–17.

Jin, X., Weber, K., and Bauer, T. (2012), 'Impact of Clusters on Exhibition Destination Attractiveness: Evidence from Mainland China', *Tourism Management*, 33, 1429–39.

Johnston, W. J., and Bonomia, T. V. (1981), 'The Buying Center: Structure and Interaction Patterns', *Journal of Marketing*, 45 (3), 143–56.

Jones, C. (2006), 'Trade Shows Big and Growing', *Las Vegas Review-Journal*, 26 Apr.

Kalafsky, R. V., and Gress, D. R. (2013a), 'Trade Fairs as an Export Marketing and Research Strategy: Results from a Study of Korean Advanced Machinery Firms', *Geographical Research*, 51, doi: 10.1111/1745-5871.12019, forthcoming.

Kalafsky, R. V., and Gress, D. R. (2013b) 'Go Big or Stay Home? Korean Machinery Firms, Trade Fair Dynamics, and Export Performance', *Asia Pacific Business Review*, 19, DOI: 10.1080/13602381.2013.814227, forthcoming.

Kalafsky, R. V., and Gress, D. R. (2014), 'How and Where Tigers Roam: The Role of Korean Trade Fairs in Supporting Firms' Export Activities', in H. Bathelt and G. Zeng (eds), *Temporary Knowledge Ecologies: The Rise and Evolution of Trade Fairs in the Asia-Pacific Region* (Cheltenham and Northampton, MA: Edward Elgar), forthcoming.

Katzenstein, P. J. (1987), *Policy and Politics in West Germany: The Growth of a Semisovereign State* (Philadelphia: Temple University Press).

Kay, A. L. K. (2005), 'China's Convention and Exhibition Center Boom', *Journal of Convention and Event Tourism*, 7, 5–22.

Kerr, M. K., and King, H. W. (1984), *Procedures for Meetings and Organizations* (Toronto: Carswell Legal Publications).

Khalid, I. A.-S., and Baker, M. J. (1998), 'Country of Origin Effects: A Literature Review', *Marketing Intelligence and Planning*, 16, 150–99.

Kirchgeorg, M. (2003), 'Funktionen und Erscheinungsformen von Messen' (Functions and Types of Trade Shows), in M. Kirchgeorg, W. M. Dornscheidt, W. Giese, and N. Stoeck (eds), *Handbuch Messemanagement: Planung, Durchführung und Kontrolle von Messen, Kongressen und Events (Handbook of Trade Show Management: Planning, Execution and Control of Trade Shows, Conventions and Events)* (Wiesbaden: Gabler), 51–72.

Kitson, M., and Michie, J. (1996), 'Britain's Industrial Performance since 1960: Underinvestment and Relative Decline', *Economic Journal*, 106 (434), 196–212.

Knorr Cetina, K. (1999), *Epistemic Cultures: How the Sciences Make Sense* (Chicago: Chicago University Press).

Kohli, A. K. (1989), 'Determinants of Influence in Organizational Buying: A Contingency Approach', *Journal of Marketing*, 53 (3), 50–65.

Kohli, A. K., and Jaworksi, B. J. (1990), 'Market Orientation: The Construct, Research Propositions, and Managerial Implications', *Journal of Marketing*, 54 (2), 1–18.

Kong, X., and Zhang, Y.-F. (2014), 'Local Characteristics and the Formation of Temporary Clusters: The Case of the Shanghai International Automobile Industry Exhibition', in H. Bathelt and G. Zeng (eds), *Temporary Knowledge Ecologies: The Rise and Evolution of Trade Fairs in the Asia-Pacific Region* (Cheltenham and Northampton, MA: Edward Elgar), forthcoming.

Kreiner, K. (2002), 'Tacit Knowledge Management: The Role of Artifacts', *Journal of Knowledge Management*, 6, 112–23.

Kresse, H. (2003), *The European Trade Fair Industry: Current Situation and Challenges.* Mimeo (Berlin: AUMA).

L'Arena (2008), 'Così Verona si mangiò la fiera' (This is how Verona ate the Trade Fair), *L'Arena*, 2 Dec., 38.

La Repubblica (1998), 'La fiera rapita a Sant'Ambrogio' (Sant'Ambrogio's Kidnapped Fair), *La Repubblica*, 11 May, 20.

Laboratorio delle Imprese (2008), *Il distretto lapideo Apuo-Versiliese (The Apuo-Versiliese Stone District)* (Verona: Banco Popolare): <http://www.videomarmoteca.it/uploads/pdf/marmo_carrara.pdf> accessed Oct. 2013.

Laboratorio delle Imprese (2010), *Il settore lapideo della Provincia di Verona (The Province of Verona's Stone District)* (Verona: Banco Popolare): <http://www.videomarmoteca.it/uploads/pdf/analisi__settore_lapideo_vr_1022010_copy2.pdf> accessed Oct. 2013.

Lampel, J., and Meyer, A. D. (2008), 'Field-Configuring Events as Structuring Mechanisms: How Conferences, Ceremonies, and Trade Shows Constitute New Technologies, Industries, and Markets', *Journal of Management Studies*, 45 (6), 1025–35.

Lanaro, P. (2003), 'Economic Space and Urban Policies: Fairs and Markets in the Italy of the Early Modern Age', *Journal of Urban History*, 30, 37–49.

Lawrence, J., Payne, T. R., and De Roure, D. (2006), 'Co-Presence Communities: Using Pervasive Computing to Support Weak Social Networks', paper presented at the International Workshop on 'Distributed and Mobile Collaboration' (Manchester).

Lazerson, M. (1993), 'Factory or Putting-Out? Knitting Networks in Modena', in G. Grabher (ed.), *The Embedded Firm: On the Socioeconomics of Indutrial Networks* (London and New York: Routledge), 203–26.

Lazzaroni, L. (1996), *Thirty-Five Years of Design at Salone del Mobile: 1961–1996* (Milan: Cosmit).

Lee, C. H., and Kim, S. Y. (2008), 'Differential Effects of Determinants on Multi-Dimensions of Trade Show Performance: By Three Stages of Pre-Show, At-Show, and Post–Show Activities', *Industrial Marketing Management*, 37, 784–96.

Lee, M., and Back, J. (2005), 'A Review of Economic Value Drivers in Convention and Meeting Management Research', *International Journal of Contemporary Hospitality Management*, 17, 409–20.

Lee, M. J. (2006), 'Analytical Reflections on the Economic Impact Assessment of Conventions and Special Events', *Journal of Convention and Event Tourism*, 8, 71–85.

Ley, D., and Olds, L. (1988), 'Landscape as Spectacle: World's Fairs and the Culture of Heroic Consumption', *Environment and Planning D*, 6, 191–212.

Li, L.-Y. (2006), 'Relationship Learning at Trade Shows: Its Antecedents and Consequences', *Industrial Marketing Management*, 35, 166–77.

Li, L.-Y. (2007), 'Marketing Resources and Performance of Exhibitor Firms in Trade
Shows: A Contingent Resource Perspective', *Industrial Marketing Management*, 36
(3), 360–70.

Li, P.-F. (2014a), 'Temporary Clustering in Developing Economies: Trade Fairs in South
and Southeast Asia', in H. Bathelt and G. Zeng (eds), *Temporary Knowledge Ecologies:
The Rise and Evolution of Trade Fairs in the Asia-Pacific Region* (Cheltenham and
Northampton, MA: Edward Elgar), forthcoming.

Li, P.-F. (2014b), 'Global Temporary Networks of Clusters: Trade Fair Dynamics in
Asian Economies', *Journal of Economic Geography*, 14, forthcoming.

LightFair International (2009a), *Official On-Site Directory* (New York: LightFair
International).

LightFair International (2009b), *General Exhibit Information* (New York: Light-Fair International): <http://www.lightfair.com/lightfair/V40/index.cvn?id=10191> accessed Apr. 2009.

LightFair International (2009c), *Thank you for Being Part of this Record-Breaking Light-
Fair Event*. Email to attendees, 15 June (New York: Light-Fair International).

Lilien, G. L., and Wong, M. A. (1984), 'An Exploratory Investigation of the Structure of
the Buying Center in the Metalworking Industry', *Journal of Marketing Research*, 21
(1), 1–11.

Lloyd, P. E., and Dicken, P. (1977), *Location in Space: A Theoretical Approach to Economic Geography*, 2nd edn (London and New York: Harper & Row).

Lorenzoni, G., and Narduzzo, A. (2005), 'Conventional Artefacts in the Digital Era', paper
presented at the American Academy of Management Annual Conference (Honolulu).

Lundvall, B.-Å. (1988), 'Innovation as an Interactive Process: From Producer–User
Interaction to the National System of Innovation', in G. Dosi, C. Freeman, R. R. Nel-
son, G. Silverberg, and L. L. G. Soete (eds), *Technical Change and Economic Theory*
(London and New York: Pinter), 349–69.

Lundvall, B.-Å., and Johnson, B. (1994), 'The Learning Economy', *Journal of Industry
Studies*, 1, 23–42.

Lundvall, B.-Å., and Maskell, P. (2000), 'Nation States and Economic Development:
From National Systems of Production to National Systems of Knowledge Creation
and Learning', in G. L. Clark, M. P. Feldman, and M. S. Gertler (eds), *The Oxford
Handbook of Economic Geography* (Oxford: Oxford University Press), 353–72.

LVCVA—Las Vegas Convention and Visitors Authority (2009), *2009 Las Vegas Year-to-
Date Executive Summary* (Las Vegas: LVCVA): <http://www.lvcva.com/getfile/ES-
YTD2009.pdf?fileID=479> accessed Aug. 2013.

LVCVA (2011), *About the LVCVA* (Las Vegas: LVCVA): <http://www.lvcva.com/about/
index.jsp> accessed Aug. 2010.

McAlexander, J. H., and Schouten, J. W. (1998), 'Brand-Fests: Servicescapes for the Cul-
tivation of Brand Equity', in J. F. Sherry, Jr (ed.), *Servicescapes: The Concept of Place in
Contemporary Markets* (Chicago: American Marketing Association), 377–402.

McCracken, G. (1986), 'Culture and Consumption: A Theoretical Account of the Structure and Movement of the Cultural Meaning of Consumer Goods', *Journal of Consumer Research*, 13 (1), 71–84.

Mcquail, D. (1994), *Mass Communication Theory* (London: Sage).

Malecki, E., and Poehling, R. (1999), 'Extroverts and Introverts: Small Manufacturers and their Information Sources', *Entrepreneurship and Regional Development*, 11, 247–68.

Malmberg, A., and Maskell, P. (2002), 'The Elusive Concept of Localization Economies: Towards a Knowledge-Based Theory of Spatial Clustering', *Environment and Planning A*, 34, 429–49.

Marmomacc (2013a), *Architecture Competition: International Award Architecture in Stone* (Verona: Marmomacc): <http://architetturaedesign.marmomacc.com/en/awards-and-competitions/international-award-architecture-in-stone/architecture-competition-international-award-architecture-in-stone/> accessed Oct. 2013.

Marmomacc (2013b), *Marmomacc Stone Academy* (Verona: Marmomacc): <http://www.marmomacc.it/en/generic/training-courses/view/marmomacc-stone-academy/> accessed Oct. 2013.

Marmomacc (2013c), *Marmomacc in the World* (Verona: Marmomacc): <http://www.marmomacc.com/it/generico/marmomacc-world/> accessed Oct. 2013.

Marshall, A. (1920), *Principles of Economics*, reprint of 8th edn (Philadelphia: Porcupine Press).

Marshall, A. (1927), *Industry and Trade: A Study of Industrial Technique and Business Organization; and their Influences on the Conditions of Various Classes and Nations*, reprint of 3rd edn (London: Macmillan).

Maskell, P. (2001), 'Toward a Knowledge-Based Theory of the Geographical Cluster', *Industrial and Corporate Change*, 10 (4), 921–43.

Maskell, P. (2014), 'Accessing Remote Knowledge: The Complementary Roles of Trade Fairs, Pipelines, Crowdsourcing and Listening Posts', *Journal of Economic Geography*, 14, forthcoming.

Maskell, P., and Malmberg, A. (1999a), 'Localised Learning and Industrial Competitiveness', *Cambridge Journal of Economics*, 23, 167–85.

Maskell, P., and Malmberg, A. (1999b), 'The Competitiveness of Firms and Regions: "Ubiquitification" and the Importance of Localized Learning', *European Urban and Regional Studies*, 6, 9–25.

Maskell, P., Bathelt, H., and Malmberg, A. (2004), *Temporary Clusters and Knowledge Creation: The Effects of International Trade Fairs, Conventions and Other Professional Gatherings*. SPACES, 2004–04 (Toronto and Heidelberg: http://www.spaces-online.com).

Maskell, P., Bathelt, H., and Malmberg, A. (2006), 'Building Global Knowledge Pipelines: The Role of Temporary Clusters', *European Planning Studies*, 14, 997–1013.

Massey, D. (2004), 'Geographies of Responsibility', *Geografiska Annaler*, 86B, 5–18.

Masterman, G. (2012), *Strategic Sports Event Management* (Oxford: Butterworth-Heinemann).

Mazzaraco, M. (1993), 'Word is out: Yellow is in for Spring–Summer '94', *Women's Wear Daily*, 20 Jan., 23.

Meffert, H. (1993), 'Messen und Ausstellungen als Marketinginstrument' (Trade Fairs and Exhibitions as a Marketing Tool), in K. E. Goehrmann (ed.), *Polit-Marketing auf Messen (Marketing Policy on Trade Fairs)* (Düsseldorf: Wirtschaft und Finanzen), 74–96.

Meffert, H. (1997), 'Neuere Entwicklungen in Kommunikation und Vertrieb' (New Developments in Communication and Distribution), in H. Meffert, T. Necker, and

H. Sihler (eds), *Märkte im Dialog: Die Messen der dritten Generation (Markets in Dia-logue: Trade Shows of the Third Generation)* (Wiesbaden: Gabler), 134–58.

Meffert, H. (2003), 'Ziel und Nutzen der Messebeteiligung von ausstellenden Unterne-hmen und Besuchern (Goals and Effects of Trade Show Participation of Exhibitors and Visitors)', in M. Kirchgeorg, W. M. Dornscheidt, W. Giese, and N. Stoeck (eds), *Handbu-ch Messemanagement: Planung, Durchführung und Kontrolle von Messen, Kongressen und Events (Handbook of Trade Show Management: Planning, Execution and Control of Trade Shows, Conventions and Events)* (Wiesbaden: Gabler), 1145–63.

Messe Frankfurt GmbH (2003), *Geschäftsbericht 2003 (Annual Report 2003)* (Frankfurt/Main: Messe Frankfurt GmbH).

Messe Frankfurt GmbH (2004a), *Light + Building, Internationale Fachmesse für Archi-tektur und Technik, vom 18. bis 22. April 2004 in Frankfurt am Main: Aussteller in Zahlen (Data Report of Exhibitors at Light + Building, 18–22 April 2004)*. Press release (Frankfurt/Main: Messe Frankfurt GmbH).

Messe Frankfurt GmbH (2004b), *Light + Building, Internationale Fachmesse für Archi-tektur und Technik, vom 18. bis 22. April 2004 in Frankfurt am Main: Schlussbericht (Final Report of Light + Building, 18–22 April 2004)*. Press release (Frankfurt/Main: Messe Frankfurt GmbH).

Messe Frankfurt GmbH (2004c), *Light + Building. Internationale Fachmesse für Architek-tur und Technik: Offizieller Katalog (Official Light + Building Catalogue)* (Frankfurt/Main: Messe Frankfurt GmbH).

Messe Frankfurt GmbH (2004d), *IFFA/IFFA-Delicat, Internationaler Treffpunkt für die Fleischwirtschaft vom 15. bis 20. Mai 2004 in Frankfurt am Main: Aussteller nach Län-dern (Data Report of Exhibitors by Origin at IFFA, 15–20 May 2004)*. Press release (Frankfurt/Main: Messe Frankfurt GmbH).

Messe Frankfurt GmbH (2004e), *IFFA/IFFA-Delicat, Internationaler Treffpunkt für die Fleischwirtschaft vom 15. bis 20. Mai 2004 in Frankfurt am Main: IFFA/IFFADelicat 2004 fest im Sattel (General Report of Exhibitors and Vistors by Origin at IFFA, 15–20 May 2004)*. Press release (Frankfurt/Main: Messe Frankfurt GmbH).

Messe Frankfurt GmbH (2004f), *IFFA: The Meating-Point. Offizieller Katalog (Official IFFA Catalogue)* (Frankfurt/Main: Messe Frankfurt GmbH).

Messe Frankfurt GmbH (2012a), *Light + Building: The World's Leading Trade Fair for Architecture and Technology. Facts and Figures 2012* (Frankfurt/Main: Messe Frank-furt GmbH): <http://light-building.messefrankfurt.com/content/light building/frankfurt/en/aussteller/messeprofil/_jcr_content/mainParsys/downloadbox/downloadboxParsys/download/file.res/MarketingdatenLB_2012_GB.pdf> accessed Dec. 2004.

Messe Frankfurt GmbH (2012b), *Annual Report 2011* (Frankfurt: Messe Frankfurt GmbH): <http://www.messefrankfurt.com/content/corporate/frankfurt/en/messe/publikationen/geschaeftsberichte/_jcr_content/mainParsys/downloadbox/downloadboxParsys/down-load_8/file.res/MesseFrankfurt_GB11_En.pdf> accessed Oct. 2013.

Metalworking and CNC Machine Tool Show (2011), *Post Show Report* (Shanghai: MWCS): <http://www.ciif-expo.com/uploadfile/mwcs/uploadfile/201012/20101217013749332.pdf> accessed Jan. 2012.

Metropolitan Pier and Exposition Authority (2011), *McCormick Place: About us* (Chicago: MPEA): <http://www.mccormickplace.com/about_us/about_us.html> accessed Aug. 2011.

Milgrom, P. R., North, D. C., and Weingast, B. R. (1990), 'The Role of Institutions in the Revival of Trade: The Law Merchant, Private Judges, and the Champagne Fairs', *Economic and Politics*, 2, 1–23.

Mintzberg, H., and Waters, J. A. (1985), 'Of Strategies, Deliberate and Emergent', *Strategic Management Journal*, 6 (3), 257–72.

Moeran, B., and Pedersen, J. S. (eds) (2011), *Negotiating Values in the Creative Industries: Fairs, Festivals and Competitive Events* (Cambridge: Cambridge University Press).

Möllering, G. (2010), *Collective Market-Making at an Engineering Conference*. MPIfG Discussion Paper, 10/2 (Cologne: Max-Planck-Institut für Gesellschaftsforschung).

Moore, E. W. (1985), *The Fairs of Medieval England: An Introductory Study*. Studies and Texts, 72 (Toronto: Pontifical Institute of Medieval Studies).

Morris, M. (1988), *Industrial and Organizational Marketing* (Columbus, OH: Merrill Publishing).

Mosbuild (2013), *Event Overview* (Moscow: Mosbuild): <http://www.mosbuild.com/About-MosBuild/Event-overview> accessed Oct. 2013.

Moser, P. (2005), 'How do Patent Laws Influence Innovation? Evidence from Nineteenth-Century World's Fairs', *American Economic Review*, 95, 1214–36.

MTCC—Metropolitan Toronto Convention Centre (2011), *MTCC Corporate Objective and Mandate* (Toronto: MTCC): <http://www.mtccc.com/> accessed Aug. 2011.

Munro, J. H. (2001), 'The "New Institutional Economics" and the Changing Fortunes of Fairs in Medieval and Early Modern Europe: The Textile Trades, Warfare, and Transaction Costs', *VSWG: Vierteljahrschrift für Sozial- und Wirtschaftsgeschichte*, 88, 1–47.

Munuera, J. L., and Ruiz, S. (1999), 'Trade Fairs as Services: A Look at Visitors' Objectives in Spain', *Journal of Business Research*, 44, 17–24.

Nanetti, R. (2013), 'Local Stakeholders: Governance Approaches to Exhibitions', in Fondazione Fiera Milano (ed.), *Exhibitions in Years 2.0: Between Internalization and Local Development* (Milan: EGEA), 45–115.

Narver, J. C., and Slater, S. F. (1990), 'The Effect of a Market Orientation on Business Profitability', *Journal of Marketing*, 54 (4), 20–35.

Nelson, R. R. (ed.) (1993), *National Innovation Systems: A Comparative Analysis* (Oxford: Oxford University Press).

Newman, H. (2002), 'Decentralization of Atlanta's Convention Business', *Urban Affairs Review*, 38, 232–52.

Nonaka, I., Toyama, R., and Nagata, A. (2000), 'A Firm as a Knowledge–Creating Entity: A New Perspective on the Theory of the Firm', *Industrial and Corporate Change*, 9, 1–20.

Nooteboom, B. (2000), *Learning and Innovation in Organizations and Economies* (Oxford: Oxford University Press).

Norcliffe, G., and Rendace, O. (2003), 'New Geographies of Comic Book Production in North America: The New Artisans, Distancing, and the Periodic Social Economy', *Economic Geography*, 79, 241–73.

Nordin, A. H. M. (2012), 'Taking Baudrillard to the Fair: Exhibiting China in the World at the Shanghai Expo', *Alternatives: Global, Local, Political*, 37, 106–20.

Oinas, P. (1999), 'Activity-Specificity in Organizational Learning: Implications for Analysing the Role of Proximity', *GeoJournal*, 49, 363–72.

Oppermann, M. (1996), 'Convention Destination Images: Analysis of Association Meeting Planners' Perceptions', *Tourism Management*, 17, 175–82.

Oppermann, M., and Chon, K.-S. (1997), 'Convention Participation Decision–Making Process', *Annals of Tourism Research*, 24, 178–91.

Osborne, B. (1980), 'Trading on a Frontier: The Function of Peddlers, Markets, and Fairs in Nineteenth-Century Ontario', in D. H. Akenson (ed.), *Canadian Papers in Rural History*, 2nd edn (Gananoque, ON: Langdale), 59–81.

Owen-Smith, J., and Powell, W. W. (2004), 'Knowledge Networks as Channels and Conduits: The Effects of Spillovers in the Boston Biotechnology Community', *Organization Science*, 15, 5–21.

Palumbo, F. A. (2008), 'Trade Show/Fair Piracy and Industrial Espionage', *Journal of Convention and Event Tourism*, 9, 277–92.

Pavitt, K. (2005), 'Innovation Processes', in J. Fagerberg, D. C. Mowery, and R. R. Nelson (eds), *The Oxford Handbook of Innovation* (Oxford: Oxford University Press), 86–114.

Peñaloza, L. (2000), 'The Commodification of the American West: Marketers' Production of Cultural Meanings at the Trade Show', *Journal of Marketing*, 64 (4), 82–109.

Peñaloza, L. (2001), 'Consuming the American West: Animating Cultural Meaning and Memory at a Stock Show and Rodeo', *Journal of Consumer Research*, 28, 369–98.

Penrose, E. T. (1959), *The Theory of the Growth of the Firm* (Oxford: Blackwell).

Penzkofer, H. (2008), 'Messen und Veranstaltungen der Messe München lösen bundesweit jährlich einen Umsatz von 2,17 Mrd. Euro aus' (Trade Fairs and Related Events in Munich Generate Annual Sales Effects of €2.17 Billion in Germany), *ifo Schnelldienst*, 61 (10), 38–43.

Perry, D. C., and Watkins, A. J. (1977), *The Rise of the Sunbelt Cities* (Beverly Hills, CA, and London: Sage).

Peterson, R. A., and Jolibert, A. J. P. (1995), 'A Meta-Analysis of Country-of-Origin Effects', *Journal of International Business Studies*, 26, 883–900.

Pharr, J. M. (2005), 'Synthesizing Country-of-Origin Research from the Last Decade: Is the Concept Still Salient in an Era of Global Brands?', *Journal of Marketing Theory and Practice*, 13 (4), 34–45.

Pinch, S., Henry, N., Jenkins, M., and Tallman, S. (2003), 'From "Industrial Districts" to "Knowledge Clusters": A Model of Knowledge Dissemination and Competitive Advantage in Industrial Agglomerations', *Journal of Economic Geography*, 3, 373–88.

Pine, B. J., II, and Gilmore, J. H. (1998), 'Welcome to the Experience Economy', *Harvard Business Review*, 76, 87–105.

Pine, B. J., II, and Gilmore, J. H. (1999), *The Experience Economy: Work is Theatre and Every Business a Stage* (Boston: Harvard Business School Press).

Piore, M. J., and Sabel, C. F. (1984), *The Second Industrial Divide: Possibilities for Prosperity* (New York: Basic Books).

Porter, M. E. (1990), *The Competitive Advantage of Nations* (New York: Free Press).

Porter, M. E. (2003), 'The Economic Performance of Regions', *Regional Studies*, 37, 549–78.

Powell, S. (2007), 'Guangzhou, a Microcosm of Global Trade', *Barron's*, 12 Mar., 57.

Power, D., and Jansson, J. (2008), 'Cyclical Clusters in Global Circuits: Overlapping Spaces in Furniture Trade Fairs', *Economic Geography*, 84, 423–48.

Première Vision (2008), *Fashion Info, September 2008 Salon*. Press kit (Paris: Première Vision): <http://www.trend-news-service.net/english/images/stories/previews/pvinfo-modegb%20june08.pdf> accessed Nov. 2013.

Prüser, S. (1997), *Messemarketing: Ein netzwerkorientierter Ansatz (Trade Show Marketing: A Network Approach)* (Wiesbaden: Deutscher Universitäts-Verlag).

Prüser, S. (2003), 'Die Messe als Networking–Plattform' (Trade Shows as a Platform for Networking), in M. Kirchgeorg, W. M. Dornscheidt, W. Giese, and N. Stoeck (eds), *Handbuch Messemanagement: Planung, Durchführung und Kontrolle von Messen, Kongressen und Events (Handbook of Trade Show Management: Planning, Execution and Control of Trade Shows, Conventions and Events)* (Wiesbaden: Gabler), 1181–95.

Pyke, F., Becattini, G., and Sengenberger, W. (eds) (1990), *Industrial Districts and Inter-Firm Co-operation in Italy* (Geneva: International Institute for Labour Studies).

Rafaeli, A., and Pratt, M. (2006), *Artifacts and Organizations: Beyond Mere Symbolism* (Mahwah, NJ: Lawrence Erlbaum).

Rallet, A., and Torre, A. (1999), 'Is Geographical Proximity Necessary in the Innovation Networks in the Era of the Global Economy?', *GeoJournal*, 49, 373–80.

Rallet, A., and Torre, A. (2009), *Temporary Geographical Proximity for Business and Work Coordination: When, How and Where?* SPACES online, 2009–02 (Toronto and Heidelberg: www.spaces-online.com).

Ramírez-Pasillas, M. (2008), 'Resituating Proximity and Knowledge Cross-Fertilization in Clusters by Means of International Trade Fairs', *European Planning Studies*, 16, 643–63.

Ramírez-Pasillas, M. (2010), 'International Trade Fairs as Amplifiers of Permanent and Temporary Proximities in Clusters', *Entrepreneurship and Regional Development*, 22, 155–87.

Rao, H. (1994), 'The Social Construction of Reputation: Certification Contests, Legitimation, and the Survival of Organizations in the American Automobile Industry: 1895–1912', *Strategic Management Journal*, 15, 29–44.

Reimer, S., and Leslie, D. (2008), 'Design, National Imaginaries, and the Home Furnishings Commodity Chain', *Growth and Change*, 39, 144–71.

Richardson, H. W. (1973), *Regional Growth Theory* (London: Macmillan; New York: Praeger).

Rinallo, D. (2008), '"It's Sort of Comical How You Think that You've Made a Choice that Exempts You from the Fashion Industry": Fashion and Consumer Agency, Revisited', in S. Borghini, M. A. McGrath, and C. Oates (eds), *European Advances in Consumer Research*, 8 (Milan: Association for Consumer Research), 60–3.

Rinallo, D. (2011a), *Event Marketing* (Milan: EGEA).

Rinallo, D. (2011b), *Competing Fashion Weeks in a Globalizing World: Exploring the Ideological Reconstruction of the Past for Commercial Purposes at Collective Events*. Unpublished research report (Milan: Bocconi University).

Rinallo, D., and Golfetto, F. (2006), 'Representing Markets: The Shaping of Fashion Trends by French and Italian Fabric Companies', *Industrial Marketing Management*, 35, 856–69.

Rinallo, D., and Golfetto, F. (2011), 'Exploring the Knowledge Strategies of Temporary Cluster Organizers: A Longitudinal Study of the EU Fabric Industry Trade Shows (1986–2006)', *Economic Geography*, 87, 453–76.

Rinallo, D., and Golfetto, F. (2014), 'European Clothing Fabric Trade Shows in Asia: Internationalization Models and Knowledge Implications', in H. Bathelt and G. Zeng (eds), *Temporary Knowledge Ecologies: The Rise and Evolution of Trade Fairs in the Asia-Pacific Region* (Cheltenham and Northampton, MA: Edward Elgar), forthcoming.

Rinallo, D., and Pinchera, V. (2013), 'Exploring the Link between Nation Branding and Commercial Mythmaking: The Construction and Reception of Italian Fashion', paper presented at the Consumer Culture Theory Conference (Tucson).

Rinallo, D., Borghini, S., and Golfetto, F. (2008), 'Building Market Knowledge Together: A Netnographic Study of Online Occupational Communities', paper presented at the Industrial Marketing and Purchasing Conference (Uppsala): <http://www.impgroup.org/paper_view.php?viewPaper=6709> accessed Oct. 2012.

Rinallo, D., Borghini, S., and Golfetto, F. (2010), 'Exploring Visitor Experiences at Trade Shows', *Journal of Business and Industrial Marketing*, 25, 249–58.

Rinallo, D., Golfetto, F., and Borghini, S. (2007), 'The Influence of Occupational Communities on Buying Behavior', paper presented at the Industrial Marketing and Purchasing Conference (Manchester): <http://impgroup.org/paper_view.php?viewPaper=5930> accessed Sept. 2013.

Rinallo, D., Golfetto, F., and Gibbert, M. (2006), 'Consocia et Impera: How the French and Italian Fabric Producers Cooperate in Order to Affirm the "Dominant Design" in the Fashion Industry', in M. Gibbert and T. Durand (eds), *Strategic Networks*. Strategic Management Society Book Series (Oxford: Blackwell), 88–106.

Ritchie, J. R. B. (1984), 'Assessing the Impact of Hallmark Events: Conceptual and Research Issues', *Journal of Travel Research*, 23, 2–11.

Robinson, P., Faris, C., and Wind, Y. (1967), *Industrial Buying and Creative Marketing* (Boston, MA: Allyn & Bacon).

Roche, M. (1999), *Mega-Events and Modernity: Olympics, Expos and the Construction of Public Culture* (London: Routledge).

Rodekamp, V. (2003), 'Zur Geschichte der Messen in Deutschland und Europa' (On the History of Trade Fairs in Germany and Europe)', in M. Kirchgeorg, W. M. Dornscheidt, W. Giese, and N. Stoeck (eds), *Handbuch Messemanagement: Planung, Durchführung und Kontrolle von Messen, Kongressen und Events (Handbook of Trade Show Management: Planning, Execution and Control of Trade Shows, Conventions and Events)* (Wiesbaden: Gabler), 5–13.

Rogers, T. (2007), *Conferences and Conventions* (Oxford: Butterworth-Heinemann).

Rosenkopf, L., and Tushman, M. L. (1998), 'The Coevolution of Community Networks and Technology: Lessons from the Flight Simulation Industry', *Industrial and Corporate Change*, 7, 311–46.

Rosson, P. J., and Seringhaus, F. H. R. (1995), 'Visitor and Exhibitor Interaction at Industrial Trade Fairs', *Journal of Business Research*, 32, 81–90.

Rothaermel, F. T. (2001a), 'Complementary Assets, Strategic Alliances, and the Incumbent's Advantage: An Empirical Study of Industry and Firm Effects in the Biopharmaceutical Industry', *Research Policy*, 30, 1235–51.

Rothaermel, F. T. (2001b), 'Incumbent's Advantage through Exploiting Complementary Assets via Interfirm Cooperation', *Strategic Management Journal*, 22, 687–99.

Rothschild, M. L. (1987), *Marketing Communications* (Lexington, MA: D. C. Heath).

Rubalcaba-Bermejo, L., and Cuadrado-Roura, J. R. (1995), 'Urban Hierarchies and Territorial Competition in Europe: Exploring the Role of Fairs and Exhibitions', *Urban Studies*, 32, 379–400.

Russo, M. (2004), *Il distretto industriale della ceramica di fronte alla sfida cinese (The Ceramic Industrial District Facing the Chinese Challenge)*. Materiali di Discussione, 460 (Modena: Università di Modena e Reggio Emilia): <http://www.dep.unimore.it/materiali_discussione/0460.pdf> accessed Sept. 2013.

Sabel, C. F. (1994), 'Flexible Specialisation and Re-emergence of Regional Economics', in A. Amin (ed.), *Post-Fordism* (Oxford: Blackwell), 101–56.

Sassen, S. (1994), *Cities in a World Economy* (Thousand Oaks, CA: Pine Forge Press).

Schätzl, L., Kramer, J., and Sternberg, R. (1993), 'Regionalökonomische Wirkungen der 1991 in Hannover veranstalteten Messen und Ausstellungen' (Regional Economic Impacts of Trade Fairs and Exhibitions in Hanover 1991), in K. E. Goehrmann (ed.), *Polit-Marketing auf Messen (Marketing Policy on Trade Fairs)* (Düsseldorf: Verlag Wirtschaft und Finanzen), 98–112.

Schmitt, B. H. (1999), *Experiential Marketing: How to Get Customers to SENSE, FEEL, THINK, ACT, RELATE to Your Company and Brands* (New York: Free Press).

Schuessler, E., Rüling, C. C., and Wittneben, B. (2013), 'On Melting Summits: The Limitations of Field-Configuring Events as Catalysts of Change in Transnational Climate Policy', *Academy of Management Journal*, 56, forthcoming.

Schuldt, N., and Bathelt, H. (2011), 'International Trade Fairs and Global Buzz, Part II: Practices of Global Buzz', *European Planning Studies*, 19, 1–22.

Scott, A. J. (1988), *New Industrial Spaces: Flexible Production Organization and Regional Development in North America and Western Europe* (London: Pion).

Seringhaus, F. H. R., and Rosson, P. J. (1998), 'Management and Performance of International Trade Fair Exhibitors: Government Stands vs Independent Stands', *International Marketing Review*, 15 (5), 398–412.

Sharland, A., and Balogh, P. (1996), 'The Value of Nonselling Activities at International Trade Shows', *Industrial Marketing Management*, 25 (1), 59–66.

Shi, Y. (2012), 'World's Biggest Exhibition Center Set for Shanghai', *China Daily*, 5 Mar., 13.

Shoham, A. (1992), 'How Exhibitors Select and Evaluate Trade Shows', *Industrial Marketing Management*, 21, 335–41.

Short, J., Williams, E., and Christie, B. (1976), *The Social Psychology of Telecommunications* (New York: Wiley).

Shultz, C. J. II. (2007), 'Macromarketing', in G. Gundlach, L. Block, and W. Wilkie (eds), *Explorations of Marketing in Society* (Cincinnati, OH: South-Western/Thomson), 766–84.

Skallerud, K. (2010), 'Structure, Strategy and Performance of Exhibitors at Individual Booths versus Joint Booths', *Journal of Business and Industrial Marketing*, 25, 259–67.

Skov, L. (2006), 'The Role of Trade Fairs in the Global Fashion Business', *Current Sociology*, 54, 764–83.

Slesin, S. (1987), 'At Milan Fair, Furniture that Surprises', *New York Times*, 24 Sept.: <http://www.nytimes.com/1987/09/24/garden/at-milan-fair-furniture-that-surprises.html?pagewanted=all&src=pm> accessed Oct. 2010.

Slesin, S. (1989), 'At Milan Fair, there's Vitality if Not Practicality', *New York Times*, 28 Sept.: <http://www.nytimes.com/1989/09/28/garden/at-milan-fair-there-s-vitality-if-not-practicality.html?pagewanted=all&src=pm> accessed Oct. 2010.

Smith, T. M., Gopalakrishna, S., and Smith, P. M. (2004), 'The Complementary Effect of Trade Shows on Personal Selling', *International Journal of Research in Marketing*, 21, 61–76.

Soskice, D. (1999), 'Divergent Production Regimes: Coordinated and Uncoordinated Market Economies in the 1980s and 1990s', in H. Kitschelt, G. Marks, and P. Lange (eds), *Continuity and Change in Contemporary Capitalism* (Cambridge: Cambridge University Press), 101–34.

Spillman, B. (2007), 'LV Still a Great Place to Show: City Tops List of Best Convention Places', *Las Vegas Review–Journal*, 1 May.

Sternberg, R., and Kramer, J. (1991), 'Gesamt- und regionalwirtschaftliche Wirkungen der Weltausstellung 2000 in Hannover' (National and Regional Economic Effects of the World Exhibition 2000 in Hanover), *Geographische Rundschau*, 43, 658–63.

Stevens, R. P. (2005), *Trade Show and Event Marketing* (Mason, OH: Thomson and American Marketing Association).

Stigliani, I., and Ravasi, D. (2012), 'Organizing Thoughts and Connecting Brains: Material Practices and the Transition from Individual to Group–Level Prospective Sense-making', *Academy of Management Journal*, 55, 1232–59.

Storper, M. (1985), 'Oligopoly and the Product Cycle: Essentialism in the Economic Geography', *Economic Geography*, 61, 260–82.

Storper, M. (1997), *The Regional World: Territorial Development in a Global Economy* (New York: Guilford Press).

Storper, M., and Venables, A. J. (2004), 'Buzz: Face-to-Face Contact and the Urban Economy', *Journal of Economic Geography*, 4, 351–70.

Strothmann, K.-H. (1992), 'Segmentorientierte Messepolitik' (Segmented Trade Show Policy), in K.-H. Strothmann and M. Busche (eds), *Handbuch Messemarketing (Handbook of Trade Show Marketing)* (Wiesbaden: Gabler), 99–115.

Syme, G. J., Shaw, B. J., Fenton, D. M., and Mueller, W. S. (1989), *The Planning and Evaluation of Hallmark Events* (Aldershot: Avebury).

Tanner, J. F. Jr (2002), 'Leveling the Playing Field: Factors Influencing Trade Show Success for Small Companies', *Industrial Marketing Management*, 31, 229–39.

Tanner, J. F. Jr, Chonko, L. B., and Ponzurick, T. V. (2001), 'A Learning Model of Trade Show Attendance', *Journal of Convention and Exhibition Management*, 3, 3–26.

Taylor, M. (1989), 'Structure, Culture and Action in the Explanation of Social Change', *Politics and Society*, 17, 115–62.

Taylor, P. J. (2004), *World City Network: A Global Urban Analysis* (London: Routledge).

Tecnargilla (2013), *Claytech* (Rimini: Tecnargilla): <http://en.tecnargilla.it/fair/claytech.asp> accessed Oct. 2013.

Teece, D. J. (1986), 'Profiting from Technological Innovation: Implications for Integration, Collaboration, Licensing and Public Policy', *Research Policy*, 15, 285–305.

Thompson, C., and Tian, K. (2008), 'Reconstructing the South: How Commercial Myths Compete for Identity Value through the Ideological Shaping of Popular Memories and Countermemories', *Journal of Consumer Research*, 34, 595–613.

Thrift, N. (2000), 'Pandora's Box? Cultural Geographies of Economies', in G. Clark, M. Feldman, and M. Gertler (eds), *The Oxford Handbook of Economic Geography* (Oxford: Oxford University Press), 689–704.

Toronto Congress Centre (2011), *The Toronto Congress Centre: Our History* (Toronto: TCC): <http://www.torontocongresscentre.com/attending/our-history.htm> accessed Aug. 2011.

Tourism Vancouver (2007), *Economic Impact of Meetings and Conventions in Metro Vancouver, 2000–2007* (Vancouver: Tourism Vancouver): <http://www.tourismvancouver.com/pdf/research/mc_economic_impact.pdf> accessed June 2013.

Townsend, C. (1914), 'The Protection of Intellectual Property at International Expositions', *California Law Review*, 2, 291–308.

Trippl, M., Tödtling, F., and Lengauer, L. (2009), 'Knowledge Sourcing beyond Buzz and Pipelines: Evidence from the Vienna Software Sector', *Economic Geography*, 85, 443–62.

TSW—Trade Show Week and CEIR (2005), *Exhibition Industry Census II: Comprehensive Resource of Exhibition Industry Data* (Chicago: TSW and CEIR).

Turgot, R. J. (1757), 'Foires', in D. Diderot and J. D'Alembert (eds), *Encyclopédie ou Dictionnaire Raisonné des Sciences, des Arts et des Métiers* (Paris: Le Breton, Durand, David).

Tushman, M. L., and Rosenkopf, L. (1992), 'Organizational Determinants of Technological Change: Toward a Sociology of Technological Evolution', in B. M. Staw and L. L. Cummings (eds), *Research in Organizational Behavior* (London: JAI Press), 311–47.

UFI—The Global Association of the Exhibition Industry (2007), *The World Map of Exhibition Venues and Future Trends* (Paris: UFI).

UFI (2008), *Recommendations for the Protection of Intellectual Property Rights at Exhibitions* (Paris: UFI): <http://www.ufi.org/Medias/pdf/thetradefairsector/ipr_recommendations.pdf> accessed Feb. 2013.

UFI (2011), *The World Map of Exhibitions Venues 2011* (Paris: UFI): <http://www.ufi.org> accessed July 2013.

UFI (2012a), *The Global Exhibition Industry Statistics* (Paris: UFI): <http://www.ufi.org> accessed July 2013.

UFI (2012b), *Eurofair Statistics 2012* (Paris: UFI): <http://www.ufi.org> accessed July 2013.

Unimev-Ojs (2013), *Bilan Chiffre 2012: Foires, salons, congrès et événéments* (Paris: Unimev-Ojs): <http://www.ojs.asso.fr/medias/fichiers/Bilan_chiffre_annee_2012_OJS_UNIMEV_2862013.pdf> accessed Oct. 2013.

Uzzi, B. (1997), 'Social Structure and Competition in Interfirm Networks: The Paradox of Embeddedness', *Administrative Science Quarterly*, 42, 35–67.

Velotta, R. V. (1999), 'Convention Center Expansion Touted as Competitive Tool', *Las Vegas Sun*, 5 Jan.

Velotta, R. V. (2009), 'Trade Shows Bringing Mobs to Vegas When it Needs it Most: Consumer Electronics Show, Which Could Draw 130,000, Starts Next Week', *Las Vegas Sun*, 5 Jan.

Verlegh, P. W. J., and Steenkamp, J.-B. E. M. (1999), 'A Review and Meta-Analysis of Country-of-Origin Research', *Journal of Economic Psychology*, 20, 521–46.

Verlinden, C. (1963), 'Markets and Fairs', in M. M. Postan, E. E. Rich, and E. Miller (eds), *The Cambridge Economic History of Europe*, III. *Economic Organization and Policies in the Middle Ages* (Cambridge: Cambridge University Press), 119–53.

Visser, E.-J., and Boschma, R. (2006). 'Learning in Districts: Novelty and Lock-in in a Regional Context', *European Planning Studies*, 12, 793–808.

Vogel, C. (1991), 'Design: A Tale of Two Cities', *New York Times*, 14 Apr.: <http://www.nytimes.com/1991/04/14/magazine/design-a-tale-of-two-cities.html> accessed Oct. 2010.

von Hippel, E. (2001), 'Innovation by User Communities: Learning from Open-Source Software', *MIT Sloan Management Review*, 42, 82–6.

Walden, K. (1997), *Becoming Modern in Toronto: The Industrial Exhibition and the Shaping of Late Victorian Culture* (Toronto: University of Toronto Press).

Wang, F.-H., and Guo, J.-R. (2010), *Blue Book of Convention and Exhibition Economy: Annual Report on China's Convention and Exhibition Economy 2010* (Beijing: Social Sciences Academic Press, in Chinese).

Watzlawick, P., Beavin, J. H., and Jackson, D. D. (2000), *Menschliche Kommunikation: Formen, Störungen, Paradoxien (Human Communication: Forms, Interferences, Contradictions)*, 10th edn (Bern: Huber).

Weber, M. (1961), *General Economic History*. Tr. F. H. Knight, from the original German edn of 1923 (New York: Collier Books).

Weller, S. (2008), 'Beyond "Global Production Networks": Australian Fashion Week's Trans-Sectoral Synergies', *Growth and Change*, 39, 104–22.

Weller, S. (2014), 'Trade Fairs in Peripheral Places: Toward a Political Economy of Australian Fashion Events', in H. Bathelt and G. Zeng (eds), *Temporary Knowledge Ecologies: The Rise and Evolution of Trade Fairs in the Asia-Pacific Region* (Cheltenham and Northampton, MA: Edward Elgar), forthcoming.

Wenger, E. (1998), *Communities of Practice: Learning, Meaning, and Identity* (Cambridge: Cambridge University Press).

Wernerfelt, B. (1984), 'A Resource-Based View of the Firm', *Strategic Management Journal*, 5, 171–80.

Yang, C. (2008), 'A Look at Las Vegas: At the Top of the Heap', *Tradeshow Week*, 12 May.

Yin, R. (1994), *Case Study Research: Design and Methods* (Thousand Oaks, CA: Sage).

Yogev, T., and Grund, T. (2012), 'Network Dynamics and Market Structure: The Case of Art Fairs', *Sociological Focus*, 45, 23–40.

Yokura, Y. (2014), 'Building Relationships at Local Trade Fairs in Japan: Case Study of the Suwa Area Industrial Messe', in H. Bathelt and G. Zeng (eds), *Temporary Knowledge Ecologies: The Rise and Evolution of Trade Fairs in the Asia-Pacific Region* (Cheltenham and Northampton, MA: Edward Elgar), forthcoming.

Young, R. (2004), 'Plastics in China: Exhibitors Mostly Tout Existing Products', *Plastics News*, 16 (24), 14–15.

Zahra, S. A., and George, G. (2002), 'Absorptive Capacity: A Review, Reconceptualization, and Extension', *Academy of Management Review*, 27, 185–203.

Zarantonello, L., and Schmitt, B. H. (2013), 'The Impact of Event Marketing on Brand Equity: The Mediating Roles of Brand Experience and Brand Attitude', *International Journal of Advertising*, 32, 255–80.

Zelinsky, W. (1994), 'Conventionland USA: The Geography of a Latterday Phenomenon', *Annals of the Association of American Geographers*, 84, 68–86.

Zeng, G. (2000), 'The Financial Crisis in Asia and the Modification of Economic Structure in Shanghai', *Asian Geographer*, 19, 37–48.

Zerbini, F., and Borghini, S. (2012), 'The Proof of the Pudding is in the Kitchen: Assessing Market Response to Signals Encoding during Supplier Selection', in Various Authors (eds), *Prodotto, consumatore e politiche di mercato, quarant'anni dopo (Product, Consumer and Market Policies, After Forty Years)* (Milan: EGEA Online), 285–302.

Zerbini, F., Golfetto, F., and Borghini, S. (2010), 'Seeing is Believing? Signalling Suppli-er's Value Potential', paper presented at the Industrial Marketing and Purchasing Conference (Budapest): <http://impgroup.org/paper_view.php?viewPaper=7379> accessed Sept. 2013.

Zerbini, F., Golfetto, F., and Gibbert, M. (2006), 'Impartive Capacity: Towards a View of Industrial Suppliers as Competence Providers', paper presented at the Euram Con-ference (Oslo).

Zerbini, F., Golfetto, F., and Gibbert, M. (2007), 'Marketing of Competence: Exploring the Resource-Based Content of Value-for-Customers through a Case Study Analysis', *Industrial Marketing Management*, 36, 784–98.

Zhu, Y.-W., and Zeng, G. (2014), 'Spatial Distribution and Influencing Factors of Chi-na's Exhibition Industry', in H. Bathelt and G. Zeng (eds), *Temporary Knowledge Ecologies: The Rise and Evolution of Trade Fairs in the Asia-Pacific Region* (Chelten-ham and Northampton, MA: Edward Elgar), forthcoming.

Index

proximity (*continued*)
  physical 56, 64, 81
  relational 258
  spatial 42, 56, 81
  temporary 2
putting-out system 41
PVE S.A. 207, 214

Reed Exhibitions 64
reference events/fairs, see also flagship trade
    shows 21, 32, 39, 91, 104, 161, 171, 224,
    241, 250, 271, 276
regional
  authorities, see government
  economic development, see economic
    development
  policy, see policy
regional/national trade shows, see also local
    trade shows 61, 76, 100, 106**f6.2**, 108,
    136, 250, 276
relational
  approach 3, 78, 86, 88, 132, 133
  experience 22, 28–9
  platform/space 2, 4, 8, 71
  proximity, see proximity
  rite 27
relationship
  horizontal, see interaction
  multiplex 49, 54, 165
  vertical, see interaction
reproduction
  of fields, see field reproduction
  of national specialization patterns, see
    national specialization patterns
Rimini Fiera 236, 237**t13.3**, 238–9

SAIE 236
sales promotion 30–2, 34–6, 40, 278
  of individual exhibitors 30–2
  of trade associations 34–6
Salon du Meuble 247, 248**f14.1**, 249**t14.1**,
    250, 257**f14.2**
Salone Bagno Arredo 253
Salone del Complemento d'Arredo 253
Salone del Mobile 25**t2.1**, 26**t2.2**, 30, 60, 233,
    245–9, 248**f14.1**, 249**t14.1**, 257**f14.2**, 281
Salone Satellite 253
sample fairs 6, 17, 20, 22–3, 38, 97, 101
Santa Croce 41
Sasmil 25**t2.1**, 26**t2.2**, 252
screening policy/process 48, 202
seminars 2, 28, 29, 67, 69, 70, 71, 72, 114, 239
sensory overload 28
Shanghai New International Expo Centre, see
    SNIEC
Shanghai, see trade show market

Shirt Avenue 196**t11.3**, 198, 199**f11.2**, 205,
    206
Singapore, see trade show market
small and medium-sized businesses/
    enterprises/firms 10, 31, 99, 114, 138,
    153, 155, 168, 170, 175, 179, 181, 189,
    208, 213, 218, 264, 269, 275
SNIEC 148–9, 149**t8.4**, 151
specialization hypothesis 75
social media 2, 66, 71, 280
South and Southeast Asia, see trade show
    market
Spain, see trade show market
spatial distribution of trade show
    activities 79, 102–9, 103**t6.2**, 106**f6.2**,
    119–20, 123–5, 130**t7.2**, 140–3, 141**t8.1**,
    143**t8.2**, 209, 267
spatial proximity, see proximity
specialization
  hypothesis 75
  industrial 10, 77, 102
  national 10–11, 77, 88–90, 105–19, 121,
    145, 243
  of capitalist varieties, see varieties of
    capitalism
  territorial/regional 12, 35, 41, 53, 75, 76,
    77, 80–4, 129–32, 223, 230, 243, 264, 277
  trade show 10, 21, 75, 76, 77, 84–90, 105–9,
    129–32, 142–6, 175–6, 264
  two-way influence model of trade show
    specialization and territorial
    specialization 9–10, 75–94, 78**f5.1**,
    90**f5.2**, 243, 264
specialized trade shows 18, 21–3, 35, 69, 101,
    152, 189, 236
spectacularization 6, 183, 267
stakeholders (of trade shows) 10, 37, 38, 49, 98,
    109, 109**t6.3**, 112, 121, 209, 243, 266, 278
stand
  closed 70
  collective 43, 274–5, 279
  content of 18, 29–30, 32, 63
  design 27, 68, 219, 274, 281
  layout 4, 39, 114, 183–4, 187
  of market leaders 28
  space distribution 31**t2.3**
standard affirmation 11, 12, 35, 36, 67, 71, 74,
    203, 211, 212, 218, 219, 220, 304
Stona 228**t13.2**
Stone + Tec 224, 225**t13.1**, 230–1
Stonetech 227**t13.2**
Stonexpo Marmomacc Americas 228**t13.2**
structure/agency debate 9, 75, 78, 92
supplier interaction 44, 48, 164, 164**t9.3**, 170,
    184, 187
support of trade shows, see policy